CONTEMPORARY PERSPECTIVES IN LEISURE

We are entering a new era of leisure. Quality rather than quantity is now the focus of researchers, policymakers and managers. Technological change, an ageing population and a harsh economic climate are changing the values and practices of leisure, as well as the relationship between leisure, society and the individual.

Contemporary Perspectives in Leisure uses a variety of disciplinary approaches to introduce the most important trends in contemporary leisure in the twenty-first century. With contributions from some of the leading international figures in modern leisure studies, the book examines key philosophical and theoretical debates around leisure, with reference to concepts such as happiness, enjoyment and quality of life, as well as the most interesting contemporary themes in leisure studies, from youth leisure and 'dark' leisure to technology and adventure.

Understanding changes in leisure helps us to better understand changes in wider society. *Contemporary Perspectives in Leisure* is a perfect companion to any course in leisure studies, and useful reading for any student or scholar working in sociology, cultural studies, recreation, tourism, sport or social psychology.

Sam Elkington is a senior lecturer in Sport Management and a teaching fellow at the University of Bedfordshire, UK. His research reflects his interests in phenomenology and pedagogy, namely, the social psychological dimensions of sport and leisure experiences and the nature, policy and practice of sport and leisure education.

Sean J. Gammon is based in the School of Sport, Tourism and the Outdoors at the University of Lancashire, UK. He is widely published in the area of sport-related tourism and continues to explore the linkages between sport, nostalgia and heritage. In addition he has researched the effectiveness of applying autotelic structures in the delivery of higher education courses to improve student creativity.

CONTEMPORARY PERSPECTIVES IN LEISURE

Meanings, motives and lifelong learning

Edited by Sam Elkington and Sean J. Gammon

Routledge
Taylor & Francis Group

LONDON AND NEW YORK

First published 2014
by Routledge
2 Park Square, Milton Park, Abingdon, Oxon OX14 4RN

and by Routledge
711 Third Avenue, New York, NY 10017

Routledge is an imprint of the Taylor & Francis Group, an informa business

© 2014 Sam Elkington and Sean J. Gammon

British Library Cataloguing in Publication Data
A catalogue record for this book is available from the British Library

Library of Congress Cataloging in Publication Data
Contemporary perspectives in leisure : meanings, motives, and lifelong learning / edited by Sam Elkington and Sean Gammon.
pages cm
1. Leisure. 2. Continuing education. I. Elkington, Sam, editor of compilation.
II. Gammon, Sean, editor of compilation.
GV174.C68 2014
790.1--dc23
2013024925

ISBN: 978-0-415-82987-8 (hbk)
ISBN: 978-0-415-82989-2 (pbk)
ISBN: 978-0-203-38173-1 (ebk)

Typeset in Bembo
by Saxon Graphics Ltd, Derby

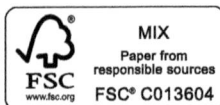

MIX
Paper from
responsible sources
FSC
www.fsc.org   FSC® C013604

Printed and bound by CPI Group (UK) Ltd, Croydon, CR0 4YY

CONTENTS

CONTRIBUTORS

Paul Beedie is currently Head of Department, PE & Sport Studies, at the University of Bedfordshire, UK. He is an active climber (a member of the Association of Mountaineering Instructors) and he teaches across a range of undergraduate and postgraduate courses. His research has been driven by an interest in adventure and includes explorations of risk, identity and community. Some key publications are: 'Media constructions of risk: a case study of the Stainforth Beck Incident' (*The Journal of Risk Research* 8(4): 331–339); 'Mountain guiding and adventure tourism: reflections on the choreography of the experience' (*Leisure Studies* 22: 147–167) and *Mountain Based Adventure Tourism: Lifestyle Choice and Identity Formation*, London: Lambert Academic Publishing (2010).

Jo Bryce is Director of Research at the Cyberspace Research Unit, School of Psychology, University of Central Lancashire, UK. Her research interests focus on the psychological, social and forensic aspects of the Internet and related technologies, with a specific focus on their use by young people, associated risk exposure and esafety. These areas focus on knowledge transfer, end user engagement, education and awareness raising, and have contributed to evidence-based policy-making at the national and European level. She was a former coordinator of the UK National Awareness Node for Child Safety on the Internet, and is a member of the Expert Research Panel of the UK Council on Child Internet Safety. As a result of this work, she regularly consults on associated issues with a variety of stakeholders in government, industry, education and enforcement.

Scott A. Cohen is a senior lecturer in the School of Hospitality and Tourism Management at the University of Surrey, UK. He is the School's Head of

Doctoral Programmes and teaches on subjects relating to the social science of tourism, sustainable tourism and tourist behaviour. Scott primarily researches sociological issues in tourism, mobility and leisure contexts, with a particular interest in the impacts of air travel on climate change. He has been awarded an 'Emerging Scholar of Distinction' by the International Academy for the Study of Tourism (2013). Scott serves as a Resource Editor for *Annals of Tourism Research*, Book Review Editor for *Anatolia: An International Journal of Tourism and Hospitality Research* and is a Fellow of the Higher Education Academy (UK).

John Haworth BSc, MLitt, PhD, is Visiting Professor of Well-being at the University of Bolton, UK, and Visiting Research Fellow in the Research Institute for Health and Social Change at Manchester Metropolitan University, UK (www.haworthjt.com). He has published extensively on work, leisure and well-being. His latest book is *Well-Being: Individual, Community and Social Perspectives* (eds) J. Haworth and G. Hart (2012). He was co-founder of the Leisure Studies Association, and the international journal *Leisure Studies*, and is currently on the editorial advisory board. He has been associate editor of the international journal *Leisure Research*. He also undertakes practice-led research into creativity in fine art, has published widely, and exhibited nationally and internationally. He has a core research interest in consciousness, creativity and well-being. He has given invited papers at international conferences in many countries.

Karla A. Henderson is Professor in the Department of Parks, Recreation and Tourism Management at North Carolina State University, USA. Her Ph.D. was completed at the University of Minnesota, USA and she holds a Doctor of Science (honoris causa) from the University of Waterloo in Ontario, Canada. Karla has given numerous presentations throughout the world. She has authored and co-authored several books such as: *Both Gains and Gaps, Dimensions of Choice: Evaluation Methods, Introduction to Leisure Services,* and *Evaluation of Leisure Services.* She is a past co-editor of *Leisure Sciences* and has contributed to the profession by serving as President of the Society of Park and Recreation Educators, the AAHPERD Research Consortium and of the Academy of Leisure Sciences. She has received many honours such as the SPRE Distinguished Colleague Award, the NRPA Roosevelt Excellence in Research Award, the NRPA Literary Award and the World Leisure Literary Award.

Steven Howlett is the author of *Volunteering and Society in the 21st Century* with Colin Rochester and Angela Ellis Paine and edited the second edition of *Volunteers in Hospice and Palliative Care: A Resource for Volunteer Service Managers* with Ros Scott. Steven has worked on many research projects on volunteering and managing volunteers over the past fifteen years. He has spoken on volunteering to audiences in Europe, Japan, South Africa and Singapore among other places. He is currently Senior Lecturer in the Business School at the University of Roehampton, UK and is convener of the Erasmus Mundus Masters programme on Human Right Policy and Practice. Previously he was Senior Research Fellow at the Institute for Volunteering Research where he edited the in-house journal *Voluntary Action*.

Lesley Lawrence is Head of Academic Professional Development based in the Centre for Learning Excellence at the University of Bedfordshire in the UK. She started her HE teaching career as a lecturer in Leisure Studies around twenty years ago and was a fairly active member of the Leisure Studies Association for many of these years, having co-edited LSA volumes and served on the Executive. Her students now are staff on the University's Postgraduate Certificate in Academic Practice, which she leads. Lesley's current research interests include studying the leisure, learning and working worlds of today's academics, triggered by the problems many face in finding the time to learn. Writing her chapter has aroused an interest in the role writing plays in our lives.

Roger C. Mannell is a psychologist and Professor of Leisure Studies, Public Health and Gerontology at the University of Waterloo, Canada where he has served as Chair of the Department of Recreation and Leisure Studies and Dean of the Faculty of Applied Health Sciences. His research, which has been funded by the Canadian Population Health Initiative, the Social Science and Humanities Research Council of Canada and the Change Foundation, deals with determinants of leisure and lifestyle choices and the impact of these choices on health. He has authored numerous publications and he co-authored the book *A Social Psychology of Leisure*. Roger was elected a Fellow of the Academy of Leisure Sciences in 1986 and he served as its president in 2004–5. He was also the 1989 recipient of the Allen V. Sapora Research Award and the 1991 U.S. National Parks and Recreation Association's Theodore and Franklin Roosevelt Research Excellence Award.

Peter McGrath is a lecturer based at the University of Central Lancashire, UK, within the School of Sport, Tourism and the Outdoors. He teaches on both the undergraduate and postgraduate programmes, and also manages the VisTrav (Sustainable Leisure Travel) Network for the Institute of Transport and Tourism in partnership with Natural England. Peter's primary research area revolves around Slow Travel and Tourism and he is currently completing a doctoral thesis on the topic.

Hayden Ramsay is Professor and Senior Deputy Vice Chancellor of the University of Notre Dame, Australia, Chair of the College of Philosophy and Theology, and Professor of Philosophy and Ethics at the University. Hayden came to Australia from Scotland in 1994. Previously, he studied philosophy at the University of Edinburgh and taught philosophy both there and at Stirling University in Scotland. Hayden worked for five years at Melbourne University and La Trobe University before beginning teaching in the Archdiocese of Melbourne at Catholic Theological College and John Paul II Institute for Marriage and Family.

He moved to Sydney in 2003, teaching at the Catholic Institute of Sydney and in Good Shepherd Seminary and then moved to Notre Dame. From 1998 until 2007 Hayden also served as an academic on the Personal Staff of the Archbishops of Melbourne and then of Sydney. Hayden has published several books and many articles in philosophy, mainly in ethics. He teaches in a number of areas of philosophy and believes passionately in the universal importance of basic philosophical thinking. His great academic interest is in the relation between a strong mind and a strong faith.

Ken Roberts is Professor of Sociology at the University of Liverpool, UK. He is a former Chair of the World Leisure Organisation's Research Commission, and also a former President of the International Sociological Association's Research Committee on Leisure. He is a founder member and now honorary life member of the Leisure Studies Association. His books include *Leisure* (1970), *Contemporary Society and the Growth of Leisure* (1978), *The Leisure Industries* (2004), and *Leisure in Contemporary Society* (2nd edn, 2006). He is also the author of *Key Concepts in Sociology* (2009), *Youth in Transition: Eastern Europe and the West* (2009), *Class in Contemporary Britain* (2nd edn, 2011) and *Sociology: An Introduction* (2012).

Richard Sharpley is Professor of Tourism and Development at the University of Central Lancashire, Preston, UK. He has previously held positions at a number of other institutions, including the University of Northumbria (Reader in Tourism) and the University of Lincoln, where he was Professor of Tourism and Head of Department, Tourism and Recreation Management. His principal research interests are within the fields of tourism and development, island tourism, rural tourism and the sociology of tourism, and his books include *Tourism and Development in the Developing World* (2008), *Tourism, Tourists and Society, 4th Edition* (2008), *Tourism, Development and Environment: Beyond Sustainability* (2009) and *Tourist Experience: Contemporary Perspectives* (2011). A second edited collection on tourist experiences, *The Contemporary Tourist Experience: Concepts & Consequences*, was published in 2012.

Robert A. Stebbins, FRSC, who received his PhD in 1964 from the University of Minnesota, USA, is Professor Emeritus and Faculty Professor in the Department of Sociology at the University of Calgary, Canada. Among his 44 books now published or in press are the following; *Serious Leisure: A Perspective for Our Time* (2007), *The Idea of Leisure: First Principles* (2012) and *Work and Leisure in the Middle-East: The Common Ground of Two Separate World* (2013). His monograph, written with philosopher Elie Cohen-Gewerc and titled *Serious Leisure and Individuality*, was published in June 2013 by McGill-Queen's University Press. Stebbins has been a visiting professor at Griffith University, University of Bedfordshire, University of Northern Iowa and the Seoul School of Integrated Sciences & Technologies. He is an elected fellow of the Academy of Leisure Sciences, Royal Society of Canada and World Leisure Academy.

Philip R. Stone is Executive Director of the Institute for Dark Tourism Research (iDTR) at the University of Central Lancashire (UCLan), Preston, UK. His principal research interests are in dark tourism consumption and its fundamental interrelationships with the cultural condition of society. Philip has a PhD in Thanatology and has published extensively in this area as well as presenting keynote addresses at numerous international conferences. Prior to academia, Philip spent 15 years in the British private sector as both a general management and management consultant. He has acted as a subject expert on dark tourism and heritage for a range of global press and broadcast media organisations. His recent co-edited/co-authored books with R. Sharpley include *The Darker Side of Travel: The Theory and Practice of Dark Tourism* (Channel View, 2009), *Tourist Experience: Contemporary Perspectives* (Routledge, 2011) and *Contemporary Tourist Experience: Concepts and Consequences* (Routledge, 2012).

Gordon J. Walker is Professor in the Faculty of Physical Education and Recreation at the University of Alberta, Canada. His research program integrates social and cross-cultural psychology and leisure theory. He is particularly interested in how culture and ethnicity affect leisure behaviour (e.g., motivations for, constraints to, experiences during, and outcomes of, leisure). To date, Gordon's research has focused primarily on Chinese, Chinese/Canadian, and British/Canadian people's leisure, with funding from the Alberta Gambling Research Institute and the Social Science and Humanities Research Council of Canada. In 2009 he was elected as an Academy of Leisure Sciences Fellow. In 2011 he co-authored the second edition of *A Social Psychology of Leisure* with Doug Kleiber and Roger Mannell, and he is currently co-editing a book entitled *Race, Ethnicity, and Leisure* with Monika Stodolska, Kim Shinew, and Myron Floyd.

Mike Watkins is a teacher-researcher in the Department of Tourism, Sport and Hotel Management at Griffith University, Australia. His teaching areas include Leisure Theory and Behaviour, Hospitality and Tourism Marketing, and Managing Cultural Diverse Workplaces. Mike's research interests focus on understanding the nature of leisure and tourism experiences and using learning theory to inform the development of pre-service and industry training programs. He has conducted several longitudinal experimental projects aimed at improving the quality of learning outcomes and teaching practice. Mike's publications appear in a variety of leisure studies and tourism management journals.

ILLUSTRATIONS

Figures

Tables

PREFACE

It may seem a little curious that an edited volume such as this has been many years in the planning. We have discussed the need for such a book over countless mugs of coffee, but it always seemed that other projects got in the way or there was no clear rationale as to why a particular time or period would be an appropriate moment to publish. So why now you may ask? It may be a little fanciful to propose that we are entering a new era of leisure but the many social, cultural and technological changes currently taking place in many modern societies are affecting the manner in which leisure is delivered and consumed, and certainly suggests that we are entering, at the very least, a new phase of leisure. To what extent this new phase of leisure impinges upon the subjective nature of leisure is a key signature of this volume, the consequence of which will, we hope, generate much timely debate and discussion.

Our initial interest in the more philosophical and experiential elements of leisure was ignited through a final year undergraduate course we have both contributed to over the past three decades. In fact it was our intention that the title of the course – Leisure in Mind – was to be the main title of the book. However, it soon became apparent that the title might limit contributors to primarily psychologically led topics and discussion – and not the broader philosophical debates that we were hoping for. Furthermore, there was a risk that it would not illustrate the contemporary nature of the volume that we were also keen on promoting. But this only explains what we wanted to cover in the book and not why we believed it necessary to revisit the debates which are without doubt the foundations of the study of leisure. Whilst teaching on the course outlined above we found that students (the majority of whom were not leisure students) would soon become quite animated, and at first distracted, by what leisure meant to them, questioning why they chose certain leisure-related activities over others. Also students were, and continue to be, fascinated by what they can do with this new-found information and insight. Such insights and personal revaluation have not been the sole preserve of the students as we, the tutors, have questioned our own leisure values and practices. There is a sweet irony that those of us teaching and researching in leisure end up unable to have the time or summon up the energy to practise what we preach. In many cases it has been the students who have reminded us of the rich benefits that leisure can bring; that valuing leisure is something which can be learnt, and above all be applied to a number of non-leisure contexts. These gentle and fortuitous reminders have led us to a number of research investigations of our own, particularly in education; highlighting the often neglected practice of teaching informed research.

But aside from the many benefits that a philosophical stance on leisure will bring to both student and tutor alike there are other reasons why and how this book came about. In the early days, those of us teaching, researching and writing in the more experiential aspects of leisure would often become quite frustrated in locating specific texts which would direct students to the key contributors and theories. Roger Ingham's (1986, 1987) invaluable psychological review quickly became required reading until more specific texts emerged (e.g., Argyle, 1996; Haworth, 1997; Mannell and Kleiber, 1997). From a positive perspective this initial dearth in related texts meant that the search for appropriate articles became quite a creative one (some readers will have to be reminded that the instantaneousness of electronic searching has not always been an option), and revealed that those writing in the more subjective aspects of leisure came from quite disparate and diverse disciplinary positions. The interdisciplinary nature of leisure should, of course, come as little surprise, though the fact that such disciplinary diversity should be so prevalent in a seemingly specialist area of leisure was, at the time, both surprising and exciting. Leisure has always been a broad church, an indication of which can be seen in the rich variety of contributors in the regular volumes published by the Leisure Studies Association. Today, such diversity is evident in the academic backgrounds of those currently writing in the areas highlighted in this volume, which are as rich and wide-ranging as they ever were. And yet there have been very few opportunities for them to collectively contribute to a single overarching text that illustrates and celebrates this inherent multiformity. It is hoped that this volume will in some way partially remedy this oversight.

A further purpose for the book was to explore the experience of leisure in the twenty-first century, and in doing so, to both re-examine time honoured theories in a contemporary context, as well as to proffer new observations and theory. In the spirit of leisure, contributors were very much given a free hand on the topics and debates they wished to cover, albeit within the broad confines of the book's three themes: meaning, motives and life-long learning. This liberty of thought has culminated in an intriguing and thought provoking collection of ideas and reflections which we believe offers important insights into the leisure condition today – and its impending future directions.

Sam Elkington and Sean J. Gammon

INTRODUCTION

Sam Elkington and Sean J. Gammon

What is this life if, full of care,
we have no time to stand and stare.

No time to stand beneath the boughs
and stare as long as sheep or cows.

No time to see, when woods we pass,
where squirrels hide their nuts in grass.

No time to see, in broad daylight,
streams full of stars, like skies at night.

No time to turn at Beauty's glance,
and watch her feet, how they can dance.

No time to wait till her mouth can
enrich that smile her eyes began.

A poor life this is if, full of care,
we have no time to stand and stare.

William Henry Davies, *Leisure*

Of all concepts that of leisure is one of the most intractable, particularly when considered in the context of modern life. Like the concept of time, to paraphrase St Augustine, we know what it is when no one asks us, but when asked what it is, we are hard put to find an answer. Relatedly, we have each found solace at various points in our careers in the unassuming language of William H. Davies's poem *Leisure*, and believe it offers a valuable organising framework for the present volume.

Written in 1911, you could be excused for thinking that Davies is referring to the trials and tribulations of living in our modern day society. He certainly appears attuned to the struggles of the modern condition. Davies laments the rushed and harried manner in which we now spend our lives which, he argues, functions only to deprive ourselves of the richness and diversity of life. We have become slaves to time and material pursuits. Davies uses satire to drive at the heart of what is a very human dilemma – how our materialistic attitude preoccupies mind and body to the extent that we no longer have any grasp of our primordial roots. At the heart of Davies's message is an imbroglio so complex and in many ways so simple that it does not transfer easily into words. And yet, it is with a modest simplicity that Davies invites us to see past the sprawl of industrialisation and urban spaces and open up to the simple pleasures of a life unhurried.

Davies's secret is form. The structure and the language of the poem are simple, hinting at leisure's inherent ubiquity – it is all around us, we need only take the time to be still and acknowledge it. A more complex interpretation of Davies's choice of simplicity relates to the naturalistic theme of the poem. Like its structure, the poem's interactions with the seemingly inconsequential details of nature, such as watching '*squirrels hide their nuts in grass*' are relatively unsophisticated. However, by utilising simplistic structure and language, Davies reinforces the human necessity to appreciate and enjoy the simple beauties in nature – we have only to take '*time to stand and stare*'.

It is telling that Davies does not use the term leisure at any point in the poem itself – it remains unlanguaged. Its implied presence instead speaks to a way of looking, a gaze to be turned on to the world. There are certain features, intrinsic to this conception of leisure, which permit us to see leisure in a new light and, crucially, in a way that reflects how we experience it today. It certainly demarcates some distinct ground from which the relationship between consumer culture and the symbolic meanings of modern leisure can be addressed.

In advanced industrial societies, leisure has now become a defining feature of the way we live, work and spend our free time. This modern leisure has evolved into a complex domain of life with myriad personal and social meanings and is recognised as significant to human and societal development. Understanding what leisure is, why it is important in our contemporary society, and why it has become a central economic consideration of many developed and developing countries, not only helps us to recognise the type of society we live in and why people value leisure time and activities in different ways, but also its growth as a major area of personal and collective expenditure (Page and Connell, 2010). Today it seems for many people the pursuit of pleasure and happiness, through leisure, much more than work shapes their sense of who they are. Leisure is meant to have edifying qualities, it is meant to lead to a better quality life.

However, in the era of modern leisure, defined by the pull of co-existent processes of freedom and consumption, while people may claim to be free and devoted to their leisure pursuits, this invariably means giving nothing of themselves, absorbing only themselves, in what is a mash-up of superficial experiences devoid of any real meaning. Indeed, as a domain of life, the social reality with which modern leisure must now grapple is one of incessant change and complexity. It may be argued that there is nothing new in any of this, that the idea of leisure has always had to contend with change and complexity given that it has ever been shaped by social and political processes; this was evident even in Davies's day. It is the pace of change inherent to the modern way of life that has no precedent.

Modern life, as it is experienced today, is at once a continuous stream of images clambering for our attention and a glut of desires and obligations, expectations and commitments, shaped by our intentions and refined and checked through hurried, and all too often, mediated social interactions. Increasing pluralisation of life choices (of which leisure is central), offered amid unprecedented exposure to new media, technologies and other forms of social communication, has resulted in the saturation of the social self. It is no wonder, then, that people seek out those leisure experiences that tell them how to live their lives: how to pose, what music to listen to, where to shop, what to eat and drink and where to travel. Working Westerners have more leisure time than any generation previously but are barely aware of the trend or its implications. In fact, the pursuit of leisure today leads to a more troubled existence. With contemporary experiences of leisure subject to increasing commercial prompting, much of the dynamic potential of modern leisure remains unrealised. That is to say it has become performative rather than expressive (Blackshaw, 2010). Over the last 30 years there has been an exponential growth in leisure, and not just the kind that is provided for by our consumer culture. Despite not being entirely divorced from the quiet hand of consumerism, many activities are marked with a significant degree of meaning, draw and devotional practices. As a consequence, the quality rather than the quantity of leisure in peoples' lives has firmly entered into the public consciousness, as well as that of politicians, researchers and managers responsible for leisure provision. The changing values and practices in leisure often act as a barometer to wider societal changes linked to, for example, the economic environment, youth culture, technological developments and an ageing population. It may be a little ambitious to posit that we are entering an altogether new epoch of leisure, though it is hard to imagine that current global developments will not have long-term effects on not only what we choose in our leisure but also the extent in which we value it.

Crucially, perhaps the greatest virtue of leisure, as intimated by Davies, is that it allows, albeit temporarily so, for suspension of the tensions of daily life, where the necessity of consumerism is replaced with the contingency of playfulness and contemplation. But even in playing and thinking there is no guarantee as we tend to get bogged down in our daily routines, to the extent that we hardly ever pause to think about the meaning of our experiences: even less often have we the opportunity to compare our private experience with the fate of others, to the social in the individual, the general in the particular (Bauman, 2000). In order to develop a contemporary interpretation of leisure we must not only break with the convention of seeing it as merely a residual category of work or other forms of obligation, but rethink our approach in nearly every way. To really understand how people experience leisure today, we must decentre the subject itself (Rojek, 2010). Here we take our lead from Davies where a focus on contemporary perspectives in leisure gives us something else to contemplate and through contemplation find new things to see.

Guided in this way by Davies, what we call the subject matter we wish to explore in all intents and purposes matters less than the mindset with which we approach it. Leisure is presented within this volume as an orientation referring to the specific ways in which individuals look at the world and to such abilities as thoughtfulness, stillness, empathy, receptiveness, resilience, courage, mindfulness, as well as criticality. Here the concept of orientation functions as a device for making visible how the subject matter of leisure constitutes a way of making sense of the world. To contemplate leisure as a way of looking is to open up to hidden nuances, distortions, contradictions, contingencies – to celebrate the ambivalence of reality – and perceive significance, and beauty, in places unexpected. This admittedly romantic ethic offers a lens through which leisure can be regarded as symbolically rich, inherently meaningful and capable of creating both presence and resonance within an otherwise directionless world. It brings with it an implicit social and moral structure comprising beliefs, values and dispositions towards leisure, brought to life by means of a way of looking that is necessarily trans-disciplinary; moving beyond the false boundaries of sociology, psychology, philosophy and history, to free the leisure imagination which aims to enhance the whole person rather than merely train the mind.

In bringing together international contributions by leading researchers from both inside and outside the field of Leisure Studies, the volume aims to examine what it means to study leisure and the individual in the context of this potential new era of leisure from various theoretical and methodological approaches. To this end, it explores the philosophical debates surrounding leisure spanning three main sections, taking in its contemporary meanings (Part I), motives (Part II) and potential for lifelong learning (Part III). The volume aims to better understand the relationship between leisure and the individual and, by extension, the nature of leisure experiences to be provided within the present and future leisure industries.

The *Meanings* section of the book begins with the familiar name of Professor Roger Mannell whose opening chapter reflects on a long and influential career, predominantly researching and shedding much needed light on our understanding of the subjective nature of leisure. Roger's chapter maps out not only his own research journey in leisure but also the general development of psychology-led research in leisure over the last thirty years or more. He reminds us of the great strides that have been made whilst also drawing attention to some important questions that remain intriguingly left unanswered. In addition he promotes the need to explore and explain leisure as a network of interrelated beliefs, attitudes and values which impact upon an individual's 'mental outlook'. Future research, he argues, should consider in what ways leisure influences the manner in which individuals reflect upon all life experiences and how such reflection impacts upon life satisfaction and well-being. Closely aligned to the debates outlined in the opening chapter Peter McGrath in Chapter Two introduces and evaluates the two concepts of slow travel and slow tourism. The main thrust of this chapter is to highlight and promote the many benefits of taking time in our leisure. There is little doubt that the slow agenda acts as both a reaction to – as well as an antidote to – the immediacy and superficiality of life lived (literally and metaphorically) in the fast lane. Continuing this theme, in Chapter Three, Robert Stebbins reflects on what part leisure plays in generating feelings of happiness and life satisfaction. Leisure in and of itself is not a single ingredient to achieving happiness, for leisure is, he argues, made up from a group of ingredients (distinguished by serious, casual and project-based components) that collectively contribute to individuals' wellbeing. Professor Stebbins' invaluable insights are no doubt born from an almost unparalleled career researching and writing in the field of leisure, and illustrate powerfully the important part leisure plays in the lives of many. Chapter Four by John Haworth highlights the significance of leisure in not just contributing to an individual's sense of wellbeing but also to the general health of a nation. In so doing he explores how the present economic downturn, coupled with an ageing society, will affect the ability to engage in meaningful leisure experiences. He calls for governments (particularly in the UK) to be more sensitive and cognisant to the direct and indirect impacts of the current austerity measures; especially to the less affluent. The closing chapter in this section takes a somewhat darker turn by exploring the moral dilemmas that are triggered through the production and consumption of dark tourism. In Chapter Five Phillip Stone and Richard Sharpley outline and discuss the many complex meanings associated with dark tourist sites, arguing that this intriguing facet of dark leisure is neither deviant nor morally questionable but offers solace and a degree of personal reflection to those that visit them.

The *Motives* section begins with Chapter Six by Karla Henderson who makes the case that the consumption of leisure comes with a price. The argument made is that although leisure can bring great personal and collective benefits to people, it can also negatively impact upon the environment as well as to other peoples. Karla believes that there should be a universal responsibility to promote *just* leisure, which can be attained through appropriate educational initiatives. It would be interesting to explore how such strategies could impact upon the quality of leisure experiences – especially with regards to freedom and guilt. In Chapter Seven Paul Beedie sheds light on why many individuals today seek out seemingly risky and adventurous pursuits in their leisure. Using climbing as an example Paul discusses that engaging in more adventurous forms of leisure offers a balance to the increasingly protective societies that many of us live in, whilst at the same time offering genuine life-affirming experiences. The following chapter by Sam Elkington (Chapter Eight) explores how the experience and practice of serious leisure is affected and influenced by the sites in which it takes place. By offering amateur actors as examples of serious leisure he found that an intense and deeply personal interaction occurs between person, activity and place. Over time, actors reported an intimacy with the site in which the performances took place, which in turn led to a sense of trust in the environment that profoundly impacted upon the quality of the experiences. In Chapter Nine Sean Gammon introduces the term *leisure identity deceiver*, which describes individuals who use leisure to deliberately mislead a third party in order to gain some form of advantage, or to simply impress on others an idealised version of themselves. To date deception in leisure has received surprisingly little research and it is hoped that Sean's discussion will act as a platform for future research. Chapter Ten by Jo Bryce evaluates the potential physical, social and psychological consequences for young people engaging in online leisure pursuits. Jo's evaluation offers an important contribution to the erstwhile sensationalist media debates that tend to frame many online activities negatively, by noting that, at least with gaming, some online pursuits offer opportunities for both personal and social development. In addition this chapter observes that many online leisure-related activities are designed and controlled from a male perspective – and although there appears to be some increase in female use, there still remains a notable divide. Next, Steven Howlett (Chapter Eleven) considers the inherent conflation between volunteering and leisure. More specifically he explores the potential results of more formal management practices now taking place in the supervision of volunteers which, if too draconian, will inhibit the *élan* of the volunteer experience. As a consequence he calls for a more sensitive approach to volunteer management; one that always keeps leisure in mind. The final chapter in this section, Chapter Twelve, is by Ken Roberts. Ken draws on his many years explaining and discussing the utility of leisure in the youth life stage. In this chapter he takes the reader through the changes that have taken place between leisure and young people since the nineteenth century, concluding that whilst today's youth have markedly more freedom and independence in their leisure choices, such choices and practices are often influenced by the choices and practices of previous youth generations.

The final section of this volume focuses on leisure and *lifelong learning* and begins with Chapter Thirteen by Hayden Ramsay, entitled 'Reflective leisure, freedom and identity'. Hayden's theme could quite easily have fit into any of the previous sections but has been placed here because we felt that his reflections have a strong educational element to them. His chapter takes a philosophical and theological direction, reminding the reader of the contemplative spiritual significance of leisure. Such values, he argues, are lost in consumer-led modern societies that propagate the materiality of leisure, rather than its simpler and often neglected intrinsic qualities. In Chapter Fourteen Gordon Walker takes a more theoretical turn by proposing a leisure participation framework that incorporates the theories of self-determination, leisure constraints and planned behaviour. The framework could be used in order to promote important theoretical positions that tend not be engaged in by practitioners – as well as generally informing the domain of leisure education. Chapter fifteen evaluates postmodern perspectives on personal identity in leisure. Scott Cohen draws the reader's attention towards the cumulative benefits of leisure involvement. He observes that previous studies have tended to focus upon the impacts and psychological rewards of specific episodes in leisure, rather than acknowledging the holistic benefits (specifically relating to well-being and personal growth) of continued leisure engagement. Chapter Sixteen by Sam Elkington and Mike Watkins reviews the current models utilised in the leisure education literature. In so doing they propose two alternative models; namely, the Leisured Pedagogic Orientation and the Learning to Experience Leisure models which, they argue, provide alternative ontological perspectives for framing students' explorations of leisure. The final chapter (Chapter Seventeen) is a candid and personal account of an academic's experience of teaching and writing in leisure over the past twenty-five years. Lesley Lawrence reflects on her fascinating journey working in higher education, revealing how her many interests and experiences in and outside of leisure have helped inform and guide her in both her writing and research. She offers invaluable advice to all of us who at times struggle in getting the right words down, and promotes the virtues of always keeping leisure in mind – whatever we're working on.

In the end, leisure understood as a contemplative way of seeing is an intrinsic quality available to anyone. However, in aiming for leisure we do not promise you, the reader, will find it in these pages; rather we humbly urge you heed Davies's message – take time to stand back from the routine cadence of daily routines and embrace that special way of feeling and seeing only permitted in leisure. In this way we can only invite the muse by creating space for the experience of leisure to be encountered from alterative contemporary perspectives; the meaning of what is said hereafter is thus something for every attentive reader to discover for themselves. In this sense the invitation is both to remember and to forget.

PART I
Meanings

1

LEISURE IN THE LABORATORY AND OTHER STRANGE NOTIONS

Psychological research on the subjective nature of leisure

Roger C. Mannell

In 1977 while finishing breakfast in the Las Vegas hotel where I was attending a research conference, I was suddenly assailed by an idea that I hurriedly transcribed on a close-at-hand piece of paper – the back of a Keno card. The recent recipient of a PhD in experimental social psychology, and newly appointed director of something called a Centre of Leisure Studies, I had been struggling to give form to an idea on which to base a research program on the psychology of leisure. The idea eventually led to the development of an experimental paradigm that provided a framework for a number of experiments that I and a succession of my graduate students completed over the next twenty years – experiments in which we examined the subjective nature of leisure (e.g., Bradley and Mannell, 1984; Mannell, 1979; Mannell and Bradley, 1986; Iwasaki and Mannell, 1999). Although I went on to study leisure experiences outside of the laboratory with colleagues using other methods such as the field experiment (e.g., Backman and Mannell, 1986) and signal-contingent sampling (e.g., Mannell, Zuzanek and Larson, 1988; Zuzanek and Mannell, 1993), these early 'experiments in leisure' provided me with some of my most interesting challenges and convinced me that the subjective nature of leisure is amenable to empirical scrutiny by psychological science.

In this chapter, I will examine the emergence as well as continued development of different approaches to 'psychologizing' and empirically studying leisure as a subjective phenomenon. In the mid-to late 1970s, along with a few other like-minded scholars scattered around North America and Britain, I began to use psychological theory and methods to study and analyze the subjective nature of leisure, that is, treat it as an empirical phenomenon as opposed to a philosophical ideal. These early efforts to use psychological perspectives to conceptualize and measure the subjective nature of leisure were an important impetus for developing the psychology of leisure as a field of study (Mannell *et al.*, 2006). Of course, empirical research on what exists only in the experiencer's mind rather than the external world is challenging and I have often joked that working in this leisure 'mind field' is akin to working in a 'mine field' (Mannell and Iso-Ahola, 1987). However, at the time of my initial experimental forays, I was well aware that social psychologists had had good success studying a variety of seemingly difficult-to-define and measure subjective phenomena experimentally in the laboratory such as the experience of time (e.g., Ornstein, 1969) and emotion (e.g., Schachter and Singer, 1962). In fact, social psychologists have continued to use laboratory experiments to study subjective phenomena that are as difficult as leisure to pin down. For example, recently Haidt and his colleagues have reported a number of successful experiments on the subjective phenomenon of 'moral elevation,' a state that individuals sometimes experience after they witness or hear about a virtuous act (Algoe and Haidt, 2009).

With respect to my own psychological experiments on the subjective nature of leisure, I was influenced by several leisure researchers who at the time were themselves advocating the use of experiments (Bishop and Witt, 1970; Neulinger, 1974). Although Bishop and Witt did not study leisure states, they carried out an experiment in which they asked research participants to imagine themselves in different sets of circumstances and then to choose the leisure activities in which they would prefer to participate. Neulinger's 1974 book, *The Psychology of Leisure*, was also very influential. The book was ground breaking in identifying a number of personality and social psychological theories that potentially could be used to explain leisure as objective and subjective phenomena. Neulinger also psychologized the concept of leisure by providing a definition based on the concepts of perceived freedom and intrinsic motivation – psychological ideas that continue to be critical for psychologists in understanding human behavior.

Another significant influence on the development of my experimental approach for studying leisure experiences in the laboratory was Csikszentimhalyi's recently published book *Beyond Boredom and Anxiety: Flow in Work and Play* (1975). On the basis of extensive interviews with people engaged in their best leisure (i.e., rock climbers, basketball players, recreational dancers, chess players), he developed his flow model, which provided insight into how the activities of everyday life come to be invested with meaning and experienced as optimal. His insightful analysis identified the key conditions and characteristics of these intensely absorbing and rewarding experiences, which include the presence of challenges that match participant skills, clear performance feedback, loss of a sense of time and awareness of self, and positive affect. My 'Las Vegas' insight involved some ideas on the ways in which flow could be operationalized and measured in the laboratory.

Experimental paradigms: a case for studying leisure experiences in the lab?

My early efforts to develop an experimental paradigm to study leisure experience in the laboratory were in part to demonstrate that leisure as a subjective phenomenon is amenable to even the most rigorous research methods used by psychologists. Experimental paradigms in psychology are tools created and used to study specific phenomena, that is, they are a standard set of procedures and arrangements (Meiser, 2011). I eventually used my experimental paradigm in a number of laboratory experiments to create or simulate a period of free time in which a game is played. This paradigm made it possible to create a laboratory environment in which I could: (1) engineer a period of 'free time' during the course of the experiment that the participants would perceive, at least within certain limits, was their own time and separate from the 'obligatory' activities under study; (2) manipulate a variety of independent variables, that is, vary the situational and personality characteristics of the participants; (3) hold constant all other features of the physical and social environment for all participants in the study; (4) measure the dependent variables used to operationalize the type of leisure experience of interest; and (5) disguise the purpose of the experiment so that the participants would behave as naturally as possible (Mannell, 1980).

In the first experiment using the paradigm (Mannell, 1979), the amount of freedom participants had in choosing a game to play during the 'free time' period and the competitiveness of the game were the independent variables that were manipulated. As predicted, participants who had greater freedom of choice and who played more competitive games experienced higher levels of flow than participants who were in low choice and low competitive conditions. The participants, who were university students, were randomly assigned to one of the four possible conditions, that is, low choice/low competition, low choice/high competition, high choice/low competition and high choice/high competition. The two-room laboratory was furnished to look like it had a testing and a waiting room. The 'waiting room' was furnished with comfortable furniture, curtains, rugs, magazines, and pictures and posters adorning the walls. Every effort was made to have the participants feel that what happened in this waiting or 'free time' period had nothing to do with the actual purpose of the experiment, which from their perspective was a learning task being carried out in the 'testing' room. All participants played the same game for thirty minutes. The manipulations led them to believe they had a little or very much choice about which game they played, and that the game was either not competitive or moderately competitive.

Of course, another critical feature of this experimental paradigm was that it allowed the measurement of flow as an indicator of optimal leisure experience. In the experiment, three features of flow were operationalized and measured. First, perceptions of the time duration of the waiting/free time period were assessed at the end of the waiting period by asking the participants to rate their perceptions of the length of waiting period – they had removed their watches for the 'testing' portion of the experiment. High levels of flow are associated with the experience of time passing quickly (Csikszentmihalyi, 1975). The second measure of flow was the participants' focus of attention on the game rather than themselves or their surroundings. Focus of attention was measured with a memory test consisting of multiple choice questions that assessed the participants' memories of the features of the game room environment. It was assumed that the less the study participant remembered about the waiting room environment, the greater their focus of attention, and consequently flow experienced. The hypotheses were supported and in subsequent experiments freedom of choice and control were always found to have a powerful influence on experiencing flow. Psychological reactance theory was used to explain the importance of freedom in experiencing optimal leisure.

We have reported a number of studies on the factors affecting these 'immediate conscious experiences' during leisure operationalized as flow or intrinsic motivation and using this paradigm or variations of it. Personality differences (e.g., locus of control, intrinsic leisure motivation orientation) have been found to interact with the level of choice and control provided participants and to influence levels of optimal experience (Mannell and Bradley, 1986; Iwasaki and Mannell, 1999). In fact, Mannell and Bradley found that in certain situations people who feel they have little control in their lives generally do not experience higher levels of flow when given more choice in leisure activities whereas those who feel they have a great deal of control in their lives do experience greater flow with greater freedom and choice in leisure.

Alternative perspectives on leisure as a subjective phenomenon

Of course, other researchers have developed different ideas about the subjective nature of leisure and ways to study it. Around the time I first became interested in the psychology of leisure, I encountered and later described a 'leisure' episode I observed when out one evening with friends in Niagara Falls, Canada not far from my hometown. It has helped me think about these various views of the subjective nature of leisure and the ways they can be studied.

In a combination theme park and shopping mall in Niagara Falls stands a machine looking not unlike a flight simulator. When I first encountered this machine, it periodically spun, bumped and twisted. When it stopped, two people emerged with slightly bemused smiles on their faces. The machine had just dispensed a simulated leisure experience – with accompanying sounds, sights and feelings of disequilibrium. This simulated environment produced an engineered lifelike experience that was advertised to duplicate that of an actual ride on the world's largest roller coaster located 800 or 900 hundred kilometers distant (Mannell and Iso-Ahola, 1987).

Of course, machine-computer simulated virtual reality environments are now common. Such systems can simulate high fidelity experiences of racing Formula One cars and flying aircraft such as the Harrier Jump Jet. However, the simulated roller coaster ride is still intriguing. It is a leisure experience at several levels. It was designed to provide a simulated leisure experience of an actual leisure experience that, itself, was engineered!

For me, this example provided a useful way of delineating three somewhat overlapping strategies or approaches to the study of leisure as a subjective phenomenon. These include what I have called the 'post hoc satisfaction,' 'definitional' and 'immediate conscious experience' approaches (Mannell and Iso-Ahola, 1987). The roller coaster simulator episode allows the illustration of these strategies and three sets of questions and measurement issues that have drawn the attention of researchers examining the subjective nature of leisure. First, what satisfactions are derived from this leisure episode? Are they distinct from the satisfactions that could be experienced through participation in another type of recreational activity (or in this case the 'real' roller coaster ride)? How can these satisfactions be observed and measured? Second, is the simulated roller coaster ride perceived as leisure by the participants? If so, what are the criteria used by the participants to judge the activity, setting or experience to be leisure and how are researchers to observe and measure these criteria? Third, what is the actual nature of the experience that accompanies participation in the simulated roller coaster ride? That is, what are the participants feeling and thinking during an episode and how can researchers observe and measure the texture and quality of these experiences? These three approaches are similar in that leisure is viewed to be most profitably understood by assessing its subjective nature, yet they differ in how they treat or conceptualize this subjectivity.

Typically only one of the three approaches has been used in any one study even though the post hoc satisfaction, definitional and immediate conscious experience approaches are interrelated or overlap. People usually participate in leisure activities and settings to have specific immediate conscious experiences (e.g., feelings of fun, curiosity, awe, competence, relaxation, excitement, freedom, escape, challenge, social connectedness). However, the extent to which these experiences meet people's needs and expectations is usually an important influence on their post hoc satisfaction with the activity. As well, whether people define or judge the episode to be leisure can be influenced by their actual immediate experience and later post hoc satisfaction. Although in the following discussion we will examine work on leisure as a subjective phenomenon from each of these three perspectives separately, it should be noted that several researchers have used two (Mannell et al., 1988; Samdahl, 1988) and even three of these (Lee et al., 1994) approaches simultaneously. Samdahl used the experience sampling method (ESM), which allowed her study participants to report not only their immediate conscious experiences during their daily activities but rate the extent to which they felt (defined) these activities were leisure. Lee, Dattilo and Howard (1994) examined leisure using all three approaches. Leisure as definitional and post hoc phenomena were assessed using in-depth interviews, while the immediate conscious experience was captured by having study participants tape-record descriptions of their experiences at the time of occurrence.

Post hoc satisfaction – leisure after-the-fact

Assessing the satisfactions derived from participation in leisure activities or settings has been a frequently used approach to getting inside the heads of people and seeing leisure from their perspectives. This approach was the earliest application of psychological theory and thinking to studying the subjective nature of leisure. Driver and Tocher (1970) defined leisure as 'an experience that results from recreation engagements' (p. 10) and along with other North American researchers interested in outdoor recreation and management issues attempted to operationalize this 'experience' as 'motivations' 'psychological outcomes', and 'experience expectations' (Manning, 1986, p. 80). These concepts are based on the idea of post hoc satisfaction. People learn through experience that participation in certain types of outdoor activities allows them to satisfy their needs or meet their expectations, and consequently experience satisfaction (Mannell, 1999). Among the best-known and tested inventory used to measure these types of expected satisfactions in outdoor recreational activities, where most of this type of research has been conducted, is the Recreation Experience Preference (REP) scales developed by Driver and his colleagues. Scales to assess the needs, motives and satisfactions associated not only in outdoor activities but a wide range of other leisure activities have also been developed (see Driver et al., 1991).

Researchers have been able to successfully measure post hoc satisfaction and a great deal of the early research was carried out based on the assumption that participation in specific types of recreation activities and settings produce specific types of post hoc satisfactions. The assumption is that people have a history of participation in various recreation activities and have learned that they can reliably experience certain satisfactions in specific recreation activities. Consequently, leisure researchers attempted to identify differences in the packages of satisfactions that different types of leisure activities or settings could provide for participants. For example, Manfredo, Driver and Brown (1983) found groups of wilderness users were seeking different 'packages' of satisfactions that in turn were related to their preferences for specific recreation environmental settings. Users attempting to satisfy their needs for risk and achievement preferred areas with rough or undeveloped access, rugged terrain and a low probability of meeting other people. Those users looking for solitude but who were not looking for achievement and challenge satisfactions preferred areas with moderate accessibility and lacking dangerous situations, although they also preferred low levels of development and probability of social encounters. A third group preferred more accessible, secure and managed settings where the likelihood of meeting other people was higher. Visitors to the latter environment saw it as providing higher satisfactions for tension release, competence, escape and family togetherness. However, subsequent research has shown that the satisfactions that people experience in recreational activities and settings exist to a large extent in the mind of the participant and not in the activity itself (Driver and Brown, 1984). The same activity can provide different satisfactions depending on the previous experience of the participant and the social and/or physical setting in which it occurs. Also, some satisfactions can be achieved in a wide variety of activities and settings while other satisfactions are highly setting and activity specific (Yuan and McEwen, 1989).

However, understanding the satisfactions people experience and the factors that influence them continues to be an important strategy and area of research for exploring leisure as a subjective phenomenon. Post hoc satisfaction has been measured immediately after completion of a leisure activity while participants are still on-site, when leaving the site or at some future time after the activity is completed. Although post hoc satisfaction is usually assessed only once following participation in a leisure activity, Stewart and Hull (1992) conducted an innovative study that had outdoor recreation participants appraise their satisfaction with a day hike a number of times while on-site during the hike itself, what they called real-time satisfaction, immediately after the hike while still on-site, and at home both three and nine months after the hike. The researchers found that ratings of satisfaction over time remained positively correlated but did change. The on-site real-time satisfactions fluctuated depending on the impact of situational factors in the recreation setting (e.g., social group, resource impacts, encounters with other participants). Stewart and Hull suggested that this on-site measure is useful for studying factors in the setting that affect people's satisfaction with their outdoor participation. It is interesting to note that although their measure of real-time satisfaction ('How satisfied are you with your experience right now?,' p. 202) comes close to being a measure of immediate conscious leisure experience, there is a distinction. They did not assess the actual nature of the experiences that accompanied participation. Stewart and Hull's measurement of post hoc satisfaction with the same activity over time is also a good example of an approach to studying longer-term changes in satisfaction and their influence on future decisions to participate. As well as assessing post hoc satisfaction, it would be interesting to have people periodically recall the immediate conscious experiences that accompanied a particular leisure activity or event and examine factors in the intervening periods between recall and at the actual time of recollection that influence both the memory of the experience and satisfaction with it (Mannell, 1980).

The post hoc satisfaction approach has continued to be a frequently used approach for assessing the subjective nature of leisure ranging from satisfaction with specific leisure activities and settings (e.g., Brooks et al., 2006) to satisfaction with the totality of people's leisure lifestyles (e.g., Walker et al., 2011).

Definitional approach – leisure in the eye of the beholder

The definitional approach to the study of leisure involves theory and research that attempt to identify the attributes or properties that lead people to perceive the activity or setting in which they are engaged, or the experience associated with it, as leisure and not something else. Neulinger (1974) made an early contribution to the psychological exploration of personal leisure definitions arguing that people are more likely to experience leisure when they perceive they have freely chosen to participate, are intrinsically motivated to do so and are more caught up in the process of involvement than achieving a goal. In an early study, Iso-Ahola (1979) used an experiment to directly test the importance of these factors suggested by Neulinger that lead people to personally perceive or define an activity as leisure. Iso-Ahola had his respondents imagine they were participating in recreational activities and settings that varied systematically according to the amount of freedom they had in choosing the activity, the extent to which their participation was intrinsically or extrinsically motivated, as well as a variety of other factors. He found perceived freedom and intrinsic motivation were critical criteria in influencing the extent to which the study participants rated these imagined activities as leisure.

Another innovative study using a definitional approach was reported by Shaw (1984) using time diaries coupled with follow-up interviews. Her research participants were asked to classify all the activities that they had listed in their diaries as either 'work,' 'leisure', 'a mixture of work and leisure', or 'neither work nor leisure'. Additionally, she had her study participants explain their choices. Activities they labeled 'leisure' were typically characterized by the perception that they had been freely chosen and intrinsically motivated. She also found that enjoyment, relaxation and a lack of evaluation by other people seemed to accompany those activities her respondents felt were leisure. Other researchers have employed qualitative research methods that involve asking people what leads them to define an activity or episode as leisure. Gunter (1987) had people describe in writing their most memorable and enjoyable leisure experiences. Feelings of enjoyment, intense involvement and separation or escape from everyday routine were commonly associated with experiences perceived as leisure.

The experiential sampling method (ESM) developed by Csikszentmihalyi and his colleagues (Larson and Csikszentmihalyi, 1983) has also been used to study personal definitions of leisure. Samdahl (1988), whose study was referred to earlier, had a group of women and men carry electronic pagers with them during their daily activities. She arranged for them to be randomly signaled throughout the day for a period of one week. Each time the pager emitted a signal, the respondents took out a booklet of brief questionnaires and completed a series of open- and close-ended items indicating their current activity, the social and physical context of their activity, and their psychological state. Samdahl also included an item that followed Iso-Ahola's (1979) procedure of asking the study's participants to rate the extent to which their current activity was leisure for them. When the respondents perceived that they had chosen to participate in an activity independently of the expectations of other people and felt that they were expressing their true selves, they were more likely to judge the activity or situation to be leisure.

Research using the definitional approach and the factors that lead people to see what they are doing as leisure has declined. However, from time to time, interesting research continues to be reported. For example, recently Watkins (2007; Watkins and Bond, 2008) explored developmental changes in leisure definitions by conducting interviews followed by open-ended discussion with university students. The students were asked to provide several different examples of leisure and what it meant to them. It was concluded that what the participants defined as leisure changed in meaning from the passing of time to exercising choice, escaping pressure and eventually to achieving fulfillment with increasing age and more diverse life experiences. Walker and Deng (2003) tackled the difficult task of examining cross-cultural differences in the way people define and characterize their leisure. They examined the extent to which Western definitions of leisure based on the characteristics of freedom of choice, flow and positive moods had a counterpart in what Chinese participants would define as the experience of Rumi.

Based on the definitional approach, a number of attributes thought to characterize what people think or judge to be leisure have been proposed (Kleiber et al., 2011). The most central and commonly agreed upon set of properties is associated with freedom or a lack of constraint. Second, activities, settings and experiences perceived to be leisure are likely to be seen as providing opportunities for the development of competence, self-expression, self-development or self-actualization. A third major set of properties is based on the nature and quality of experiences derived from participation including enjoyment, fun and pleasure. Other characteristics found to lead people to feel they are engaged in leisure include feelings of relaxation as well as its opposite intense involvement or flow, feelings of separation or escape, a sense of adventure, spontaneity and loss of the sense of time. Additionally, experiences with cognitions involving fantasy and creative imagination have been suggested as properties leading to perceptions of engaging in or experiencing leisure.

Immediate conscious experiences – topography of subjective leisure

In addition to my leisure experiments described earlier, researchers have attempted to examine the actual on-site experiences accompanying involvement in leisure activities and settings in people's daily lives to further understand the subjective nature of leisure. In other words, there has been interest in the anatomy and topography of the experience, its evaluative (e.g., moods, emotions, feelings) and cognitive components (e.g., thoughts, images). These immediate conscious experiences are experiences of the present moment. The metaphor 'stream of consciousness' used by William James (1890) probably best characterizes mental experience and suggests that conscious states are perceived as continuous and constantly changing. Pope and Singer (1978) describe the stream of consciousness as 'the flow of perceptions, purposeful thoughts, fragmentary images, distant recollections, bodily sensations, emotions, plans, wishes, and impossible fantasies… [it] is our experience of life, our own personal life, from its beginning to its end' (p. 1). Describing these experiences during leisure and studying person and environmental determinants of these experiences has been seen as an important area of study in the psychology of leisure. Not too surprising, a number of the factors that lead people to define what they are doing as leisure as well as the satisfactions they derive from their leisure involvements are also properties of immediate conscious experiences occurring during leisure.

There also has been considerable interest in what constitutes a 'good' leisure experience. Is it characterized by higher positive moods, greater intensity or relaxation, flow with the experience of time going quickly or slowly and lesser or greater self-consciousness, rich fantasy, etc.? Some theorists have conceptualized the existence of unconditional (Kelly, 1983) and pure (Neulinger, 1974) leisure, and philosophers like de Grazia (1962) have viewed leisure as a special state of mind, 'which few desire and fewer achieve' (p. 5). There also are leisure scholars (Tinsley and Tinsley, 1986) who see the ultimate leisure experience as being primarily characterized by a high level of psychological involvement or absorption and best described by Csikszentmihalyi's concept of flow. As noted earlier, Csikszentmihalyi's (1975) concept of flow has been a particularly attractive model of leisure experience for leisure researchers, since his theory identifies a variety of features that can be used to define and measure it. In fact, it can be argued that the first systematic empirical studies of immediate conscious leisure experiences were reported by Csikszentmihalyi (1975) in his study of people during what they considered their best leisure activities.

Other pioneering studies of immediate conscious leisure experiences involved monitoring mood changes during the course outdoor recreation activities. More and Payne (1978) studied a day trip to a park by having visitors fill out surveys when they entered and then again when they left – positive moods increased but so did negative moods! Hammitt (1980) measured the moods of students at four different times during a trip to a marsh and once several days later. Their moods changed predictably depending on the phase of the outdoor recreation experience. In fact, a good deal of the research on immediate conscious leisure experience has been carried out by researchers interested in outdoor recreation experiences, the factors in the natural environment that influence them and the management of the environment to enhance these experiences. This area of research has continued to be very active and a variety of data gathering strategies have been developed to monitor leisure experiences in outdoor environments. For example, Hull, Michael, Walker and Roggenbuck (1996) examined the 'ebb and flow' of people's experiences in different environments that included walking along a rural road and in a city centre and sitting indoors with a view of a rural setting or no view. By having the study participants fill out self-administered questionnaires at various times during each of the activities it was found that the experiences were dynamic, multi-dimensional and complex. However, the researchers did not find that the rural versus urban or indoor versus outdoor settings predicted systematic variations in experience. Lee and Shafer (2002) also studied the dynamic nature outdoor experiences. They asked participants to recollect five events that occurred while hiking, such as seeing fish and meeting others on the trail and to rate their feelings at these times. The interaction between events encountered by the hikers in the outdoor environment and their self-identities were found to influence their emotional experiences during the activity. The hikers' experiences of challenge, satisfaction and absorption in the same outdoor environments varied according to whether they as individuals tended to be adventurous or meditative.

The development of the experiential sampling method (ESM) has contributed substantially to uncovering regularities in perceptions and feelings of happiness, self-awareness, concentration, sense of time and other features of conscious experiences in leisure activities and settings. Researchers have examined the feelings of intrinsic satisfaction experienced in recreational compared to non-recreational and work activities (Graef et al., 1983; Csikszentmihalyi and LeFevre, 1989), the meaning and quality of experiences derived from different types of leisure activities engaged in by adolescents (Kleiber et al., 1984), the moods of older adults in different types of social leisure (Larson et al., 1986) and experiences in a variety of conditions predicted to foster optimal leisure states (Havitz and Mannell, 2005; Mannell et al., 2005; Mannell et al., 1988; Samdahl, 1988).

Flow experiences during leisure and other domains of life have also been studied using specially designed survey questionnaires. In study of working women, Allison and Duncan (1987) used a questionnaire they devised to measure enjoyable flow. They found that work was the primary source of flow for professional workers, whereas for blue-collar women it was leisure. They provided a paragraph describing enjoyable flow and asked study participants to indicate how frequently during a week they experienced a similar state in their work and leisure. Bryce and Haworth (2002) examined well-being and flow among office workers using Allison and Duncan's questionnaire items, and Delle Fave and Massimini (2003) also used a questionnaire to examine flow among teachers and physicians. Study participants were invited to read three quotations describing optimal experience, to report whether they ever felt any of them during their daily lives, and to list the activities or situations in which they occurred. They were then asked to select from their list the activity in which flow was most intense and pervasive. Subsequently, participants were invited to describe the average quality of experience associated with the selected activity using a Likert-type scale.

Mannell (1993) and Elkington (2011) have suggested that serious leisure is a context particularly likely to foster flow. Using ESM, Mannell found that the older adults in his study were more likely to experience flow in leisure activities to which they were strongly committed and those who experienced flow more frequently during their daily lives had higher life satisfaction. Elkington has argued that serious leisure and flow are structurally and experientially mutually reinforcing and that experiencing flow is what makes serious leisure most rewarding and experienced as optimal. In a study of students involved in amateur acting, hobbyist table tennis and voluntary sport coaching, he used a phenomenological approach with open-ended group discussion and follow-up individual interviews based in part on a modification of the flow questionnaire. His findings suggest that flow-based serious leisure experience is the richest because of people's 'total personal commitment of self to its achievement, continuity and progress' (p. 278).

As already noted, most of the research on the ebb and flow or the dynamic nature of immediate conscious leisure experiences has occurred in outdoor recreation settings. There are a few exceptions. For example, Kubey and Czikszentmihalyi (1990) used data from an ESM study and found that participants' experiences (i.e., feelings of activation, positive affect, challenge and concentration) changed differently from before to during and after participation in three types of leisure activities (watching TV, athletic sport and other active leisure). McIntyre (1998) used the ESM to obtain measures of the dynamic nature of outdoor recreation by signaling canoeists on a wilderness river and asking them to record their level of activity, focus of attention and feelings of connection with wilderness at the moment signaled. Borrie and Roggenbuck (2001) used the ESM to monitor the environmental and wilderness experiences of visitors to a wild life refuge. They found that the cognitive content of the participants' experiences during the visit, that is, the extent to which they were focused on themselves, others, the task and the environment, changed throughout the visit. Change included greater focus on the environment, the self and internal experience at the end of the visit compared to the start. They also focused less on others and social acceptance during the middle phase of the visit. Jones (Jones, 2008; Jones et al., 2003) had kayakers complete a series of one-page questionnaires to measure flow and other variables during a river trip. The kayakers' perceptions of time, intrinsic motivation, involvement, merging of action and awareness, concentration on the task at hand, awareness of the physical surroundings, and moods were assessed using Likert-like scales. An interesting innovation on this approach has been reported by Mackenzie, Hodge and Boyes (2011). Data from novice whitewater river surfers was collected during interviews near the riverbank at the end of each day. However, helmet-mounted video camera footage of their participation was replayed during the interview to facilitate re-immersion in the experience and specificity of recall. These methods were used to examine hypotheses that two types of flow states may occur in adventure activities.

The dynamics of outdoor recreation experience has also been examined using other types of experience than flow. Scherl (1988) used personal narratives in logbooks to study the day-to-day affective states, perceptions and cognitions of adult participants on an Outward Bound program in the Australian wilderness. Hull, Stewart, and Yi (1992) found that significant changes in mood (e.g., excitement, boredom, calmness) occurred during a day hike and that the changes correlated with physical characteristics of the trail and stages of the hike. Arnould and Price (1993) used a combination of qualitative and quantitative approaches to study the dynamic nature of a lengthy raft trip on the Colorado River in the Grand Canyon.

Research on outdoor recreation experiences also has led to interesting work on the multi-phasic nature of immediate conscious experiences. In fact, the idea that experiences accompanying recreation activities change over the course of participation in an activity was proposed by Clawson and Knetsch (1966) before systematic research began. They suggested that the phases include: (1) anticipation – a period of imagining and planning the trip or event; (2) travel to – getting to the recreation site; (3) on-site – the actual activity or experience at the site; (4) travel back – the return trip home; and finally (5) recollection – the recall or memory of the activity or experience. The Hammitt (1980) study of a trip to a marsh referred to earlier was the first to empirically examine variations in the nature of the experience over the five phases and researchers have continued to explore the phenomenon. A special issue of the *Journal of Leisure Research* edited by Stewart (see Stewart, 1998) was devoted to the subject with articles addressing experience changes in adventure activities, multi-day competitive events, trail users, wilderness activities and vacations. Although most of the multi-phase immediate conscious experience research has been carried out in outdoor recreation settings, researchers are beginning to apply the idea to other types of leisure activities. Mitas, Yarnal, Adams and Ram (2012) measured positive emotions on a daily basis in twenty-five adult participants before, during and after two leisure travel experiences.

Research on immediate conscious experiences has provided a number of insights into the complex and multiphasic nature of leisure experiences as well as the situational and individual or personality differences that influence them. A rich variety of methods have been used including the experimental laboratory, experiential sampling method, personal accounts, completion of journals and questionnaires at assigned or random times during the experience.

A final note – neglected types of leisure experiences and subjective approaches?

Although this chapter began with a discussion of my own attempts to study the subjective nature of leisure experimentally in the psychological laboratory, the psychology of leisure is not today an experimental field like much of mainstream psychology (Mannell and Kleiber, 2013). However, as I argued earlier, in addition to the insights provided by this research, it demonstrates that even the seemingly difficult to define and measure subjective nature of leisure can be studied with even the most rigorous of empirical psychological methods. Although psychologically oriented leisure researchers have not embraced experimental methods, they have been highly innovative in the use of a variety of methods for studying leisure as a subjective phenomenon. These methods have been used along with the post hoc satisfaction, definitional and immediate conscious experience approaches to successfully empirically investigate the subjective nature of leisure. Efforts to understand and promote positive and healthy leisure lifestyles and ultimately higher quality of life are likely to be far more successful if the subjective nature of leisure is understood rather than just what people do during their free time or leisure. Much of the research on the subjective nature of leisure has been done in Western cultures and with a few exceptions little cross-cultural analysis has been reported. Fortunately, this state of affairs is changing as the study of leisure is becoming increasingly international (Mannell and Kleiber, 2013).

Although a variety of types of leisure experience have been identified, more intense and optimal experiences have been given much greater theoretical and research attention than those that are relaxing, reflective and meditative (Kleiber, 2000). However, more reflective experiences and processes have been receiving theoretical and empirical attention by psychologists outside of leisure studies with the development of positive psychology (Kleiber *et al.*, 2011). For example, Langer's (1989) theory on mindfulness has stimulated the development of measurement strategies and research (e.g., Brown and Ryan, 2003). Mindfulness is seen as a way of paying attention and experiencing the present moment that originated in Eastern meditation practices. It has been described as bringing one's complete attention to the present experience on a moment-to-moment basis in a non-judgmental way. Recently, Gim (2009) has argued that mindfulness practice can enhance the quality of leisure. Also, Bryant and Veroff (2007) have explored the idea of 'savoring,' an immediate conscious experience and process by which people focus on, appreciate and enhance positive experiences in life. They argue it is characterized by sharing with others, memory building, self-congratulation, sensory and perceptual sharpening, behavioral expressiveness, temporal awareness and counting blessings. Kleiber *et al.* (2011) have noted that savoring has similarities to flow. It is a positive experience, yet it also is different. Rather than being absorbed in the experience itself, it is a process of considering and reflecting on the experience. Savoring may often follow immediately after flow-like leisure experiences.

This idea of considering new or alternative leisure experiences such as mindfulness and savoring is a reminder of more philosophical views of leisure as a state of mind such as that of de Grazia (1962). Subjective phenomena like savoring and mindfulness can be parts of broader more global perspectives on life – perspectives amenable to systematic empirical study – where the subjective nature of leisure is a network of interrelated beliefs, attitudes and values providing a perspective or mental outlook on life. Leisure as a 'mental outlook' appears to have been neglected, and although there is periodic reference to leisure as a personal philosophy or an outlook on life (e.g., Leitner and Leitner, 2004; McNamee, 2000), little or no theory and research have been reported. Leisure researchers have studied relatively stable subjective leisure states such as attitudes and developed measures of them (see Manfredo, 1992). However, a great deal of this research is focused on assessing the extent to which people feel negative or positive about leisure in general or specific leisure activities (Kleiber *et al.*, 2011). When attitudes toward leisure in general have been assessed, it has been to predict people's satisfaction with their leisure lifestyles, the size of their leisure repertoire or frequency of participation in leisure activities. Yet, outside of leisure studies there are a number of 'mental outlooks' on life and ways of living that have been proposed that appear to be relevant to the idea of leisure as a mental outlook. For example, the ideas of 'voluntary simplicity' (Elgin, 2010) and 'in praise of slow' (Honoré, 2004) have been widely discussed in the popular media.

Perhaps, it would be useful to propose a fourth approach to conceptualizing and studying the subjective nature of leisure in addition to the post hoc satisfaction, definitional and immediate conscious experience approaches. Leisure as a 'mental outlook' could be viewed as a habitual way of looking at one's life and the daily events that comprise it. Researchers could study the range, variety and complexity of leisure outlooks and their impact on people's behavior, experience and well-being.

2

ESCAPE FROM TIME

Experience the travel within

Peter McGrath

> Take off the watch. Get rid of the time pressures, the deadline, the agenda.
> Escape from time.
>
> Krippendorf (1984)

Introduction

Leisure is often associated with 'discretionary' or 'unobligated time' (Borsay, 2006), which transpires to time when one is not working or occupied. Leisure is a key dimension for quality of life yet as a society we're pushed to our physical, psychological and emotional limits in the amount of time we spend at work, or even the time we spend thinking about work. There is currently no English word for working yourself to death; however, possibly the West will have to follow the lead from the Japanese and Chinese who have coined the terms 'karoshi' and 'guolaosi' respectively. In 2012 the UK government urged the country to work harder, after slipping back into recession but what does this default recovery position mean for the future of leisure and our leisure time? Increased productivity is usually converted into higher wages and increased production instead of more free time (Reisch, 2001). With the ever-demanding pressures of time the need to compress our leisure activities into reduced time frames has become apparent. Nijkamp and Baaijens (1999) explain in terms of leisure and tourism, high travel speed has become deeply rooted in our modern society. The paradox is, however, that people often do not use the extra time saved for alternative leisure purposes (e.g., reading, walking), but seem to spend it immediately on other trips. Thus, there seems to be a drive towards a 'restless society,' characterized by 'hypermobility' (Nijkamp and Baaijens, 1999). As a consequence the 'art of travel' has fallen out of fashion and the words of William H. Davies that open this book could not be more pertinent as we no longer have the time to stop, to stand and to stare. Countering the acceleration of life is the slow movement; a socio-cultural phenomenon, which aims to re-address our relationship with time and offer enough time for meaningful things (Reisch, 2001) with an emphasis on quality over quantity. In essence slow living could be described as a life that is outwardly simple and inwardly rich (to quote the title of the influential 1981 book by Duane Elgin). The interpretation of 'slow' therefore in this sense is a lifestyle choice and could be linked to the concepts of voluntary simplicity and downshifting as a way of seeking a more meaningful and balanced life. This chapter explores the concept of 'slow' and its relation to leisure with a particular focus towards holidaymaking and the development of the terms, *slow travel* and *slow tourism*. Essentially it is premised by a need to rethink time; it is argued that in order to improve quality of life it is essential to change the pace from one which is rushed and time compressed to one that revolves around doing things at the "right" speed, it is not simply a fast versus slow discussion. This argument is aligned to the earlier work of Virilio (1991) who argues speed is a major destructive force changing societies at a pace which will be difficult to reverse.

Shifting priorities: the search for a more balanced life

In recent decades the West has got wealthier and living standards risen yet it is thought this has not been matched by a rise in people's happiness (Easterbrook, 2003). Over time we have convinced ourselves that the pursuit of material acquisition will help satisfy our needs and ultimately this has led to a lack of time free from working. Not surprisingly, long working hours, the acceleration of pace, stress and pressure 'to keep up' in consumption terms has been leading to a backlash against work and spend since the 1980s (Schor, 1998). For the more we want, the more we must work for it and the more extra time is required to purchase and maintain all of these things (Young and Schuller, 1988). Consequently we have had to cut corners in many aspects of our lifestyles which Cross (1993) terms 'domestic speedup' whereby we try to fit everything into shortened periods of time; eating fast foods, shopping online and fundamentally missing quality time spent with family and friends. This trend has increased in more recent years. The materialistic culture of fast living and unsustainable consumption can be neatly summarized as follows:

> We have bigger houses but smaller families;
> more conveniences, but less time;
> We have more degrees, but less sense;
> more knowledge, but less judgment;
> more experts, but more problems;
> more medicines, but less healthiness;
> We've been all the way to the moon and back,
> but have trouble crossing the street to meet
> the new neighbor.

We build more computers to hold more
information to produce more copies then ever,
but have less communication;
We have become long on quantity,
but short on quality.
These are times of fast foods
but slow digestion;
Tall men but short character;
Steep profits but shallow relationships.
It's a time when there is much in the window,
but nothing in the room.

(Moorehead, 1995)

This summary is clearly rooted in spirituality and is somewhat idealistic though perhaps does re-iterate our priorities in modern society. While aspects of our modern day living may be brought into question, there is still a need for both money and time as these are seen as resources for well-being. However, the two are becoming increasingly in competition with one another and most of us complain that we do not have enough of one or perhaps of either. It could be argued that as society grows more affluent, money becomes less effective and time takes its place; Reisch (2001, p. 377) reports that once a certain income level has been reached, the marginal utility of more available time is higher than the marginal utility of more available income, in other words 'wealth in time' is of ever increasing importance to many of us. The desire for more time, specifically free time is common place (Parkins, 2004) and Reisch (2001, p. 374) found that people are seeking 'enough time for meaningful things'. This quest often begins in specific economic conditions (boom and bust) when people decide to re-evaluate their place in life. Newspaper articles and popular books about work pressures, 'anti-careerism,' 'downshifting,' and a need to 'slow down' proliferate at these times, outlining the increasing difficulty people encounter in finding time in everyday life, while extolling the virtues of free time and family life. So what is the cure for what Dossey (1982, p. 50) coined 'time-sickness' in which he described our obsessive belief that 'time is getting away, that there isn't enough of it, and that you must pedal faster and faster to keep up'. The 1990s saw a surge in downshifting when people made a conscious decision 'to opt out of the culture of consumerism and the career rat race ... cutting back on purchasing, reducing working hours, and perhaps bailing out of conventional work in search of greater quality of life and control over one's work' (Ghazi and Jones, 1997, p. 46). The concept was premised on a need to prioritize, to adjust values and approach life with a different mindset. Hamilton and Mail (2003) highlighted several primary motivations for downshifting in the pursuit for a more balanced and fulfilling life; people may want to spend more time with their families; they may well be motivated by a desire to live a less materialistic and more sustainable life. Yet individuals who made the choice to downshift usually stressed that they were not dropping out of society. They did not see themselves as part of a movement but simply as individuals who wanted to make a change to the balance of their lives. Although the term no longer gains the abundance of media attention as it did over a decade ago people are still trying to take back time and seek more meaning and balance within their lives.

Taking time to slow down

> We have lost our sense of time ... We believe that we can add meaning to life by making things go faster. We have an idea that life is short – and that we must go fast to fit everything in. But life is long. The problem is that we don't know how to spend our time wisely. And so we burn it ... Ultimately, 'slow' means to take the time to reflect. It means to take the time to think. With calm, you arrive everywhere.
>
> Petrini (2001, p. 1)

The story of Western modernity is often told as a story of constant acceleration and speed has long been synonymous with success yet in our non-stop-society, leisureness and unhurriedness are becoming increasingly attractive. If downshifting was a term for the 1990s then perhaps the most recognised phrase in the 2000s has been 'slow' which has now become familiar shorthand for leading a more balanced life. The slow movement is deeply rooted in slow food with a guiding philosophy to preserve the environment, local identities, local produce and seeking to enjoy once more the pleasure of food. Founded by Carlo Petrini as a non-profit, eco-gastronomic, member-supported organization it is seen as a direct riposte to globalization and in particular to counter the rise of fast food and fast life spurred by a protest (organized by Petrini) to the opening of a McDonalds next to the Spanish Steps in Rome. The movement has since expanded globally to include 10,000 members in 150 countries and the manifesto reads in part 'we are enslaved by speed and have all succumbed to the same insidious virus: fast life, which disrupts our habits, invades the privacy of our homes, and forces us to eat fast foods' (Slow Food, 1989). Honoré (2004) agrees that 'slow' is a countercultural perspective, which rails against the structures in Western society that encourage fast consumption. He suggests that the quest for 'fast' brings about poorer diet, health, relationships, communities and environment thus to live slowly is to engage in 'mindful' rather than 'mindless' practices. Meredith and Storm (2011, p. 1) explain slow living means

> structuring your life around meaning and fulfillment. Similar to 'voluntary simplicity' and 'downshifting,' it emphasises a less-is-more approach, focusing on the quality of your life ... Slow Living addresses the desire to lead a more balanced life and to pursue a more holistic sense of well-being in the fullest sense of the word.

A fundamental concern in slow living is time, and the movement aims to claim back the quality of time in our hurried lifestyles (Bowen and Clarke, 2009) and offer us more time for everyday life activities. It can be thought that 'slow' amounts to *taking* time for something and *investing* the time to think, reflect and evaluate. The prefix 'slow' has since been added to a range of concepts including art, cities, education, fashion, gardening, media, money, tourism, travel, parenting and sex. An abundance of leisure activities are listed yet it is interesting to note that 'slow leisure' has largely been ignored in current writings, an anomaly that this chapter aims to subtly address. Before doing so a closer examination of some of the developing terms will be given.

From fast to slow: the emergence of slow travel and tourism

As a leisure activity, tourism has become an important aspect of our lives and can be linked to well being. In 1770 William Gilpin, who is often acknowledged as the father of modern day tourism, wrote 'we travel for various purposes – to explore the culture of soils, to view the curiosities of art, to survey the beauties of nature, and to learn the manners of men, their different politics and modes of life' (Gilpin, 2005). Our obsession with fast travel in recent decades has for many distorted our view of tourism and it could be suggested that the 'art of travel' has been lost. Speed is seen as necessary to economic development and governments drive forward advances in technologies to allow us to travel greater distances in shorter time frames. For instance at the time of writing the UK government are in the final stages of consultation for the High Speed 2 rail network citing economic boost for the country as an underlying rationale for the proposed development. Meanwhile aerospace engineers in Oxfordshire, England are developing a supersonic aircraft designed to travel at five times the speed of sound with the capability to commute 300 passengers from Brussels to Sydney in between two and four hours. This increased mobility has driven the time and space compression further since the early introduction of modern transport. There is in this sense an overwhelming need to re-scale the planet. People often suggest that the world is 'small' yet this is very much a superficial construct built upon fast travel. To experience beyond the superficial one can switch to a slower mode of transport (walking, cycling) as suddenly one becomes more aware to the scale of our planet. The slower we travel the more engaged we become with our surroundings and notice the complexities and richness Gilpin spoke of. We can perceive the scale of the landscapes around us and notice the subtle differences in light and shade whilst also capturing the feelings we have which become etched in to our memories. The different segments of the journey create 'triggers' that enable us to effortlessly travel back and forth through our memory and in this respect time is no longer linear. Holidays are widely acknowledged to be multi-sensory activities and travelling slowly facilitates engagement with all of our senses. When walking we can feel the stones beneath our feet, the taste of the cold wind on our lips, and we see, hear and smell our surroundings. If more meaning is what we desire then this can be further enhanced through a continuative human experience as when we travel along a footpath, for instance, we are not just in touch with ourselves but also with the people who created the path. To further continue the construct that the world is getting smaller, people talk of the 'sameness' each city offers. The mass tourism product allows tourists to sustain their own small worlds at extended distances. Tourists collect images and experiences in predicted spatial contexts that confirm their socio-cultural expectations, and local providers of tourist facilities make all possible efforts to construct the idealized tourism space visitors are looking for. However as tourism advances so too does the tourist and the words of William H. Davies again echo as to stop, to stand and to stare will allow us to see that there are fundamental differences in all people of the world, which, for a traveller, is an enriching part of the experience.

Many tourists are in search of authenticity and are more aware of the benefits low impact tourism brings, whilst also seeking to engage and give something back to the communities they visit. Slow travel is a relatively new term that encapsulates some of these ideals. The term has received wide coverage in the quality media and an array of guidebooks devoted to the concept (see, for example Bradt Guides (Ferguson, 2012) and Sawday Guides, 2010). The term has been creeping into the academic literature over the past decade (Dickinson & Lumsdon, 2010; Dickinson et al., 2011; Lumsdon and McGrath, 2011; Markwel et al., 2012; Matos, 2004) and has since been extended to include slow tourism. The origins of the term(s) are rather unclear and there is little consensus as to what 'slow' actually means in relation to travel and tourism. Matos (2004, p. 94), one of the earliest authors to explore the concept, suggests slow tourism has two defining principles: 'taking time' and having an 'attachment to place.' He explored slow tourism as a catalyst to reinvigorate the tourism offering and explains it allows for a 'deeper awareness, for a more authentic discovery of a locality, of its people, and of its culture'. Sustainable development is at the very heart of this argument and Matos highlights this by suggesting it is a pillar of the philosophy of slow tourism. In many ways the debate is built upon earlier work of Krippendorf (1984) and the advocacy of Poon (1994) for an alternative to mass-tourism. Ceron and Dubois (2007, p. 201) agree that the concept is underpinned by sustainability and highlight the travel experience as being key: 'stays are longer and the travel between home and destination is often slower (more train and bus), and considered as pleasant and interesting'. Slow travel has also become popularized through television series for instance Around the World in 80 Days (BBC, 1989), Long Way Down (BBC, 2007) and Long Way Round (Sky One, 2004). This coupled with a surge in media interest provided Gardner (2009, p. 11) with a platform to compile a 'manifesto for slow travel' whereby she outlines some of the guiding principles as follows:

- Start at home. The key to travel is a state of mind. That can be developed at home.

- Travel slowly. Avoid planes if at all possible, and instead enjoy ferries, local buses and slow trains. Speed destroys the connection with landscape. Slow travel restores it.
- You may eagerly look forward to the arrival at your chosen destination, but don't let that anticipation eclipse the pleasure of the journey.
- Check out local markets and shops.
- Savour café culture. Sitting in a café, you become part of the cityscape and not merely a passing observer.
- Take time to get a feel for the languages and dialects of the areas you visit. Learn a few phrases, use a dictionary and buy a local newspaper.
- Engage with communities at the right level. Choose accommodation and eating options that are appropriate to the area where you are travelling.
- Do what the locals do, not only what guidebooks say.
- Savour the unexpected. Delayed trains or missed bus connections create new opportunities.
- Think what you can give back to the communities you visit.

As a concept it could be argued as nothing new. Until the twentieth century the majority of travel was slow by its very nature with travellers exploring the world on foot, by horse and sailing boat (Towner, 2002). The 'guiding principles' presented by Gardner are, however, rather stringent and perhaps somewhat elitist. Academics have since aimed to debate the topic(s) though thus far no universally accepted definition has been provided. Depending on the author's stance it may be premised by mode of transport, specific destination, ecological importance or purely experiential. Of course in academic terms this could be argued to be healthy as to develop a detailed definition can tie a noose around a subject; nonetheless a definition does allow attention to be drawn and ideas progressed. Lumsdon and McGrath (2011, p. 12) suggest:

> Slow travel is a sociocultural phenomenon, focusing on holidaymaking but also on day leisure visits, where use of personal time is appreciated differently. Slowness is valued, and the journey is integral to the whole experience. The mode of transport and the activities undertaken at a destination enhance the richness of the experience through slowness. Whilst the journey is the thing and can be the destination in its own right, the experience of locality counts for much, as does reduced duration or distance of travel.

A need for a simpler approach

The foundations to slow travel and slow tourism have been set but continue to evolve. The two terms are often used as one or interchangeably leading to the conclusion that perhaps a simpler approach to the topic is now needed. In essence, to understand 'slow' is the key to this process. There is a temptation to align the term with negative connotations such as not being convenient or effective, moving backwards and bringing dull or boring experiences. However 'slow' in the context presented here is positive and aims to re-engineer time, to transform it into a commodity of abundance rather than scarcity by 'taking time' and 'investing time' in all that we do. Misinterpretations are inevitable but as the term evolves the true benefits will be realized – similar to the French 'flâneur' of the nineteenth century who strolled the boulevards, parks and arcades of Paris. In this era flâneurs were considered 'lazy' and synonymous with 'wasting time' though later considered as men who developed a deep and rich appreciation of the landscapes they travelled. The key to slow travel considers the travel time taken to be a valuable part of the holiday experience, opposing the view by many that travel time is 'wasted'. Slow tourism, however, extends the concept to the destination level and encourages one to take the time and invest the time to explore and better understand the local landscapes and people (similar to the flâneur). In this sense slow travel and slow tourism allow people to re-engage not just with their surroundings, which as Matos (2004) explains encourages people to look rather than to see, to experience rather than to endure the area but also to re-connect with one another. Whilst many authors premise their 'slow' argument around travelling at a slower pace I contend that physical speed is irrelevant but deceleration (within) is required. To travel slowly should be to engage in mindful rather than mindless practice, to take time and invest time. Where better to be slow therefore than on a moving plane, ship or train, as there are fewer places conducive to internal conversations (De Botton, 2002). Time 'stands still' and offers us the opportunity to invest and make mindful use of our time (to read, reflect, talk, gaze). To this end the mode of transport becomes a facilitating factor to slow travel and provides 'a visual "cinematic" experience of moving landscape images' (Larsen, 2001, p. 80). In some circumstances, it could well include interludes of stillness where a tourist is totally absorbed in the experience or where there is an absence of disturbance. Perhaps the best aid to slow travel in this sense is the train; the views have none of the potential monotony of those on a ship or plane, they move fast enough for us not to get exasperated but slowly enough to allow us to identify objects. They offer us brief, inspiring glimpses into private domains, letting us see a woman at the precise moment when she takes a cup from a shelf in her kitchen, then carrying us on to a patio where a man is sleeping and then to a park where a child is catching a ball thrown by a figure we cannot see (De Botton, 2002, p. 57). To this end slow travel facilitates a 'dual journey,' the literal and the journey within. This deeper meaning suggests an identity affirming experience where at the end of hours of train dreaming, we may feel we have been returned to ourselves – that is, brought back into contact with emotions and ideas of importance to us. Similarly with slow tourism specific settings become facilitators: for example a café in the market square allows the tourist to stop, to stand and to stare. This level of deceleration further emphasises the link between the twenty-first-century slow traveller and the nineteenth-century flâneur. In both cases one seeks to become less visible and immersed with the local landscape and culture, in contrast to other tourists who are clearly visiting and their visibility notable to all.

Conclusion: slow leisure, a new notion?

> To be able to fill leisure intelligently is the last product of civilization.
>
> Bertrand Russell

The essence of this chapter has been to provide insight to a counter-cultural movement based around quality over quantity and premised on an unsustainable consumptive society. The movement is clearly gaining momentum and the surge of slow initiatives is only set to continue in future years but as with the concept of downshifting it has the potential to fade in time. The prefix 'slow' in many instances could be argued as no more than a re-emphasis to the early interpretation of the suffix as opposed to the one placed by modern society. For instance travel has been transformed through the ages, propelled by the development of technology. Slow travel seeks to re-invigorate an earlier interpretation of travel with the intent of meeting others from different lands and to be educated in their arts and literature. This transposes nicely to leisure and thus it is pertinent to give this the final thought. For the purpose of this discussion leisure will be classified as time available to an individual when work, sleep and other basic needs have been met. It is duly noted that leisure has varying meanings but 'the primary task is not to discover what leisure is...rather to make a decision as to which of the phenomena labelled by this term, one intends to address oneself to' (Neulinger, 1981, p. 26). Our current need to cram as many leisure activities into our free time frames as possible to help satisfy our needs is a characteristic 'slow' aims to reverse. The emerging slow revolution is largely based around leisure activities (art, cities, education, fashion, gardening, media, money, tourism, travel, parenting and sex) thus the slow philosophy easily extends to leisure. The term *slow leisure* has not been the focus of academic interest thus far but it is predicted that it will in future years. It could be seen as an umbrella term for the varying facets allowing one (no matter what activity) to decelerate, to think, reflect, evaluate and affirm identities. Slow leisure quite simply is to take time and invest time in activities. Similarly for slow travel and slow tourism the activity is the facilitating mechanism for slow (for instance exploring an art gallery or cycling along a nature trail). Self development and discovery is fundamental to the argument and not only does the term allow academics to debate and critique but also more importantly it encourages people to re-evaluate their relationship with leisure and leisure time. It is unclear how leisure and leisure time will evolve and questions remain unanswered as to how much time we will have away from work, sleep and other basic needs but what we can assume of the future is that people will continue to seek a more balanced and meaningful life. 'Slow' offers this through an experience within, to stop, to stand and to stare in all walks of life; it encourages one to take time and invest time in one's actions. Undoubtedly many will see this stance as too simplistic; however the concept should remain simple as in essence the ideal is to return to simple living.

3

LEISURE, HAPPINESS AND POSITIVE LIFESTYLE

Robert A. Stebbins

Interlaced among all the dreary news of the day are the persistent and mellifluous observations about happiness in our lives. Even though there is in this trendy interest a certain amount of phony and simplistic advice and thought, it is on the whole a good thing. At least it accentuates the positive and gets people thinking about their lives in such terms.

Richard Layard (2005, p. 12) defines happiness as the state of feeling good and enjoying life. It is a descriptive term. Moreover some thinkers see happiness as momentary: '[it] is considered to reflect a person's more temporary affective feelings of the present moment' (Mannell and Kleiber, 1997, p. 208). Examples include: 'I was happy with my performance on the test', 'I am happy that my party turned out so well', 'I was very happy to receive that award the other day'. Let us label this *short-term happiness*, so-called because the 'present moment' might last for a few minutes or even a few days.

By contrast, others see happiness as a description of a broad swath of life, as expressed in such observations as: 'I was happy as a child', 'My years in this community have been happy ones', 'I will be happy in retirement'. In this vein Diener (2000) holds that happiness and subjective well-being are the same. For him well-being is a combination of positive affect and general life satisfaction. In a similar vein Keyes (1998, p. 121) defines social well-being as 'the absence of negative conditions and feelings, the result of adjustment and adaptation to a hazardous world'. To put the matter positively, let us say that well-being comes with having good health, reasonable prosperity and, in general, being routinely happy and content. This is *long-term happiness*.

Short or long term, happiness is the result of a huge variety of personal and social conditions leading to this state in individuals. Thus, it is interesting to describe people's (usually long-term) happiness, to know how many of them are happy, think they will be happy, once were happy, and so on. In this regard it is now common to compile national happiness ratings (see Datablog, 2010), while Britain's Prime Minister, David Cameron, has decided to create a national happiness index. These are major undertakings, which by the way appear to ignore the short/long-term distinction just set out.

Yet even more complicated is the project of explaining such tendencies as well as explaining the condition of happiness itself. A substantial part of the explanation of happiness has been driven by the question of whether money makes people happy. And, from what I will be saying about fulfillment in this article, it should be easy to conclude that, much of the time, no direct link exists between happiness and money. Layard (2005) determined from his review of comparative research on this issue that 'comparing countries confirms what history also shows – that above $20,000 (USD) per head, higher average income is no guarantee of greater happiness' (p. 34). Once food, clothing, shelter and the like are secure, having more money is not necessarily a source of increased well-being (Franklin, 2010, p. 5).

Subjective or social, the concept of well-being rests on the presupposition that, to achieve it, people must be proactive, must exercise personal agency to arrive at this state. Well-being is therefore also a goal, which when reached will demonstrate a person's overall happiness. The same may be said for obtaining a decent quality of life. Both concepts speak to a process of personal betterment, as the individual defines this state. Happiness is therefore further explained by our willingness to work toward our well-being and agreeable quality of life.

Moreover psychological and sociological positiveness are sources of happiness. Happy people are positive about their lives, whether at the moment or over a long period of time. This observation describes the result of positive living, of the pursuit of positiveness in a life seen as attractive and worth living. Be that as it may, positiveness is both a condition *and* a goal. As a condition it may be seen as an aspect of long-term happiness. As a goal, however, it stresses finding worthwhileness; it emphasizes getting something desirable out of life. Personal agency is also a prerequisite of positiveness (Stebbins, 2009b, p. 7). It stresses actively finding a life that is, in combination, rewarding, satisfying and fulfilling. Here people direct their own efforts to find worthwhile activities, even while those efforts are inevitably framed and sometimes constrained by broader social, cultural and structural conditions.

The limits of the idea of happiness

Before tackling this matter of the limits of the idea of happiness, we must review some of the leisure theory directly related to it. To this end, let us consider the central concepts of the serious leisure perspective (SLP), which may be described, in simplest terms, as the theoretic framework that synthesizes three main forms of leisure showing, at once, their distinctive features, similarities and interrelationships.

The three forms of leisure

The three forms are the serious pursuits and casual and project-based leisure, which are briefly defined as follows (Stebbins, 2012):

- Serious pursuits
    - *Serious leisure* is the systematic pursuit of an amateur, hobbyist or volunteer activity sufficiently substantial, interesting and fulfilling for the participant to find a (leisure) career there acquiring and expressing a combination of its special skills, knowledge and experience.
    - *Devotee work* is activity in which participants feel a powerful devotion, or strong, positive attachment, to a form of self-enhancing work. In such work the sense of achievement is high and the core activity endowed with such intense appeal that the line between this work and leisure is virtually erased.
- Casual leisure is immediately intrinsically rewarding, relatively short-lived pleasurable activity requiring little or no special training to enjoy it. It is fundamentally hedonic, pursued for its significant level of pure enjoyment, or pleasure.
- Project-based leisure is a short-term, reasonably complicated, one-off or occasional, though infrequent, innovative undertaking carried out in free time, or time free of disagreeable obligation. Such leisure requires considerable planning, effort and sometimes skill or knowledge, but is for all that neither serious leisure nor intended to develop into such.

Over the years extensive exploratory research and grounded theoretic analysis of data on a wide variety of free-time activities have made it possible to create a typological map of the world of leisure (see Figure 3.1). That is, so far as can be determined at present, all leisure (at least all leisure in the West) may be classified according to one of these three forms and their several types and subtypes. More precisely the serious leisure perspective offers a classification and explanation of all leisure activity and experience, as these two are framed in the social-psychological, social, cultural and historical contexts in which each activity and its experience take place.

Additionally, some kinds of work – referred to as 'devotee work' (Stebbins, 2004) – can be conceived of as pleasant obligation, in that such workers, though they must make a living performing this work, do so in a highly, intrinsically appealing pursuit. Work of this nature is therefore essentially leisure and has been conceptualized as such in a recent book (Stebbins, 2012). This theoretic adjustment is compatible with the serious leisure perspective, particularly since the latter stresses human agency, 'intentionality' (Rojek, 2010, p. 6), or what 'people want to do' and distinguishes the satisfaction gained from casual leisure vis-à-vis the fulfillment flowing from the serious form. The new concept of 'serious pursuits' presented in Figure 3.1 encompasses both serious leisure and devotee work.

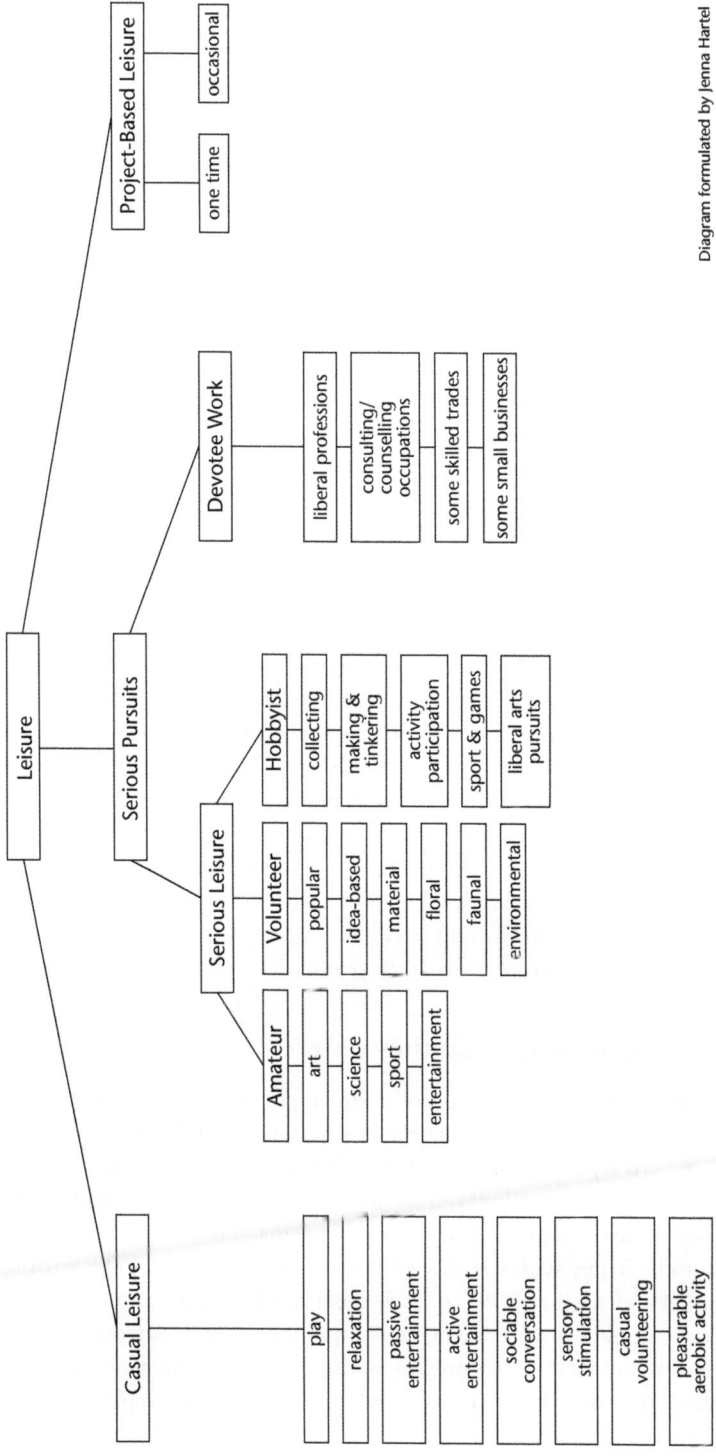

Types explained in Stebbins (2007a, 2007b, pp. 6–10, 38–39, 45–47)

FIGURE 3.1 The serious leisure perspective

Diagram formulated by Jenna Hartel

Casual leisure is fundamentally hedonic, engaged in for the significant level of pure enjoyment, or pleasure, found there. It is also the classificatory home of much of the deviant leisure discussed by Rojek (1997, pp. 392–393). Casual leisure is further distinguished from the serious pursuits by the six qualities of the latter; only in these pursuits do we find need to persevere at the activity, availability of a leisure career, need to put in effort to gain skill and knowledge, realization of various special benefits, unique ethos and social world, and an attractive personal and social identity.

Eight types of casual leisure have been identified to date, namely, *play* (including dabbling), *relaxation* (e.g., sitting, napping, strolling), *passive entertainment* (e.g., TV, books, recorded music), *active entertainment* (e.g., games of chance, party games), *sociable conversation, sensory stimulation* (e.g., sex, eating, drinking), and *casual volunteering* (as opposed to serious leisure, or career, volunteering). The last and newest type – *pleasurable aerobic activity* – refers to physical activities that require effort sufficient to cause marked increase in respiration and heart rate, but nevertheless are still considered fun to do. The children's game of tag and the adult exercise routine of walking on a treadmill to the challenges of an electronic game exemplify this type (explained further in Stebbins, 2007b).

Project-based leisure is a short-term, moderately complicated, either one-shot or occasional, though infrequent, creative undertaking carried out in free time (Stebbins, 2005). Such leisure requires considerable planning, effort and sometimes skill or knowledge, but for all that is not of the serious variety nor intended to develop into such. Nor is it casual leisure. The adjective 'occasional' describes widely spaced undertakings for such regular occasions as arts festivals, sports events, religious holidays, individual birthdays or national holidays while 'creative' stresses that the undertaking results in something new or different, showing imagination, skill or knowledge. Though most projects would appear to be continuously pursued until completed, it is conceivable that some might be interrupted for several weeks, months, even years.

Leisure and happiness: how do they differ?

Leisure can generate happiness, but is not itself happiness. Happiness is a state of mind; it is positive affect and a component of emotional well-being (Snyder and Lopez, 2007, p. 71). By contrast leisure is activity; it is what we do in free time to make life attractive and worthwhile. We may describe ourselves as 'happy', but we may not say we are 'leisure' (however happy we may be).

In general to be happy with a leisure activity is, at least in part, to be satisfied with it. Mannell and Kleiber (1997, p. 208) observe following Campbell (1980) that satisfaction implies a judgement, a comparison of the outcome of, for example, a leisure activity in the present with what the participant expected. Thus low satisfaction with that activity would fail to generate happiness at that moment.

So, by no means all leisure activity results in a happy state. I am not speaking here of boredom, which I have argued elsewhere is not leisure (Stebbins, 2003). Whereas people try to avoid becoming bored, some of them find that certain leisure activities have minimal appeal such that they are only marginally better than boredom. Bruno Frey (2008) found in his studies of happiness conducted at the University of Zurich that results were mixed on whether watching television makes people happy. But it is clear from his group's research and the relevant literature that such activity, if it leads to happiness at all, generally leads to low satisfaction and hence a low order of this mood. Moreover they found indirect evidence to support the hypothesis that: 'television consumption significantly lowers the life satisfaction of individuals with high opportunity costs of time, whereas as it has no discernible effect on the life satisfaction of individuals with low opportunity costs of time'. In economics the concept of 'opportunity cost of time' refers to time lost in an activity that could have been used to pursue a more satisfying one such as self-employment or high-level salaried work (e.g., professional jobs, top bureaucratic positions). It takes good self-control to avoid the high opportunity costs of time attendant on the excessive consumption of television.

What has been referred to elsewhere as 'volitional abandonment' (Stebbins, 2008) constitutes another free-time situation where leisure fails to engender happiness. Volitional abandonment takes place when a person consciously decides to participate no further in an activity. I dealt with this antecedent in my comparison of devotee work and serious leisure (Stebbins, 2004a, pp. 88–89). There it was observed that some people eventually come to realize that their formerly highly appealing work or leisure is no longer nearly as enjoyable and fulfilling as it once was. It has become too humdrum, possibly no longer offering sufficient challenge, novelty or social reward (e.g., social attraction, group accomplishment, contribution to development of a larger collectivity). Perhaps they have become discouraged with one or more of its core tasks, so discouraged that they believe they will never again find deep satisfaction in it.

Nevertheless some people hang on for a period of time, unhappily participating in the activity while finding it difficult to extricate themselves from it. This is a common fate among volunteers who have served well in responsible positions, often because they have established a standard of performance few others are willing or able to meet. Amateurs and hobbyists in team-based activities may reluctantly stay with them, when others in the group complain that, if the first leave, the orchestra, sports team, bridge club or barbershop quartet, for example, will deteriorate, if not cease to function. In this half-life it is questionable whether such participants are truly at their leisure; perhaps for them the activity has slid into disagreeable obligation. Does the notion of obligation and how it relates to the capacity to participate in certain activities need to be developed in greater depth here?

The presence of disagreeable obligation in leisure might appear at first blush to be a contradiction of terms. People are obligated when, even though not coerced, they do or refrain from doing something because they feel bound in this regard by promise, convention or circumstances. The obligation is not, however, necessarily unpleasant. For example, the leading lady is obligated to go to the theatre during the weekend to perform in an amateur play, but does so with great enthusiasm because of her passion for drama as a leisure activity. By contrast, her obligation to go to work the following Monday morning after a most fulfilling leisure weekend comes as a letdown. In fact, she could refuse to honour both obligations, for no one is likely to force her to do so, but such refusal is unlikely, because it would very probably result in some unpleasant costs (e.g., a fine for missing work that day, a rebuke by the director for being absent from the performance). Another example might centre on people, among them a fair range of professionals, for whom their occupation is as much a passion as acting is for the actress and for whom going to work each Monday, however obligatory, is viewed as a good thing.

Casual leisure, because it is evanescent hedonism, is subject to losing its appeal and drifting toward low levels of satisfaction and short-term unhappiness, if not completely out of the zone into boredom. Frey's data from his study of television fit here. In addition, it is certainly possible that some kinds of sociable conversation lose their appeal after a protracted period of it. And most of us like to eat and sleep, but can become satiated with either after too much. In serious and project-based leisure participants may be dissatisfied, or unhappy, with how their activities or projects have turned out. The relatives get into a vicious quarrel at a family picnic; the soloist in the community orchestra concert, gripped with stage fright, plays badly off key; the board member of a non-profit has at every meeting acrimonious exchanges with the organization's executive director. Some of these examples depict only short-term unhappiness, allowing thus for the possibility that long-term happiness in the activity remains intact.

The shopaholic offers a good case in point. *Merriam Webster's New Collegiate Dictionary* (11th edn) traces the origin of the word 'shopaholic', defined as one who is extremely or excessively fond of shopping, to 1983. The *New Shorter Oxford Dictionary* (5th edn) adds that shopaholics are compulsive shoppers. But when shopping becomes compulsive, the leisure quality of such activity vanishes, subtly but inexorably overridden by psychological anxiety and lack of self-control. This is not a happy state.

Observing that participation may be coerced brings us to the problem of obligatory shopping, which it turns out upon closer examination, is not always unpleasant (Stebbins, 2009a). Put otherwise leisure may be obligated, as I have just argued. And this may be true of shopping as well. Shopping as obligatory leisure is probably relatively rare, but yet, consider the fulfillment some people experience when buying, for example, a new house or automobile. Let us assume that they are not upset by the financial implications of such a purchase and that they have worked up a solid knowledge of the product and its market, carefully searched out the best buy, and realized the best deal, all of which can be deeply rewarding. The purchase was necessary for these shoppers, however, for their old car had been demolished in an accident or their old house sat on land over which a new highway would soon be built.

These buyers of the new car or house are probably happy with their obligatory purchase. But it may be argued that, given the effort they put into finding the best buy, the activity is better described as a leisure project rather than as an instance of casual leisure (on project-based leisure see Stebbins, 2005b). There is a sense of fulfillment gained from having profoundly investigated the alternatives and having subsequently made a reasoned choice, a state of mind that is not part of the casual leisure experience.

Happiness in leisure: authentic and profound

Martin Seligman (2002) brings us to the jumping off point for relating leisure and long-term happiness, when he states that 'authentic happiness' comes from realizing our potential for enduring self-fulfillment. This observation opens the door to the central relationship that leisure has with happiness. Putting his thoughts into a leisure studies framework, we may say that enduring self-fulfillment springs primarily from serious leisure and devotee work activities, where it commonly takes several years to acquire the skills, knowledge and experience necessary to realize this personal expression. Leisure projects are often capable of producing some sense of self-fulfillment, but not at the level of the 'serious pursuits' (summary term for serious leisure and devotee work, Stebbins, 2012, ch. 1). Casual leisure, because it is based, at the most, on minimal skill and knowledge, is incapable of producing self-fulfillment and therefore long-term happiness by means of it.

But there is reason to question Seligman's use of the adjective 'authentic'. Is the happiness achieved through serious pursuits any more real or genuine than that achieved through casual leisure? Surely casual leisure happiness is real enough, as in the thrill of a roller coaster ride, an entertaining night at a comedy club, an enjoyable sociable conversation or a bus tour offering breath-taking natural scenery. Rather, the central issue is how long does such happiness endure and how profoundly related is it to our personal history, acquired skills and knowledge, and special gifts and talents? Most leisure leads to real, authentic, happiness but only some of that happiness is profound, whereas some of it is superficial, falling thus at an intermediate point on the happiness-unhappiness dimension.

Seligman, by the way, does not mention leisure in his discussion. Instead it is I who has extended his observation into free time and called into question the way he applies 'authentic' to happiness as experienced in the activities there. This brings up a more general observation central to this discussion, namely, that outside the various descriptive indicators of happiness associated with leisure, leisure is far from being a prominent theme in the literature on the subject. Perhaps this is to be expected, for a growing proportion of that literature is written by economists and psychologists (for a partial review see Frey, 2008, pp.

13–14). On this account Nobel laureate Gary Becker (1965, p. 504) concluded that 'although the social philosopher might have to define precisely the concept of leisure, the economist can reach all his traditional results, as well as many more, without introducing it at all!' Nonetheless, the economist Richard Layard (2005, pp. 74–75), to his credit, does recognize leisure of the serious kind (he does not use the term) at which point he cites Csikszentmihalyi and flow. There would appear opportunity here to develop this linkage in greater depth here.

Samuel S. Franklin (2010), a psychologist, approaches the relationship of happiness and fulfillment from the angle of his discipline. Starting with Aristotle's concept of happiness, he brings together theory and research from psychology, philosophy and physiology in support of Aristotle's views on this psychological state. Franklin's main premise is that happiness is the fulfillment of human potential and not a series of transient pleasures, accumulated wealth or an outcome of religious belief. For him happiness is long term, a way of living that characterizes such fulfillment. This said, there are few words in his book about leisure. As with economics this should come as no surprise. For what is known about leisure from the standpoint of psychology has been described as a 'social psychology of leisure' and 'a child of leisure studies' (Mannell *et al.*, 2006, p. 119). These authors hold that 'leisure has all but been ignored by social psychologists in the field of psychology during the past 100 years' (pp. 112–113).

Returning to flow, its analyses have helped broaden the scope of happiness experienced while pursuing leisure. I have noted elsewhere (Stebbins, 2010) that the majority of serious leisure activities generate flow during all or a significant portion of the time spent engaging in their core activity. Only the liberal arts hobbies produce little or no flow. The yardstick with which I examined serious leisure for the presence of flow is Csikszentmihalyi's (1990, pp. 48–67) set of eight components of this psychological state:

1   sense of competence in executing the activity
2   requirement of concentration
3   clarity of goals of the activity
4   immediate feedback from the activity
5   sense of deep, focused involvement in the activity
6   sense of control in completing the activity
7   loss of self-consciousness during the activity
8   sense of time is truncated during the activity.

One might therefore be forgiven the inclination to paint all serious leisure with this brush, since the non-flow liberal arts hobbies are in the minority, often overlooked (hobbyist readers commonly attract little attention) and seldom studied scientifically. So it behooves us to be more discriminating about the ways in which we conceive of the place of flow in serious leisure. Furthermore, some of the casual leisure activities, especially the sensory stimulation type, look as though they offer flow-based experiences. But application of the eight components fails to support this impression in that components 1 and 6 are, by definition, not part of the casual leisure experience. And by no means every leisure project is capable of producing flow for its participants. In other words here, too, each project studied requires close scrutiny to determine its potential for flow.

Conclusion

Although leisure is not happiness it clearly plays a pivotal role in generating this state. We should never lose sight of this relationship with one of today's most vibrant spheres of life, for to do so would be to miss an opportunity to promote leisure's relevance to matters that count with science and the general public. Even if some (mostly casual) leisure leads only to short-term, superficial happiness, it is nonetheless a kind of happiness many people like. We in leisure studies should be showing them the many free-time avenues that may be taken to reach this goal and the nature of the benefits that may be found along the way. Indeed, it is the only kind of happiness that the majority of members in any society ever experience. Nevertheless, we should also single out serious and project-based leisure as additional routes to happiness, albeit of a more profound and enduring sort. In effect we are arguing, in doing this, that, whereas money is generally a poor currency for buying happiness, leisure offers a much more profitable route to this goal. Serious and project-based leisure are far more likely to lead to long-term happiness, especially when, with the casual form, all three are integrated in an optimal leisure lifestyle.

In fashioning their leisure lifestyles people blend and coordinate their participation and allocation of free time in one or more of the three forms. In this regard, some people try to organize their free time in such a way that they approach an 'optimal leisure lifestyle' (Stebbins, 2007b). The term refers to the deeply rewarding and interesting pursuit during free time of one or more substantial, absorbing serious pursuits, complemented by judicious amounts of casual leisure or project-based leisure, if not both. People find optimal leisure lifestyles by partaking of leisure activities that individually and in combination help them realize their human potential, leading thereby to self-fulfillment and enhanced well-being and quality of life.

Discussions of happiness and optimal leisure lifestyle inevitably lead to the broader question of how to find positiveness in life. A key point for this chapter is that positiveness consists of much more than happiness. Thus positive psychology revolves around a large set of emotions leading to this state, among them, love, respect, laughter, altruism, accomplishment and, of course, happiness. Positive sociology adds to this some crucial propositions about striking a favourable balance in an even broader swath of personal life: in work, leisure and non-work obligation (Stebbins, 2009b). To a degree, this balance depends on finding one or more 'formative careers'. This is my label for a person's sense of continuous, positive self-development and self-fulfillment as it unfolds over the years in certain kinds of work and leisure. Fulfilling work and leisure – activity that expresses, often maximally, one's gifts and character – are most commonly found in the professions, consulting occupations, certain skilled trades and some small businesses. In free time, fulfillment is experienced through the serious leisure activities of amateurs, hobbyists, and skilled, knowledgeable volunteers.

Sociological positiveness is further enhanced through attractive interpersonal relationships. Warm relations with close friends, relatives and marital or live-in partners can add tremendously to personal well-being in everyday life. The same may be said for the positiveness experienced from being agreeably involved in the community. The two principal avenues for this latter process are volunteering and the various collective hobbies and amateur pursuits (e.g., playing a team sport, performing in a community orchestra, participating in a quilting club).

At bottom sociological positiveness rests to a very large extent on leisure, which is one of society's institutions. This includes, as stated earlier (Stebbins, 2004a), the claim that even fulfilling work is essentially leisure; it just happens that some people make a living in such activity. Moreover, positive interpersonal relationships are founded and maintained in substantial part on a leisure base. But, alas, as with happiness, leisure does not invariably engender positiveness. The sorts of leisure just discussed have been described as 'serious'. They stand apart from free-time activities qualified as 'casual'. The latter – it includes play, entertainment, sensory pleasure, relaxation and social conversation – can be most helpful as, for example, in alleviating stress, establishing personal relationships or simply allowing for a change of pace, all positive processes in life, to be sure. Nevertheless people can also overdo casual leisure to the point where it becomes deadening and therefore negative, evident in the all-too-common lament that 'Life is dull, all I do is come home from a boring job and watch television'. Frey's research supports this assertion about 'low order of happiness'.

4

LEISURE, LIFE, ENJOYMENT AND WELL-BEING

John Haworth

Leisure is important for the individual, the community and the state. Iso-Ahola and Mannel (2004) consider, on the basis of considerable research, that active leisure is important for health and well-being. Participation in both physical and non-physical leisure activities has been shown to reduce depression and anxiety, produce positive moods and enhance self-esteem and self-concept, facilitate social interaction, increase general psychological well-being and life satisfaction, and improve cognitive functioning. Recent research has also shown that middle-aged men who work long hours, but remain physically active, have a reduced risk of heart disease, than those who do not remain physically active, who in turn are more than twice as likely to die of heart disease than those who devote less time to their jobs. General physical activities, including walking, cycling, gardening, DIY, have been advocated to help with physical fitness. Veenhoven (2009) includes the importance of leisure for enjoyment of life, which he considers lengthens life.

Of course, leisure is not a panacea. If it is used as avoidance behaviour in order not to face up to something that has to be done, it can increase stress. Iso-Ahola and Mannell (2004) recognise that many people are stressed because of financial difficulties and the dominance of work, and that leisure is used for recuperation from work. The result is a passive leisure life style and a reactive approach to personal health. The authors argue that trying new things, and mastering challenges, is discouraged and undermined by the social system and environment.

Stebbins (2004c) argues that an optimal leisure life style includes both serious and casual leisure. His extensive studies of serious leisure activities, such as astronomy, archaeology, music, singing, sports and career volunteering, show that it is defined by six distinguishing qualities. These are: the occasional need to persevere at it; the development of the activity as in a career; the requirement for effort based on specialised knowledge, training or skill; the provision of durable benefits or rewards; the identification of the person with the activity; the production of an ethos and social world. It also offers a distinctive set of rewards, satisfying as a counterweight to the costs involved.

The experiences of leisure and unpaid work in the household are not gender neutral. Kay (2001) argues that within households, the capacity of male and female partners to individually exercise choice in leisure is highly contingent upon explicit or implicit negotiation between them. Many studies have shown that, even when both partners are working, women still make a significantly greater contribution to domestic tasks, and there are key differences between men's ability to preserve personal leisure time, and the much more limited capacity of women to do so. As individuals, men and women appear to give different priority to the work, family, leisure domains of their collective life, while simultaneously striving to achieve a mutually satisfying joint lifestyle. Kay (2001) argues that leisure is a significant domain of relative freedom and a primary site in which men and women can actively construct responses to social change. She considers that the recognition of this can contribute, at both a conceptual and empirical level, to a holistic understanding of contemporary lived experience; but that it raises the question about the extent to which we can realistically talk of families, collectively, being equipped to resolve the work–life dilemma. Sarah Womack (2012) reports that new research from the Understanding Society Study shows that although the gender gap in housework has been narrowing gradually, even when women are the main breadwinner, they still do more housework than their partner.

Rojek, Shaw and Veal (2006) indicate that considerations of leisure are intertwined with those of urban industrial resource allocation, health and well-being, social order, social inclusion and exclusion, affluence, deprivation and distributive justice. They contend that leisure is perhaps the primary setting for active citizenship. Social capital has been viewed as the notional commodity of community engagement and cohesion which can be associated with better health and well-being. Yet preliminary studies are beginning to show that social ties have the potential to both improve and constrain health and well-being; and that an emphasis on increasing social capital has the potential to exclude those who are different (Sixsmith and Boneham 2002). Sixsmith and Boneham (2007) also argue that emphasis on the role of social capital in enhancing health might divert attention away from the more urgent need to improve health through reducing income inequality. The Marmot Report of 2010 gives extensive evidence in the UK for the importance of tackling health inequalities, and that the fair distribution of health, well-being and sustainability are important social goals (www.ucl.ac.uk/gheg/marmotreview). Dorling (2010) shows dramatic differences in health and inequality across the UK. Unemployment, which has been shown to be, for many people, detrimental to health and well-being (Warr 1987), is significantly greater in the north than the south of England. Wilkinson and Pickett (2009) argue that more equal societies always do better. The Equality Trust has been established in the UK to promote a healthier, happier, more sustainable society (www.equalitytrust.org.uk).

Work

For the majority of people, work is the central life activity, though issues of work–life balance are of increasing importance. Work can be considered central to human functioning. Both Marx and Freud extolled the potential importance of work for the individual and society. The historian of work Applebaum (1998) states that 'The work ethic is the human ethic'. Kohn and Schooler (1983) indicate that where work has substantive complexity there is an improvement in mental flexibility and self-esteem. The social psychologist Maria Jahoda (1982, 1984, 1986; Haworth 1997, Chapter 2) in her ground-breaking analysis of employment and unemployment, argued for the centrality of the social institution of employment in providing five categories of psychological experience which are conducive to well-being and that, to the extent that the unemployed are deprived of these experiences, this contributes to the decline in their well-being. These experiences are: time structure, social contact, collective effort or purpose, social identity or status and regular activity. The wage relationship present in employment provides traction for people to engage in work, providing these categories of experience as unintended by-products of purposeful action, which they may or may not find enjoyable. While the detrimental effects of poverty on the well-being of the unemployed are acknowledged, Jahoda was concerned to bring into visibility the important supportive effects social institutions can have on behaviour, habits and traditions. Considerable research has shown the importance of these categories of experience for well-being (see Haworth 1997, chapter 3). They have been incorporated in the environmental factors proposed by Warr (1987, 2007) as important for well-being.

Jahoda emphasised that in modern society it is the social institution of employment which is the main provider of the five categories of experience. While recognising that other institutions may enforce one or more of these categories of experience, Jahoda stressed that none of them combine them all with as compelling a reason as earning a living. Jahoda recognised that the quality of experience of some jobs can be very poor and stressed the importance of improving and humanising employment. Jahoda also emphasised the important influence the institution of employment has on shaping thought and behaviour. She considered that since the Industrial Revolution employment has shaped the form of our daily lives, our experience of work and leisure, and our attitudes, values and beliefs.

Yet stress in employment is viewed as a major problem (www.hse.gov.uk/stress). Many individuals experience long hours of work, increasing workloads, changing work practices and job insecurity. Many have to change jobs more frequently, and increasing numbers of people are forced to spend periods without jobs. Schor argues that

> In the absence of deliberate intervention to reduce (working) hours, it seems likely that the trend towards a US-style increase will grow, rather

than subside. However, it is recognised that the link between ecological degradation through consumption and long hours could provide an added impetus for reducing hours.

(Schor, 2006, p. 214)

In the US the trend towards increasing hours of work is driven by the rise in married women's labour force participation, worsening income inequality, new technology and the desire for increased profits. Similar factors are occurring in the UK. Research by Zuzanek (2004) and Schneider *et al.* (2004) indicates that increased hours of paid work done by the average household is one of the contributors to the perceived increases in levels of stress experienced by contemporary families.

Although experiences of work vary across different socio-political and cultural contexts, Haworth and Lewis (2005) indicate that some general trends are nevertheless emerging across national boundaries. A qualitative study looking at work, family and well-being in young adults in eight European countries (*Transitions*) showed a drive for more efficiency and an intensification of work across all the countries as fewer people are expected to do more work. The study also revealed a widespread implementation gap between policies to support the reconciliation of work and family, whether at the state or workplace level, and actual practice; and persisting gender differences in work–life responsibilities and experiences in a range of social policy contexts. The *Transitions* case studies (Lewis and Purcel 2007) also showed that both managers and work colleagues have a decisive role in creating the organisational climate and culture that contribute to the well-being of employed parents. While workplace policies and practices are shaped by national and local regulations, they are also increasingly a matter of daily and informal negotiation with managers in local organisations. Well-being for parents varied across departments, highlighting the discretionary application of informal, trust-based policies. However, even when managers and their working practices did enhance parents' flexibility and autonomy over work and family boundaries, this tended to be undermined by other factors, particularly long hours and the intensification of work. Combating the intensification of work may require joint effort by cross-national institutions.

Rojek (2004) addresses the polarisation between the over-worked section of the community identified in Juliet Schor's (1992) *The Overworked American* and the increasingly marginalised and insecure mass identified by Ulrich Beck (2000) in the 'Brazilianisation thesis'. In examining the question of solutions to the 'post-work' world, including the idea of a guaranteed income and the possibility of harnessing unpaid *civil labour* to undertake work of community benefit, he notes that proposals do not go beyond national solutions to what are global problems.

Taylor (2002) in a report on The Future of Work programme, funded by the Economic and Social Research Council, advocates that a determined effort is required to assess the purpose of paid work in all our lives, and the need to negotiate a genuine trade-off between the needs of job efficiency and leisure.

The report considers that class and occupational differences remain of fundamental importance to any understanding of the world of work. The UK Cabinet Office has produced a report on Life Satisfaction (Donovan *et al.*, 2002). This found strong links between work satisfaction and overall life satisfaction, and also between active leisure activities and overall satisfaction, concluding that there is a case for government intervention to boost life satisfaction, by encouraging a more leisured work–life balance.

Ageing

For retired people, keeping active, including active leisure pursuits, is seen as an important way of enhancing well-being for the financially secure. Older people are a growing segment of the leisure market. Haworth and Roberts (2007) note that it is possible that the baby boomer cohorts (the products of the relatively high birth rates from the 1940s to the 1960s) will import a higher propensity to consume into later life than their predecessors. They are the first cohort historically to have grown up in post-scarcity conditions, and who throughout their lives have regarded it as normal to buy fashion clothing, purchase recorded music, take holidays abroad etc. It is possible that they will be less willing than their predecessors to cut back, more willing to take on new debt and to spend the equity in their dwellings. However, approximately half of those retired in the UK will depend primarily on state benefits: they will not be among the Woopies (well-off older people). Up until now public leisure provisions have been particularly valuable to the less well-off, not because they have been more likely to benefit than the better-off (the reverse has applied) but because most of these services (broadcasting, parks, playing fields, the countryside, the coast, galleries, museums and other amenities) have been free or accessible at modest cost; in effect access has been a right of citizenship. In the future it is likely to become more difficult for the public sector to be run in this way, particularly when governments are concerned with cutting the public financial deficit.

Harahousou (2006) points to the pressing demographic trend that by 2025 one billion people will be aged 60 and over; and that in the developed world ageing is becoming less associated with dependency and more with activity and independence: '"Active ageing" is the new definition of "ageing" which has emerged and reflects the desire and ability of many seniors to engage in all life's activities such as work, retirement, education and leisure' (p. 232). The gerontologist, Tom Kirkwood, in the Reith Lectures 2001 'The End of Age' argues that life-expectancy will go on increasing in developed economies, and that we need equitable solutions that will meet our needs at all future stages of our life cycle.

A report by the ONS (www.ons.gov.uk) in June 2012 'Comparison of UK and EU at-risk-of poverty rates 2005–2010' indicates that among those aged 65 and over, in 2010, the at-risk-of-poverty rate in the UK was considerably higher than the EU average, a difference of 5.5 percentage points. In 2010, the UK had the 10th highest at-risk-of-poverty rate among the 27 EU member states. A report from the IPPR dated 4 June 2012 'The Long View: Public Services in 2030' by Rick Muir (www.ippr.org), notes that we cannot predict the future with any degree of certainty, but that there are some long-term trends which we can predict with greater confidence. The demographic trend we can predict with the greatest confidence is that the British population will age over the next two decades. In part this is due to the continuing transition of the particularly large baby boomer generation into old age. But it is also because we are all living longer: the Office for National Statistics (ONS) projects that the average (median) age will rise from 39.7 years in 2010 to 39.9 years in 2020 and to 42.2 years by 2035. The number of people aged 85 and over is estimated to rise from 1.4 million today to 3.5 million by 2035. By 2035 there will have been an eightfold increase in the number of people living beyond their 100th birthday (ONS 2011). This trend is relatively predictable and will have a significant impact on the public finances of almost every advanced society. The report notes that we can also be fairly confident that there will continue to be a rise in the prevalence of chronic diseases such as diabetes, cardiovascular disease and hypertension that are linked to relatively affluent but unhealthy lifestyles.

Drawing on official forecasts the report projects a significant increase in expenditure by 2030, the main drivers of this increase in expenditure being health, state pensions and long-term care costs, due largely to an ageing population (OBR 2011). As a consequence of this large rise in demand and relatively stable revenue position, the primary budget balance is projected to move from a surplus of 1.3 per cent of GDP in 2015/16 to a deficit of 0.6 per cent of GDP in 2030/31 and 3.2 per cent of GDP in 2060/61: a deterioration of 4.5 percentage points of GDP or £66 billion in today's terms. The report notes that there are considerable uncertainties in such projections over a long time period. We don't know how healthy we will be as we age, a variable which has a huge impact on the projections. But the report stresses that there will unquestionably be policy decisions in the future that will have an impact on the public finances, such as future tax increases, spending reductions and new spending commitments. The report notes that whichever party is in power over the next two decades the fiscal environment will remain tight and will impose upon our leaders the need for difficult and unpopular decisions; and that they would be wise to lead a public debate now on the kind of choices that will confront us. The report sets out some of the big choices policymakers will have to make to ensure long-run fiscal sustainability. The report stresses that given the importance of these decisions for all of us, the debate needs to involve as many people as possible, reflecting the views of people from different walks of life. And given the magnitude of the task, it needs to start now.

Enjoyment

Seligman and Csikszentmihalyi (2000, p. 12) distinguish between pleasure and enjoyment. They note that:

Pleasure is the good feeling that comes from satisfying homeostatic needs such as hunger, sex, and bodily comfort. Enjoyment on the other hand, refers to the good feelings people experience when they break through the limits of homeostasis – when they do something that stretches them beyond what they were – in an athletic event, an artistic performance, a good deed, a stimulating conversation. Enjoyment, rather than pleasure, is what leads to personal growth and long term happiness.

In a pioneering study, Csikszentmihalyi (1975) set out to understand enjoyment in its own terms and to describe what makes an activity enjoyable. He found that when artists, athletes and creative professionals were asked to describe the best times experienced in their favourite activities they all mentioned a dynamic balance between opportunity and ability as crucial. Optimal experience, or 'flow' as some of the respondents described it, could be differentiated from states of boredom, in which there is less to do than what one is capable of, and from anxiety, which occurs when things to do are more than one can cope with.

Enjoyable flow experiences come from a wide range of activities. In a study of young people, using the Experience Sampling Method, where participants answer questions on activity and subjective well-being several times a day in response to a signal from a bleeper, Haworth and Evans (1995) found that highly enjoyable flow experiences were most frequently associated with the job, followed by listening to music. Csikszentmihalyi and LeFevre (1989) found, contrary to expectations, that the vast majority of flow experiences, measured as perceived balanced skill-challenge experiences above the person's average level, came when people were at work rather than in free time. A study by Haworth and Hill (1992) of young adult white-collar workers shows similar results.

Studies by Clarke and Haworth (1994) and by Haworth and Evans (1995) showed that activities described as highly challenging with skill equal were highly enjoyable about only half of the times. Further, these studies showed that high enjoyment could be experienced when individuals engaged in activities which were described as only of a low challenge, such as watching TV. It is important to note, however, that high enjoyment was more often associated with high challenge met with equal skill (flow). Also, when high challenge met with equal skill is found to be enjoyable this seems to be beneficial for subjective well-being, as measured by standard questionnaires,

In a study using the Experience Sampling Method conducted within an academic setting by Siddiquee, Sixsmith, Lawthom and Haworth (forthcoming), the results show that level of enjoyment is significantly correlated with level of happiness, level of interest and visual interest. The study indicates that enjoyment can come from low, moderate and high challenge activities. Analysis of skill-challenge balance and enjoyment at both work and leisure showed that a greater level of enjoyment was obtained if skills were higher than moderate challenge. The study also highlights that high enjoyment (score 3 on a 3 point scale) in relation to both work and leisure is greater when moderate challenge and high challenge are met with equal skill, traditionally termed 'flow'. It must be reiterated that as in other studies (e.g., Clarke and Haworth 1994), high enjoyment also came from both moderate and low challenge activities and could be associated with high interest and happiness. In many cases, a cluster of positive subjective experiences came from social activities in leisure. Delle Fave and Massimini (2003) note that creative activities in leisure, work and social interaction can give rise to 'flow' or 'optimal' experiences, and that these experiences foster individual development and an increase in skills in the lifelong cultivation of specific interests and activities.

Csikszentmihalyi and Csikszentmihalyi (2006), in an edited book on what makes life worth living, highlight the importance of personally meaningful goals, individual strengths and virtues, and intrinsic motivation and autonomy, in what makes people happy and life meaningful. Positive emotions and the development of personal resilience are also important in optimal functioning Fredrickson (2006) advocates from her research that people should cultivate positive emotions in themselves and in those around them not just as end states in themselves, but as a means to achieving psychological growth and improved psychological and physical well-being over time. She considers from her 'Broaden and Build' theory of positive emotions that they broaden attention and thinking; aid psychological resilience, helping to build personal resources, enhancing psychological and physical well-being. The understanding of enjoyment could also enhance the investigation of human flourishing. Seligman (2011) argues that while happiness is a part of well-being, happiness alone does not give life meaning. Central to enhanced well-being is the ability to flourish. He proposes that Positive Emotion (of which happiness and life satisfaction are aspects) is one of the five pillars of Positive Psychology, along with Engagement, Relationships, Meaning, and Accomplishment – or PERMA, the permanent building blocks for a life of profound fulfilment.

The Office of National Statistics (ONS) in the UK in its 'Approach to measuring well-being' is 'Aiming to build a deeper understanding of how internal psychological factors and personal attributes can mediate external determinants and contributions of individual well-being' (Beaumont, 2011). Research by Haworth, Jarman, and Lee (1997), using the Experience Sampling Method, indicated the important role of enjoyment in well-being, linking personal factors (locus of control) and situational factors (Principal Environmental Influences). (See also Haworth 1997 and Haworth 2004.) Locus of control (Rotter 1966), measured by a standard questionnaire, is the degree to which an individual feels that behavioural outcomes are due to personal effort (internal locus of control) rather than to chance (external locus of control).'Situational factors', or 'Principal Environmental Influences' (PEIs) identified by Warr (1987) as important for well-being were: opportunity for control, environmental clarity, opportunity for skill use, externally generated goals, variety, opportunity for interpersonal contact, valued social position, availability of money and physical security. They include categories of psychological experience identified by Jahoda (1982) provided by the social institution of employment. The Principal Environmental

Influences are considered to interact with characteristics of the person to facilitate or constrain psychological well-being or mental health. The results from the ESM study by Haworth, Jarman and Lee showed that several of the PEIs were associated with measures of well-being; and that locus of control was associated with measures of well-being, with internal locus of control individuals having better scores. Internal locus of control individuals also had better scores on several PEIs; and also greater levels of enjoyment, interest and control, and wished to be doing activities more, than external locus of control individuals, measured over the week of the study. Path analysis showed that for some measures of well-being, locus of control had a greater indirect effect on well-being through the PEIs than a direct effect. The study suggested that enjoyment and feelings of control might enhance locus of control, which in turn may lead to enhanced well-being either directly or through greater access to PEIs. Clearly, there is an interaction between opportunities provided by social institutions and the experiences and characteristics of the person, in relation to well-being.

The state and financial institutions

The recent global financial crisis has had significant deleterious effects on work, leisure and well-being in many countries. In addressing the crisis and the failure of the banking institutions, Hutton and Schneider (2009) point to the failure of the philosophy of regulation through market failure. They note that the presumption has been that in general markets work and that states do not. Only in exceptional circumstances – where a particular market is proven to fail – is there any case for government action, which should, in any case, be temporary. The paper argues that this idea of the self-regulatory effect of market failure has failed, and that state regulation on a permanent basis is essential.

After the pioneering lead of the British Labour government in financially supporting the failing banks, other countries followed. The British government continued to support the economy through making money available, termed quantitative easing, to support businesses and industry, and reduce the degree of unemployment caused by the banks' failures, even though this increases public debt, which was opposed by opposition parties. Paul Krugman, a Nobel Prize winner for economics, and professor at Princeton University, commenting on the situation in America at that time, said that it seems that there isn't going to be a second Great Depression after all; and that what saved America is, basically big government. He said that

> unlike the private sector the federal government hasn't slashed spending as its income has fallen. This has helped support the economy in its time of need, in a way that didn't happen in the 1930s, when federal spending was a much smaller percentage of GDP. And, yes, this means that budget deficits – which are a bad thing in normal times – are actually a good thing right now.
>
> (*The Guardian*, 11 August 2009, p. 26)

The Bank of England has acknowledged that there was a systemic failure to anticipate the financial crisis. *The Guardian* (3 March 2012) reporting on a speech by the Governor of the Bank, Sir Mervyn King, noted that

> The governor was critical of a banking system that had 'overextended' itself, noting that, by the end of 2006, the banks had borrowed £50 for every pound provided by their shareholders. Problems were building in the banking system, he said, noting 'on all sides there was a failure of imagination to appreciate the scale of the fragilities and their potential consequences'.

Forecasting the future of the economy includes assessing risks, and requires judgements, which inevitably involves the perspectives of the forecasting group. In this process the voices of other experts may not be given sufficient credence. Paul Krugman (2012) in his book *End This Depression Now* points to the influence of the social circle on the views of economists and financiers, for whom the system has been highly beneficial, a similar point also made by Ha Joon Chang an economist at the University of Cambridge, and author of *23 Things They Don't Tell You About Capitalism*. In an article in *The Guardian* (5 June 2012) on the failure of austerity, he says that the reason our leaders focus on austerity is they want to preserve an economic system that has served them so well in the past three decades. While critical anaylsis and policy uses methods which make use of a conscious rational appraisal of situations, a greater recognition and understanding is needed of the subconscious processes influencing social institutions and the functioning of organisations. The financial regulation of British banks is slowly proceeding. The Governor of the Bank of England, Sir Mervyn King, is now advocating the implementation of the recommendations of the independent Vickers commission on banking, but also said there should be a review in the future to decide 'whether we need to go further' (*The Guardian*, 23 October 2012, p. 37).

Unemployment

The Guardian (12 April 2012) reported that according to the European Commission unemployment amongst Europe's young people has soared by 50 per cent since the financial crisis of 2008. It is rising faster than overall jobless rates, and almost half of young people in work across the European Union do not have permanent jobs. In some countries in Europe one in two young people are currently out of work. Unemployment, with its potentially serious consequences for health and well-being, is additionally deleterious in young people with its impairment of the development of positive life trajectories. The New Economics Foundation in its 2012 document *Well-being Evidence for Policy: A Review* (www.neweconomics.org) reports that 'Unemployment is strongly negatively correlated with various measures of subjective well-being. This relationship exists over a range of national and international datasets'. The report indicates that in order to promote high well-being, minimising unemployment should be made even more of a priority than it already is.

The Equality and Human Rights Commission (EHRC) in the UK is a public body set up to challenge discrimination, to protect and promote equality and respect for human rights, and to encourage good relations between people of different backgrounds. Every three years the Commission is required to report to Parliament. In its first review (2012) 'How fair is Britain?' (www. equalityhumanrights.com) the report states, regarding employment, that the recent recession has hit some groups harder than others. As in most countries, men have been more adversely affected than women and young people more than older people. People over 50 have fared better than expected during the recession, perhaps due to their propensity to be flexible in the workplace. Black people and disabled people in their early 20s are twice as likely to be not in employment, education or training (NEET) as White people and non-disabled people. Regarding health and unemployment, the EHRC report states that there is a strong association between low socio-economic status and poorer health: in England and Wales, those who have never worked or are long-term unemployed have the highest rates of self-reported 'poor' health;

There are legitimate concerns about the future of the Eurozone, and the adequacy of its financial institutions, which impinge on the UK economy, and influence investment in growth by private business, and hence influence employment. Proposals have emanated within the Eurozone to introduce a banking union. The Eurozone is also likely to introduce a growth plan to accompany its deficit reduction plans. The growth plan may focus on spending on infrastructure, which will improve national assets and create employment. In the UK, reduction of the public deficit is an important policy of all the main political parties. The coalition government has succeeded in producing 'a safe haven for investors' and reduced borrowing costs to service the national debt. The coalition government is pinning its hopes on the private sector creating growth. However, a 'double dip recession' occurred in 2012 and borrowing by the government has increased, due in part to the increase in unemployment.

The coalition government has been accused of planning to cut the deficit deeper and faster than is actually required for ideological reasons in order to reduce the working of the state, which it considers to be inefficient. The IMF believes that in most advanced countries tackling unemployment is better than excessive early deficit reduction; and that the process of fiscal consolidation would benefit from some plans for economic growth. The IMF was also reported (*The Observer*, 5 October 2010) in a paper on 'Taxing Financial Transactions: Issues and Evidence' to argue that a small levy on transactions may help to dampen the 'herding behaviour' encouraged by computer trading behaviour. This would be an additional organisational benefit to that of the revenue-raising potential of a levy on transactions which may ease deficit reduction. However, progress with such a tax is not considered desirable by the coalition government in the UK because of its possible deleterious effect on the financial institutions of the City. But progress on the tax may occur in the Eurozone as it attempts to stimulate growth. The National Institute of Economic and Social Research in the UK in its quarterly report *National Institute Economic Review April 2012* indicates that employment could be boosted by temporary increase in infrastructure spending without breaking budgetary rules. Climate change concerns are also resurfacing; and the government is proposing to invest significantly more in green energy, though without the hoped for level of caps on carbon dioxide emissions, which will also aid in the creation of jobs. Many infrastructure projects can, however, take time to implement. In the UK a reduction in VAT and National Insurance is additionally advocated by the Labour Party for a more immediate boost to spending and growth, leading to a reduction in unemployment.

The coalition government Budget in March 2013 introduced an employment allowance from 2014, which removes the first £2000 off the employers' national insurance contribution. However, the budget was seen primarily to reinforce plans for austerity, even though growth forecast for 2013 had been halved to 0.6 per cent by the Office for Budget Responsibility. In response, many economists, and others, called for policies for economic growth (letters to *The Guardian,* 21 March 2013). The New Economics Foundation (Nef) also published a document *New Macroeconomic Strategy* (2013) on the first steps needed for a fair and sustainable economy. Amongst these it called to

> End austerity and sustain demand. When no one else is spending, government has to. We must act to boost demand and redistribute wealth to the regions. Rising inequality and a falling share of wages in output are a direct driver of economic stagnation and must be reversed.
>
> (Executive Statement)

Nef argues for an economic strategy that is more equal, will provide good jobs, minimise environmental impact and maximise well-being.

Well-being

Well-being has been viewed variously as happiness, satisfaction, enjoyment, contentment; and engagement and fulfilment, or a combination of these, and other, hedonic and eudaimonic factors, including resilience and flourishing. Well-being is also viewed as a process, something we do together, and as sense making, rather than just a state of being. It is acknowledged that in life as a whole there will be periods of ill-being, and that these may add richness to life. It has also been recognised that well-being and the environment are intimately interconnected. Certainly, well-being is seen to be complex and multifaceted, and may take different forms (Haworth and Hart 2007/12). Happiness and well-being are now crucial topics for research and policy in many countries. Layard (2003, 2005) reviewed evidence showing that above a certain level, economic growth (GDP) does not increase overall societal well-being, as people evaluate their income in relation to changing standards. A movement for happiness has been established (www.movementforhappiness.org/movement-manifesto). The New Economics Foundation (www.neweconomics.org) considers that sustainable well-being should be at the forefront of government policy. The Centre for Well-being at Nef has produced the Happy Planet Index, which tracks national well-being against resource use, showing that it is possible for a nation to have well-being with a low ecological footprint. It is also important to recognise the interconnectedness of nations. Leisure plays an important part in the economy of many countries. In Greece, for example, 20 per cent of those employed work in the leisure industries, primarily tourism. In the current Eurozone financial crisis in May/June 2012 tourism to Greece was significantly down, particularly from Germany.

In recent years in the USA there has been a focus on 'Positive Psychology' concerned with factors leading to well-being and positive individuals. A European positive psychology network (www.enpp.org) and a Centre of Applied Positive Psychology (www.cappeu.com) have also been established. The positive psychology programme is very praiseworthy, and is stimulating much needed research in many countries. However, it focuses primarily on individual influences on well-being. It is strongly influenced by the individualistic American culture. Yet recent advances in research in social neuroscience show the essentially social nature of human mind and brain (www.socialmirrors.org and the Social Brain project of the Royal Society for the Arts). The positive psychology programme could thus be enhanced by the study of the influence of social institutions on behaviour and well-being (e.g. Jahoda 1982). Prilleltensky and Prilleltensky (2007) argue from extensive studies that wellness is achieved by the simultaneous and balanced satisfaction of personal, interpersonal and collective needs.

Chapters in the edited book by Haworth and Hart (2007, 2012), 'Well-Being: individual, community and societal perspectives', which has its origins in a series of transdisciplinary seminars on well-being funded by grants from the Economic and Social Research Council in the UK, collectively show that

- Well-being is complex and multifaceted. It is considered as a state and a process. It is a contested concept.
- Well-being includes personal, interpersonal, and collective needs, which influence each other.
- Well-being may take different forms, which may conflict across groups in society, requiring an overarching settlement.
- Well-being may also take different forms over the life-course of an individual.
- Well-being is intimately intertwined with the physical, cultural and technological environment, and requires a global perspective.
- Interventions to enhance well-being may take different forms. They should be conducted at individual, community and societal levels, ideally in concert.

Interventions need to recognise diversity and socio-economic inequalities in society, and be concerned with the unintended as well as the intended consequences of action.

Measuring national well-being

Currently in the UK, at the behest of the UK government, the Office of National Statistics (ONS) (www.ons.gov.uk) is developing new measures of national well-being. The aim is that these new measures will cover the quality of life of people in the UK, environmental and sustainability issues, as well as the economic performance of the country. The ONS has added four questions to its annual Integrated Household Survey. These are: Overall, how satisfied are you with your life nowadays?; Overall, how happy did you feel yesterday?; Overall, how anxious did you feel yesterday?; Overall, to what extent do you feel the things you do in your life are worthwhile?. The questions are answered on a scale from 0–10. Smaller surveys addressing other aspects of well-being are being conducted each month. Initially, results will be regarded as experimental to see if the questions work, and that they meet public policy and other needs, including international developments. The monthly Opinion Survey conducted in August 2011 by the ONS included a measure of enjoyment, and other aspects of experience, as well as the four overall measures of well-being. The question on enjoyment asked: 'Overall how much enjoyment did you experience yesterday?' answered on a 10 point scale from 0 no enjoyment at all to 10 as much enjoyment as possible. The mean rating was 6.4, compared to a mean rating of 7.4 to the question 'Overall how happy did you feel yesterday'. Enjoyment correlated 0.58 with happiness. Nearly 20 per cent had a rating of under 5, while 35 per cent or more had a rating of between 8 and 10. Obviously there are significant differences in enjoyment amongst sections of the population. It would be valuable to analyse in more detail how enjoyment is distributed amongst the population by variables such as age, gender, employment/unemployment, income and geographical place etc. It would also be useful to have a question on level of enjoyment, in addition to quantity of enjoyment, and be able to analyse the incidence of high enjoyment.

Sustainable well-being

It is increasingly important to recognise that leisure is crucial not just to the well-being of individuals but also to the state of the health of the nation. The value of well-being to quality and length of life has been recognised by The New Economics Foundation (Nef, www.neweconomics.org) which considers that sustainable well-being should be at the forefront of government policy. Unemployment, shown for many people to be detrimental to health and well-being (Warr 1987), has increased significantly recently and is greater in the North than the South of England, with unemployment amongst young people now at a record level of over one million. The New Economics Foundation in its document '21 Hours: why a shorter working week can help us all flourish in the 21st century' suggests that a 'normal' working week of 21 hours could help to address a range of urgent, interlinked problems: overwork, unemployment, over-consumption, high carbon emissions, low well-being, entrenched inequalities and the lack of time to live sustainably, to care for each other and simply to enjoy life. Nef claims that experiments with shorter working hours suggest that they can be popular where conditions are stable, pay is favourable and that a new standard of 21 hours could be consistent with the dynamics of a decarbonised economy. Nef recognises that moving from the present to this future scenario will not be simple. The proposed shift towards 21 hours must be seen in terms of a broad, incremental transition to social, economic and environmental sustainability.

The present chapter commenced with the statement that leisure is important for the individual, the community and the State. Rojek (2010) argues that leisure is contextualised by how one is situated in relation to society. We have seen in the present chapter that there is a significant interaction between the person and the social situation in relation to work, leisure and well-being. Rojek (2010) also considers that the subject of inequality is absolutely pivotal to understanding leisure forms and practice. While it may be the case that some aspects of leisure have increasingly become to be regarded as a right of citizenship, the austerity cuts applied to local authorities have significantly influenced their ability to continue to provide many facilities. The home is also a site for leisure, yet housing is a scarce resource, becoming more difficult to access for some groups, particularly in different parts of the country. There are also gender differences in the impact of austerity, which can potentially affect participation in leisure activities. *The Independent* (6 December 2012) reported that Labour claims that women will be hit harder than men; turning to research by the House of Commons Library showing that of the £1bn expected to be raised from new direct tax, tax credit and benefit charges in 2014–15 81 percent (£867m) would be coming from women. If the aim of government policy is to increase well-being, it would seem essential that interventions need to recognise diversity and socio-economic inequalities in society, and be concerned with the unintended as well as the intended consequences of action.

5

DEVIANCE, DARK TOURISM AND 'DARK LEISURE'

Towards a (re)configuration of morality and the taboo in secular society

Philip R. Stone and Richard Sharpley

> Leontius ... was coming up from the Peiraeus ... when he saw some dead bodies lying near the executioner, and he felt a desire to look at them, and at the same time felt disgust at the thought, and tried to turn aside. For some time he fought with himself and put his hand over his eyes, but in the end the desire got the better of him, and opening his eyes wide with his fingers he ran forward to the bodies, saying 'There you are, curse you, have your fill of the lovely spectacle.'
>
> Plato, *The Republic IV*, 360 BC

Introduction

Travelling to meet the dead has long been a feature of the tourism-leisure landscape. In ancient times, for example, state-sanctioned death and killing provided the mainstay for leisure consumption at Roman gladiatorial games. In the Middle Ages, death provided for a spectator event as journeys to witness public executions offered a valid excuse for leaving home. Moreover, during the Romantic period of the eighteenth and nineteenth centuries, touristic visits to deceased authors' homes, haunts and graves were perhaps the most compelling technique for imaginatively contacting the dead. However, today, in a (Western) secular society where death and dying is largely sequestered and institutionalised behind medical and professional facades, death and the dead, or at least *certain kinds* of death and the Significant Other Dead, are mediated in the public realm for contemporary consumption (Stone, 2012). This modern mediation of mortality includes the 'darker side of travel' whereby tourists now visit commoditised sites of death which, in turn, have been packaged up and rendered into performative leisure experiences for tourism consumption (Sharpley and Stone 2009). Commonly referred to as 'dark tourism' (Lennon and Foley, 2000), tourists can now make traumascapes such as Auschwitz-Birkenau, Ground Zero, the Killing Fields of Cambodia, or Chernobyl – the site of the world's worst nuclear accident – an integral part of leisure itineraries. However, despite ethical dilemmas of the practice and processes of dark tourism, dark tourism as a contemporary leisure experience can constitute ceremonies of life and death. These, in turn, have the capacity to expand boundaries of the imagination and to provide the contemporary visitor with potentially life-changing points of shock. Indeed, dark tourism and the inherent 'leisure' experience it entails may be perceived as a rite of social passage, given its transitional elements and its potential to influence the psychology and perception of individuals (Biran et al., 2011). Furthermore, dark tourism occurs within liminal time and space and, as such, locates the activity within constructivist realms of meaning and meaning-making (Stone and Sharpley, 2008). Arguably, therefore, dark tourism provides a contemporary lens of leisure through which life and death may be glimpsed, thus revealing relationships and consequences of the processes involved that mediate between the individual and collective self.

While dark tourism as a subject for scholarly scrutiny remains theoretically and empirically fragile, the provocative and emotive nature of dark tourism in commodifying seemingly taboo topics such as death has attracted increasing academic and media attention (Stone, 2011). Much of this attention has focussed on specific aspects of the phenomenon, including for instance, dark tourism and collective memory and politics, interpretation and commodification of tragedy and atrocity, as well as exploring fundamental interrelationships between consuming dark tourism and the cultural condition of contemporary society. Particularly, however, an increasing number of critical spotlights are being shone on the moral and ethical dimensions of dark tourism, with significant moral commentary being generated by the media. For instance, Marcel (2004, p. 1) proclaimed in The American Reporter that 'death makes a holiday' and, as such, 'dark tourism is filled with moral ambiguities' and that it is the 'dirty little secret of the tourism industry'. Avis (2007) writing in the Turkish Daily News argued that dark tourism was 'sick' and, as a result, should be abolished in that it signified the moral end of humanity. Similarly, Halley (2004) commenting in The Sunday Independent suggested dark tourism was a negative vessel to expel our own miseries in that it allowed individuals to have a narcissistic 'therapeutic blubber' without the debilitating side-effects of having experienced actual tragedy. Meanwhile, West (2004), in his journalistic monologue Conspicuous Compassion, argues collective outpourings of grief by so-called 'grief tourists' in the aftermath of tragedy, or what he calls 'mourning sickness', is more about individuals seeking a common identity and new social bonds to replace those that have withered in the post-war era. West goes on to assert tourists' cynical use of the death of strangers in shows of public memorialisation is not about genuine empathy but mere ersatz emotion.

Debatably, what these selective moral commentaries suggest is that dark tourism is somehow aberrant in both its production and consumption of taboo topics such as death and the (re)presentation of the dead. Particularly, moral criticism and the subsequent moral panic it may create is often levied at the assumed deviant nature of not only the individuals who partake in dark tourism but also, and perhaps more importantly, the apparent deviance and immorality of their (leisure) experience. Of course, deviance arrives from partaking in social and cultural taboos which, in turn, are prohibitions placed on exposing what is good as well as what is bad. Prohibited by authority or social influences, taboos are rooted in an unconscious guilt and insulated from our psychosocial life-worlds by mediating institutions of religion and politics. Yet, in an age of secularisation and liberalisation, new mediating institutions of the taboo are emerging, particularly within contemporary museology and the visitor economy. Presently, therefore, a number of time-honoured taboos, such as talk of death and presenting the dead within public places, are becoming increasingly translucent and, consequently, there is a new willingness to tackle inherently ambiguous and problematic interpretations.

However, despite criticism from an emotionally charged media of dark tourism and its interpretation of death and disaster and, subsequently, the morality of dark tourism and ethics of consumption, any ostensible deviance of leisure experiences within dark tourism have not been interrogated or conceptually informed. Thus, the aim of this chapter is to commence a theoretical interrogation of the interrelationships between dark tourism and the leisure experience – or what might be termed *dark leisure* – with notions of deviance, morality and boundaries of the taboo. In other words, specific dark tourism experiences may be considered a facet of broader dark leisure in the touristic (re)presentation and contemporary consumption of taboos. Drawing upon and updating previous work by Stone (2009) and his analysis of constructing morality in dark tourism places, this study critically addresses the role of dark leisure experiences in the secular (re)construction and (re)configuration of the taboo, morality and deviance. Of course, deviance is engineered by established moral codes and policed by secular and religious gatekeepers; yet deviance and the taboo it is derived from is often socially, culturally and individually relative. Therefore, this chapter argues that the notion of deviance is currently being challenged by dark tourism and that embodied dark leisure experiences provide for a potential (re) construction of morality and a reorientation of moral codes within secular society. Consequently, the chapter suggests that against a backdrop of secularisation, provoking notions of deviance and a reconfiguration of the taboo within (new) dark leisure experiences allows contemporary morality to be confronted. Ultimately, the study contends that because the secular (re) construction of morality and the challenging of taboo boundaries in new communicative (leisure) spaces is often misconstrued as deviant, dark leisure is neither 'dark' nor 'deviant' but divergent in challenging taboo gatekeepers. However, the question remains of what is deviance in dark leisure, and it is to this that the chapter now turns as a basis for subsequent discussions on reconfiguring morality and the taboo in dark tourism places.

Leisure and 'deviance': constructions of dark leisure

The thought of deviance – that is, the transgression of social, religious and cultural orthodoxy – can titillate the imagination. Indeed, deviance is a daily bastion of popular culture in which deviant topics such as death, sex, gambling, drug use and violence are visually and textually offered for casual consumption (Bryant, 2011). Yet, leisure as a consumption activity is often lauded with 'goodness' and the benefits to participants and society. Subsequently, within the leisure literature there is an inherent bias in favour of a positivist paradigm that continues to adhere to assumptions of disembodied universals that 'prove' the existence of beneficial characteristics of leisure (Reible, 2005; Stenseng et al., 2011). Leisure theorists often remain faithful to a moralising construction of what is good and what is bad that renders imperceptible leisure activities that might be deemed 'deviant'. Inherent in this imperceptibility are concomitant, if not naive, assumptions that only 'normal' or 'legitimate' leisure is beneficial to society, essential to wellbeing, a means of providing an opportunity to find truth, freedom and beauty, and which are embedded with meaning (Rojek, 1999a). Of course, leisure activity in this context is concerned with reinforcing and maintaining social order or improving social conditions (Rojek, 1999a). Yet, arguably, such a view has limitations in understanding individual meanings in collective leisure settings, as well as limiting understanding of what might be considered popular 'deviant' activities. As a result, discourse on 'deviant leisure' – that is, dichotomies between what is considered negative or immoral leisure activity and that which is considered legitimate – has received increasing academic attention (Rojek, 1999b).

Disentangling concepts of leisure and deviance is extremely difficult and contentious, and has even warranted academic debate on fallacious 'leisure' activities such as serial killing and murder (Rojek, 1999c; Gunn and Caissie, 2002). While such discourse is unhelpful in extricating deviance in what might be considered mainstream leisure, leisure is not a definite category of social behaviour (Horna, 1994). Unsurprisingly, therefore, a lack of consensus in defining what is and what is not deviant leisure assumes that deviant leisure relates to a negative and immoral activity (Stebbins 1996a; Stebbins et al., 2006). In other words, deviant leisure may be deemed 'deviant' in violating common and accepted norms of behaviour and society (Bryant, 2011). Importantly, however, leisure which is socially constructed as 'deviant' dispossesses those who choose to participate in it. Moreover, the social and cultural construction of deviant leisure lies in the central assumptions of its origin, the lexicon used to describe and discuss it, the perceptions of the beholder, and the rules and sanctions enforced by those with hegemonic power. Consequently, deviant leisure can provide the backdrop for the formation of identity, for finding a sense of being and purpose in a secular and fragmented world, or for rejecting religion, conformity and creating alternative cultural values. As Rojek (1999a) suggests, deviant leisure serves to exhibit disdain and to reject social controls that otherwise would eliminate it. In short, deviant leisure is not inherently deviant but is relative both as a perception as well as a cultural practice.

However, while deviant leisure may be a subset of leisure, which is informed by sociology and social psychology, it has its conceptual origins in *deviance* – and deviance has been medicalised. As Conrad and Schneider (1992) note, the medicalisation of deviance is not a morally neutral approach to gathering knowledge but, rather, an approach that reflects an epistemological shift from 'badness to sickness'. Williams (2009) goes on to argue that deviant leisure tends to rely heavily on Western Judeo-Christian perspectives and psychiatric and forensic discourses. As a result, deviant leisure is often assumed to be bad, pathological, dangerous or even criminal. Of course, while this study does not dismiss these assumptions, the increasing recognition of the complexity of deviant leisure calls for a widening of what might constitute legitimate 'healthy' or 'positive' deviant leisure and the processes involved in its constitution (Biran and Poria, 2012). Particularly, Williams (2009) argues many forms of deviant leisure, when additional methods and disciplines are considered, may be viewed as legitimate healthy experiences. Arguably, therefore, those dark leisure experiences located within dark tourism, which as noted earlier are often perceived as morally suspect and deviant by an unfettered media, might be viewed as legitimate and healthy when the broader cultural condition of secular society is taken into account. In other words, against a backdrop of contemporary society and culture, dark leisure which might be construed as deviant by some may have positive, if not fundamental, characteristics. This is particularly so when secular society has cultivated a process of individualisation, whereby the individual self feels isolated and morally confused due to the negation of dominant religious and moral frameworks. Consequently, as individuals attempt to seek (moral) meaning on their own terms and from alternative cultural institutions (such as tourism and leisure), new moral orders are mediated by collectivities of embodied individuals who are emotionally engaged with their social world. Thus, it is these embodied dark leisure experiences which add to a potential reconfiguration of morality within secular society that this chapter now turns.

Secularisation, individualism and moral confusion – the role of 'dark leisure'

The issue of morality, as defined by good or bad conduct, has been subject to increasing scrutiny by those interested in its purpose, especially within the ambivalent character of contemporary society (Stone, 2009). Consequently, an increasing secularisation of modern (Western) societies has given rise to fundamental questions of religion, morality and the moral frameworks in which we are located. Indeed, an increasing rejection of institutionalised religion as a formal framework for social and cultural control raises the notion of not only religiosity, but also how the moral well-being of the individual self can be met within an ever fragmented and polarised world. Moreover, questions of moral well-being in contemporary society become more pronounced when established taboos such as the representation of death are tested and religious gatekeepers are challenged. Thus, as 'secularisation is an inevitable outcome of social processes, which causes a realignment of the entire social fabric' (Oviedo, 2005), the *sacred canopy* (after Berger, 1967) which once embraced society and provided for an overarching meaning system in terms of moral endeavours, has become fractionalised. However, secularisation is not a simple, one-dimensional transformation of a sacred world-view into a profane one. Instead, it is 'a complex process of reconfiguration that re-invents, translates, or cites moments of sacrality in a new concept' (Skolnick and Gordon, 2005, p. 7). Certainly, one key aspect of contemporary society and the secular values attached to it has been to detach individuals, or at least loosen them, from any sense of obligation which they may have felt towards traditional and established religious institutions which previously had provided a dominant framework in which to find meaning and moral guidance. Indeed, individualisation is regarded as one of the most important processes to have dramatically changed society (Beck and Beck-Gernsheim, 2002). As a result, the individual self has become free and independent from traditional, social and religious foundations. Thus, the emphasis on individual freedom lessens the control and influence of traditional institutions upon society, whereby institutional religion has become polarised and personalised. As Halman (1996, p. 199) states, 'religious and moral values are no longer imposing themselves on societies'.

However, individualisation should not be confused or equated with individualism; as Halman (1996, p. 198) points out, 'individualisation denotes a process in which traditional meaning systems and values diminish in importance in favour of personal considerations and decisions concerning values, norms and behaviours'. Individualism, meanwhile, focuses on the individual's self-development, convictions and attitudes as the basis upon which to make decisions, whereby individual ethics are (morally) relative (Harman, 1975). Arguably, however, increased individualism which has resulted from individualisation, combined with a reduced scope of the sacred, has resulted in moral confusion for the individual self. In other words, the lack of a consistent framework of substantive norms, values or moral principles to define and understand personal identity leaves many individuals feeling disoriented. Moreover, when taboo boundaries are pushed ever forward for contemporary tourism consumption and potential deviant labels are being assigned to both the process and practice of dark leisure, this disorientation takes on added significance. Therefore, the process of individualisation has made people more reliant upon themselves for moral instruction and less dependent on traditional institutions which, in turn, raises issues of how individuals within contemporary society seek and utilise (moral) meanings from non-traditional institutions.

Hence, if we accept the individual self, as a result of secular inspired individualism, is experiencing moral confusion and disorientation, then the self must begin to seek meanings and identity formulation in a complex and fragmented world. Conventional religious institutions which once provided moral space, both in the mind of the individual self and as a physical outlet for moral reflection and guidance, have largely been negated. In its place is a post-conventional society that demands 'an open identity capable of conversation with people of other perspectives in a relatively egalitarian and open communicative space' (Hyun-Sook, 2006, p. 1). It is these new *communicative spaces* that we must consider in framing contemporary approaches to morality (Stone, 2009). Above all, if we view dark leisure in its various manifestations within dark tourism as contemporary communicative encounters which dialogically interpret tragic events and, subsequently, convey a sense of morality, then we can adopt a multidimensional approach towards constructing morality. Ultimately, however, dark leisure experiences and the ensuing moral dilemmas which surround them often result in a vibrant discussion of not only the taboo topic represented, but also the actual (re)presentation itself. This, in turn, could potentially inform contemporary moral instruction to the individual self, and it is to this point that this chapter now turns.

Reconfiguring morality and the taboo through dark leisure

The process and consequences of dark leisure as a mediating force in (re) constructing morality and influencing the boundaries of established taboos can greatly benefit from engaging with the philosophy of Emile Durkheim. In his seminal text, *The Elementary Forms of Religious Life*, Durkheim (2001 [1912]) developed a deep concern with society as a moral, religious force which stimulated in people an effervescent propulsion towards actions productive of either social cohesion or dissolution. Termed by Durkheim as *collective effervescence*, the asocial capabilities of the embodied individual, as well as the potentialities of embodied humans at the collective level, meant that boundaries of morality can be shifted, translated and (re)invented by people engaging with their social world (Shilling, 2005). As Shilling and Mellor (1998, p. 196) note, 'it is the collective effervescence stimulated by assembled social groups that harnesses peoples' passions to the symbolic order of society'. Thus, the emotional experience of these assembled social groups allows individuals to interact on the basis of shared ideas and concepts. Fundamentally, the concept of effervescence and its consequent emotional 'rush of energy' (Durkheim, 2001, p. 215) permits social gatherings to infuse individuals and, thus, for people to become embodied and informed about particular tragic events that may have perturbed their life-world. Hence, collective effervescence has the potential to substitute the world immediately available to our perceptions for another, more moral world (Durkheim, 2001). It is this gathering of social groups within secular society, often in socially sanctioned environments, such as in the case of dark tourism, that a contemporary reality of *la société* is observed (Stone, 2009). Indeed, the social binding of individuals by dark leisure experiences in subtle, if not quiet emotional effervescence influences and informs moral conversations about death or disaster, whereby the self can extract individualised and thus morally relative meaning about a particular tragic event (Stone, 2009). Particularly, in the case of violent events, or where communities have suffered disaster, Durkheim (2001, pp. 302–303) suggests a collective response has implications for the individual:

> When emotions are so vivid, they may well be painful but they are not depressing. On the contrary, they indicate a state of effervescence that suggests a mobilization of all our active forces and even an influx of external agencies. It matters little that this exaltation was provoked by a sad event; it is no less real and does not differ from the exaltation observed in joyous festivals … Just by being collective, these ceremonies raise the vital tone of the group … thus they are reassured, they take heart, and subjectively it is as though the rite really had repelled the dreaded danger.

Consequently, a Durkheimian perspective allows for an understanding of the construction of secular moral orders as mediated by collectives of embodied individuals who are both cognitively and emotionally engaged with their social world (Shilling and Mellor, 1998; Shilling, 2005). However, whilst Durkheim's insight of morality was an expression of what was perceived to be sacred, a contemporary application of Durkheim's work goes beyond that of the relationship between religion and morality. When applied to contemporary assembled social groups and experiences thereof, such as those which exist in some dark tourism sites, it is suggested that inherent dark leisure experiences influence and inform, thus allowing the self to become embodied about the tragic event which they are consuming. This may result, in relative terms at least, in a transformation of personal emotional insights and moral orders. In other words, morality is generated, maintained, challenged or confirmed within these new vitalised leisure spaces, albeit with varying degrees of intensity, through embodied individuals who are engaged with their secular and individualised life-worlds. In turn, this stimulates a kind of collective emotional energy, or *effervescence*, which socially binds individuals through their consumption of dark leisure experiences. Consequently, it is this, the fact that individuals collectively assemble in seemingly 'dark spaces' and gaze upon sordid human activity, or collectively consume grief and tragedy, that is often reported upon by the media as 'moral panic' or somehow deviant (Seaton and Lennon, 2004). However, fundamentally, this apparent deviant kind of leisure is not as unequivocal as some media reporting might assume. Indeed, when examined from a Durkheimian perspective, the deviance dark leisure experiences seemingly provoke might be viewed as ethically relative to the individual but, at the collective level, has profound implications for secular society in its attempt to create and maintain new moral frameworks through the expansion and testing of taboo boundaries. In short, the perceived deviance of leisure behaviour in dark tourism is the consequence of discourse generated by dark tourism practice and the taboo it seeks to represent. Consequently, deviance as in deviant leisure is *not* the end result of dark leisure, but merely *a symptom* of secular society attempting to negotiate and mediate morality in new communicative spaces. Indeed, it is against a backdrop of individualisation and construction of new secular moral orders that the communication and negotiation of 'moral meaning' within collective contemporary 'dark spaces' is often misconstrued as deviant. Quite simply, there is *no* deviance as a result of dark leisure experiences, only talk *of* deviant behaviour. It is this 'talk', frequently conveyed by media commentaries of dark tourism, which is an integral element of the social effervescence that reconfigures and translates moralities which surround the contemporary consumption of death, disaster and tragedy.

Conclusion

This chapter arises from a simple yet fundamental interest in the social and cultural construction of morality within secular society and the interrelationships of contemporary leisure experiences. Therefore, this chapter set out to enhance the theoretical foundations of the dark tourism phenomenon and inherent 'dark leisure' experiences by considering them within a broader framework of emotion and morality. In so doing, the study has not only developed a conceptual basis for the future empirical testing of ethics and morality within dark leisure experiences, but has also contributed to a wider social scientific understanding of morality within contemporary societies.

The summative model in Figure 5.1 illustrates a number of emergent issues from this chapter. First, secularisation and the negation of religion as a traditional dominant framework, in which meaning and moral guidance is provided, has seemingly left some individuals isolated, disoriented and morally confused. Second, as post-conventional societies cultivate a process of individualisation and moral confusion, individuals seek morally relative meaning on their own terms and from non-religious and non-traditional institutions, enabling dark tourism places in their representation of taboo topics to become contemporary communicative spaces. Third, individuals collectively assemble in these new communicative (dark) spaces, resulting, potentially, in both the provision and extraction of moral meaning about a particular tragic event, which in turn allows the self to become embodied through a dark leisure experience. Finally, collective effervescence and its resultant emotional energy is discharged through and by embodied individuals within these new socially sanctioned dark spaces, whereby morality is conveyed not only by official interpretation of the death or tragedy, but also by the actual presence and emotional engagement of the individual visitor. This, in turn, can be interpreted by the media and other commentators as moral panic or deviant behaviour which, to them at least, means an apparent dissolution of ethics at the collective level. In short, dark leisure may provide new communicative encounters in which not only are immorality and taboos (re) presented for contemporary consumption, but also in which morality is communicated, reconfigured and revitalised. This reconfiguration and revitalisation of moral issues through dark leisure is *not* deviant, nor should it

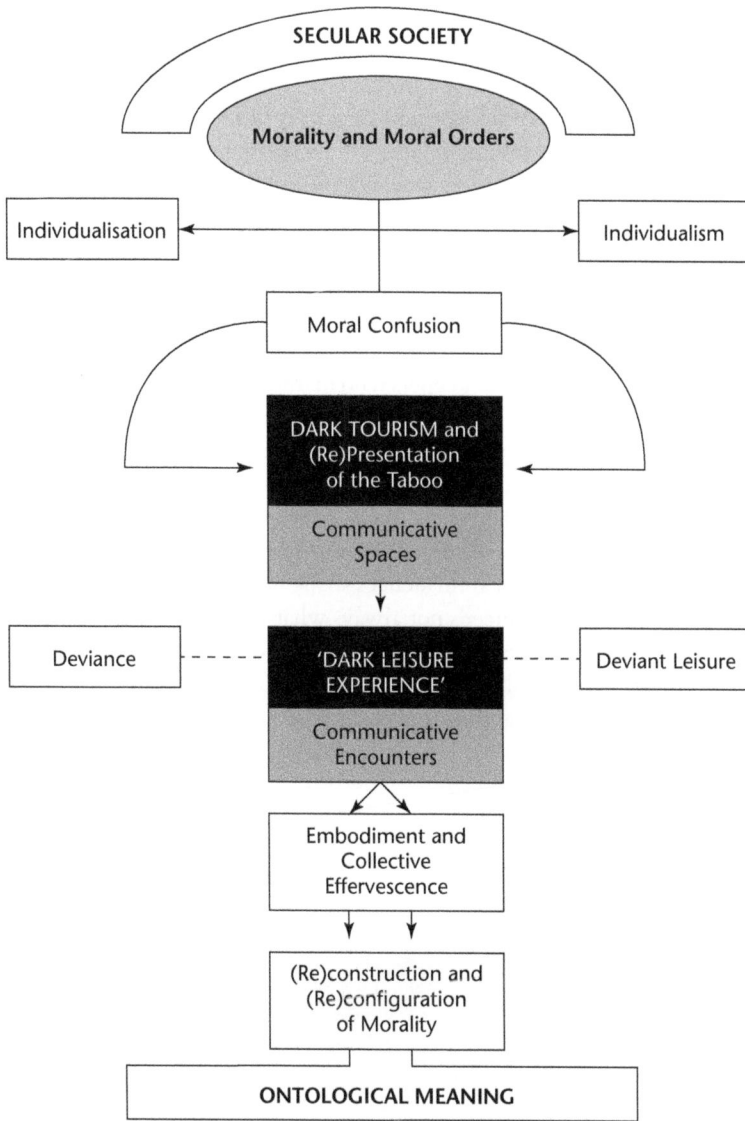

FIGURE 5.1 A conceptual model of dark leisure experiences and the reconfiguration of morality within secular society

generate discourse about deviance, but instead it should be viewed as a process of contemporary society in which we renegotiate moral boundaries and ethical principles through consuming the taboo. Therefore, it is, perhaps, the process of dark tourism which attracts individuals to consume death in new insulating spaces that generates a perceived deviance, in addition, or even rather than, the actual death, disaster or tragedy that dark tourism seeks to represent.

Of course it would be naive to advocate that the process of dark tourism, both in its production and consumption, provides for defining communicative encounters for contemporary moral instruction. It does not. Given the extensive and complex array of dark tourism sites in a variety of social, cultural and political contexts, actual dark leisure experiences will no doubt both *provide* and *be provided* with a myriad of potential moral meanings. Nonetheless, locating dark tourism and concomitant dark leisure within a broader conceptual emotion-morality framework allows for moral orders and their construction within contemporary society to be interrogated. Dark leisure is neither deviant nor dark in the usual accepted sense, but an often widely reported upon, if not misunderstood phenomenon. Indeed, dark leisure challenges the very idea of deviance within deviant leisure as well as the gatekeepers who maintain the concept. In conclusion, however, the primary complication remains in that leisure researchers appear to have difficulty in extricating themselves from the socialisation that has allied deviant leisure practices with immorality, psychopathology and dangerousness. Whilst this socialisation is entrenched and pervasive, this study advocates that future deviant/dark leisure research becomes more attuned with how social, cultural, historical and political influences shape perceptions of morality, taboos and deviance. Indeed, deviance is not always what it first appears. Within a dark leisure context, so-called deviance can embody and even strengthen notions of human connectivity, translate and reconfigure boundaries of morality and, ultimately, create ontological meanings for the secular self.

PART II

Motives

6

THE UNSUSTAINABILITY OF LEISURE

The sustainability of just leisure

Karla A. Henderson

Leisure is a human right (World Leisure, 2005). In other words, leisure is a fundamental, universal, and natural right to which individuals should be entitled just because they are human beings. If this supposition is true, then everyone in the world should have the right to have leisure with all its benefits. However, having the right or freedom for any endeavor also requires responsibilities in being accountable for actions. Thus, leisure is a human right that is fundamental only when it is associated with universal responsibility.

Assuming leisure is a human right suggests that it has social, physical, mental, and spiritual benefits for individuals. Leisure, however, is not inherently good. Leisure can have *disbenefits* for individuals as well as for society. One concern about leisure is that it can be highly consumptive.

According to the World Wildlife Federation (2012), the worldwide consumption of natural resources has doubled since 1966, and people are currently using the resources equivalent to 1.5 planets each year to support current activities. High-income countries have a greater footprint than low-income countries. Further, if everyone lived like an average citizen of the US, a total of four earths would be required to regenerate humanity's annual demand. The Intergovernmental Panel on Climate Change (Solomon *et al*, 2007) concluded that as a species human beings are living lifestyles that are, in the long term, unsustainable. Although leisure may be a right, it also means that along with those rights come responsibilities related not only to ensuring environmental sustainability but also social and economic sustainability.

Much of my research over the past twenty-five years has focused on gender and other dimensions of diversity, inclusion, and social justice (e.g., Henderson 1997, 1998, 2009; Henderson and Ainsworth, 2003; Henderson *et al.*, 1996; Henderson and Hickerson, 2007). My emphasis has been on enabling women, as well as other disadvantaged groups, to achieve equality and equity regarding leisure. However, having access to leisure may be a moot point without considering the interface between social and environmental justice related to sustainability. The challenge for the future regarding leisure as well as other human behaviours is to critically analyze unsustainable ways of living to assure more sustainable approaches can address social, economic, and environmental benefits.

Sustainability as a term relative to leisure has been most visible in addressing tourism and sustainable development. Further, the notion of a *triple bottom line* is often linked to how organizations and businesses of all types address social responsibility and sustainability. The purpose of this chapter is to emphasize that considering leisure as a right also means that it carries a responsibility for sustainability. Leisure scholars, practitioners, and educators have a role in ensuring that leisure addresses sustainable living and that when individuals exercise their right to leisure, they also recognize their moral obligations to society.

A quandary lies, however, with the reality that every choice made in people's lives and about leisure impacts others. Every leisure choice made impacts someone – either the self or others. Further, leisure can be harmful when it exploits other people (e.g., the low paid workers in developing countries who make athletic shoes), or when it creates pollution (e.g., noise and carbon dioxide emissions as a result of allowing motorized recreation vehicles to operate on public lands). The question is whether the impact of leisure is unnecessarily harmful, and in what ways leisure can be more just and sustainable.

I acknowledge that perhaps not all leisure should promote justice, but I believe leisure scholars and practitioners as well as the general public should be aware of how leisure can contribute to addressing social problems by minimizing potential harm. Some people might argue that to define leisure as freedom means that each individual should be free to choose what he or she does during leisure. However, just leisure is an option that also can be chosen. Just leisure is not a mandate, but it is worth considering. Further, I recognize that sustainability is a term that raises many questions. Some people believe that sustainability means to maintain a status quo when, in fact, the status quo is not currently sustainable. Other individuals interrogate the term related to sustainability asking who sustainability is for and what sustainability means in terms of the length of time (e.g., for the coming decade, century, or forever). Further, the conditions of sustainability must also be considered if it infringes on people's perceptions of their rights. The implications of just leisure and sustainability are not entirely clear.

Nevertheless, I contend in this reflective chapter, which admittedly is biased and perhaps highly idealistic, that leisure can be sustainable relative to social and environmental justice if individuals and organizations recognize that leisure is more than an individual right, privilege, or personal freedom. In the current trajectory, leisure along with most other human behaviours is globally harmful and unsustainable. At the same time, by advocating for and rendering leisure as just (i.e., *just leisure*), sustainability can be facilitated. The solution is not to deny people the right to leisure or to make leisure drudgery, but to connect rights to responsibilities. I believe just leisure makes this connection and contribution to sustainability.

Background

The title of this book is *Contemporary Perspectives in Leisure*. The editors suggest this text aims to examine what studying leisure and the individual will mean in the context of a new era of leisure. The editors suggest that many disciplines should be involved in examining leisure, and I agree. I also believe that psychological perspectives are important, but I would argue that a focus on the individual is incomplete without recognizing the impact of individuals on society. A focus primarily on psychological perspectives and the individual associated with the right to leisure will not be sustainable. Therefore, in thinking about individuals and their leisure as this book emphasizes, the universal responsibilities necessary for sustainability must be considered. For the most part, leisure is meaningless unless it is just.

From a US perspective, I would argue that leisure has typically been defined from psychological perspectives. The common definitions offered in American introductory textbooks usually relate to time, activity, and state of mind (e.g., Henderson *et al.*, 2001). An individual's free or unobligated time, specific recreation activities valued and undertaken, and the perceptions or attitudes a person has about his or her leisure behaviour mostly focus on psychological perceptions. Involvement in leisure often includes others, but for the most part leisure has been viewed as an individual experience aimed at maintaining personal core and balance engagement. To talk about global sustainability requires that leisure be defined beyond psychological aspects. Attaching justice to leisure mandates sociocultural analyses as well as global considerations.

Sustainability as it is frequently discussed today is about creating communities that can maintain and improve the health and well-being for residents. I want to emphasize the aspect of improvement since maintenance may only result in status quo, which is not viable given the current environmental crisis, for example. Further, sustainability is more than a green or environmental concern. It means a society where wider social concerns and economic opportunities are related to environmental limits. Justice and sustainability are the basis for action.

Some people describe the triple bottom line of sustainability as like a three-legged stool. If any one of the legs (i.e., social, economic, or environmental elements) related to leisure is removed or broken, the stool will become unstable, and basically unusable. Without a natural environment with clean air and water, leisure would not be possible. The social implications are huge when examining the benefits of leisure experiences as well as the commitment to be inclusive and fair such that all individuals have the right to leisure and are able to access meaningful and responsibility opportunities. Further, leisure must be economically sustainable regardless of whether it relates to people's access to leisure or to the financial resources necessary to facilitate leisure opportunities. For the context of this chapter, I describe the economic leg as closely connected to social sustainability, although I recognize they are not the same.

Sustainable leisure, therefore, includes elements that address social needs and interests by considering economic implications while preserving the environment and respecting people's lives. The foundation of sustainability emphasizes how highly interdependent these dimensions are. Sustainable leisure also means that opportunities for leisure will be available for today's generations and generations to come.

The term I have used in the past to describe the value of leisure is *just leisure* (i.e., not mere leisure) as a means to transform individuals and society toward greater inclusion (e.g., Henderson, 1997; 2000; 2009; 2012). Just leisure can challenge, broaden, and deepen leisure as not only an individual experience but as a social force. Just leisure relates to the notion that leisure can contribute to social as well as environmental justice. Fain (1991) suggested, 'Every act of leisure has moral meaning' (p. 7). Therefore, the morality and justness of leisure must be emphasized to understand its contribution to sustainability.

Just leisure has its roots in the notion of justice. Justice refers to fairness, reasonableness, and doing what is right. Fairness, rather than sameness, is required to achieve justice. The definitions of justice also depend on people believing that they can make a difference in the world whether they are scholars, educators, students, or citizens. Regardless of the type of justice (i.e., social, environmental, economic), fairness to benefit everyone is at the heart of justice.

Social justice includes a vision of society with an equitable distribution of resources and where individuals feel physically and psychologically safe. In this society, individuals are both self-determining and interdependent. It involves a sense of one's own agency and a sense of social responsibility toward and with others and for society as a whole (Adams *et al.*, 1997). Social justice also refers to an understanding of present and historical social inequities to address positive social change.

Just leisure further encompasses environmental justice. Environmental justice is an outgrowth of social justice with a focus on how the environment influences people's lives and vice versa. It goes beyond environmentalism that emphasizes species and land preservation (Warren, 1996), although these aspects are important relative to environmental sustainability. With its roots in problems resulting from environmental racism (i.e., a concern that people of colour tend to be ignored regarding environmental problems), environmental justice today proposes that individuals and communities practicing just leisure cannot abdicate their responsibility to examine the impact on the environment from ecological and social perspectives. Environmental justice can also relate to disparities among people concerning leisure or other activities connected to both the quantity and quality of the opportunities (Taylor *et al.*, 2007).

The meanings and values of leisure in the twenty-first century, therefore, must be broad based. Because of globalization, the interconnections of people to one another and to the earth are more evident than during the twentieth century. The psychological and sociological motives for leisure are important, but moving people beyond diversity to unity, from freedom to common good, and from short-term to long-term outcomes will determine the sustainability of leisure and of the earth (Earth Charter Commission, 1992).

Linking sustainability and leisure

The relationships and interconnections between social inequities, environmental degradation, and leisure should be evident. The connections are both simple and complex. For example, Agyeman, Bullard, and Evans (2002) described how environmental problems bear down disproportionally on poor people. Ironically, however, the poor are not the major polluters. As noted earlier, most environmental degradation and pollution come from high consumptive nations and especially by people who are more affluent. The challenge is to ensure a better quality of life in a just and equitable way while living within the limits of sustainable ecosystems for all individuals.

Agyeman *et al.* (2002) indicated that the solution to environmental concerns is a more careful use of resources and a change in high-consumption lifestyles experienced by some, and aspired to by most, people across the globe. However, altruism regarding the exploitation of resources will be almost impossible to secure without a commitment to a shared future. The quandary is that to facilitate social justice so that all people have equitable opportunities for personal well-being and a basic quality of life requires environmental resources. Agyeman *et al.* concluded that globalization has eroded sustainability because of the world's awareness of how people live, particularly in high income (i.e., high polluting) countries. This unsustainable standard, unfortunately, is desired by everyone in the world. Justice, however, should offer more than how people share the good(s) and the bad of something. Justice should eliminate the bad such as environmental overconsumption and pollution. The preservationist goals of many environmental movements must be combined with greater social equity concerns, which is a huge challenge. Regardless, unjust leisure is not likely to be sustainable in any terms.

Understanding what just leisure can mean and the implications for sustainability can be viewed from several perspectives. These aspects are related when considering implications for individual lifestyle changes, research and scholarship, curriculum development, and management of leisure services. To play on words, the issues of quality and quantity associated with leisure can be *juxtaposed* or *justaposed* when these ideas are linked to sustainability.

The most important element that contributes to unsustainable and unjust leisure for the future relates to consumption of *things*. The consumption of goods is not all connected to leisure but many of the commodities that people buy are connected directly or indirectly back to leisure. Lessening consumption of leisure products or services will require a new mindset. I am reminded of a story that I read several years ago about mindsets and perspectives. The story goes like this:

One day the father of a very wealthy family took his son on a trip to the country with the express purpose of showing him how poor people live. They spent a couple of days and nights on the farm of what would be considered a very poor family. On their return from their trip, the father asked his son, 'How was the trip?'

'It was great, Dad.'

'Did you see how poor people live?' the father asked.

'Oh, yeah,' said the son.

'So, tell me, what did you learn from the trip?'

The son answered, 'I saw that we have one dog and they had four. We have a pool that reaches to the middle of our garden and they have a creek that has no end. We have imported lanterns in our garden and they have the stars at night. Our patio reaches to the front yard and they have the whole horizon. We have a small piece of land to live on and they have fields that go beyond our sight. We have servants who serve us, but they serve others. We buy our food, but they grow theirs. We have walls around our property to protect us. They have friends to protect them.'

The boy's father was speechless.

Then his son added, 'Thanks, Dad, for showing me how poor we are.'

Thus, the mindset that moves beyond consumption is a beginning and relates directly to leisure meanings, motives, and learning. Education related to just leisure is important in moving toward sustainability. This education can focus on educating for and about just leisure as well as education through and during leisure. Education about sustainability requires learning about people's relationships to the world and the role leisure plays. What may be especially important when exploring sustainability and just leisure is how the behaviour of individuals, scholars, educators, and managers matches the ideals.

Implications for lifestyles: individual satisfaction to universal responsibility

The implications of just leisure and sustainability cannot focus solely on the individual, but understanding something about individuals and their mindsets may be necessary to address sustainability issues. Sustainability often is not easy to implement because it is future-oriented. Leisure, on the other hand from a psychological perspective, is generally present-oriented. Leisure for many people is about the here and now, whether defined as free time, recreation activity, or personal experience. In considering what leisure in the twenty-first century should resemble, the focus of this text on personal meanings, motivation, and learning must all be taken into account. At the same time, universal responsibility (Earth Charter Commission, 1992) can be a part of addressing leisure lifestyles. Universal responsibility does not have to be detrimental to freedom, but can be a way to make a freely chosen contribution to the greater good of society and the earth, and to just leisure.

Universal responsibility requires an understanding of what consumerism does related to social, economic, and environmental sustainability. Unfortunately, the economy and environment are often at odds with one another. People are encouraged to consume to boost the economy. Economic development is often more important than environmental protection. Further, the exploding population of the earth means that social equity cannot mean the same access to natural resources, which are rapidly being depleted. Universal responsibility underlines how the Golden Rule comes into play: do unto others as you would want them to do unto you. If leisure in the twenty-first century could be viewed less as an individual right and more as a universal responsibility, leisure could move beyond a consumption model.

A starting point for just leisure relates to understanding how people live their lives and examining what a sustainable leisure lifestyle might resemble. Because of the mindset described in the story above especially for the *haves* (as contrasted to the *have nots*) in the world, tremendous challenges lie ahead. A sustainable lifestyle is not meant to deny individual happiness or enjoyment. However, a sustainable lifestyle requires dedication to learning, exploring, and committing to practices that are sustainable. Further, the behaviour needs to have meaning so that an individual will be motivated, willing to learn, and devoted to practice sustainable behaviours. Behaviour change is not easy, particularly when globalization suggests that what promotes the economy is consumption of goods and services.

Natural resource depletion as well as social inequality can be attributed to the consuming public's desire for satisfaction, convenience, and novelty. One solution is to reinforce satisfaction outside of consumption. Individuals need guidance to recognize that satisfaction comes not only through individual experience but also through having a shared vision (i.e., universal responsibility) about the future. 'Reduce, reuse, recycle' is one mantra for environmental sustainability. For example, greening various leisure spaces such as sports and special events has been implemented to some degree with a special focus on recycling. Recycling, however, may only be the tip of the iceberg. Reducing consumption may have the greatest implication for environmental sustainability, but it is also difficult to mandate and measure in societies focused on consumerism.

One idea that emerged almost three decades ago related to reduced consumption was the notion of voluntary simplicity as a sustainable way of living (Elgin, 1981). It is also sometimes called living simply and making a commitment to that lifestyle. The focus is not about living in poverty, but living in *balance*. Elgin claims that people can change their lives by embracing partly or wholly the tenets of voluntary simplicity such as frugal consumption, ecological awareness, and personal growth. He claimed that in the process, people have the power to change the world.

Means have been presented for how individuals can move away from high consumption toward sustainable/beneficial leisure experiences. Examples might include spending more time with family and friends, time in nature and involvement in non-consumptive (e.g., non-motorized) outdoor activities, biking or taking public transportation, exercising, playing music, becoming more self-reliant (e.g., gardening, making gifts), reading, buying used equipment instead of the newest gear or leisure gadgets, and community volunteering.

Many people find that happiness comes from strong family ties, close friendships, community service, and good health as illustrated in the story presented above. Intrinsic satisfaction can occur in many ways during leisure. Enjoying what one is doing as well as being mindful of the social and environmental footprint being made can be intrinsically motivating. Mindfulness is non-judgmental awareness in the present moment. Research has shown that a correlation exists between mindfulness and sustainability (Jacob *et al.*, 2009). Jacob *et al.* also suggested that sustainable living will not diminish quality of life in terms of subjective well-being if the mindset is focused on not only individual satisfaction but on universal responsibility. This responsibility applies not only to individuals but also to scholars.

Implications for just leisure, sustainability, and scholarship

Any leisure researcher committed to quality of life issues should also be committed to the fundamental values of justice, equity, and empowerment (Henderson, 1997). Therefore, research and scholarship can be just and focus on the implications of the research for sustainability and social change. Research is defined as an intentional act deliberately designed to bring about positive outcomes for individuals and communities. If justness is to occur, then researchers should intentionally consider the ethics and aims of research, and not leave matters to fate. Equity is demonstrated by the commitment to the protection, growth, health, and well-being of people as well as of environments.

Justice researchers have asked what implications leisure research has for society and the environment. Therefore, I have argued (e.g., Henderson, 2012) as have others that justice scholarship must move from the periphery (Allison, 2000) to the center of the leisure studies research agenda (Arai and Kivel, 2009). Social change as well as sustainability in its broadest sense can be a deliberate outcome of scholarship. The challenge for the future lies in asking critical questions about the implications that leisure research has for social and environmental justice. The relatively easy questions have involved documenting injustices. The challenge is to scrutinize what leisure research does to mitigate injustice and to create a more sustainable world.

Some leisure research has focused specifically on justice. The explicit outcome has been to address injustice and empower the individuals who are studied. However, many published leisure research papers do not specifically ask questions related to justice. Given the human rights and environmental crises in society, I have suggested that all leisure research regardless of the topic should consider what the findings contribute to justice and sustainability (Henderson, 2012). If there are no implications, then why should the research be undertaken? I believe that leisure research could contribute to social responsibility if most topics were interpreted at least partly through a justice and sustainability lens. I have confidence that researchers can have a role in addressing how leisure and leisure research can empower individuals and change social and environmental systems. The answers may not come easily but intentional critical reflection is necessary.

Implications for just leisure, sustainability, and education

A common cliché is that knowledge is power. As noted in the earlier section on lifestyle changes, learning and education are prerequisite to behaviour changes. In addition to individual learning, however, educators have an important role to play in teaching for justice and sustainability as it pertains to leisure as well as other behaviours. The role of education is to empower people with ideas and resources. The emphasis can be on integrating a sustainable way of life through lifelong learning.

A good deal has been written for almost a century about justice education. Teaching for social justice in many ways was a tenet of what John Dewey (1916) espoused regarding student engagement in classrooms. He argued that education was a necessity and a vantage point for living a meaningful life. Paulo Freire (1971) emphasized the idea of praxis or the necessity of combining education with action. Hooks (1994) also advocated for praxis and stressed the importance of critical awareness and engagement to push the boundaries of traditional education.

Educating for justice and sustainability related to leisure is not value-free. Education and curriculum development will require the interrogation of traditional ideas that have both implicitly and explicitly privileged certain groups of people as well as the idea that humans are dominant over nature. A focus on just education requires critical insights regarding the dichotomies between individual freedoms verses universal responsibility.

Further, the emphasis in addressing justice and sustainability must merge the relationship between awareness and doing. As I have argued throughout this chapter, teaching about and enabling leisure requires that students understand the connections between freedom and responsibility. Just to learn about social injustice or concerns about resource depletion is not enough without showing students their responsibility and giving them an opportunity to do something both in terms of individual lifestyle changes as well as through their future work in research or leisure management,

Implications for just leisure, sustainability, and leisure management

As I have implored, any professional committed to leisure services management and other related areas should consider the fundamental values of justice and sustainability. Further, leisure opportunities should be intentionally designed to bring about positive outcomes in individuals, groups, communities, and the environment. Leisure is not inherently good and facilitating services cannot be left to fate. Just leisure is embodied in demonstrating an interest in the protection, growth, health, and well-being of people as well as of their communities and natural environments.

Leisure should embody freedom and finding meaningful options, but the choices will only be as good as the organizational and environmental opportunities that are available. Much has been written, for example, about social ecological models of health promotion. Stokols (1992) suggested that the core assumption of social ecology is that multiple facets of the physical and social environments influence the well-being of people. Multiple aspects enhance a range of behaviours by promoting and sometimes requiring certain actions while discouraging or prohibiting other activities. Just leisure is a multifaceted phenomenon associated with intrapersonal psychological aspects, interpersonal or social influences, community based environmental factors, and policy implications. Social ecology as a framework or model can bridge multiple approaches to just leisure. The framework places an emphasis on not only the environment or the individual, but the relationship between them leading to particular behaviours. Therefore, organizations committed to just leisure and sustainability have roles to play in providing appropriate choices as well as assuring that their operations do not contribute to social inequities or environmental degradation. These organizations should have responsibility for addressing environmental problems such as climate change.

Climate change is a long-term issue that will affect everything including leisure management. For example, many parts of the world have seen changes in rainfall, which has resulted in an unusual number of floods, droughts, and/or more frequent and severe heat waves. Oceans are warming and becoming more acidic, ice caps are melting, and sea levels are rising. As these changes have become more pronounced, leisure opportunities have been affected. Although leisure managers are not going to reverse this global crisis, they can assure that they are not contributing further to the problem. For example, sustainability as it relates to the *green* environment can be addressed by supporting environmentally friendly products and services as opposed to those that pollute or harm the environment, and by encouraging recycling in facilities and at events.

The foundation for addressing environmental sustainability in the future will start with strategic plans that make environmental management central to everyday operations. This approach is a form of prevention in that in addition to addressing the environmental consequences, steps are taken to avoid these consequences in the future. For example, ecotourism is a form of tourism that revolves around the meanings and importance of the environment to visitors as well as to the community hosts. Ecotourism is one way to mitigate the problems associated with some forms of mass tourism. The National Park Service (NPS) in the US is another example of an organization implementing sustainability as a part of its mission. Recommendations have been adopted concerning policies, partnerships, and the education of the workforce to make sustainability integral to park operations. NPS is also making the education of the public about the benefits and values of sustainable recreation a high priority. In addition, the NPS is committed to monitoring its own ecological footprint to assure that the organization is not contributing further to environmental issues.

Thinking about the environment, however, also must be considered within the broad spectrum of sustainability that includes social justice. Social justice is often more difficult to pinpoint and not as easily addressed, although certainly a commitment to diversity and equal access is necessary. Environmental impacts and social injustice, however, cannot be addressed by only one discipline or organization. Professional leadership by example is important in showing commitment to the sustainability in all its forms relative to leisure.

Conclusion

In this chapter I have emphasized the interdependency of just leisure and sustainability. Although some people might argue I'm unrealistic, I believe that the future of leisure lies in recognizing that the right to leisure also requires universal responsibility for the integrity of humans and the conservation of environmental resources. Individual rights and social responsibilities must be linked. Although the benefits of leisure to individuals are important, the satisfactions and convenience of leisure should not be sacrificed for injustice to other people or environments. Universal responsibility will require nurturing a shared vision and identifying with the whole earth and its people.

The first step in moving toward more just leisure lies in recognizing the current problems and what the implications are to sustainability if the global society continues in its current trajectory. As suggested in this chapter, many options exist. One way to elicit the first step is in the education of students who wish to pursue careers in recreation and leisure services. Textbooks and coursework that link ideas about justice and sustainability to professional practice are worth pursuing. Professionals currently working in leisure services might be offered continuing education opportunities to explore how to make their practices more socially, economically, and environmentally sustainable. Further, as I have argued elsewhere (Henderson, 2012), researchers should also consider how their research contributes to justice. Most research undertaken has implications for social and environmental justice if the links are considered, regardless of the topic.

To re-emphasize, justice and sustainability will require linking diversity with unity, freedom with common good, and short-term with long-term objectives (The Earth Commission, 1992) for personal lifestyles, professional practice, and leisure scholarship. Therein lies the challenge. Foremost to consider in examining contemporary roles of leisure are; to focus on how applying justice principles influences a greater understanding of the sustainability of leisure, how just leisure can make leisure better for all people, and what the implications of just leisure analyses are for policy, practice, and everyday living. Leisure if it is business-as-usual will likely be unsustainable. Just leisure is a means for moving toward the sustainability of leisure opportunities as well as the sustainability of the planet and its people into the future.

7

PLAYING IN THE GREAT OUTDOORS

Risk and adventure activities in the twenty-first century

Paul Beedie

Origins

This really happened. 'Doomwatch' is a spectacular climb up a pillar of rock rising above the Horseshoe Bend section of Cheddar Gorge. Tony told me the top pitch was 5c, which I knew was at the limit of my technical climbing ability. I had a new partner who expected me to lead all the pitches. From a comfortable ledge below the final overhang I saw the line: it moved up and left to a wall which appeared to give access to the exposed rock above the overhang, and thereafter the top of the climb. Breathe, relax, move; slot in and clip the small wires for protection; right rope, clip, left rope clip; feel the stillness; caress the rock; feel the crenulations; feet move, hands move and I am in the moment. Then I am at the top (how did I get here?), aware of the sun and the gentle breeze – I had floated up the pitch.

He is lucky who, in the full tide of life, has experienced a measure of the active environment that he most desires. In these days of upheaval and violent change, when the basic values of today are the vain and shattered dreams of tomorrow, there is much to be said for a philosophy which aims at living a full life while the opportunity offers. There are few treasures of more lasting worth than the experience of a way of life that is in itself wholly satisfying. Such, after all, are the only possessions of which no fate, no cosmic catastrophe can deprive us; nothing can alter the fact if for one moment in eternity we have really lived.

(Shipton 1944, pp. 221–222)

This much should be understood from the beginning: that above everything else, and beyond the solid worth of weather and auroral observations in the hitherto unoccupied interior of Antarctica and my interest in these studies,

I really wanted to go for the experience's sake. So the motive was in part personal. Aside from the meteorological and auroral work, I had no important purposes. There was nothing of that sort. Nothing whatever, except one man's desire to know that kind of experience to the full, to be by himself for a while and to taste peace and quiet and solitude long enough to find out how good they really are.

(Byrd 1938, pp. 3–4)

Introduction

This chapter will endeavour to illuminate why people today appear to need risk and adventure in their lives. In the origins section above there are a number of clues. In the reflective account of a rock climb, there is recall of a powerful and enduring memory of outdoor adventure. This experience of what might be described as 'flow' (Csikszentmihalyi 2002) is over 25 years old now, but the memory is sharp. Flow, and its commensurate model of 'serious leisure' (Stebbins 2005a; 2007b) are useful theoretical ideas for discussing adventure sports in the twenty-first century which will be illustrated by examples from mountain based activities, notably climbing, hiking and mountaineering. But there are more clues in the extended quotations from first Shipton and then Byrd. Each author, reflecting upon their own adventures in the Himalayas and Antarctica respectively, suggest a connection between what we do and the way we choose to live. Both men subscribed to the scientific ethos which drove twentieth-century exploration in wild places (the development of surveys and charts for those 'blanks on the map' for Shipton and meteorological observations for Byrd) yet as work and leisure merged into a distinct lifestyle choice, each was looking for, and to a large extent found, something deeper, more serious and profound.

The common themes from the accounts of these adventurers, and from many others that have been inspired to pursue their own explorations, can be summarised in this way: the accumulation of material wealth is replaced by that of symbolic capital; life becomes more meaningful if risk is understood and to some extent embraced; emotions are heightened if we can experience connectivity to the natural world and align to its rhythms and, lastly, discard much of the complexity of everyday life to experience a simpler, perhaps more atavistic way of being. This set of ideas captures something of the qualitative dimension of leisure in that it suggests doing something for its own sake, albeit in a counter-intuitive way to the dominant social concerns of risk reduction and control in the modern world. Frank Furedi (2007) has written extensively about a 'culture of fear' which pervades our times, arguing persuasively that fear and risk have become interchangeable and that, as our lives reach unprecedented levels of security, fear (and risk) is socially constructed in ways that benefit those with the power to shape these things (media and politicians for example). Furedi develops the concept of 'vulnerability' through which he argues fear has become 'normalised as a force in its own right' (2007, p. 8). This analysis has important implications for ideas of 'freedom' in leisure choices – especially so for engaging in risk activities such as climbing – as it suggests each of us has absorbed and internalised a social determined 'risk thermostat' which will shape our decisions as we move closer to the 'edge'.

However, these ideas are also aspirational and relative to the social, economic and cultural conditions of the twenty-first century. The fascination lies in understanding how leisure opportunities today support the adventure 'instinct' – which Mortlock (1984) among many others claims resides in us all – in the context of life in developed countries today. Anderson (1970) for example, argues for a 'Ulysses Factor' inside us all. His key idea is that adventure and human advance have always been directly connected and he cites many examples of exploratory journeys and voyages throughout history which led to multiple discoveries of minerals, food, fertile lands, communication lines for trade and many other markers of progress. Anderson argues humans have always had an innate curiosity to explore which sets us apart from other life forms, and this 'instinct' has not gone away just because planet earth is now largely 'known', populated and its resources identified. He argues that the instinct has mutated into a desire to engage in exploration for its own sake and this manifests itself – more so in certain people – as the present day adventure sports of climbing, mountaineering, ocean sailing, pot-holing and more recently activities such as BASE jumping (parachuting from Buildings, Antennae, Spans to Earth). For Anderson (1970) these present day 'edge-workers' (Lyng 1990) are keeping the Ulysses Factor alive. Such analysis uses an interpretation of historical data to make the case, but it is too neat and complete when, as will be demonstrated, the circumstances of adventure as leisure today are rather more complex. For example, a person might be attracted to outdoor adventure activities precisely because someone else has already 'been there, done that and written the (guide) book': the risks integral to adventure become more generally known and to some extent, therefore, more controllable. This focus might be summarised as, in a modern world which purports to control and manage risk, why are adventure pursuits (such as climbing and mountaineering) continuing to grow in popularity? This chapter will endeavour to use the clues introduced above into a more developed set of answers to this question of paradox.

One reason might be that leisure has become an extension into the value systems of work (in that it needs to be measurably productive) rather than the re-creation of self through the constructive use of free time. Following work by Kleiber (2012) in 'leisure education', the case can be made that notions of flow and serious leisure reflect a passionate, dedicated, 'career' development dimension to leisure – for example Csikszentmihalyi (2002, p. 162) discusses 'the waste of free time' and states: 'the flow experience that results from the use of skills leads to growth; passive entertainment leads nowhere'.

Leisure today, then, is a product of the social, cultural, economic and political conditions of our times. People are discursively influenced to conform to expectations of productivity and progression – often shaped in the rhetoric of self empowerment and personal growth – hence the idea of leisure 'education' and career enhancement. When leisure choices become lifestyle defining in ways which don't conform to societal norms, such people are often marginalised. Jillian Rickly-Boyd (2012) illustrates this point well as she presents the findings from her research into the American rock climbing community: she found a loosely connected group of young (and not so young) climbers who move around North America like seasonal nomads pursuing their climbing dreams and living in tents or the back of vehicles off minimal means, disconnected from family and mainstream life but bonded through their shared climbing experiences. She calls these people 'lifestyle climbers' and concludes: 'the pursuit of rock climbing is crucial to existential authenticity, as that which informs the mindset of this lifestyle' (2012, p. 101). These climbers locate at one end of a leisure continuum, the existential life defining end which narrows a person's sense of identity to 'climber'; these people may even be beyond 'serious leisure' in that, certainly for the years that they follow such a lifestyle choice, there is no balance with the more mundane and quotidian ways of living that most of us follow. At the other end of such a continuum there are people that dabble in climbing as a sporting diversion which – increasingly commonly this occurs on indoor climbing walls (see, for example, www.bigrockclimbing.co.uk) – is a leisure choice and brings its rewards of the pleasures of physical activity and the social sharing that accompanies the activities. But crucially the identity of 'climber' is one of many that such people absorb and support through an endless round of social presentation in different settings.

Adventure, climbing and leisure

There are a number of contributory factors to climbing in the twenty-first century that have led to greater leisure participation from a broader range of people but three are especially important. First there is the development of technologies; of primary importance here is more appropriate footwear and mountain clothing – lighter and more comfortable boots and breathable waterproof jackets for example. But other technologies are equally important including walking poles and satellite navigation (GPS) tools, especially in the way that they define mountaineering as a lifestyle choice through consumption as the primary driver ahead of (authentic) participation. Second there is the development of robust risk management procedures. There is a huge debate about how we might reconcile the definition of adventure as 'uncertainty of outcome' with the propensity of those with responsibility for risk management (e.g., the Health & Safety Executive, National Park authorities, head teachers and organisations such as the Duke of Edinburgh's Award scheme) to constantly make things safer by, for example, building footpaths and adding signposts to wild places, publishing guidance about appropriate mountain equipment for different conditions and the establishment of a complex but comprehensive system of qualifications for mountain leaders. Nevertheless, despite media sensationalising of the rare incidents of serious mishaps in the mountains – the death of a schoolboy in Glenridding Beck in the Lake District in 2002 is an example – the mechanisms through which most mountain adventure activities operate today benefit from the accumulated experience of many years in the demonstration of systematic risk assessment and management as required by the 1974 Health and Safety at Work Act. The law requires people responsible for leading adventure activities to be able to demonstrate that 'risks must be reduced until: As Low As Reasonably Practicable' (ASLARP), but this does not require the elimination of risk (otherwise no one could go to the mountains), only that reasonable controls can be evidenced. This safety framework has collectively helped increase the number of people making climbing based leisure choices. The third significant contributing factor has been the growth of commercial and business activities connected to adventure and the outdoors in general and aiming to provide and support leisure lifestyle choices. The range of examples that might be cited is considerable as it covers mountaineering providers such as Jagged Globe (who specialise in taking clients on expeditions to the highest mountains in the world; see www.jagged-globe.co.uk), leisure centres who sell access to indoor climbing walls and all the shops and retail outlets which sell specialist adventure activities equipment and clothing. A person who is interested in active participation with climbing, hiking, rambling or mountaineering today can thus do so in relative comfort, in the knowledge that the risks integral to these activities can be managed (although never eliminated) and via a range of opportunities from extreme big mountain expeditions to valley walks and from cutting-edge new rock climbing exploration to indoor artificial climbing complexes engineered to replicate 'real' climbing but without the drawbacks of travel to remote places (such as national parks), inclement weather or the limitations of daylight.

The idea of leisure choice and its integral identity construction is fundamental to the role that leisure has in the fluid and fast moving times of the twenty-first century as adventure activity choices become more extensive and commodified. Moreover, as Kleiber (2012, p. 10) points out, these processes are not fixed but change over the course of a person's life, emphasised by the more fluid and accelerated social conditions today:

> Finding security, becoming capable, establishing an identity and finding intimacy and integrity are core issues throughout the lifespan, but each becomes particularly salient at different points and in response to different life events.

The democratisation of mountaineering is an example of how things change. This might have increased the casual leisure participants in the sport but it still retains the capacity for serious leisure career development, as the leisure continuum model suggests. Climbing and mountain recreations in general have the capacity to attract and retain a full range of people who might be interested in a fun and healthy outdoor experience in a general sense or a deeply engaging technically demanding adventure challenge: or each of these, but at different times. A strength of mountain based activities is the breadth of experiential possibilities: valley walks, summit hikes, technical rock climbs, gorge ascents or descents, abseiling, zip-wires or scrambling. A further strength is its capacity to offer different levels of engagement which can vary by individuals and can change for any one person over time. As a person ages for example it is likely that margins of safety expand in that person's methodology for engagement of risk (Hodgkin, 1978; Drasdo, 1978). What this does mean is that, unlike some sports which are highly competitive and may lead to elite performance consistent with winning medals (but what thereafter?), mountain based sports have the capacity to be lifelong. The following section discusses theoretical ideas that can illuminate how people make their leisure choices; this will be followed by a more applied discussion about mountain activities today.

Leisure as freedom of choice

According to Rojek (2005, p. 32) leisure is an expression of individual choices which are: 'made from patterns of behaviour and options of conduct laid down by factors of location and context'. The echoes of Marx are evident here in the notion that choice is only possible in the context of the social and economic conditions of our times, and in most areas of life today commercial agendas operate to construct what is generally acknowledged to be a consumer society. Sport and in particular adventure sports are not immune to the processes of commodification (Beedie & Hudson 2003; Varley 2006; Fletcher, 2008; 2010), much of which is concerned with the increasingly complex social processes of identity construction.

Identity is, therefore, a central concern of current times:

> The accelerated pace of change, the multiplicity of roles assumed by the individual, the deluge of messages that wash over us expand our cognitive and affective experience to an extent that is unprecedented in human history ... The search for a safe haven for the self becomes an increasingly critical undertaking, and the individual must build and continuously rebuild her/his 'home' in the face of the surging flux of events and relations ... The self is no longer pinned to a stable identity; it wavers, staggers and may crumble.
>
> (Melucci 1996: 2-3)

There is a social frontier in leisure, a set of activities that we freely engage with, as individual choice is conducted in the context of requirements of systemic control and regulation that simultaneously opens up possibilities and shapes how we engage with these. In mountain based activities there are different levels at which a person can engage depending upon their propensity for adventure.

Robert Stebbins (2007b) has developed and modified over time a model of leisure engagement that distinguishes between 'serious' and 'casual' forms of participation. He presents the case for the life-enhancing, educational and developmental possibilities of the immersion required by the former over the latter form. He has also written more specifically about adventure sports, which includes mountaineering. Although his 2005 book is about 'hobbyists' in different adventure sports, there is still a tendency to connect adventure sport to deep or serious leisure, a connection that diminishes more casual or shallow forms of participation.

Stebbins (2005) argues that between the micro focus on the motivation for engaging in adventure activities that threaten life and the macro analyses of adventure sport in modern society that is essentially risk averse lies a meso level of analysis. He argues, following Lyng's (1990) essay on edgework, that people who engage with adventure sports do not have a death wish but, rather, are interested in the idea of personal challenge, and in particular of self testing their competence to deal with the emotional and physical demands of being 'on the edge'. In this respect an analysis becomes apparent that offers an alignment to Csikszentmihalyi's (2002) concept of 'flow' and clearly connects to the components of serious leisure outlined above.

Flow is an aspirational state that can be achieved when a person becomes actively involved in a challenging task, such as a climbing activity, and it results in: 'a sense of exhilaration, a deep sense of enjoyment that is long cherished and that becomes a landmark in memory for what life should be like' (Csikszentmihalyi 2002, p. 3). The elements of flow experienced in the climbing example cited in the origins section include: a challenge at the limits of a person's skill; total immersion in the activity; enhanced concentration; control over movements; a sense of transcendentalism or oneness with the environment and an apparent suspension of time so that one is completely in the moment. This model and its integral assumptions of serious engagement with challenge (in this discussion mountain based adventure), indeed the implicit diminishing of casual leisure as a kind of subservient level of leisure participation, is not consistent with the democratisation of mountaineering characteristic of life in the twenty-first century. Flow is an interesting concept but highly individualised and subjective in the way it is experienced, and therefore difficult to study empirically. Additionally, there are variables which have changed, or at least evolved, since Csikszentmihalyi and Stebbins developed their models and the most relevant of these have already been set out, namely technology development, risk management systems and the development of adventure as business. This process of evolution can be illustrated through a brief overview of how mountaineering has developed as a sport – or more accurately today, a series of sports. Developing Rojek's framework of leisure shaped by the social and economic conditions of the times, the choices we make are contextualised by the construction of values and meanings commensurate with those conditions. As will be discussed, answering the basic question of why more people are becoming involved in outdoor activities such as climbing requires unpicking a complex picture that encompasses: the value of symbolic capital, an increasingly efficient media promotion of all things adventurous together with a greater number of adventure celebrities, a higher profile for environmental issues and sustainability, effective risk management systems and an expanding awareness of the concept of risk intelligence (Evans 2012) as well as the dynamic circumstances of personal affluence and access to resources for leisure more generally. All these developments, and all this choice, are set against having the time to do these things.

Mountains, adventure, freedom and leisure choice

Donnelly (2004) discusses the history of mountaineering through three key indicators: that the Eurocentricity of that history is fallacious, that meaning is socially constructed and, of particular importance to the discussion here, that there are generational differences amongst mountaineers with an older resistance set against a younger ambition to re-write the rules. The mid-nineteenth-century emergence of mountain climbing, geographically focused on the Alps and driven in no small measure by a British educated elite (the Golden Age which began with Wills' ascent of the Wetterhorn in 1854 and ended with the Matterhorn tragedy in 1865) established mountaineering as a recreation in which 'rules' were agreed (by the people active in the sport) that minimised the risk and recorded ascents via the easiest routes. According to Donnelly (2004) it only became a sport when risk was embraced, completion was acknowledged and the rules (or ethics) were re-written to retain the notion of challenge. Challenge sets risk against a person's competence to deal with the specific target (e.g., to achieve an ascent) and a certain 'adventure' is the resultant, when adventure is defined as uncertainty of outcome. When the balance of risk set against competence for any one person is right 'flow' is possible (Csikszentmihalyi, 2002).

It was the second generation of climbers, the Silver Age of mountaineering (Donnelly 2004, p. 141), that turned mountains into 'playgrounds' and developed the sport of mountaineering. However, this was a sport that could not be institutionalised but was organised around consensus and adherence to a set of ethics that retain the essential 'freedom' of the participant. Part of the attraction of mountaineering as a leisure activity was taking responsibility, which is the hub of the risk-competence models. The commodification of climbing, and other adventure activities (Beedie & Hudson 2003; Fletcher 2010) has changed that, so guided climbing became normalised.

In mountaineering, the sport is 'governed' by ethics which are socially determined and debated in climbing magazines, websites and club meetings but do not represent a system of enforceable rules. With competition growing, each new generation of climbers has had the capacity to rewrite the 'rules'. Mountaineering and climbing are essentially *residual* activities with a long history but there are *emergent* sections such as bouldering, deep water soloing and sport climbing (the first two are simple climbing activities where the climber is un-roped either on boulders and small crags or on sea cliffs; the latter is roped climbing on rock that has pre-placed bolts which the climber can use for safety protection). These fragments collectively represent the diversification of the sport into a number of sporting variants – the outcome is an extension of choice for people attracted to climbing activities. According to Donnelly (2004: 143), 'institutionalisation has a petrifying effect on sports, tending to freeze them at the moment the rules were written and enforced and stifling the creativity of subsequent generations of participants'. He concludes that climbers can go on 'playing with gravity'.

This in-built developmental potential is important because Rojek (2005, p. 32) argues that humans are 'learning animals' and that we gain pleasure by mastering skills and knowledge: 'we move on to new challenges in order to test and enhance our competence and through achieving fulfilment our sense of autonomy is enhanced' (Rojek 2005, p. 33). Moreover, because leisure occurs in a social context competition with others is an important part of people's intrinsic rewards. From this social perspective 'freedom' is only possible through 'webs of interdependency' (in climbing: equipment manufacturers, transport systems, communication media). For Rojek, leisure has four primary functions: representation (the moral regulation of activities through the state and market media – 'don't go into the mountains without a map'; identity (leisure as a marker of inclusion or exclusion, that is ascribed or achieved status – 'what ascents have you done?'); control (leisure connections to regimes of power – 'the ongoing allure of the romantic tradition of escape to wild places'); and resistance – which Rojek argues is problematic in that 'consumerism has colonised leisure time and space so thoroughly that leisure forms that involve no level of commercialisation seem culturally anomalous' (2004, p. 97) and 'withstanding the colonising logic of consumer culture is formidably difficult' (p. 102). It has already been suggested that commercial activity concerned with adventure has had an important role to play in the democratisation of mountaineering, however, to suggest it is the primary driver for participation is to overstate the case.

The idea of sport in the mountains is captured by the idea of 'nature challenge' (Stebbins 2005, p. 16). Stebbins, developing his concept of deep leisure, argues that those outside adventure sports (the public, media, managers and legislators) do not see the insider view. Developing a similar argument to Walter (1984) who wrote an articulate essay called 'Death as Recreation', the case is presented that those people who make leisure choices to participate in adventure activities do so from an informed perspective as edge-workers not mad-caps with a death wish. Stebbins (2005) argues that those people who choose adventure activities are not adrenaline junkies who need a high risk fix but rather people who are motivated in many different ways to participate and that this spectrum of motivations is not fixed but does flex and change before, during and after the activity. This acknowledgement of a range of participants is important, as is the point that participants are aware of risk but recognise controls (such as one's level of skill and experience in meeting the challenge) can reduce this.

Storry (2003) offers a further critique of Rojek's assertion that we can't escape the commodification process. He argues that we all have a propensity to develop competence, and that this is human nature, but that those people who engage with adventure in the original meaning of the term – that is, with uncertainty of outcome as risk set against a person's capacity to rise to the challenge – set themselves apart from thrill seekers (such as those who pay for a bungee jump) for whom competence, or indeed any skill, is not a pre-requisite for participation. Storry was a professional mountain guide and is here recognising that, although the social context for climbing is important, in adventure sports he suggests that, although socially determined, it is the individual who participates. He goes on to explain that motivation is complex, but can be explained by positioning on two 'axes of motivation': one polarises a *performance* orientation (which is intrinsic to the person) to an *outcome* orientation (which is extrinsic to the person) and the other polarises a *self regarding* orientation (which is exclusive) with an *other regarding* orientation (which is inclusive). This model is combined with the conceptualisation of climbing as a series of games – freely entered in to and regulated by the ethics first set out in written form in an essay by Lito Tejada-Flores called 'Games Climbers Play' (1978) – in which the participants' motivations are tempered not by the external controls of a risk managed adventure thrill activity but by a propensity to seek out a flow state through a peak adventure experience. Storry identifies four primary games that climbers – and by extension other adventure activists operating outside the commodified adventure framework – play. A self regarding–performance orientation results in 'deep play'; a self regarding–outcome orientation results in 'personal achievement'; an outcome orientation to others results in 'social bonding' and another regarding–performance orientation results in 'nature life'. None of these orientations are inclusive of a death wish; additionally they are not fixed but flex and change and will probably occur in overlapping and even simultaneous episodes in the holistic experience of climbing. However, the games do have a common genesis and that is the idea of competence being tested through a freely chosen engagement with a risk activity: although people do not commonly set out to achieve a sense of flow, this can be an outcome of the peak adventure experience of working the edge. Storry's conceptualisation thus retains recognition that the leisure choice that is climbing is not fixed but flexes and changes in ways that fit the leisure continuum model. Climbing is no longer ring-fenced as person and place specific – which suggests inclusion of some and exclusion of others – but is a less clearly defined and bounded set of activities, highly personalised but still capable of generating a sense of well being, and possibly flow.

Flow operates in the zone between boredom and anxiety. In terms of physical enactment, Csikszentmihalyi discusses the potential of the human body (2002, p. 95) and he suggests: 'the simple act of moving the body across space becomes a source of complex feedback that provides optimal experience and adds strength to the self' in ways that facilitate the production of flow. In this respect he sees flow as commonplace and achievable in everyday settings; however, when one combines Storry's (2003) model of motivation the picture becomes more complicated because 'the simple act of moving the body' is subjected to a series of potential motivations and outcomes. People do not make leisure choices just because they want to achieve flow, but if this happens then it is likely to have a positive effect on continued participation in that activity. In sports like climbing and mountaineering there is always likely to be an element of challenge because of the proximity of risk.

The presence of risk, and risk perceptions shaped by the social construction of the values and meanings integral to mountaineering, is likely to have an important role in the choices we make. There are many ways that mountaineering in the twenty-first century continues to evolve and accommodate more people and a greater diversity of people. These are developments of the three areas (technology, risk management and commerce) set out above. First, technology continues to improve levels of comfort and safety through enhanced potential to control the impact of the environment on the activity (Drasdo, 1978); examples of these increased margins of safety include lighter but stronger ropes and helmets, 'sticky' rubber soled climbing footwear and detailed climbing guide books which indicate where the route goes and how hard it might be at specific points. A particularly important development has been the use of stainless steel bolts as anchors for climbers to protect themselves: these are pre-placed and permanent and eliminate the need for a climber to 'place' protection whilst making it easier to 'see' the line of the climb so that, for some climbers, the challenge is diminished but for others the activity becomes a physical challenge of technical execution in a risk controlled setting. Such bolted climbs have been labelled 'sport' climbs to distinguish them from 'adventure' climbs. Nevertheless, technology has created a choice of climbing forms through which a person can control the margins of safety.

Second, there has been a proliferation of experts in mountaineering. Mostly this is guides and instructors, but there is also a growth of technical officers, Health and Safety officials and administrators. This trend is illustrated by the proliferation of awards and qualifications available for outdoor leaders. It is a moot point whether this development is a consequence of or a catalyst to the democratisation of mountaineering; nevertheless the range of awards does reflect current levels of engagement from basic low level walks to highly demanding technical snow and ice climbs. For walking, rambling and hiking, in the UK, the Walking Leader's Award allows a person to work in areas up to 600m but to lead groups in the bigger mountains requires a Mountain Leader's Award. To manage climbing scenarios on crags and small outcrops requires a Single Pitch Award but to progress to multi-pitch climbing in summer conditions requires a Mountain Instructor's Award, and if snow and ice is involved a Mountain Instructor's Certificate. Qualified experts generate confidence among participants and have led to sustainable outdoor careers for well-qualified instructors (as work, not leisure), which in turn is changing the more traditional idea of a mountaineering apprenticeship that Hodgkin (1978) discusses. Traditionally a person interested in mountaineering spent years literally learning the ropes, guided by those more experienced who were the guardians of the sport, a status achieved mostly by experience and the recognition of peers as awards are more recent developments. In many respects the proliferation of experts in mountaineering has created a professional dimension. Such changes have accelerated the development of adventure as a commodity (Beedie & Hudson, 2003; Varley 2006).

Third, climbing and walking activities have become more populous in wild outdoor places where, when the wind is howling, the cloud down low and rain falling there is a confidence that comes from knowing you are not the only one out on the hills. Moreover, the social organisation of these activities is also moving with the times in that social networking via Facebook, for example, is as likely to generate group based activities in mountains as the more traditional structures of climbing and rambling clubs. Perhaps the greatest manifestation of this fluidity and mobility characteristic of our times is the arrival of climbing locations in places where most of us live (towns and cities) far removed from the wild and isolated places where the real crags and mountains are found. Climbing walls have been around since the 1960s when they were clunky after-thoughts added to leisure centres and new school sports halls by well-intentioned architects and planners who used unimaginative combinations of bricks and concrete plinths to create truly artificial climbing environments. Apart from the obvious limitations of design and location (indoors was good but not when other sports were using the hall), the principle of moving the climbing to the people was a watershed moment in the democratisation of mountaineering. Climbing walls developed quickly towards the end of the twentieth century as climbers became involved in both their design and management: first design innovations in wall texture, interchangeable specialist holds and degrees of slabs, overhangs and bulges arrived; soon after 'living stone' did away with the artificial holds and created a textured feel of nicks, slots and crevices which accurately replicated real rock. Then the location shifted to dedicated centres such as the disused steel works in the centre of Sheffield that became The Foundry in the early 1990s and the walls became climbing centres with big and little climbs, bouldering areas (climbing low down, un-roped), cafes, shops and dedicated (and qualified) staff to organise and deliver climbing courses as well as monitor the adherence to safety rules by casual climbers. The climbing centre in Milton Keynes (www.bigrockclimbing.co.uk) caters for all these aspects of leisure, and more, including taster sessions, parties for adults and children, 'social climbing' sessions, climbing competitions and corporate training. Choice has proliferated and come to the people: this venue is so successful (it has its own membership incentive scheme) that for some participants this controlled indoor environment has become an end in itself so that climbing becomes another sport to be experienced before moving on to others rather than the start of a climbing career that through deep immersion will lead to a life-long career of serious leisure in the mountains.

So, choice has increased in climbing and mountaineering and this has been facilitated by the social and economic conditions of the twenty-first century.

Technical innovation combined with commercial developments such as climbing walls have had a significant role to play in this. In some considerable measure this supports Rojek's (2005) contention that we are captured by the 'webs of independency' and have become entangled in the processes of consumption and its commensurate concerns of identity construction. However, to argue that these casual forms of leisure define participation in climbing and walking activities today is wrong because it ignores the possibilities that the 'learning animals' within us (Rojek 2005, p. 32; Storry, 2003) have the potential to deepen our level of involvement, especially in our capacity to move from artificial adventure sites to activities in wild places. As our engagement deepens so our experience increases and our assessment of risk becomes more nuanced. The challenge is retained as we gain control over our decision making rather than yielding completely to commercial expediency – and climbing and mountaineering activities offer such potential. Evans (2012) calls this capacity to understand 'risk intelligence', and although he is writing about navigating everyday life, the concept applies well to negotiating leisure choice today. He says (Evans 2012, p. 68): 'Learning to feel comfortable in the twilight zone ... is crucial in many areas of life where certainty is rarely justified ... Developing risk intelligence requires getting the balance right, steering between the extremes of uncertainty, intolerance and endless calculation'. In many ways this challenges Furedi's (2007) analysis which suggests omnipresent vulnerability sustained by discursive agendas by suggesting that experience and education can provide self-empowerment to offer a purer template of choice in how we use our leisure time: the experiential experience of climbing – whether guided or self determined – will develop degrees of risk intelligence as a counterpoint to the ubiquitous 'culture of fear' so that it is possible to claim that leisure as freedom still exists.

Conclusion

From the emergence of the Romantic movement in the nineteenth century wild places (and mountains in particular) have been constructed as escape locations from the dominant urban locations that most of us live and work in. This nostalgia remains with us, and becomes heightened as a counterbalance to the intensity of contemporary lives and our cravings to avoid boredom. Adventure is discursively ubiquitous in our lives – from its connection to entrepreneurialism and advancement to carbonated drinks and shampoo advertising and the picture of the Himalayan mountain Ama Dablam as the logo for an insurance company – so it is contained in leisure. The complex answer to the question of why people feel the need to become involved with risk based activities contains all the elements introduced in 'origins' at the start of this chapter: the enduring qualities of 'experiences' above the ephemerality of material possessions; the attractions of peace and quiet and the opportunity to slow down and be in control of one's motility and thoughts (the concept of 'slow adventure' is currently being developed by Peter Varley) and the magnetism of the adventure instinct, even if it leads to a commodified and managed adventure experience such as that of the white-water rafting company investigated by McGillivray and Frew (2007).

Perhaps the best way of understanding the attractions of outdoor adventure for any one person is to think in terms of fluidity. The continuum model introduced at the start of this chapter suggests a way of thinking about this issue that embraces flexibility and is supported through the work of Shen and Yarnal (2010) who critically evaluate the Stebbins model of serious versus casual leisure and conclude that the serious-casual dichotomy does not capture the nuances of leisure choices: 'the proposed continuum conception may shed new light on the understanding of typical leisure experiences by clarifying widespread misconceptions associated with the SL-CL dichotomy' (p. 101).

Playing in the outdoors is an important part of leisure whether this is through a shallow, recreational and fun based experience or deeper, more structured and committed form of adventure sport engagement. The leisure choices made can enhance our sense of identity which, it has been suggested, evolve, develop and change in keeping with the fluid conditions of contemporary times. There are established identities – such as mountaineer – which resist infiltration by people who may not subscribe completely to the established identity template; however a combination of commercial and technological developments is changing access to mountaineering by increasing active leisure choices at the same time as the essential core of adventure activities can be seen to be fragmenting and diversifying. Nevertheless, the experiential drivers for engaging in adventure sports still allow for people to make active choices, particularly through the search for competence (in skill and judgement acquisition) and challenge (through a conscious engagement with risk) that is at the centre of the flow experience. Finally, leisure choices vary from person to person and by the stages that we are at in our life cycles. Mountaineering is different from more conventional sports (such as power based team sports) in that it offers a genuine capacity for life-long active participation. This is partly because of the range of activities encompassed by the sport – different forms of climbing, hiking, rambling and expeditioning are examples. Moreover, within that life-span what starts as casual leisure could become deep leisure over time – thus resisting attempts to dichotomise – and, as margins of safety generally increase as we age the reverse is also possible, as is the potential to deepen one's engagement but via a different form of mountaineering. Such fluidity is entirely consistent with social conditions in the twenty-first century.

8

SITES OF SERIOUS LEISURE

Acting up in space and place

Sam Elkington

Introduction

It is a widely held view in the study of leisure that certain spaces and places matter to people, and that personal bonds commonly develop between people, places and activities, taking on an identity of their own (Stedman, 2003; Hammitt *et al.*, 2004). Serious leisure is a concept used to describe the nature of involvement in leisure activities that are sufficiently substantial and interesting in nature for the participant to find a career there, acquiring and expressing a combination of its special qualities, skills, knowledge and experience (Stebbins, 2007b). Serious leisure participants may develop a strong attachment to their chosen pursuits. However, to what extent the leisure setting mitigates serious leisure involvement has received little scholarly attention. To this end, the chapter builds upon research undertaken by Elkington (2010, 2011) exploring the complex phenomenology of individuals' experiences of flow in amateur acting. Flow theory (Csikszentmihalyi, 1992) is a person–environment interaction theory in which optimal, flow, experience is triggered by a good fit between a person's skills in an activity and the challenges afforded by that activity; this creates a very positive state of consciousness and leads to deeply enjoyable and intrinsically motivating experience. The chapter draws together the fields of Leisure Studies, Human Geography and Environmental Psychology, to examine, for the first time, the intersection of time, activity, state-of-mind, and meanings of space and place as distinct and yet interrelated dimensions of the serious leisure experience – as it happens.

Serious leisure in space and place

Leisure happens and is produced in space. These spaces may be material and related to concrete locations, yet the spaces, and therefore geographies, of leisure may be metaphorical, even imaginative (Crouch, 2000). Space, then, can be important in shaping the meaning of leisure sites and leisure experience may be transformed by the way in which people encounter those spaces and activities and give them meaning (Stebbins, 2012b). Stebbins (2012b) notes that there is a multitude of places and spaces popularly thought of as being used exclusively for leisure – the skate park, the shopping mall, the coffee shop, the nature reserve – indicating there are many geographical aspects to leisure study. Stebbins (2009a) has observed that many of these spaces represent sites for mass, or what he terms casual leisure, defined as immediately, intrinsically rewarding, relatively short-lived, pleasurable activity requiring little or no special training to enjoy it. It is fundamentally hedonic and, as such, is engaged in for the significant level of pure enjoyment, or pleasure, found there (Stebbins, 1997). Among its types are: play (including dabbling), relaxation (e.g., sitting, napping, strolling), passive entertainment (e.g., TV, books, listening to music), active entertainment (e.g., games of chance), sociable conversation and sensory stimulation (e.g., sex, eating, drinking). Casual leisure is unlikely to evoke a particularly strong attachment to or identification with these sites, however, for many of these spaces serve other important interests besides leisure, and therefore cannot be counted as uniquely geographic leisure spaces. Stebbins (2012b) sees geographic leisure space as constituting a unique principle of contemporary leisure, but only when that space is of a pure type; that is, when it is used for the purposes of serious leisure.

Serious leisure is defined as

> the systematic pursuit of an amateur, hobbyist, or volunteer activity that people find so substantial, interesting, and fulfilling that, in the typical case, they launch themselves on a (leisure) career centred on acquiring and expressing a combination of its special skills, knowledge and experience.
>
> (Stebbins, 2007b, p. 5)

A serious leisure activity is defined by six distinctive qualities, found among amateurs, hobbyists and volunteers alike. One such quality is the need for a degree of *perseverance*. A second quality of serious leisure, as identified by Stebbins, is the 'tendency for amateurs, hobbyists, and volunteers to have *careers* in their endeavours' (Stebbins, 2001b, p. 6). The construction and maintenance of careers often rest on a third quality of serious leisure: the requirement of *significant personal effort* based on specifically acquired knowledge, training, skills, or occasionally all three (Stebbins, 2001b). Stebbins's research also turned up eight *durable benefits* commonly found by amateurs in their chosen pursuits, namely: self-actualisation, self-enrichment, self-expression, regeneration or renewal of self, feelings of accomplishment, enhancement of self-image, social interaction and belongingness, and long lasting physical products of the activity. A fifth quality that further defines the serious leisure concept is the *unique ethos* and *social world* that evolves around each serious leisure activity. Stebbins based the sixth and final quality of serious leisure on evidence that participants in serious leisure activities *identify* strongly with their chosen pursuit – an identity that grows through substantial emotional, moral, and often physical investment. Stebbins has considered individual involvement in amateur leisure and professional work, focusing on barbershop singers, jazz musicians and stand-up comedians, sporting and artistic hobbies, as well as volunteering as a leisure pursuit.

In recent work, Stebbins (2012b) offers a detailed conceptualisation of leisure's context and an understanding of leisure as space and domain. In particular, he considers what he sees as the three spaces of leisure: institutional, temporal and geographical. Leisure, suggests Stebbins, can be defined and examined as it fits within *institutional space*, the cultural and social organisation of community and society, as it fits within *temporal space* and the span of daily, weekly and yearly time, and as it fits within *geographical space*, the places and surrounding environment where leisure activities are pursued, whether artificial or natural. In this way it is seen as a location, a site where particular leisure happens, a distance between things. However, Stebbins's treatment of leisure space and place as context fails to consider that feature which distinguishes place from surrounding space, or from simple location – a human focus. Stebbins's general sketch of context is basic to an understanding of place, but by being basic and general it does not say enough about what is distinctive and memorable about these place encounters. Space is not synonymous with place, for the latter applies to a complex field of perceptual experience involving person and setting together with the range of historical and cultural influences, knowledge and meaning that invariably imbue that field. A central concern in searching for the heart of place lies in identifying the human role, and while Stebbins acknowledges that both people and places make a contribution in the context of serious leisure, this does not capture what is exceptional about our most compelling experiences of these sites of serious leisure; for example, when participants find the intensely absorbing experiences associated with Flow (Csikszentmihalyi, 1992; Elkington, 2010, 2011). In its purest form, suggests Stebbins (2001b), 'psychological flow is more likely to be felt in certain serious leisure activities that are rewarding for their self-expression, cherished experiences, self-gratification and tendency to refresh mind and body' (p. 21). Stebbins (2005a) has since conceptualised psychological flow as an optimal example of the thrills available in serious leisure. These thrills or high points are 'the sharply exciting events and occasions that stand out in the minds of those who pursue a kind of serious leisure' (Stebbins, 2007b, p. 15). Thrills in serious leisure may be seen as situated manifestations of certain more abstract rewards; they are what many participants seek as concrete expressions of the rewards they find there. They are deemed of great importance, in substantial part, because they motivate the participant to continue their pursuit of an activity in the hope of finding similar experiences again in future leisure episodes. Elkington (2010, 2011) has found it to be highly prized in amateur theatre. In his study of the complex phenomenology of flow experience in serious leisure, Elkington found that experiencing the qualities of flow is what makes leisure for participants most rewarding. Flow is taken here to refer more generically to an optimal psychological state in which complete absorption in the task at hand leads to a number of positive psychological qualities which include: the perception that personal skills and the challenges provided by an activity are in balance, centring of attention, loss of sense of self, unambiguous feedback to a person's actions, feelings of control over actions and environment, and momentary distortion of time. Crucially, the complex phenomenology of flow-based serious leisure sketched out in Elkington's research revealed a dimension of experience that is easily overlooked in accounts of leisure, a dimension that may be the most critical of all because it concerns experience of the most primary sort; namely that of an aesthetic character.

Aesthetics in leisure place

Aesthetics is ordinarily thought of as referring to art, to the value that distinguishes the arts from other, more ordinary and mundane objects or activities. A general meaning of place as aesthetic reveals a perceptual environment that joins a distinctive physical identity and coherence, a resonance, with a memorable character, or form, with which an individual actively engages through action (Berleant, 2003). It is through perception and experience, argues the human geographer Yi-Fu Tuan (1977) that we get to know the world through places. Tuan coined the term 'topophilia' to refer to the 'affective bond' between people and place (Tuan, 1975). This bond, this sense of attachment, is fundamental to the idea of place as a 'field of care'. Tuan defines place through a comparison with space. He develops a sense of space as an open region of action and movement while place is about stopping and becoming involved. Place philosopher Edward Relph (1976) has claimed that to be human is to be 'in place'. Places in this deeper sense need not have any fixed location at all; rather priority is given to immersion in place. Building on Heidegger's notion of Desien (approximately *dwelling*), Relph describes what he terms as practical knowledge of places – the very everyday fact of our knowing where to enact aspects of our lives. We live in one place, work in another and find leisure in another. But we are also willing to protect our places against those who do not belong and we are frequently nostalgic for places we have left. These human responses, for Relph, reveal the deeper significance of place to human 'being'. For both Tuan and Relph, then, places resonate with the human condition at an essential level. Places are experienced.

Elkington found the flow experiences of amateur actors was invoked through a similar resonance with the environment. The defining features of actors' descriptions of being 'in flow' during serious leisure were characterised above all by an intense experiential involvement in moment-to-moment activity in a leisure setting. In flow-based serious leisure, everything is experienced as optimal. Mind and body are in harmony, negative thinking and self-doubt is absent, and functioning is enhanced. When all of a person's skills are needed to successfully manage challenges of a situation, that person's attention is so completely absorbed by the demands of the immediate activity that any awareness of the individual as being separate from the actions performed disappears. So involved are these individuals in what they are doing it could be said they share a unity with that setting. The comments of one actor best illustrates this:

> When you're on stage … you almost build a barrier, well the lights do it for you in a way … but it's almost like there's a fourth wall there, like you're in a room … and you forget that there's an audience watching because you get so involved in what you're doing on stage (Actor 1).

In this experience of appreciative immersion, awareness is no longer split between individual and environment. Rather individuals are so involved in what they are doing they stop being aware of themselves as separate from actions they perform, creating a unified state wherein actions are both effortless and spontaneous. Berleant (2003) has termed the perceptual experience of total absorption captured here as 'aesthetic engagement'. It was obvious from the way participants spoke about such experience that these were special and highly valued moments, offering willing participants a high degree of aesthetic engagement that is intensely positive. But much more is at stake in matters of aesthetics in place, as revealed in flow-based serious leisure, than what is identifiably human – what is cultural, social or historical. Much of what is traditionally discussed as 'time' and 'space' is also to be understood in terms of place, as two actors describe.

> Your focus is just so intense that it puts you outside of that space … outside of time, you're just caught up in the moment (Actor 4).

> You're more aware of things like timing when you're taking on smaller parts because you're off and then on and then off again … you don't won't to interrupt the flow of the performance so your timing has to be perfect (Actor 8).

Such is the intensity of experience in flow for these actors that it gives the impression of having been somewhere not accessible normally. Flow-producing activities, suggests Csikszentmihalyi (1990), have the ability to 'provide a sense of discovery, a creative feeling of transporting the person into a new reality' (p 74) where time is experienced more subjectively 'so that at various times it seems to speed up, slow down, or stand still' (Csikszentmihalyi, 2003, p. 54). In flow, time and space meet and are experienced within the single structure that is place. Rather, the unusual level of personal involvement when in flow means the sense of time tends to adapt itself to the activity at hand. Evidently, the transformation of time, in amateur theatre, can be both a by-product of being completely involved in an activity and part of the challenge for that activity, wherein in normal clock-time is replaced by experiential sequences structured according to the demands of the presently engaged situation. For actors, rehearsals and a run of shows differed in this respect. Place, in this sense, is not limited to its social, historical or geographical parameters, since whatever is meant by them, time and space exceed the particular cultural and historical contexts which they embrace and support. The flow aesthetic repositions time and space as forms for intuition with place, not as an instance of sheer physical landscape, but as a material condition of possibility for action. A distinctive quality of this aesthetic engagement with a setting is the individual's lack of an analytical stance towards that space. Since the flow experience described by amateur actors occurred in situations where they were able to manage, at least theoretically, with the demands for action, there is a sense of personal agency over the unfolding of the activity.

> Occasionally during rehearsals but mainly at the time of the performances I reach a place where I am completely content with myself and the task before me … my focus is clear and my intentions true … anything is possible (Actor 3).

Implicit here is what Malpas (2001) has described as a 'transcendental condition of possibility'; a sense of going beyond the unknown, of stretching individual capacity for action. According to Bloch (2000), this experience is not 'conceived as a delusion in which the person has lost his/her critical powers, but rather as a revelation in which a more profound reality is encountered' (p. 56). Giving up or surrendering to the demands of the situation and suspending any concerns about doing so was certainly a powerful and emotive sensation for actors as one participant attests:

> Reaching this place … It's the best feeling in the world … like you're untouchable … when I'm in this place I move effortlessly, there's no conscious thought involved. I'm lost in the moment and anything is possible (Actor 2).

The momentary sensing of place encountered here gives rise to an open region for action and movement within which a variety of elements are concealed or brought to light through their mutual interrelation and juxtaposition with the region. Most notably, in flow, due to deep concentration on the activity at hand, the individual not only suspends concern for the implications for their actions, but temporarily loses an awareness of self. The ability to forget the self on a temporary basis has special meaning to actors allowing for a permissiveness that is not found outside of this experience of place. According to one actor:

> You can forget yourself and just play … play with your character, play with the audience, play at being someone else other then yourself (Actor 9).

The grasping of leisure space, and so of place, at least in flow-based serious leisure, is tied, in large part, to this possibility for pre-reflective action which includes the capacity to be affected, or acted on, by one's surroundings. This is not sheer spontaneity of the individual acting in undelimited freedom but a responsive appreciation and sensitivity to the possibility of place that in turn requires an active grasping of both subjective and objective space. Space, then, is not derived from abstraction from place, but the very concept of place would appear to entail an understanding of space from the start. In the words of one amateur actor:

> I know exactly where I need to be mentally and physically to perform at my best. For me it's a package deal, if my head's not right or the performance space isn't right it throws me. I need it to be just so (Actor 7).

Clearly physical characteristics alone do not make place; whether this connection comes through action or through the simple presence of involved others, human sensibility to a physical location, together with positive aesthetic engagement, was found to give rise to the simultaneous absorption and presence that actors associated with the serious character of place. That is, the appreciative awareness of flow invites sensations of mind and body simultaneously in both suspension and animation, of being somewhere in between thinking and feeling, of being in motion through space and time, as a lived experience with an open character. However, though the open structure and form of stage acting appears well-adapted to the inducement of the aesthetic engagement characteristic of flow, it was clear that the way in which the possibilities for action are structured within such leisure activities and settings affects the ease with which participants are able to enter flow. Some actors, for instance, appeared to rely on more structured activity (i.e., ritual, routine and/or superstition), while others seemed to need fewer structural supports. How this is manifest appears to be a purely personal affair, one requiring the investment of significant personal effort on the part of the participant. The comments of one actor emphasised the sense of personal obligation and commitment that necessitates the purposeful and significant investment of energy in order to perform well:

> This is a purely personal thing. It's not a matter of waiting for things to be right, you react to the situation and how you feel in that time and place you sometimes have to work hard ... and sometimes you just don't get that balance right and you're left just going through your lines (Actor 9).

To slip into flow at all, then, actors must attain certain levels of experience, skill, knowledge and conditioning appropriate to the challenges presented by the activity so that there is a confidence on behalf of the individual that they possess the specific abilities necessary to perform well in that place at that time. Confidence of this sort appeared to be founded upon a distinct sense of trust, itself built up over repeated exposure to and experience of a leisure setting:

> I've grown to trust this space, and the people in it ... over time and through experience a strong bond has formed between us, we're in it together ... it's this connection that gives you the energy and motivation to perform again and again (Actor 1).

Trusting in themselves, in others and in the leisure setting appears to be an important condition for actors to let go of the prevailing conscious controlling tendencies of their non-leisure lives. In the words of one actor:

> In time you develop the confidence to let go of it all, when you feel completely confortable with those around you and your surroundings ... I'm familiar with what happens in that space and how it works. I don't give it much conscious thought anymore (Actor 12).

Examining the aesthetic character of flow-based serious leisure not only identifies, in place, another aspect of this complex idea but also reveals something of the qualities and characteristics, the form, of the situations of which that experience is a part. What is valued here lies in the conditions under which participants encounter their leisure and in what takes place 'in-place'. But in order to create meaningful form this encounter must be a lasting one. Indeed, what characterises such an encounter is the emotion revealed in how actors articulate sensations, movements and experiences in relation to place. Crucially, the articulation of emotion appears to be spatially mediated in a manner that is not simply metaphorical. Emotional relations and attachments weave through space and time and help form the fabric of unique personal geographies (Crouch, 2000). The emotio-spatiality of flow-based serious leisure experience signals the presence of complex occurrences in excess of and elsewhere than that at the surface of cognition and awareness. While the folk phenomenology of flow often substitutes for any further elaboration about what comprises it, this glancing is merely the tip of what appears to be a much deeper experiential iceberg. For instance, the ability to establish a distinction between everyday reality and that of flow turns on the level of personal commitment to and involvement in a particular setting. It is likely that the typical beginner does not know of such structures, while the typical expert probably incorporates them automatically into his or her interactions with that space. This kind of discussion of place is much more than a discussion of location since place is undoubtedly a product of pausing, of becoming involved, and a chance of attachment that, in reality, exists as a matter of degrees – strong to weak, serious to casual. The challenge for the individual is to learn to manage time, space and the activity, to internalise as many of these supporting place structures as possible. Lived experience of space is what renders its features as visible and remarkable, while concomitant occurrences 'in' space constitute the materiality of place experiences. This in turn makes experiences of place, experiences of dwelling in and inhabiting place the proper object of attention here. Accordingly the ability of actors to engage in an aesthetic experience is based, in large part, on context, manifested in a personal bodily and perceptive experience prolonged beyond the immediate experience. Place, in this sense, is not a physical location, nor is it a state-of-mind; it is the engagement of the conscious body with the conditions of a specific site, with particular ways of thinking and seeing, of being-in-the-world. In short, place is embodied.

Embodied place and the 'serious encounter'

We have seen in the comments of actors that place possesses a certain resonance and form as a repository of social, cultural or personal significance in the form of knowledge and memories. Knowledge and memories are part of a culture and depend, in various ways, upon the physical setting for how people remember the course of events leading up to the present (Roberts, 1996). This was best captured by one ex-professional actor:

> I've been part of the group for nearly 15 years and in that time have seen a lot and have had some memorable experiences ... it's familiar to me, we have always rehearsed and performed in the same place, and for those, like me, who have been around a while there's a history, a heritage, and an energy here that takes hold of you ... sort of becomes part of you ... and you try and re-live and do justice to that history, that heritage in each performance (Actor 10).

Place familiarity involves the pleasant memories, achievement memories, cognitions and environmental images that result from acquaintances and remembrances associated with certain leisure places, and which serve as the initial stages of the human-place bonding process (Roberts, 1996). Traces of the past are visible in perceptual form as a kind of projected memory and may even confer an enhanced presence on a location that is otherwise undistinguishable. Material form together with sensory apprehension and social and/or personal significance can together create the special phenomenal experience of aesthetic engagement in flow that distinguishes place from simple geographical location. These phenomenological insights into the 'feeling of doing' interpret more directly a process of embodiment, through which individuals engage, encounter and grasp a sense of place, gradually refining the aesthetic engagement of individuals to ever-subtler levels of awareness of and encounters with a leisure setting. This is most eloquently captured by one actor:

> I had come through a focused slice of life that had affected me so intensely and emotionally that you never quite experience things in the same way again ... it changes you, not just as an actor and how you act, but as a person and how you approach life (Actor 5).

The aesthetic engagement of devotees from amateur theatre shares a degree of intensity that is consistent with experiencing flow, experience that is usually associated with high-quality performance and a pattern of commitment that joins them with others in a unique ethos of shared meaning and perseverance, in a personal and collective sense. This commitment and personal endeavour forges a connection with other individuals or groups that share interests, reinforces shared commitment and creates the experience of being part of a defined social world containing clearly defined activities and roles, perhaps only known to members and/or the individual. For amateur actors, this social world was experienced as somehow separate from wider society, with this separation largely based upon the special skills, knowledge and attributes required to perform well there. In this social world, it was not uncommon for participants to have their own language or terminology, their own behaviours, norms, values and attributes that, over time, had reinforced this separateness:

> Not everyone can do what we do ... some of us have had a taste of the profession and want to continue it on without all the stress and just enjoy ourselves, others have spent years developing themselves as amateur actors. But all of us share a love of acting and are committed to producing quality performances as a group (Actor 6).

The clear emphasis on 'us' and 'others' substantiates the fact that the meaning of leisure is embedded in participatory forms of social practice and is subject to the structuring influences of socio-cultural beliefs and traditions that surround these practices (Hamilton-Smith, 1991). Such meaning, thus, takes on the norms and values of that particular leisure group by providing positive practice models to emulate and negative models to be avoided. Serious leisure settings are sites of social engagement and become meaningful through the ways in which people are encountered there. Maffesoli (1996) has noted the significance of social relations or 'sociations' in the place-making process. Flexible social relations support and sustain the ritualistic practices that render these spaces distinct from everyday life. Place is an important part of this practice because people invariably define social relationships and identities through the spaces where they meet (Maffesoli, 1996). These forms of social relationships are developed through particular kinds of behaviour linked with particular kinds of spaces that hold distinctive features through practice and whose materiality, in turn, colours those relations. In this way, the meaning ascribed to serious leisure space, and so place, is not static, rather it is continually shifting through reflection and recollection, and by doing so, facilitates continuity and progression of place experiences through the creation of intentions and expectations that provide future focus for attention.

> When there's been a particularly successful run of performances you do try and channel that positive energy into the next production ... there's an

integrity to it, and an expectation that what you do next is of just as good a quality, like it's an extension of yourself (Actor 3).

While encounters with this social world can be expressive of particular cultural practices, place also made different sense to actors depending on the expressive feeling at that time:

> There's a definite rhythm to performing well as part of the group. It's not something you're always aware of, it's a feeling, a kind of whole body sense that each of us are present in the moment and in complete control (Actor 9).

These temporal moments of expression elucidate the embodied character of place wherein the body permits transportation of sensual feeling so that objects and other people are lent significance through the way in which they are encountered. Material content of places becomes significant in this process. In theatre acting, actors are surrounded by others and by the material configuration of the theatre through which the active geography of acting is configured. Acting is an explicitly expressive practice. The space in which rehearsal and performance happens is the expressive space through which the individual self, as actor, is both constructed and reaffirmed. The features of place and the pace of activity may be understood as embodied through the actions of the people there as participants. For instance, each actor utilised a highly personalised configuration of ritualistic practices, particular means of engagement, physical activities and artistic production to recreate the much coveted sensation of 'presence' associated with performing well as part of the group. Subjective definitions of place and the attributes contained within, therefore, reflect self-definitions conditioned by social (and cultural) affiliation. For actors, the sensation of presence is symbolic of achieving what Tuan (1980) has termed as rootedness in place, of being 'at home' in a prereflective sense, supporting an overarching identification with a locale and its landscapes that is largely taken for granted. The strength of this identification and affiliation with place has emerged and evolved through ongoing interactions with other actors and the environment and is largely defined by what has occurred there and with whom, rather than the physical attributes existent within the setting.

Serious place affiliation and 'centres out there'

Places are embodied by the way people use and value them. Moreover, people are encountered in terms of space and are associated with and symbolised by configurations of space. Space will also feel differently for different people, standing as it does for the embodied practices and sociations that are themselves sprung from human dwelling in place. But place's role in dwelling runs deeper than this. It is a force that cannot be reduced to the social, the natural or the cultural. It is, rather, a phenomenon that brings these areas together and, indeed, in part produces them. It is within the structure of place that the very possibility of the social arises (Malpas, 2001). In this way, places are never complete, finished or bounded, but are always becoming, subject to the peculiar processes and practices of the leisure setting. For instance, continued involvement in amateur theatre was found to lead to the accrual of certain personal and social benefits, including the enhancement of self-concept, self-actualisation, feelings of accomplishment, enhanced self-esteem and social interaction. Elkington (2011) found that the majority of these benefits occurred as a consequence of flow-based serious leisure experience and were associated with increased perceived competence and affectivity. This suggests it is not enough for an individual to just do an activity to feel good about themselves, but some expression of skill is necessary to create that affect, forging a strong attachment to or identification with that leisure setting as being one that is flow-producing. It seems the strength of attachment is at least partly determined by the functional utility of a leisure setting concerning its ability to facilitate desired flow-related leisure experiences consistent with Williams and Roggenbuck's (1989) notion of 'place dependence' (see also Bricker and Kerstetter, 2000; Kyle *et al.*, 2003; Williams *et al.*, 1992). Such an association is likely to forge a strong attachment through the emotional and symbolic meanings ascribed to particular leisure settings. Low and Altman (1992) have used the term 'place attachment' to refer to the phenomenon of human-place bonding. However, though they claim that 'affect, emotion, and feeling are central to the concept' (Low and Altman, 1992: p. 4), they have also indicated that these emotional elements 'are often accompanied by cognition (thought, knowledge and belief) and practice (action and behaviour)' (ibid., pp. 4–5).

Activity involvement of devotees of amateur theatre reveals a distinctive connection to and affiliation with the spaces and places associated with acting that forges a degree of commitment and sense of belonging or seriousness. Crucially this serious place affiliation was found to extend to sites other than those immediately engaged by actors, to particular theatrical sites that held significant symbolic meaning for their craft and for which they were willing to travel considerable distances to visit. One professionally trained amateur actor tells of an example of his own special affiliation with such a site:

> I was fortunate enough to perform at the Old Vic in London early on in my training. It was awe inspiring to be performing where so many of the greats had performed … the history was palpable. It's something that I draw on to this day … the distinctive musky smell backstage and how the original stage boards moved and creaked beneath your feet when you moved. I also got a job there as a stage hand and so have a particular affinity for the theatre. I now try and see at least one show a year there and very often will do the theatre tour just to re-live it (Actor 11).

While the signification ascribed to such sites certainly resembled the affective human-place attachment of Tuan's Topophilia, it is also akin to Cohen's (1992) notion of 'centres out there', offering a realm in which, alongside a sense of awe, individuals had constructed modes of being other than that of routine everyday life. A tangible relatedness to these 'other sites', these 'centres out there' is revealed that accentuates an embodied emotional sensing of place for those actors who had visited and in rare cases worked and/or performed in these sites. For these individuals there were particular features capable of triggering memory of, and past encounters with, this 'other' place. In this way, near and far spaces are not separate, nor are the metaphors and the materiality of the associated place experiences. They are mutually embedded, embodied and composed through experience rather than by a formal framework or social convention, where everything has a clear, ordered, relationship. More significantly, embedded in the physical landscape is a landscape of personal, as well as social and cultural, history. But this intimate bonding between place and culture does not mean that place is a simple product of cultural configurations any more than it is of social structure. Similarly, the fact that we can affect changes of place as well as be affected by the places we are in is not tantamount to saying that individually or collectively we create places. When people visit places such as these they encounter, embody, recall similar places, trigger other experiences and engage notions of landscape and space so that they (re)discover the places in their own way. Tied to these experiences and the emotion embedded in them is the social context in which experience occurs. Meaningful place experiences most often occurred for actors in the presence of significant others. Their strong ties to the social world of acting were reflected in the homogeneity of their perspectives relating to place and their experiences shared within these places. Over repeated exposures with particular places and through social psychological processes of people-place interactions they had developed an affective-memory and memory-achievement familiarity: a sense of trust, of belonging, identity, dependence and even possessiveness towards places, to the extent that these places had become 'their place' or their 'favourite place' or 'the only place' for a variety of positive leisure experiences. Crucially the degree to which place identities are tied to the individual was determined by the strength of affiliation – the *seriousness* – with which the individual pursues, encounters and becomes involved in their leisure. This process of emotional and symbolic place affiliation also serves to reinforce and shape individual identity (Kyle and Chick, 2007). Leisure identities, in this sense, become highly salient to the self-concept of actors for three reasons: first, and perhaps most significantly, these identities express and affirm individual talents and competencies in relation to a particular leisure setting. Second, they provide some degree of social recognition within that setting. Finally, they affirm central values and interests for continued commitment to that setting. This identification not only describes individuals as members of the group, as insiders, but also prescribes their behaviours as part of the group *in-situ*. These situated behaviours allow individuals to clearly distinguish between themselves, as participants, from non-participants, as outsiders.

This *seriousness* component functions as a social psychological marker characterised by an important degree of personal commitment to, and trust in, the core activity and its setting. However, the embodied character of such serious encounters suggests the concepts of continued and situational involvement may not be synonymous with positive flow-like experiences, for even though a person may be very involved in a particular activity and hence somewhat predictable, specific circumstances will impact decisions leading up to participation in a leisure episode, the experiential outcomes of a leisure episode and ultimately how that episode is interpreted. It is likely that in addition to continued involvement, factors present in the immediate circumstances surrounding participation in a specific episode of the activity (i.e. work and non-work obligations) also influence the level of situational involvement. Thus, the nature and intensity of involvement will vary over time, from individual to individual and context to context. The individual may gain a profound sense of continuity of experience (and leisure career) from their continued and steady development as a skilled, experienced and knowledgeable participant in a particular form of serious leisure and its setting, and from the deepening fulfilment that accompanies such personal growth. Actors are seen as both building and marshalling a repertoire of interpretations, clues and tropes to account for their actions. In order for the setting to become familiar enough to be deemed trustworthy, it needs to have been experienced several times. In this way, an actor's sense of the unfolding of his or her career in any complex leisure role can be a powerful motive to act therein (Stebbins, 2007b). It is also possible the inverse of this effect may occur, where repeated episodes of low activity involvement and failure to achieve aesthetic, flow-like, engagement, over time, deflate the willingness for continued involvement. To the extent that continued involvement is long-term involvement, it also seems possible that some participants will reach a plateau in their level of seriousness. That is, they will continue to participate in the serious leisure activity, but no more seriously than earlier. Others may even cut back on their seriousness, as for example, work forces reduction in leisure time or when physical skills wane. It is reasonable to suggest, from this initial sketch, that the activities, and so places, people continue to take seriously, over time, are those that are likely to be intrinsically enjoyable and flow-producing, in many cases forming the back-drop for broader leisure lifestyles. These places are often experienced as an extension of the self through knowledge of place with particular features acting as reminders and confirmers of leisure-based identities (i.e. as actor). Significantly, the embodied character of leisure place comes across as comparatively persistent in the order of things: certainly not eternal, but also not merely momentary either.

Understanding serious leisure *as it happens*: a new pragmatism?

The ideas considered in this chapter offer an alternative pragmatic approach for the study of serious leisure in space and place. This rethinking of the subtleties of serious leisure involvement is suggestive of a kind of transitional space out of which experiences, and knowledge, of serious leisure emerge. Here the experience of the materiality of the setting, or site, is crucial to its understanding. In particular for actors the sensations of movement and duration are crucial in coming to understand and know the church hall or theatre as a space and place for leisure. Over time and through continuous commitment and perseverance, these personally meaningful transactions are woven together to create personal pathways with varying temporal and spatial qualities that, when successfully negotiated, culminate in a peculiar, dynamic and holistic sense of trust in that setting. The aesthetic experiences and embodied practices of theatre acting provoke precisely such engagement and, to the extent that they are provocative of thought, are crucial to understanding leisure space and place. Time is thus a crucial element in how such sites are viewed and perceived by participants, not as a still moment but rather as a movement through space, an experiential path. Sensations of time and space as they are put in motion along this experiential path, be it of building or landscape, are significant to what individuals make of its history, people or events.

Articulating the variety of experiences comprising the aesthetic engagement of flow reveals something of what makes this serious leisure as it happens for actors and is tied to a distinctive space component. The space component of a serious leisure activity, or 'core activity space', is not something that can be pointed to in its content; rather it can be detected only through the nature of responses to a particular setting. The response, in effect, constitutes the materiality of what happens in that space. Schatzki (2002) argues that the concept of 'happening' is closely connected to that of a performance. The happening of serious leisure (of theatre acting) is the performance of its constituent actions. More broadly, suggests Schatzki, the happening is the carrying out of its constituent practices, which have four principal phenomena: 1) understandings of (complexes of know-hows regarding) the actions constituting the practice; 2) the written and unwritten rules and codes of conduct that participants observe or disregard; 3) Purposive-Affective structuring encompassing a range of ends, projects, actions and emotions acceptable for participants to pursue and realise; 4) general understandings, taking in the nature and craft of theatre acting. Together with the aesthetic and embodied character outlined earlier in this chapter these principles provide a set of concepts that allow fuller articulation and elaboration of the bundle of practices and arrangements that constitute the amorous places of serious leisure and the peculiar experiences that they invite. Arrangements, claims Schatzki, are assemblages of material objects – persons, artefacts and things – that help configure space and are central to the process of building an intimate familiarisation and union between individual and setting. The dynamics of the relationship between the human and non-human entities which compose familiar surroundings are, for actors, highly dependent on personal and local clues made out as salient features in the process of human-place bonding. Guided by a wide range of sensory data, including not only the visual but also tactile, auditory and olfactory clues, as well as indications of spatial positioning, are widely distributed in the web of connections which sustain familiarity. None of this familiar accommodation is social in the sense of social practices which designate ways of acting or behaving in that particular space. Others might become accustomed to the same setting through a different configuration of clues. It does not follow that members of the same social group have identified the same clues for their use, since these markers are dependent on the person and his/her pathway into and through the core activity and its context. Equally, these clues are not available to the unfamiliar visitor. Such mannerisms will appear unworldly to any lacking the intimate knowledge that has been learned through the long process of familiarity.

Discussion of place familiarity challenges us to approach the question of space in terms of sensation of movement and duration, of the unfolding of leisure in real time. There are two forms of real time revealed in the descriptions of actors; one quite familiar in discussions of leisure, the other considerably less so. The familiar type of real time is objective time, alternatively known as clock time or the time of the world. This category of time is defined by succession, a series of events or moments that occur before and after one another. To occur in objective time is to occupy a place in the sequence of events/moments that constitute that time. Most serious leisure activities, amateur theatre included, are not instantaneous. This means that their occurrences take time, laying down or coinciding with a duration of objective time. The less familiar type of real time is the unfolding or passage of the events or moments that form performances. This movement is real time in the sense of real time presently at issue, what Schatzski has termed as the 'time of the activity'. The time of the activity represents acting toward some end from what motivates participants to continue with a serious leisure pursuit. The objective real time in which action is played out is the unfolding of its performance. In contrast, the activity real time in which actions are performed is the structure of the performance itself as it is played out between motive and end. The unfolding of performances and the materiality of their constituent practices and actions are interfused with one another exhibiting temporal features described by actors as finding the 'rhythm' of the activity and as establishing 'presence' therein.

From this perspective, the happening of serious leisure is, above all, the real time performance of its constituent actions through practice. But this seems somehow incomplete. Serious leisure as it happens is not simply the core activity of theatre acting or, say, volunteer fire fighting, happening, for there is more to a happening than that which is outwardly observable. As the practices and actions of serious leisure are performed, how do things stand with those dimensions and structures that are perhaps not immediately apparent in the performances? Evidence suggests that they are partly held in the cultural and collective memory of the social group, and partly in the practice-memory of individuals. Cultural and collective (social) memory is the form of accumulated knowledge about the activity's past and that passed-on subset of this knowledge that stabilises a collective identity for members as participants (Assmann, 2005). In addition to this, while individuals are the entities who remember in a strict sense, what, as well as how, they remember is, in large part, shaped by a confluence of their own and the group's practices. This 'practice-memory' implies memory as a property of particular forms, structures, of persisting practice (Schatzki, 2006), from past into the present. Its content, this structure, is a complex of understandings, rules, purposive-affective orderings and general understandings pertaining to a distinctive space component. Practice memory, in turn, rests on a complex of non-instantaneous actions, thoughts, abilities and readiness. The performance that constitutes the happening of amateur theatre as serious leisure and the phenomena that maintain memory are thus spread through time and space and are revealing of an evolving practice ecology and the diverse ways in which sites come to provide the circumstances to encourage something of the aesthetic engagement that some leisure settings have the capacity to evoke so forcefully. Wherever it be the aesthetic experience of place is one of inhabitation, or dwelling to use Heidegger's term. Here we feel beauty, attraction or awe not merely as affect, we feel them materially as processes, as events, as performances of the body. Leisure space, in this sense, is not something individuals merely observe, they live through and are changed by it – it is a transitional space. Such a notion of transitional space is not simply a metaphor or theoretical abstraction of space; for it has itself a materiality. More specifically, 'inside' and 'outside', 'near' and 'far' are not simply metaphors for referring to the psyche or to some reality 'out there'; they refer to the inescapable materiality of embodiment. The material qualities of transitional space and their impingements on embodied experiences of dwelling in relation to space have been shown to be crucial to the serious leisure encounter. Transitional space, so conceived, does not appear spontaneously or simply because we will it to, but it is ever-present and everywhere as potential. Whether this potential is actualised, however, depends in part on how a setting holds its form and draw for participants through real time and upon such criteria as commitment from participants, high levels of effort and skill in the activity, time involvement and willingness to maintain and/or increase their involvement in the activity in the future – in short, the *seriousness* with which they approach their leisure.

This seriousness component has been found to characterise an important degree of attachment to and trust in the core activity of amateur acting. Though a point that must be understood is that individuals only become committed to and trusting in/of a leisure role (i.e. as actor) based on their deepening involvement in and attachment to its highly valued core activities and settings; individuals will discover in the course of their involvement therein just how fulfilling the core activity can be (Stebbins, 2007b). So tightly connected are encounter and context that serious leisure participants tend to see the space in which they are pursuing their core activities according to those activities. However, Stebbins's conceptualisation of the context of leisure and its composite institutional, geographic and temporal spaces overlooks space at the level of the core activity.

The subtleties of serious leisure involvement revealed in this chapter are suggestive of the need for further differentiation in the conceptualisation of leisure space, out of which experiences, and knowledge, of different serious leisure pursuits emerge. When considered at the level of the core activity, the Serious Leisure Perspective implies a variety of leisure spaces that have been recently acknowledged by Stebbins (2013): there is *space to be conquered*: sports/board games, nature challenge activities. *Space in which to showcase*: the arts and entertainment fields. *Space as a resource*: practice/training space for musicians, dancers, athletes. *Space for selling goods or services*: shops and outlets for hobbyist makers of, say, quilts, knit goods, ceramic objects. *Space in which to provide help*: volunteer/professional caring. All these spaces combine in peculiar ways distinctive visual, olfactory, tactile, and auditory (including distinctive, little or no sound) qualities. It is also likely that some serious leisure pursuits will have core activities that are pursued in more than one of these five types of space. Thus, athletes have space to be conquered and space to use as a resource; both the painter and actor has a spatial resource (i.e., atelier, set or props) and one or more exhibition or performance venues (showcase) (Stebbins, R.A., personal communication). In addition to this, the practice ecology of amateur theatre acting reveals a complexity and continuity to the aesthetic engagement characteristic of flow-based serious leisure not evident in conventional expressions of either Csikszentmihalyi's flow or Stebbins' serious leisure frameworks. Elkington (2011) has posited that flow-based serious leisure experience represents the richest, most nuanced portrayal yet of what might more accurately be referred to as deep or optimal leisure experience. The term *optimal* is not used here to imply some utopian leisure state, nor the presence of a true or pure form of leisure experience for which each individual should strive. Rather it denotes intense, purposeful action and personal commitment of self that has been shown to bring about a meaningful resonance between an individual, a leisure activity and its setting. Such a resonance is experienced and described by participants more as an existential balance, both a state of being and process of becoming, as opposed to some experiential end.

Conclusion

While the notion that people may develop a strong attachment to leisure settings is acknowledged in Stebbins's work, the nature of this attachment has always been treated from the perspective of the prescribed qualities of serious leisure, and does not adequately represent the emergent nature of human-place bonding outlined in this chapter. Too often ignored is the capacity of the individual to make their own sense of these features, through their own experiences. Here materiality and metaphor are not confined to particular events, geographical space or practices. The serious place affiliation of amateur actors has unveiled the different landscapes experienced during serious leisure, the palpable landscapes and the impalpable mindscapes that continuously interact and form internal relations, personal meanings, with each other. This initial sketch of serious place affiliation offers a pragmatic guide to what gives certain leisure places their special qualities and force. But the world is made up of less than serious places. Many of us in the modern age inhabit anonymous, bland and ubiquitous leisure spaces (i.e., the shopping mall, the cinema complex, the bowling alley), experiencing them with weaker intensity on less profound occasions. Yet however vivid it may be, the peculiar force of experiencing sites of serious leisure lies in the fact that we do not just grasp leisure space by our senses, we project our personalities into it, we are tied to it by emotional bonds; space is not just perceived, nor is it pre-figured – it is, at once, lived and the back-drop by which all leisure is seen and rendered meaningful.

Place has been presented in this chapter as being an organising principle for an individual's engagement with and immersion in leisure. But the opportunity to be expressive and to be able to make sense of what is done as leisure is varied and influenced by all sorts of contexts – both leisure and non-leisure. Everyday individual practices are not limitless but equally their contexts and structures are not over-arching. Nor is knowledge of and practice in leisure space and place pre-constituted. It is in their interaction that meaning is made and embodied. Leisure places, along with their associated experiences, practice and repertoires are not so much pre-formed as performed. Here the notion of context is hugely important and provides dimensions through which closer analysis can develop how people in different circumstances develop distinctive knowledge and values of place and how these may be interpreted and sketched out. Situating place and its constitutive sites and landscapes within Stebbins's serious leisure framework signifies a conceptual and theoretical innovation for the study of leisure, for it is across these sites of serious leisure that emotional and symbolic place affiliation appears to occupy a more central role in formulating the serious leisure experience than has been heretheto acknowledged. The significance of this more pragmatic interpretation of context makes it increasingly important to investigate and to interpret how these work and are worked out in practice. Acknowledging a human focus suggests more attention needs to be paid to the relative complexity and subtlety of negotiation, even if that negotiation is always understood to be incomplete, fragmented and temporary. Leisure space and place are themselves resources worked and negotiated through time and space to form the one thing that is felt to be of most value and significance in what happens there – the sensation of human dwelling.

9

I AM WHAT I PRETEND TO BE

Performance and deception in leisure

Sean J. Gammon

Introduction

Leisure literature is replete with well-reasoned arguments supporting the notion that leisure identities offer individuals opportunities to both become and find their true selves (Argyle, 1996; Haggard and Williams, 1992; Kelly, 1983; Shamir, 1992; Stebbins 1992b). Undoubtedly, such personal attainment is boosted by leisure's ability to encourage action and behaviour that is driven by perceptions of choice and intrinsic interest. Indeed, it is these qualities that separate leisure from many other life domains. In addition to the personal identity virtues that leisure brings to an individual (such as fulfilment and meaning), there is a further purpose related to its ability to emit the right type of messages of ourselves to the right type of people. Our leisure choices not only have the potential to realise who we truly are, but also to communicate to others a more informed sense of who we are as well as who we would ideally like to be. Therefore leisure identities act as a means to communicate particular individualities about ourselves that would not normally be obvious in other social contexts. However, to what extent such leisure pursuits *genuinely* reflect our interests, and in doing so our characters, is unclear. Leisure as a potential source of deception has received scant attention in the literature which is curious given the abundance of studies that have focussed upon fraudulent impression management strategies undertaken in everyday life (Bednar *et al.*, 1989; Buss and Briggs, 1984; Goffman, 1959). As a consequence this chapter aims to explore in what ways fabricated leisure identities can be used by individuals to influence others' impressions of them. It is hoped that the discussions and propositions mapped out below will not only shed light on a hitherto unexplored facet of leisure but will also encourage further empirically led research.

However it is important to mention here that it is not the intention of this chapter to question leisure's positive role in identity development, but rather to suggest that some leisure activities and interests have the potential to be used and exploited by individuals in order to communicate specific personal characteristics – many of which they don't have.

Leisure and identity

The proposition that leisure is a place and space in which we truly become ourselves has been much debated over the last 2000 years or so. The Aristolian idea that leisure (contextualised as freedom from life's necessities) is an opportunity to achieve personal improvement through reflection and the pursuit of knowledge and truth still holds currency today. More recent research, however, has extended the notion that leisure identities are key components of the self by addressing issues related to the symbolic value of leisure (Haggard and Williams, 1992), as well as to its ability to promote well-being (Haworth 2004) and 'safe' opportunities for role enactment (Kelly, 1983). Leisure, it seems, offers sanctuary from the superficial performances that we must practise in the many roles we are forced to assume during a lifetime. Whether it be the role of the student, the worker or the parent, leisure encourages us to drop the well-rehearsed enactments that such roles demand and allows us to immerse in activities and behaviour that are more aligned to our true selves. Such implicit consent no doubt reflects the Latin root of the term leisure *(licere)* as being allowable or permitted. But how can we be sure that we are undertaking activities that enable us to get closer to our true selves? How can we be sure what our true selves are? Such questions of course have lain at the nub of philosophical debate for millennia. For example the ancient Hellenic philosophy of eudaimonism proposed that individuals have almost an ethical duty to be true to their selves, or to be more precise, to live in accordance with the *daimon*. The *daimon* refers to those special qualities that all individuals have the potential to realise:

> These include both potentialities that are shared by all humans by virtue of our common specieshood and those unique potentials that distinguish each individual from all others.
>
> (Waterman, 1993, p. 150)

To recognise and achieve such potentials gives those that accomplish them a profound sense of fulfilment and life meaning. More simply put, a life worth living is one that not only acknowledges the specific goals that should be aspired to but also the manner in which they should be achieved. Such eudaemonist perspectives are not just laudable virtues resigned to history but have been, and continue to be, heavily influential in contemporary theoreticians' writing – in and outside leisure (Csikszentmihalyi, 1975, 1997; de Grazia, 1962; Kelly, 1983; Maslow, 1968; Neulinger, 1981). However, it is the work of Alan Waterman that is more firmly aligned to directly interpreting the eudaemonist perspective in a contemporary situation. Waterman (1990, 1993) has taken a psychological application to eudaimonism, offering the term 'feelings of personal expressiveness' (PE) to conceptualise its psychological equivalent. In so doing he identifies six conditions that are more likely to generate such identity affirming experiences:

> a) an unusual intense involvement in an undertaking; b) a feeling of a special fit or meshing with an activity that is not characteristic of most daily tasks; c) a feeling of intensively being alive; d) a feeling of being complete or fulfilled while engaged in an activity; e) an impression that this is what the person was meant to do; f) a feeling that this is who one really is.
>
> (Waterman, 1993, p. 152)

The feelings expressed above share some notable similarities with optimal leisure experiences, demonstrating effectively why leisure is often acknowledged as particularly pertinent to achieving and/or searching for identity affirming experiences (Haggard and Williams, 1992; Kelly, 1983; Schlenker, 1984; Kleiber *et al.*, 2011). But, personal expressiveness can only be achieved if first; there is an awareness of the person we truly are, second; that we have the opportunity to be true to ourselves, and third; that we truly care about being who we are, and desire 'to live the life that is one's own' (Norton, 1976, p. 26). For those who have never been able to find themselves, what Waterman (1993) refers to as the *identity diffuse,* the life journey is a passive affair that involves little self-reflection, and follows a life-path based upon the expectations of others. In this case leisure becomes a source of hedonic enjoyment, rather than any meaningful search for personal growth and selfhood (Ryan and Deci, 2000; Waterman *et al.*, 2006). As way of contrast there are also individuals who *choose* to be someone else; those who can be referred to as *identity disguised* (Waterman, 1993). In this case an individual may have an awareness of where their talents and aptitudes lie though are coerced into pursuing interests and goals that are assigned by others. Pressure can be exerted through cultural practices as well as from significant others such as parents, spouses and peer groups. Unsurprisingly, the *identity disguised* will experience feelings of regret, frustration and in some cases despair (Horney, 1950; Soloman, 2006). But there are others who freely choose to be someone else, whose motive for disguise is more cynical; where identities are carefully selected in order to deliberately mislead and/or to emit idealised representations of the self. It is likely that such behaviour stems from either a disinterest in expressing their true selves or issues related to low self-esteem. Presenting idealised versions of ourselves is, of course, quite natural and a fundamental part of impression management for many of us (Goffman, 1956, 1959; Schlenker, 1980), but when such identity engineering becomes the sole method of portraying ourselves to others, the practice can become pathological. Horney (1950) famously described this type of behaviour as the neurotic search for glory; where false identities are used in order to achieve a perceived advantage over others, or to communicate misleading information for personal gain. The strategy therefore is to distract others from seeing the true self by presenting and promoting fabricated images and information of how we would ideally like to be, in order to influence others' perception of us. So:

> To accomplish the idealized self, the character disorder engages in a search for glory through various means: a need for perfection; compulsive ambition; striving power, popularity, admiration and deference.
>
> (Soloman, 2006, p. 86)

Leisure identities would then be used as a tool in which to impart information about ourselves to people with whom we interact, in mostly non-leisure domains. It is important to point out that the focus here is upon adults and consequently does not include the leisure and non-leisure identity development processes which have been discussed in considerable detail in children and adolescents elsewhere (Coatsworth *et al.*, 2005; Erikson, 1968; Kivel and Kleiber, 2000; Kroger, 1989; Larson, 2000; Marcia, 1966; Tarrant *et al.*, 2001). What is being suggested here is that leisure is more than just an opportunity to work out identities; it is a relatively self-contained practice that potentially enables individuals to (re)invent and concoct idealised versions of themselves. The more cynical practitioners of this type of behaviour can be termed as *leisure identity deceivers*. Kelly (1983) believes that leisure environments are perfect for trying out new role identities; to explore hitherto undiscovered facets of who we are, and in doing so become more of ourselves in the event. This playful approach to identity acquisition differs from the cynical practice outlined above, in that it illustrates a search for self – rather than a method by which to disguise or hide it. But is such camouflage and deception rare, or is it something we all do to a greater or lesser extent throughout the life-course? Simply put: is leisure-related identity deception, far from being a pathological condition, a natural and commonly adopted mode of communication? In order to explore this further it is necessary to focus upon the manner in which leisure identities are acquired and communicated.

Leisure roles and self-presentation: is it me I'm looking for – or someone else?

There is little doubt that leisure offers special conditions for identity development and affirmation (Kelly 1983). In the first instance it offers opportunities for competence; as to do something well nourishes both personal and social identities. There is also indeterminacy in many leisure activities that encourage exploration, 'a trying of the untested' (Kelly, 1983, p. 99) is more likely to take place when outcomes are unknown. A further element is that leisure is relatively self-contained, enabling identity-related experimentation to take place away from the scrutiny of more judgemental eyes. However, there is little doubt that social networking sites may now limit such containment, where life's experiences are almost instantaneously recorded and shared with the virtual community. But nevertheless, records do not always have to be shared, and even when they are – they can be carefully edited. Leisure still remains relatively remote from many other life contexts, and because of this, is arguably more open to deception and subterfuge. As Leary (1995, p. 170) succinctly states, 'people are more likely to make false claims the less likely others are to detect the deception'.

As discussed in the previous section, the primary aim to deceive through leisure is to emit idealised versions of how we appear to others. As a consequence it is the social identity that seems to take precedence over the personal, because the salient concern is not only how we imagine we appear to others but also how we imagine others' judgement of us (Woodward, 2002, p. 8). Of course the idea that we attempt to control how others see us is not new – and in many cases is quite a normal process of human interaction (Argyle, 1996). Studies on impression management discuss in intricate detail the many ways we choose to present ourselves to others. There is little uncertainty that the majority of self-presentation strategies aim to highlight important features about our true selves, though it is the work of Erving Goffman that highlights the more performative aspects of social interaction, and so is an appropriate starting point when exploring the nature and practice of deception.

Goffman (e.g., 1959; 1963; 1983), drawing and later augmenting from the work of, amongst others, Kenneth Burke, Victor Turner and Marcel Maus (see Burns, 1992), is considered as offering the most comprehensive explanation of the construction and portrayal of the social self. Using theatrical and dramatic metaphors Goffman (1959) argues that within any given social establishment individuals are constantly performing and/or spectating for or towards other actors and other audiences. Therefore, the dramaturgical perspective incorporates the individual as a key determinant in social order, a point highlighted by Burns (1992, p. 82) who notes that 'individuals are constantly at work not only promoting, reinforcing and repairing the social order, but creating, recreating and arranging it'. As already discussed, the idea that individuals are keen to impress upon others an ideal or desirable perception of them can be found in anthropological, sociological and social psychological literature (Jenkins, 1996; Kelly, 1983). Goffman (1959) however was the first to contextualise the nature of the performance according to a number of situational, personal and motivational constructs. He contends that:

> A 'performance' may be defined as all the activity of a given participant on a given occasion which serves to influence in any way any of the other participants.
>
> (Goffman, 1959, p. 26)

The 'participants' can either be the audience or fellow 'actors' who can be considered analogously as cast members or players delivering a collective impression. Performances are not exclusively undertaken in order to impart information to a third party or parties but are also carried out for the satisfaction and reassurance it generates within the individual. The performance represents not only how the actor wants to be perceived but also how they would ideally like to be. If the performance goes well and is received positively by the audience then this will help reinforce and validate the particular characteristics of the performance to the actor as natural to, or representative of, their true selves. The degree to which an individual is aware that they are performing is dependent upon the situation and the motivation that lay behind the performance. In some cases the individual will be duped by their own performance – believing it to be real. Whilst on the other hand the act may be knowingly and cynically performed by individuals all too aware of the deception they have concocted:

> At the other extreme, we find that the performer may not be taken in at all by his routine … When an individual has no belief in his own act and no ultimate concern with the beliefs of his audience we may call him cynical.
>
> (Goffman, 1959, p. 28)

A prominent feature of the dramaturgical model is that region or place largely determines behaviour. The region is therefore closely linked to the setting but differs in that not all regions are reserved for performing. Goffman believed that the nature and degree of a performance is determined by the actor's perception of whether they were on stage or not. Performances therefore are only maintained in front of and towards a front region (front stage) whilst back regions (back stage) are reserved for relaxation and recuperation from the rigours of the role. To what extent leisure represents a type of back stage is unclear, though there is no doubt that for some, it represents an opportunity to relax and to shed the taxing performative demands that other roles demand. For others it may, paradoxically, offer opportunities for performance and pretence: time to forget who we are – in essence to become someone else, albeit for a short period. In most cases identity acquisition in leisure is playful with any pretence knowingly and openly engaged in for the potential therapeutic experiences it offers. Yet, there are also situations when roles are assumed for the sole purpose to influence others' impressions of us – impressions that imply particular personal characteristics we may not possess. To what extent either of these cases represents a form of cynical deception is unclear, and will be explored further in the next section.

Deception or pretence in leisure?

Oscar Wilde has been attributed to stating that it is important to 'be yourself, everyone else is taken'. Given Wilde's renowned self-confidence, it is likely that even if Wilde was not responsible for the phrase he would have agreed with it. Evidently Wilde had not accounted for those individuals for whom pretending to be other people is part of who they are. But the ways in which leisure can be used to fabricate personal characteristics is both complex and context specific.

The following examples of potential *leisure identity deceivers* act as only a starting point for discussion. The degree to which any activities can be truly perceived as being cynically deceptive is very much dependent upon the motive, the audience that the fraud is aimed at, and the extent that the deception is embraced and internalised by those that practise it. In the first instance there are those that participate in an activity in order to achieve perceived positive responses from an audience they are unfamiliar with. In some cases the pretence may be hidden from those that know them; for participation is primarily driven by the desire to feel more positive when assuming the role. The need to raise self-esteem may lie behind some actions, though in this case validating responses from others are mostly imaginary; for feedback is sought from the activity itself, and so satisfaction is derived from the performance and enactment potential of the role (Kelly, 1983). As way of illustrating this, in most developed cities bike messengers are used by companies as an efficient and effective method to send documents and parcels through the increasingly congested streets. Messengers have a reputation for being fit, courageous with an in-depth knowledge of the streets in which they apply their trade. They can be often identified by the type of bike they use (fixed wheel – sometimes called fixed gear) which will be customised for urban travel such as removing all brakes or having only one on the front wheel, and cut-down handlebars allowing more room to traverse between other vehicles. In addition messengers will sport cut-down or rolled-up trousers and of course a large messenger bag. In recent times the messenger 'look' has been adopted by non-messenger cyclists who ride similar bikes and dress correspondingly, and have been termed by the cycling fraternity as *fakengers* which has been defined as a 'bike riding poseur who dresses in messenger gear and rides a fixed gear but is not a messenger. They can be found in most major cities' (Urban Dictionary, 2013). In this event the performance will be supported by the setting, i.e., using the backdrop of urban locales where authentic messengers are more likely to operate. However to suggest that the behaviour of the *fakenger* is deliberately deceiving is questionable, as very few will cycle around towns and cities for the single purpose of posing as a messenger. The majority of *fakengers* will be regular cyclists who playfully imitate the appearance of the messenger whilst travelling to and from a destination – and in doing so will hope to symbolically associate themselves with the positive characteristics of the messenger outlined above. But the performance is no more than a light-hearted role play, rarely will it stem from a desire to calculatingly deceive. This type of role play is common in many leisure pursuits; and can be observed in the average skier assuming the dress, equipment and demeanour of the instructor, or the twenty handicap golfer whose golfing paraphernalia produces admiring glances from the professionals. It could also include the tourist who saves up all year in order to afford exclusive hospitality, and thus to be treated as a person of means – if only for two weeks (Gottlieb, 1982).

Another method in which leisure interests can be shared with others is through symbolic presentation, whereby individuals will non-verbally communicate their leisure interests through symbols. Music tastes can be highlighted through style of dress, team shirts and jerseys will indicate fans' affiliations, and general sports interest can be transmitted via wearing related clothing. The desire here is to both publicise the kind of person they are whilst attracting others with similar interests. There is, as Kelly (1983, p. 101) observes, "a symbolic 'leisure ethnicity' in which actors seek not only symbolic identity, but also to signal others with the same leisure identification". Yet there are some who will use a variety of leisure-related symbols that they have no connection and/or affiliation with in order to gain some kind of advantage or to impress on others specific personal characteristics that they wish to be associated with. Feigning symbolic attachment can be blatant or more subtle; ranging from individuals wearing rugby shirts in order to appear more of a team player or to suggest that they are fit, strong and gutsy – to those who opt for wearing a badge or some other emblem to promote lifestyles which they may not practise. If indeed leisure choices have a backstage quality to them then the motive for deception is to create a *pseudo backstage* that reveals personal qualities about an individual that they do not possess. In reality leisure represents an establishment in which both front and back stages are visible, though for those who practise deception the back stage signifies little more than an imaginary place where imaginary activities take place.

Whilst false symbolic attachment strategies may take place independently, it is more common for them to be reinforced and supplemented by self-description. This simply involves an individual telling others of their interests and achievements as, 'by telling others about their personalities, likes and dislikes, previous experiences, accomplishments, families, occupations, emotional reactions, fears, and so on, people can create particular impressions in others' eyes' (Leary, 1995, p. 17). For the *leisure identity deceiver* self-description offers more scope to paint a picture of their leisure 'preferences' and 'practices', and as a consequence is more likely to make an impression. As way of an example, during the 1980s and 1990s a popular TV programme in the UK named *London's Burning* focussed upon the lives and struggles of members of the London Fire Brigade. One of the characters in the drama was ironically named Charisma (as he had little) whose life outside the brigade consisted of a make-believe world where he achieved great sporting successes and was supported by a wide circle of adoring friends. Charisma would often buy and engrave trophies that evidenced his fabricated life outside the brigade which over time was questioned by his suspicious workmates. The initial success of the deception was that the character's leisure was distinct and separate from his workmates so remained relatively undetectable. It was only when they decided to support one of his sporting achievements unannounced (a final of a snooker competition where Charisma was not one of the finalists as he had indicated – but the referee) that the fraud came to light. This, albeit fictional, example demonstrates that in some circumstances the deception has an element of truth to it, that in fact any duplicity is based more upon exaggeration than out-and-out fabrication.

To exaggerate our interests and/or achievements in leisure does not necessarily equate to deliberate deception as in many social contexts we have little time and opportunity to communicate important aspects of ourselves to the people we wish to influence (Leary, 1995; Schlenker and Weigold, 1992). However, in some situations we may exaggerate connections or relationships with prominent, successful or famous people in order to bask in their reflected glory (BIRG). A study by Cialdini *et al.* (1976) found that less committed fans were more likely to BIRG after their team won and CORF (cut off reflected failure) when they lost. This may manifest itself by wearing team colours, shirts and scarves after a win, or displaying dissociative behaviour and distance after a loss (Gammon, 2012).

In some situations self-presentation will involve the careful management of what is not revealed as much as what is. This can take place during self-description episodes where specific interests and activities are edited out and in some cases replaced by interests that are more likely to impress. This type of life editing is today quite commonly practised in cyberspace where individuals project, via social network sites, carefully chosen images and information about themselves that represent an ideal self. The digital self can with ease be manipulated and regularly edited to promote and endorse successful, fun and interesting lives (Schau and Gilly, 2003; Zhao, 2005). Issues revolving around the applicability of Goffman's dramaturgical approach to social media design have been extensively discussed in the literature (Donath, 1998; Hogan, 2010; Lewis *et al.*, 2008; Robinson, 2007) and as a consequence are beyond the scope of this chapter to discuss in any significant detail. Nevertheless, it is worth mentioning that one of the key debates concerns to what extent social networking sites represent some form of backstage. For example some have suggested (Tufekci, 2008) that Facebook acts as a private space where there is some control over who has access, whilst others argue that there still remains information potentially open to all:

> Online, the notion of a backstage fails to capture the role of a third party in regulating who has access to information about an individual. That Facebook allows only friends or 'friends of friends' to see specific content does not suggest that this content signifies a backstage to other possible content that is available for anyone to see.
>
> (Hogan, 2010, pp. 379–380)

Social networking sites therefore potentially offer an additional space in which to manage the self. Virtual friends will often significantly outnumber those whom individuals are truly close to, and posted news and images will be carefully chosen and crafted to help reinforce whatever image is desired. Indeed, there are instances of individuals buying virtual girlfriends and boyfriends in order to be perceived as more popular or romantically successfully than they actually are. For as little as five dollars it's possible to get a week's worth of 'in a relationship with' on a profile which will be supported by some status comments and 'likes'. As David Lee, the BBC's technology reporter found: 'Now, instead of hiring someone to grasp your arm and go out to a party or dinner – it's all about looking good online' (BBC News 2013).

The reasons as to why individuals deliberately aim to deceive through the pretence of leisure interests and activities are many and numerous. It may well be as a reaction to the ever increasing opportunities of identity investment available in many modern societies. Notions of self are today made up of a plethora of identities, resulting in a sense of identity loss or distinctiveness – that in turn can lead to feelings of confusion and anxiety. Gergen (1991) described these states of social saturation as a condition of *multiphrenia* where the self is divided into a multiplicity of identity investments. Individuals no longer can devote the necessary time and energy to new leisure interests and projects, and so make them up. As discussed above, leisure identities have the potential to project powerful messages about the type of person we would like to be, and so they become an effective and resourceful method in which to communicate personal and social identities. But this does not account for the fact that some individuals will deliberately deceive, whilst others, for a range of personal and situational circumstances, will choose leisure interests that they would normally aspire to but are unable to engage in. It may be that for some, the practice of leisure invention *is* their leisure; that they enjoy the playful deception of pretending to be someone else, and that the deception itself reveals something about them. To what extent the act and experience of the pretence equates to being true to the *daimon* is as yet unclear.

The purpose behind deception will vary, from those whose motive stems from a desire to distract others from their true identities, which may be explained by self-esteem issues (Leary and Kowalski, 1990) – to those whose motives are to deliberately trick another party in order to gain some personal or social advantage. The latter are undeniably more focussed upon what they can achieve by appearing to be someone else, rather than what they can hide. It is, as yet, unclear how such deception impacts upon the lives of those that practise it, though in many cases it will depend upon the extent of the fraud and the implications of being found out. Leisure has traditionally been viewed as a space and place in which we can safely experiment and practise at the type of person we would like to be. It is an environment that promotes self-discovery primarily because any awkward or unsuccessful performances do not generally leak out into any other life domains. But when leisure deception is detected the implications to the social life and psychology of an individual can be potentially extremely damaging. The humiliation of being caught, together with *potentially* being branded a liar can have long-term consequences illustrating well leisure's potential to inhabit and impinge upon non-leisure settings and contexts.

The idea that self-presentation is as much about pretence as it is about portraying the true self is not new (Bednah, 1989; Buss and Briggs, 1984) but the notion that leisure activities and values are chosen specifically for reasons of deception has had scant coverage in the literature. In a world where it is becoming progressively challenging to work out individuals' identities through the more traditional routes of work and class, people are now increasingly turning to leisure in order to communicate who they are and how they would like to be viewed. There appears to be a growing appreciation that leisure pursuits have the potential to differentiate identities, not only as a method in which to find and become our true selves but also as a means to become who we are not. Fabrications are built upon participatory imitation, or carefully crafted self-description strategies which can be validated through symbolic attachment, as well as social media. Leisure unquestionably offers potent opportunities for identity development but by the same token offers opportunities for pretence and deception.

10

THE TECHNOLOGICAL MEDIATION OF LEISURE IN CONTEMPORARY SOCIETY

Jo Bryce

Historical changes in the organisation and experience of leisure activities have traditionally been associated with technological developments in entertainment, transport and production (Argyle, 1996; Bryce, 2001; Rojek, 2000). This is perhaps most apparent in the changes associated with the emergence of the Internet and related technologies as important spaces for leisure participation and experiences in recent years. Computer gaming, social networking and consumption of media content are all popular technologically mediated activities which form a significant component of the leisure lives of many individuals in contemporary society. These developments have led to societal concerns about the psychological, social and physical effects of these activities, particularly for children and young people. This chapter reviews current research examining the potential effects of computer gaming, exposure to sexually explicit material (SEM) and sexting. It aims to demonstrate the utility of considering the motivations, experiences and outcomes associated with these technologically mediated activities within the context of the social, developmental and identity-related functions of leisure as an alternative framework for understanding their dynamics. In order to achieve this aim, the chapter considers the implications of established concepts within leisure theory to developing a deeper understanding of these behaviours. This includes a consideration of dichotomous leisure classifications (e.g., serious v casual) and constraints, and demonstrates the contribution of such an analysis towards reflexive development of these concepts.

Computer gaming

Computer gaming is a popular and profitable contemporary leisure activity. Recent research suggests that 83 per cent of young people aged 9–16 in the UK play games online (Livingstone *et al.*, 2011). The activity has also been found to rank as the favorite leisure activity for males aged 12–24, and third most popular for those aged 25–44 (Vorhaus, 2008). The popularity of computer gaming led to concerns being expressed by policy makers, researchers and the general public about the outcomes of frequent gaming, high levels of violent content, displacement of physical leisure activities and academic work, particularly for children and young people (e.g., Bryce and Kaye, 2011; Gentile, 2009; Gentile *et al.*, 2004).

Such concerns reflect the traditional characterisation of computer gaming as a passive and casual leisure activity which is potentially detrimental to mental and physical health (Bryce, 2001; Bryce and Kaye, 2011). However, the diversity of game genres, contexts of play, interactions and experiences facilitated by the activity problematise such classifications. The experience of flow and identified positive outcomes of the activity suggest that gaming can facilitate similar levels of commitment, skills and knowledge as other serious leisure activities (Bryce and Kaye, 2011). It can also be engaged with as a more casual leisure activity, facilitating associated experience of play, relaxation and passive entertainment (Bryce, 2001; Stebbins, 1997). This suggests that gaming cannot definitively be classified as either serious or causal, but is situated on a continuum between the two which can vary between and within individuals depending on a range of specific characteristics (e.g., available time, motivation, gaming context, genre). The classification of gaming as casual, passive and without commitment is consistent with the negative effects perspective on the outcomes of the activity, both in terms of displacement of healthier leisure activities and the encouragement of aggressive attitudes and behaviour. However, this fails to adequately account for the range of potentially positive psychological and physical outcomes associated with the activity which have been empirically identified (see later section of the chapter).

The distinction between active and passive leisure (Iso-Ahola, 1997), and their differential physical and psychological outcomes, also has relevance when considering computer gaming as a leisure activity. Active leisure involves physical activity and social interaction, and has been found to be related to reduced levels of depression, anxiety and stress, as well as improved physical and mental health (Caltabiano, 1995; Iso-Ahola, 1997; Iso-Ahola and Mannell, 2004; Pressman *et al.*, 2009; Trainor *et al.*, 2010). Conversely, participation in passive or escapist leisure activities (e.g., watching TV, reading) has been claimed to lead to reduced physical and mental health (Iso-Ahola, 1997). However, research has found that gaming provides opportunities for mood management by enabling individuals to cope with negative affect by exerting control over the virtual world and achieving in-game goals (Ferguson and Rueda, 2010; Nabi *et al.*, 2006; Zillmann, 1988a, 1988b). This suggests that even casual gaming can have psychological benefits for gamers as they provide a technologically mediated environment in which the established functions of leisure can be fulfilled.

The classification of gaming as a passive leisure activity is also consistent with concerns about the potentially negative and indirect effects of gaming on health by reducing participation in active and health-enhancing leisure activities (Bryce, 2001). However, recent developments in active games technology (e.g., Nintendo Wii Sports, Xbox Kinect) provide players with opportunities to engage in physical activity which can have positive effects on health and well-being (Bryce and Kaye, 2011). Recent research suggests that these games can increase levels of physical activity, particularly in children and adolescents (Daley, 2009; Graf *et al.*, 2009; Graves *et al.*, 2007). This demonstrates that technological developments have facilitated a change in the dynamics of gaming which present some challenges to claims about the potentially negative effects on the health of players. This is also consistent with the increasingly social nature of gaming and its associated beneficial outcomes described later in this chapter.

Deviant leisure

The concept of deviant leisure also has relevance to understanding computer gaming. The increasing popularity of Internet use during leisure has been accompanied by concerns over its use for activities which could be considered as deviant or illegal. These exist on a continuum with legal and 'normal' leisure activities, and include activities which may be considered deviant (e.g., substance use, sexual deviance) or criminal (e.g., violence, vandalism) which also provide experiences of enjoyment and excitement (Bryce, 2001; Katz, 1988; Rojek, 2000). This highlights the potential for leisure to be the site of legal and moral conflict about the legitimacy of freely chosen activities (Bryce, 2001; Rojek, 2000). An examination of the dynamics and outcomes of deviant leisure has been marginalised in this research area as it contrasts with the underlying moral view of leisure as inherently good, and has subsequently been viewed as a forensic or clinical issue (Rojek, 2000). The ability for the Internet and online spaces, as significant locations for the leisure activity in contemporary society, to facilitate activities which would generally be considered deviant has raised concerns for policy makers, law enforcement and society in general.

The availability and circulation of deviant or illegal information and images, together with the formation of ideographic online communities based around similarly deviant or illegal interests, raises a number of challenges associated with freedom of expression, regulation and public protection (Bryce, 2001). For example, online communities based around deviant sexual interests (e.g., rape, paedophilia) test the limits of established legal and moral standards by providing a forum for users to exchange content, and legitimate ideologies and activities which are unacceptable to wider society (Bryce, 2001). The socially supportive aspects of such virtual groups are also of concern as the associated legitimisation of beliefs may facilitate criminal behaviour by encouraging individuals to act on their beliefs or interests offline (Bryce, 2001). This also relates to groups organised around extremist political and religious ideologies which may be illegal in many countries (e.g., Neo-Nazi, Islamic extremism).

It has also been argued that the Internet can be characterised as a liminal leisure space in which opportunities to debate and evaluate cultural values can facilitate social change (Bryce, 2001; Rojek, 2000; Turner, 1992). Many online communities and newsgroups focus specifically on debate and discussion about a variety of interests and issues. This can range from 'normal' leisure interests (e.g., sports, entertainment), but also news and politics which may question mainstream perspectives on various issues and challenge consensus opinions. Such communities can themselves be seen as deviant or dangerous in their challenge to mainstream explanations of events (e.g., 9/11 and other topics discussed on 'conspiracy sites' such as David Icke and Abovetopsecret.com).

Rojek (2000) distinguishes between invasive and mephitic leisure, and characterises mephitic activities as being participated in by individuals who lack respect and trust for others, and view individuals as objects or commodities. This is reflected in leisure activities which would also be deemed immoral or deviant (e.g., sex tourism, sexual abuse of children) (Bryce, 2001; Rojek, 2000). Invasive deviant activities are those participated in by individuals who lack self-respect, feel alienated from others and use leisure to repress disliked aspects of themselves (Rojek, 2000). The online environment provides a variety of possibilities for engaging in activities which enable the construction of identities that could mask individual perceptions of inadequacy and the construction of virtual ideal selves. Online gaming in which avatars are constructed and controlled could be classified as falling within this category of leisure, as could individual gaming in which the individual seeks to escape from themselves and the world (Bryce, 2001). However, the potential benefits of identity play as a form of mood management have also been recognised by researchers (Greenwood and Long, 2009; Olson, 2010).

The routine construction of the computer gaming as a deviant social problem which requires regulation is consistent with the negative effects perspective on the activity (Bryce and Rutter, 2006; Bryce and Kaye, 2011). It is also reflected in claims that exposure to violent game content has been a significant casual factor in a number of murders and school shootings (e.g., Columbine High School shootings, 1999; Virginia Tech Massacre, 2007) (Bryce and Kaye, 2011; Thompson, 2007). This has led to calls for further regulation of violent media content as providing training and preparation for criminal and violent behaviour (Thompson, 2007). This is particularly relevant given the relatively large number of games in which successful performance requires virtual participation in extreme violence, torture and murder (e.g., Left 4 Dead 2, Soldier of Fortune 2), and the claimed negative behavioural and attitudinal effects of engaging with them (Whitty et al., 2011).

Such concerns have led to the development of a large body of academic research addressing the potentially negative psychological and social outcomes of computer gaming. Many researchers claim that there is clear evidence that exposure to violent game content increases aggression-related cognitions, attitudes and behaviour in both children and adults (Arriaga et al., 2008; Gentile and Anderson, 2003; Markey and Scherer, 2009). However, the failure of other empirical studies to replicate such findings has led other researchers to identify a number of theoretical and methodological limitations of the literature (e.g., Colwell and Kato, 2003; Ferguson *et al.*, 2008). These include weak effect sizes for the relationship between violent content exposure and aggressive behaviour, poor external validity of laboratory measures of aggressive behaviour and sampling issues (Bryce and Kaye, 2011; Ferguson and Kilburn, 2010; Valadez and Ferguson, 2012). The existing evidence has also been contested in relation to the claim that violent game content has similarly negative effects on all gamers (Bryce and Kaye, 2011; Kaye, 2012). The role of trait variables, motivations for play and the emotional experiences of interacting with violent game content have been identified as additional factors likely to influence the outcomes of engaging in the activity (Kaye, 2011). For example, the ability to engage in aggressive behaviours which violate real-life social norms has been found to provide intense emotional experiences (Bertozzi, 2008; Whitty *et al.*, 2011). This highlights the importance of developing further understanding of the meanings which gamers derive from their experiences, particularly those which involve performance of extreme violence, and their potential influence on attitudes and behaviour. It is also important to recognise that the liminality of gaming spaces provides opportunities in which social norms and moral judgements associated with violence and aggression can be explored, without necessarily having a detrimental effect on the individual. This also highlights the importance of research identifying the characteristics of individuals who may be at greater risk of associated negative psychosocial and behavioural effects (Bryce and Kaye, 2011).

Gaming as leisure activity

It has recently been argued that given the existing limitations of research on the negative effects of the activity, examining gaming as a form of motivated action which can facilitate similar positive experiences and outcomes as other leisure activities is an alternative framework for understanding the activity (Bryce and Kaye, 2011; Jansz and Tanis, 2007). This is consistent with studies indicating that positive social experiences, challenge, enjoyment and alleviation of negative mood are motivations for playing videogames (Colwell, 2007; Ferguson and Rueda, 2010; Greenwood and Long, 2009; Olson, 2010; Russoniello *et al.*, 2009; Yee, 2007). These studies suggest the potentially positive social and experiential value of the activity, though recognition of this body of literature is largely absent from the negative effects literature.

Researchers examining gaming from a more positive, leisure-related perspective have utilised flow theory (Csikszentmihalyi, 1975) to conceptualise the enjoyable psychological experiences and outcomes of the activity (Bryce and Kaye, 2011). Flow is an established concept within leisure research, and is characterised as a rewarding and positive psychological state experienced by an individual when they are engaged in an enjoyable and intrinsically motivated activity (Csikszentmihalyi, 1975). The key dimensions of the flow experience are a distorted sense of time, intense involvement, a sense of control and an equal balance between the capabilities of the individual and the challenge of the specific activity (Csikszentmihalyi, 1975; Csikszentmihalyi and Csikszentmihalyi, 1988). The experience of flow has been found to be associated with states of enjoyment, positive affect and psychological well-being (Bryce and Haworth, 2002; Clarke and Haworth, 1994). This framework has been used to examine the positive psychological experiences of a wide range of leisure activities including sports (Jackson, 1992; Jackson and Eklund, 2002; Stavrou et al., 2007) and a variety of online activities (Novak et al., 2003; Siekpe, 2005; Thatcher et al., 2008). Recent research also suggests that flow is experienced during gaming, and is associated with enjoyment, positive affect, self-esteem and well-being (Klimmt et al., 2007; Ryan et al., 2006; Wan and Chiou, 2006; Weibel, Wissmath, Habegger, Steiner and Groner, 2007). This demonstrates that gaming can facilitate positive experiences and outcomes in ways consistent with other leisure activities, and demonstrates the utility of a leisure-related approach to understanding its dynamics and outcomes.

Social aspects of gaming

Research has also begun to examine the influence of the social contexts in which gaming occurs as part of the motivational and experiential dynamics of the activity (Kaye and Bryce, 2012). Although playing videogames is stereotypically conceptualised as a solo activity, it is increasingly a social activity facilitating online and offline interactions (Bryce and Kaye, 2011; Yee, 2006, 2007). Online gaming environments provide an important location for leisure and social interactions for those who engage in the activity (e.g., Cole and Griffiths, 2007; Filiciak, 2003; Ng and Wiemer-Hastings, 2005). Similarly, many people play computer games within existing offline social networks during their free time, consistent with the identified importance of social factors in facilitating leisure participation and involvement (Kyle and Chick, 2007 Mannell and Kleiber, 1997). These have also been found to be both a motivational and experiential factor associated with gaming, and a predictor of online game enjoyment (Cole and Griffiths, 2007; Colwell, 2007; Kim and Ross, 2006).

Research examining the social dimensions of the activity has also examined its relationship with the experience of flow in gaming (e.g., Weibel et al., 2007). The original individualised flow model did not consider the social dimensions of autotelic experiences, though the concept of shared or 'group flow' was later proposed to characterise situations which facilitate such experiences (Kaye and Bryce, 2012; Nakamura and Csikszentmihalyi, 2001). Research also found that the sense of social belonging and companionship provided by group contexts can enhance the enjoyment and intrinsic rewards of an activity in addition to the established flow components (Kaye and Bryce, 2012; Csikszentmihalyi, 1975; Sato, 1988). The previously discussed ability of gaming to facilitate flow experiences has also been demonstrated in social gaming situations. Kaye and Bryce (2012) found that task-relevant skills, knowledge of the skills of other players, feedback from others and being seen were antecedents for the experience of group flow in both cooperative and competitive gaming. The study also identified collective competency, interdependence, collaboration, coordination, complementary participation and a shared task focus as additional antecedents of group flow in cooperative gaming environments. These factors appear to differentiate group and individual flow, although the determinants of individual optimal experiences must also be present (Kaye and Bryce, 2012; Walker, 2010). The group-level unit of performance, interdependence and cooperation are the defining characteristics of the experience, consistent with previous models of social flow (Kaye and Bryce, 2012; Walker, 2010). This expands current theoretical knowledge about the relationship between flow and gaming, and suggests that these concepts can be used to develop further understanding of the dynamics of group flow in other leisure activities which are characterised by similar shared experiences (e.g., team sports) (Kaye and Bryce, 2012). This further highlights the utility of reconceptualising established dichotomous classifications of leisure activities as being located on a continuum to recognise that group flow can occur in both casual and more serious, competitive contexts. It also demonstrates that examining this activity from a leisure perspective has the potential to inform further development of established conceptual frameworks within this research area.

Leisure constraints – gender

There are also a number of constraints to participation in technologically mediated leisure activities, including gaming. Freedom, choice and access are central to the concept of leisure (Iso-Ahola, 1997; Neulinger, 1974). However, research suggests that there are a number of factors which influence an individual's ability to gain access to, and participate in, desired activities in online and offline leisure spaces (Bryce, 2001; Bryce and Rutter, 2003; Jackson and Henderson, 1995). Gender, ethnicity, SES, disability and sexual orientation have all been identified as leisure constraints in the literature (Shaw, 1994, 2001). There is a large body of research which suggests that females of all ages are disadvantaged in their leisure choices by a number of constraining factors (e.g., time, SES, marital and parental status), and that gender influences access and participation in leisure spaces and activities (Bryce, 2001; Shaw, 1994).

The advent of the Internet and related technologies led to hopes that online anonymity and other characteristics of mediated communication would free individuals from the restraints imposed by group membership, interactions and stereotypes by removing physical and social cues which characterise interaction in offline environments (Dubrovsky et al., 1991; Postmes and Spears, 2002; Sproull and Kiesler, 1991). However, early experimental studies found no evidence for this 'equalisation hypothesis', suggesting instead that stereotypes and associated behaviours were persistent and potentially intensified online, particularly in relation to race and gender (Burkhalter, 1999; Herring, 1993; Postmes and Spears, 2002; Smith and Kollock, 1999). This research demonstrated that established access and interaction constraints were reproduced in online environments, and reduced the potential for virtual leisure spaces to challenge and resist associated traditional stereotypes (Bryce, 2001).

This is consistent with research examining barriers to female access to technology, ICT use and technologically mediated leisure activities such as Internet use and computer gaming (Bannert and Arbinger, 1996; Schumacher and Morahan, 2001). It has been argued that these technologies are associated with a highly gendered and masculine culture (Cockburn, 1986), and that this is reflected in the societal perception that computer gaming is a masculine activity which excludes females (Bryce and Rutter, 2003). However, Colwell and Payne (2000) found that 88 per cent of females aged 12–14 years old played computer games on a regular basis. More recent research also found that 83 per cent of young people aged 9–16 years in the UK play games online alone or against the computer, and this did not vary by gender (Livingstone *et al.*, 2011). The study also found that males were more likely to play games online against others than females, particularly in the 13–16 age group. This is consistent with other research which found that males aged 12–15 were more likely to use the Internet once a week or more to play games than females (59 per cent vs. 33 per cent) (Ofcom, 2011). This is consistent with research on young adults which found that 70 per cent of male undergraduates had engaged in the activity that week compared to 25 per cent of females (Winn and Heeter, 2009), a gender difference consistent with previous research in this demographic (Ogletree and Drake, 2007). There is also evidence that gender differences in frequency of play increase with the transition from adolescence to young adulthood (Roberts *et al.*, 2005). This suggests that gender differences in the frequency of engagement in the activity are more marked in adolescence and young adulthood, and related theoretical explanations for this focus on the gendered nature of the activity.

Game content

The claim that gaming is a gendered activity was initially based on the dominance of masculine game themes (e.g., war, competition, sports), stereotypical representations of females and high levels of violence in games (e.g., Dietz, 1998; Kafai, 1996). This was claimed to make the activity uninteresting, offensive or excluding to females (Bryce and Rutter, 2003). However, these claims are based on content-based research from the early 1990s, and the increasing diversification of game genres and platforms since then suggests that this may not necessarily be representative of contemporary game content (Bryce and Rutter, 2003). This also highlights the need to consider the reception and interpretation of gendered and stereotypical representations by females, and recognise the potential for alternative meanings to be derived, as well as the possibilities that females could identify with masculine characters (Gailey, 1993; Yates and Littleton, 1999; Bryce and Rutter, 2003). This is consistent with the identified need to challenge gender stereotypes and perceptions of female gaming based on claimed preferences for supportive rather than active gaming roles, and avoidance of competitive gaming situations (Behnke, 2012; Kafai *et al.*, 2008). It is also supported by research finding that in-game violence and gender representations have less impact on female game preferences than the levels of social interaction afforded by the game (Hartmann and Klimmt, 2006). This suggests that there is greater diversity in the gender representations available in the contemporary games market, though it is likely that certain genres may continue to be dominated by masculine themes (e.g., First Person Shooters). The issue of the construction of gender in online gaming is also of relevance as individual gamers have free choice in the nature of the characters they create for themselves.

Spaces

The spatial dynamics of computer gaming are also linked to its gendered nature, reflecting the relationship between spaces and the development of gendered identities (Ahrentzen, 1992; Bryce and Rutter, 2003). Computer gaming spaces are temporal and spatially diverse, and the activity can occur within established public (e.g., arcades, bars and service stations), domestic and online spaces (Bryce and Rutter, 2003). Public leisure spaces have been claimed to be highly gendered, and the association of these spaces with masculinity places constraints on female access and concepts of 'appropriate' female behaviour within them (Hey, 1984; Wearing, 1998). Despite the growth in public gaming environments (e.g., cybercafés and gaming competitions), the gendering of these spaces has meant that female gaming generally remains a domestic activity (Bryce and Rutter, 2003; Kerr, 2003).

Private and domestic spaces have been conceptualised as the primary site of female leisure as a result of their relationship with domestic and family labour (McRobbie, 1991). This is especially the case for girls and female teenagers whose leisure is often dominated by 'bedroom culture' (McRobbie, 1991). The associated expectation that constraints on female participation and access to computer gaming in these locations should be reduced is challenged by research suggesting that males assume the role of 'expert' in these spaces and undermine female skills even in situations where they own the console (Bryce and Rutter, 2003; Schott and Horrell, 2000). This highlights the utility of examining the gendered nature of gaming in the context of everyday life, domestic structures and leisure practices (Yates and Littleton, 1999). It also demonstrates that examining the dynamics of technologically mediated activities can further inform understanding of established leisure concepts such as constraints, and the extent to which these continue to exert an influence on the leisure access and experiences of females within contemporary society. This indicates that virtual environments represent locations for both resistance and reinforcement of gender roles and stereotypes, and this is an area which has been examined in relation to the dynamics of online gaming.

These environments provide a temporal and geographical blurring of the distinction between public and private leisure spaces, and their anonymity can potentially provide female gamers with the opportunity to compete against male opponents free from the markers of gender (Bryce and Rutter, 2003). The associated potential for increased participation and reduced stereotypical behaviour towards female gamers is consistent with the equalisation hypothesis (Postmes and Spears, 2002). However, the perception of these spaces as competitive and masculine potentially makes them threatening and constrains female participation (Bryce and Rutter, 2003; Morris, 1998). This is further evidenced by recent research highlighting the dominance of hypermasculine discourse among male gamers, as well as sexist and offensive behaviour towards female World of Warcraft players (Behnke, 2012; Nardi, 2008).

Despite this, there is evidence that gendered perceptions of gaming are changing as female online gaming clans and online communities demonstrate that gaming can be a serious leisure activity for some females, regardless of the attitudes and behaviour of male gamers (Behnke, 2012; Bryce and Rutter, 2003). It has been argued that some females enjoy playing competitive and violent games despite the gendering of the activity and the associated constraints which this can place on participation (Behnke, 2012; Cassell, and Jenkins, 1998; Kafai *et al.*, 2008; Pearce, 2006). This highlights the ability of gaming to provide opportunities for resistance and renegotiation of gender stereotypes, consistent with increased female participation in other leisure activities traditionally conceptualised as masculine (Bryce and Rutter, 2003; Shaw, 2001; Wearing, 1998). This suggests that examining gaming from a leisure perspective can lead to a clearer understanding of the potential for challenge to the constraints placed on female leisure in contemporary society, as well as theoretical concepts in the leisure literature.

Young people, leisure and mediated sexual activity

Current debates about the sexualisation of children and young people through the entertainment media, advertising and contemporary consumption practices also have relevance to considering the dynamics of technologically mediated leisure activities. Consumption of media content is an important aspect of young people's leisure in contemporary society. In addition to music, films and computer games (as previously discussed), there are also concerns about the content to which they may be exposed online or through mediated peer interaction. The associated pressures to which young people are exposed occur largely in their free time, and reflect wider concerns about the potential effects of changes in the organisation and experience of their leisure. This section of the chapter considers the potential experiences and outcomes of exposure to adult sexually explicit material (SEM) and 'sexting' for young people as technologically mediated leisure activities. These are both examined within a leisure framework to understand their potential effects and outcomes, gender dynamics and developmental perspectives.

Exposure to adult sexually explicit material

The Internet has created the opportunity to have relatively anonymous access to a variety of sexually explicit content online. This has created concerns over the lack of effective age verification systems, the relatively low uptake of parental controls and the potential impact of exposure to SEM on the sexual attitudes and behaviour of young people (e.g., Carroll et al., 2008; Peter and Valkenburg, 2006, 2009; Stulhofer et al., 2010).

There are only a small number of studies examining the frequency of young people's exposure to SEM online, but the available evidence suggests that this is a relatively common experience. Recent research found that 11 per cent of young people in the UK aged 9–16 had seen sexual images online, and that 24 per cent of these young people were distressed as a result (Livingstone et al., 2011). A similar US study found that 34 per cent of young people aged 11–17 had been exposed to unwanted SEM online, though 74 per cent of these did not perceive the experience to be upsetting (Mitchell et al., 2007). Sabina, Wolak and Finkelhor (2008) found that 12 per cent of male and 19 per cent of females who had viewed SEM before the age of 18 felt it had a strong impact on their attitudes and emotions. Females reported experiencing negative emotions (e.g., embarrassment, guilt), whereas males reported experiencing excitement. Another recent study found that 23 per cent of young people aged 11–17 years old in America reported intentional exposure to SEM (Ybarra et al., 2011). These studies suggest that a number of young people are exposed to SEM as part of their online leisure activities, and the majority do not experience any distress as a result. However, this research focuses on direct emotional responses to exposure, and there are other potentially indirect impacts which have also been addressed in the literature.

Impact of viewing SEM on young people

Adolescence and young adulthood are developmental periods characterised by sexual exploration and development (Arnett, 2004; Lefkowitz and Gillen, 2006). These processes are complex and dynamic, and involve biological and psychosocial changes associated with the development of sexual identity (Ponton and Judice, 2004; Ybarra et al., 2011). The media and SEM have been identified as important sources of information about sexual attitudes and behaviour for young people (e.g., Brown, 2006; Peter and Valkenburg, 2007; Træen et al., 2006; Ward, 2003). Whilst it is recognised that this could have potentially positive outcomes (Hald and Malamuth, 2008; Luder et al., 2011), a number of potentially negative effects have also been proposed. These include negative influences on normative beliefs about gender, sexual behaviour and relationships, and increased sexual risk taking (Brown and L'Engle, 2009; Braun-Courville and Rojas, 2009; Wingood et al., 2001).

In addition to the proposed effects of exposure to SEM described above, there are also concerns over the potential objectification of women and encouragement of sexual aggression. A number of studies suggest that sexually aggressive behaviour and attitudes are elevated for adults who regularly use SEM, particularly those identified as high risk for sexual violence (Carroll et al., 2008; Malamuth et al., 2000; Vega and Malamuth, 2007). Drawing on research examining the influence of violent media content on behaviour, some researchers have claimed that exposure, particularly to violent SEM, has the potential to increase sexual aggression (Ybarra et al., 2011). However, it is recognised that not all sexually aggressive individuals have been exposed to SEM (and vice versa), and such effects are likely to be the result of complex interactions between a number of psychological and social factors (Ybarra et al., 2011). This is consistent with previous research which found no evidence of a relationship between exposure to SEM and sexual aggression in non-offender populations, indicating that this material is more likely to be used by individuals to reinforce established deviant sexual beliefs and behaviours (Malamuth et al., 2000; Marshall and Fernandez, 2000; Seto et al., 2001). This suggests that exposure to SEM in absence of other predisposing characteristics is unlikely to lead to sexual aggression in young people.

This brief review of the literature demonstrates that some young people accidentally or intentionally access SEM during their leisure time. To an extent this is not unexpected or a particularly new phenomenon, though the ease of access and the extreme nature of some of the imagery which is available to young people is of obvious concern. The potential outcomes of exposure to SEM are difficult to determine empirically, particularly the impact on perceptions of normal sexual behaviour. It has been claimed that there has been a lack of attention to SEM within the context of leisure, particularly as a popular activity for males (Shaw, 1999). Within certain sections of society, viewing SEM and associated behaviours are perceived to be deviant and damaging for adults as well as young people. However, there are also possibilities that access to SEM for some young people is part of developmental processes associated with exploring sexuality and relationships, and may provide access to information that is difficult to find elsewhere (Peter and Valkenburg, 2007). This further illustrates the problematic nature of dichotomous classifications of leisure and the value of their reconceptualisation in terms of a continuum to reflect the potentially developmental function of exposure to SEM for young people. This approach provides a clearer basis to consider its ability to shape sexual attitudes and behaviour, and identify characteristics of those individuals who may be particularly vulnerable to the potentially negative effects of exposure. There is also a need for further research examining young peoples' interactions with such material, particularly their interpretation and derived meanings. There are also issues relating to SEM, objectification and gender stereotypes which require further consideration, and this also relates to young people's wider consumption of media during their leisure time. The issues are examined further in relation to young people producing and circulating their own SEM or sexting during leisure.

Creating, disseminating and receiving SEM or 'sexting'

The potential for young people to engage in risky sexual behaviours online is also of concern given that this could make them vulnerable to receiving unwanted requests for SEM and making unsafe sexual contacts (Liau *et al.*, 2005; Livingstone and Haddon 2008; Ybarra *et al.*, 2007). This is particularly relevant given the increasing popularity of young people creating and sharing sexually explicit user-generated content (e.g., images, video clips) with peers and romantic partners online (Bryce, 2010; Livingstone *et al.*, 2011). This material can subsequently be widely disseminated to peers and more generally online, exposing those involved to ridicule and bullying (Boyd, 2007; Bryce, 2010). Such outcomes can have a range of negative psychological consequences, including feelings of humiliation, psychological distress and suicidal feelings (Koefed and Ringrose, 2012; Cassidy *et al.*, 2009).

There is significant variation in prevalence figures for young people engaging in this behaviour. Initial research in the UK found that 38 per cent of 11–18 year olds had received sexually explicit or distressing messages (Cross *et al.*, 2009). More recent research found lower prevalence rates for sexting. Livingstone *et al.* (2011) found that whilst 12 per cent of 11–16 year olds in the UK had seen or received sexual messages online, only 4 per cent had posted or sent someone else such material online. Another study in the USA found that 2.5 per cent (N = 39) of 10–17 year olds appeared in or created nude/nearly nude images, and 7 per cent received images but did not appear in or create them (Mitchell *et al.*, 2012). Approximately a quarter of young people in both these categories reported feeling upset, embarrassed or afraid in response (21 per cent for production, 25 per cent for receipt).

These studies demonstrate large variation in prevalence rates for the behaviour, with larger and representative samples reporting lower proportions of young people engaging in the behaviour, and definitional differences in the behaviours measured (Lounsbury *et al.*, 2011; Mitchell *et al.*, 2012; Ringrose *et al.*, 2012). However, it is clear that some young people engage in this behaviour and that it can have potentially harmful impacts on the individual, particularly when images are circulated more widely or utilised in victimisation. This highlights the importance of understanding the motivations associated with engaging in the activity, and the extent to which it is a new technologically mediated risk or consistent with adolescent sexual development (Livingstone and Haddon, 2008; Ringrose *et al.*, 2012).

A recent UK study examining the motivations, experiences and outcomes associated with sexting among young people found that whilst the behaviour can be sexually motivated, it is frequently utilised within the context of coercion and harassment (Ringrose *et al.*, 2012). The study also found that sexting involves normative constructions of male and female sexual behaviour, which create pressure on females to conform to, and reproduce, body image and sexual attractiveness stereotypes which are dominant in the media and wider society. These results are also consistent with research indicating the reproduction of social and cultural norms relating to gender and physical attractiveness in young adults' identity construction on their Facebook profiles (Zhao *et al.*, 2008). Other research suggests that many female self-representations on dating sites frequently use 'glamour shots' (Whitty, 2008), and that similar sexualised self-presentations of both genders are common in online profiles (Managao *et al.*, 2008; Kapidzic and Herring, 2011). This suggests that social networking is a location for development and expression of identity in ways which reproduce existing stereotypes about sexual attractiveness and behaviour.

This is consistent with the emergence of the Internet as an important space for young people's leisure in which the developmental processes associated with exploration of identity, sexuality and intimacy which characterise adolescence are managed (Caldwell and Witt, 2011; Pempek *et al.*, 2009; Subrahmanyam *et al.*, 2009). This involves exploration risk-taking and exploring normative boundaries for behaviour and communication (Hope, 2007; Livingstone, 2008; Wolak *et al.*, 2007). As a result of these processes, it is unsurprising that young people are accessing and producing SEM, developing online romantic relationships and engaging in other online behaviours perceived to be risky by adults. Many of these are based around the disclosure of personal information online as a central component of the development of intimacy and communication in their relationships (Bryce and Klang, 2009). This is also related to the ability of technology to connect individuals who are not already known to young people in online spaces, leading to their potential to be sexually exploited and victimised by adults as well as each other during their leisure. Young people may not be fully aware of the public and persistent nature of the information which they post and share online, and its potential use for harassment and victimisation (Bryce and Klang, 2009). However, there is evidence that some young people are generating strategies for protecting themselves from online risks, paradoxically through behaviours which they are routinely advised against in educational messages (Bryce and Fraser, under review). This suggests that young people are developing resilience to online risk, and that this may be transferrable to their offline activities. It also suggests that the leisure activities and experiences of young people which adults may perceive to be risky or deviant actually fulfil important developmental functions in ways similar to other adolescent leisure activities.

Conclusion

The activities considered in this article are all potentially part of young people's leisure in contemporary society. They have also been considered as problematic due to their potentially negative psychological, social and physical outcomes. The intention of the chapter is not to deny that the associated concerns are unjustified or that negative effects do not occur, but to suggest the utility of examining their dynamics from a leisure studies perspective. Such an approach recognises the importance of understanding motivations for engaging in these activities and the variety of psychological and social functions which they fulfil for individuals. It also highlights the importance of considering the processes by which motivations influence the associated derived meanings and experiences as additional determinants of both positive and negative outcomes. This also enables the development of a clearer understanding of factors which increase individual vulnerability and resilience to the negative outcomes associated with the technologically mediated activities examined in this chapter.

The focus on negative effects in much of the existing literature contrasts with increasing importance of technology within the everyday lives and leisure of young people as a means of communicating and exploring sexual identity and relationships (Bryce, 2010). It is, however, consistent with the frequent characterisation of adolescent leisure as problematic or deviant due to the potential to engage in risky or harmful behaviours (e.g., consumption of alcohol, sexual activity). The implied moral judgements about the appropriateness of such activities often fail to sufficiently recognise their importance in the development of identity and sexuality. The associated testing of boundaries which these activities involve often creates conflict with the perceived standards of normative behaviour of adults and wider society. However, there is a need to recognise that a certain level of risk–related behaviour is developmentally adaptive for young people in building resilience, the ability to manage risk and the transition to adulthood (Livingstone, 2008). Leisure activities are the primary focus for such experimentation and experiences, highlighting the important developmental functions of leisure for adolescents (Caldwell and Witt, 2011). This suggests that a more holistic approach to examining young people's engagement with technologically mediated leisure activities, which includes a consideration of developmental functions and associated positive outcomes, will enable a deeper understanding of their potential effects and outcomes. This also requires a consideration of the gendered aspects of adolescent leisure (particularly in relation to SEM and sexting), including the reproduction of existing gender stereotypes and their shaping of attitudes and behaviours, as well as leisure experiences and associated outcomes. It is also important to consider the potential for young people to challenge and resist the messages about sexuality and relationships that they may convey. Whilst there is evidence that computer gaming is an activity in which females can challenge existing gender stereotypes, the representations of females in SEM are potentially more problematic and appear to provide less opportunity for resistance or renegotiation. This highlights the need for further research examining the gender dynamics of the representation and reception of SEM, and its influence on attitudes and behaviour.

There is also a need to develop a clearer understanding of the role of fantasy in technologically mediated leisure activities and the potential encouragement of specific behaviours, particularly engagement with media content which contains realistic or graphic representations of violence and sexual activity. This represents an important area for future research, though there are obvious associated methodological and ethical challenges. The potential opportunities for virtual performance of these behaviours and exposure to SEM has implications for understanding leisure experiences and outcomes, as does the potential to meet people who may share similar interests which are generally considered deviant in wider society. This is particularly relevant for young people who may be more easily persuaded into engaging in specific online activities which are risky or harmful.

The activities examined in this chapter also raise the issue of whether technologically mediated activities are transformative or reflect a continuous evolution in the relationship between technology and the organisation of leisure (Bryce, 2001). Regardless of the activity and whether it is online or offline, the individual and social functions of leisure (e.g., mood management, developmental) have not fundamentally changed. However, they do challenge the dichotomous classifications that characterise theoretical perspectives on leisure (e.g., serious v casual, deviant v normal), and highlight the greater utility of a continuum-based approach. This also demonstrates their ability to enable a reflexive consideration of established concepts with leisure theory, and provide opportunities to refine and develop contemporary approaches to understanding the organisation and function of leisure at both the individual and societal level. The affordances of technologies and online spaces to create ideal online selves or perform virtual actions which break offline moral and legal codes highlights the need for further theoretical and empirical research examining their influence on the dynamics of both potential positive and negative leisure experiences and outcomes over time. This will enable researchers and policy makers to anticipate and mitigate the associated possibilities for young people to be exposed to risk and harm during their everyday leisure lives.

11

HOW NOT TO TAKE THE FUN OUT OF EVERYTHING

Facilitating volunteering and leisure

Steven Howlett

Introduction

Rushing from paid work in order to make a meeting of the school governing body, it would be easy to understand someone asking themselves 'why do I do this?' Could this role, performed in spare time, be seen as a leisure activity? The person who relaxes by singing in a choir is probably thought of as engaging in leisure and not as volunteering; but when the choir sings carols at Christmas in the local hospital, is that person now a volunteer? Being a room steward in a museum seems like it is a volunteer role. Is it leisure too? What if the person is doing it to gain experience for a future paid job? What if it is being done because the person is interested and enthusiastic about the museum collection, about which they too want to learn more? And because the steward's role helps facilitate others to visit the museum, should we then call this leisure volunteering? You have helped restore a beautiful steam engine because of your passion for steam railways. Now your work will be on display to the public with visitors able to pay for a ride on the train along a section of restored track. Your group has asked you to help draw up rotas to tend the engine, but also to organise people to take the money and open the gift shop and the café; oh, and you need to check that the organisation has complied with health and safety, has the right insurance for volunteers and visitors and so on. Has your hobby extended to something beyond? Has your group of fellow enthusiasts mutated into a different form of volunteering? Are people who will volunteer in the café leisure volunteers too? And has the need to manage a variety of elements over and above your initial commitment pulled the rug from beneath the enjoyment you have thus far experienced? When is somebody volunteering *in* leisure and *for* leisure? Does this distinction imply that it is possible to volunteer in say, sport, but not be seeking a leisure experience? Or to be volunteering in a charity, but be doing it as a leisure activity?

These examples perhaps begin to illustrate the fuzziness when it comes to thinking about what is a leisure activity and what is volunteering. Why does this matter? Maybe because leisure and volunteering are often studied separately and yet the ideas and concepts used to understand them means that one speaks to the other. It could be very useful to both fields of study to examine the areas of similarity and difference. Stebbins (2004b) for example noted that it is relatively rare in both the study of leisure and the study of volunteering, to find the two considered together. While many academic articles and books have been published since Stebbins made that observation, many do, as Lockstone-Binney et al. (2010) (citing Aitchison, 2006) note focus around sub-fields of tourism, sport and events. But if we move to a different level of abstraction, maybe those studies in tourism, sport and events will say something about volunteering more widely. And conversely, work that addresses aspects of volunteering, for example access, motivations and where appropriate, management, can speak to leisure.

This chapter will try to apply some ideas about volunteering to leisure. The general theme outlined below is that the trend in managing volunteers is moving towards a more formal approach (see for example Rochester et al., 2012). And while more formality may be appropriate in some cases, volunteering is too diverse for it to be a given in all situations. This chapter will argue that introducing ideas about leisure adds a new dimension to thinking about management. Studying volunteering in a leisure context may involve considering the leisure of the volunteer and how that facilitates the leisure of others (working in a museum for example). Alternatively, it may include thinking about when hobbyists could also be said to be volunteers as in the steam railway example above. The extent to which a more formal approach to management is appropriate, or whether another form of organisation is better, and what circumstances influence the choice of management style is important in practice. The seeming trend to a formal approach, if applied uncritically, could be counter-productive; below I will argue that formalising volunteering to make it look like work could detract from volunteering as a leisure activity.

To examine this we need to consider the definitions of volunteering and leisure, the motives of volunteers and the expectations of volunteers and organisations. The chapter begins with an outline of the boundaries between leisure activity and volunteering. It does this from a perspective closer to the field of volunteering study than leisure study, and so looks to extend the idea that the volunteering and leisure nexus is found beyond tourism, sport and events. By using the model created by Rochester (Rochester, 2006; Rochester et al., 2012) which incorporates Stebbins' idea of serious leisure into a model that incorporates unpaid work or service and activism, we will be able to examine the ambiguities that mark the cross-over between leisure and volunteering (see for example Stebbins, 1982; 1996b; 2004b; 2007a; 2009c).

The chapter then considers meaning and motivations. There are studies that show volunteers ascribe a leisure meaning to their roles (Stebbins, 2009c). That is to say, irrespective of how the academic debate is shaping up to delineate between leisure and volunteering, volunteers themselves may identify their volunteering as a leisure pastime. We can also look to what extent the motives for leisure and for volunteering have some congruence, and this in turn can help us to understand both how and why people become involved, and the support they need. This last point draws together a number of critical issues that follow on from the discussion of the overlap of volunteering and leisure. It is here that the chapter focuses on the issue from a volunteer management perspective to examine the extent to which there is a move within volunteer involving organisations to more formal ideas of management. But, if the motivation to volunteer is primarily one directed to satisfy leisure, what forms of management are helpful to enhance, and which may undermine, the voluntary impulse?

Leisure and volunteering

It is not difficult to make the case for an examination of volunteering and leisure as two sides of, if not the same, then very similar coins. Stebbins (2004b, p. 4) states that 'Notwithstanding the relative lack of scholarly attention given to volunteering by leisure studies specialists, making a case for it as leisure poses little logical difficulty'. Once the general case is made however, the edges that mark where volunteering and leisure overlap are not so crisp. But it is in the fuzzy overlap that leisure and volunteering practitioners and academics can find areas of mutual interest. Stebbins (2004b, p. 4) helpfully begins by arguing that if we consider the etymology of volunteering we will see that, just like leisure, it is a non-coerced activity. Furthermore, like leisure, leisure volunteering is built upon the notion of a satisfying and/or enjoyable experience. Already we can see that the basic material for our consideration is cut from the same rock.

The idea of an enjoyable experience looms large in Argyle's (1996) work on the social psychology of leisure. In it he appears to make little distinction between volunteering and leisure. For him all voluntary work is leisure.[1] Indeed, volunteering provides him with his first example of a leisure activity; and he states that 'Leisure raises some interesting issues for psychology. For example, how is voluntary work motivated and how are people socialized into it?' (Argyle, 1996, p. 1). Delving further into this, Argyle found that when he asked people to rate their moods 'by the end of a typical meeting of the club' the results enabled him to rank activity by, what he called, indicators of 'joy'. On this ranking, voluntary work as a leisure activity resulted in 'joy' that out-scored socialising, classes, politics, hobbies and drama (Argyle, 1996, pp. 82–83). Clearly there is some difference here between volunteering and hobbies, but it is not clear what it is and it is not hard to argue that some form of hobby involvement, some socialising and some aspects of drama and politics could involve voluntary work. Stebbins (1982) also works in broadly the same area and he draws on Bosserman and Gagan (1972) and Smith (1975) who argue that at the level of the individual, all leisure is voluntary action since it is uncoerced and unpaid; Stebbins then goes on to make the case for volunteering as a type of 'serious leisure'.

Swinging in the other direction, Musick and Wilson (2008) make the case for volunteering *not* being considered as leisure. In their comprehensive work *Volunteers: A Social Profile* they argue that:

> Volunteering is simply work done outside the home and outside the job market in an organizational setting performed during the time left over from housework, childcare and paid work. It is not really a form of leisure because leisure time pursuits tend to be abandoned once they no longer provide intrinsic gratification, whereas people will continue volunteering even though it is sometimes unpleasant.
>
> (Musick and Wilson, 2008, p. 16)

Perhaps the person who has done more than most to untangle this and square the circle is Stebbins who makes at least two significant contributions to the field. The first is that he begins to categorise leisure participation in such a way that we can locate activities on a continuum with (serious) leisure at one end and volunteering at the other and with stops along the way for hobbyists and amateurs. Where Stebbins' work adds a new perspective is that, at the volunteering end of the spectrum, volunteering is an activity characterised by commitment but is still a source of leisure, and we shall cover Stebbins' criteria below. Second, he tackles the gritty issue of how the presence of compulsion and coercion can alter an activity which seems to be leisure and/or volunteering into one that may be considered neither.

Volunteering as serious leisure

The argument put forward by Musick and Wilson (2008) above is that leisure is directed by a need for gratification while volunteering can sometimes be 'unpleasant'. And yet, as we have seen, Argyle finds that volunteering is a source of not inconsiderable joy. Stebbins' argument is that volunteering can be seen as a form of 'serious leisure' (see Stebbins, 1982, 1992a, 1996b; Stebbins and Graham, 2004). It is a concept that has been used in many of the interdisciplinary academic studies of leisure and volunteering.

To arrive at the idea of serious leisure we need to contrast it with two other types of leisure – casual and project-based. Casual leisure is immediate and enjoyable – including 'Play, relaxation, entertainment' (Stebbins, 2009c, p. 156). But, it can also include volunteering and, again Stebbins provides examples 'It is seen in such activities as handing out leaflets, stuffing envelopes, soliciting money on the street (e.g., the Salvation Army), picking up litter, and directing traffic in a parking lot' (Stebbins, 2009c, p. 156), or 'Cooking hot dogs at a church picnic or taking tickets for a performance by a community theatre' (Stebbins, 2004b, p. 5). Project-based leisure on the other hand includes 'a short-term, reasonably complicated one-off or occasional, though infrequent, creative undertaking (Stebbins, 2004b, p. 7), such as 'giving pro bono legal service (one-time only), volunteering at an arts festival, working on an election campaign, working (one-time) on a Habitat for Humanity project and serving on a publicity campaign for an environmental cause' (Stebbins, 2009c, p. 156). In contrast to this, serious leisure is something that implies more time, skill, knowledge and effort: 'Serious leisure is the systematic pursuit of an amateur, hobbyist, or voluntary activity sufficiently substantial, interesting, and fulfilling for the participant to find a (leisure) career there acquiring and expressing a combination of its special skills, knowledge, and experience' (ibid: 156). Once again Stebbins is parcelling activities for definition; the 'serious' element separates out persistent participants from causal toe-dippers. Using Stebbins' ideas enables us to re-examine Wilson and Musick's assertion that volunteering is not leisure – clearly under some circumstances it can be.

It should now be evident that these definitions are fluid. Even with the help of Stebbins's work it is not easy to locate some activities in relation to casual or serious leisure, or whether a particular volunteering role is leisure at all. Stebbins himself, in the quotes above, has to qualify 'one-time' working, presumably because any more slides the example from project based leisure into casual; and in the examples that opened this chapter presumably the person singing carols in the hospital is a casual volunteer where the choir leader is a serious volunteer. Stebbins (2007a) latterly has produced a typology that helps further. By dividing leisure into six forms (popular, idea-based, material, floral, faunal and environmental) and crossing with type of volunteering – serious, casual or 'project-based' – Stebbins has produced 18 'types' through which the leisure basis for volunteering can be explored. The choir volunteers can be explored around the notion of popular volunteering, we can explore whether this is serious or casual by looking at interests and motivations.

It is also interesting to note that there is a growing interest in episodic volunteering (Macduff, 2005) and the new ways of thinking about this within the leisure domain (Handy *et al.*, 2006). It may imply, for example, that project-based volunteering repeated as episodic events is very much akin to serious leisure with implications for how volunteers are managed, as we shall see later.

Even recognising the imprecision of definitions, we do have criteria against which to judge an activity as leisure volunteering. These are set out by Stebbins (1992a, 2001a) and listed by Misener *et al.* (2010, p. 269), who argue that they have been empirically validated in several studies. The qualities are: 1) the occasional need to *persevere* in order to continue experiencing fulfilment, 2) the opportunity and tendency to follow a leisure *career*, that is to have longevity and development within the role, 3) there is significant *personal effort* involved, based on a knowledge, training and skill, 4) the participants realise *durable benefits*, such as self-fulfilment, enrichment and expression and an enhanced self-image; feelings of accomplishment. A sense of fun is important too, and although also a figure for casual leisure, should not be thought of as at all unimportant for the serous leisure volunteer, 5) is a *unique ethos* that is associated sharing interests in a particular field over an extended period of time, 6) a *distinctive identity* develops through identifying strongly with the chosen pursuits.

The second aspect of defining volunteering that Stebbins helps with is to look at what we mean by voluntary. This is important because it further addresses the point made by Wilson and Musick, that volunteering cannot be seen as leisure because volunteering can be, at times, unpleasant. The concept of the serious volunteer addresses this through the idea of the need sometimes to persevere. But, Stebbins (2001a, p. 2) also argues that when volunteering is seen in economic terms, the leisure motivation is 'neatly side-stepped' and although Musick and Wilson (2008) spend a lot of time looking at motivations, their dismissal of volunteering as 'not leisure' appears to be on economic terms – it is unpaid work outside of the paid labour market. However, Stebbins moves the argument to new ground. He argues that, even if volunteers are engaged in something 'unpleasant', they can feel as though they are engaged in something worthwhile. As a result, a 'key element in the leisure conception of volunteering is the felt absence of moral coercion to do the voluntary activity' (Stebbins, 2001a, p. 2). This puts us in a different place; to understand leisure volunteering, we must not only have some notion of knowledge, commitment, the benefits derived and the identity forged; but we must also listen to the volunteer. Once we take the views of volunteers into account, a wide range of volunteering can be seen as leisure if the volunteer feels that they get a 'leisure reward' and they feel they have a choice. Conversely, something that appears a leisure choice may not be if the 'volunteer' has no choice. In the first instance the 'unpleasant' element is accepted by choice and persevered through; in the second, the unpleasantness is not accepted and the 'volunteer' has to endure it because they feel that they have no choice.

Stebbins (2001a) uses the terms 'mainstream' volunteering where the volunteer has choice and feels no coercion or obligation; where there is some form of coercion, Stebbins introduces the term 'marginal volunteering'. Stebbins lists six types of marginal volunteering; these are 1) extracurricular activities at work, 2) time money schemes, 3) exploratory volunteering in search of a work career, 4) assigned volunteering in training and corrections programmes, 5) help for friends or relatives, and 6) busy work as job replacement for retired people.

Two examples from these six types will suffice to illustrate the main thrust of this work. In the first, Stebbins uses the example of an employee who is asked to organise the firm annual picnic. The employee has a knack for organisation and so could have found the task enjoyable (and so maybe this could have been a leisure activity). Having done it the previous year, the person knows that the task is thankless and doesn't want to do it again; but, not wanting to appear uncooperative, takes the task on. Really however the employee would have liked a simpler task of talking to people to find out who would want to come. This would have been casual leisure because the employee likes talking to colleagues and actually enjoys the picnic. The second example is of a retired person who takes on a role to replace the working day. In this instance, the volunteer only wants the structure of the day, expects to work and so is accepting of the role even if it is too 'unsatisfying' and 'uninteresting' to be considered a leisure role in the eyes of the person involved (Stebbins 2001a, p. 7).

At the root of this work are questions of choice and identity – the extent to which a volunteer has choice and identifies the role they perform as leisure. Stebbins argues that '[T]he distinction between marginal and mainstream volunteering is worth converting to an operating principle for guiding research on and management of volunteers' (Stebbins 2001a, p. 9). We will return to the implications for management later.

A further exploration of the boundaries between volunteering and leisure comes with the work of Rochester (2006, and Rochester *et al.*, 2012), who maps the various permutations as shown in Figure 11.1. Rochester adapts the conceptual framework of Billis (1993, 2010) and explicitly draws attention to the areas (of what Billis would term) ambiguity and hybrid forms. Billis pioneered the study of voluntary organisations in the UK and rooted his work in maintaining that to understand, and manage, voluntary organisation requires a recognition that at the heart of voluntary organisations is a fundamental tension. Organisations will in some way reflect bureaucratic forms, but these can often be at odds with the values of association that underpin voluntary organisations. The result is that voluntary organisations are hybrids of this bureaucratic/associational tension. Rochester transposes this idea to consider volunteering and produces a model that outlines three 'worlds' of volunteering – those of serious leisure, of unpaid work/service and of activism as shown in Figure 11.1. Rochester deals with the fuzzy boundaries, not through trying to define them, but by accepting that there is always overlap which will produce hybrid volunteering – shown in Figure 11.1 where the forms of volunteering overlap. The model gives:

> four hybrid forms where either the nature of the organisation through which the volunteering takes place or the combination of roles undertaken by the volunteer means that more than one perspective is required to understand the kinds of volunteering involved.
>
> - Volunteering which can be seen as a combination of unpaid work and activism
> - Volunteering which can be seen as a combination of activism and serious leisure
> - Volunteering which can be seen as a combination of serious leisure and unpaid work
> - Volunteering which can be seen as a combination of all three elements.
>
> (Rochester *et al.*, 2012, pp. 15–16)

We have an armoury of perspectives if we draw upon Stebbins' emphasis on choice and identity and typology of volunteers, and Rochester's ideas of the significance of the volunteer role and the organisational setting. Bringing these perspectives to bear, we are ready to try to understand better the relationship between leisure and volunteering. An example here will demonstrate how the complexity can be examined using these different viewpoints. The perennial

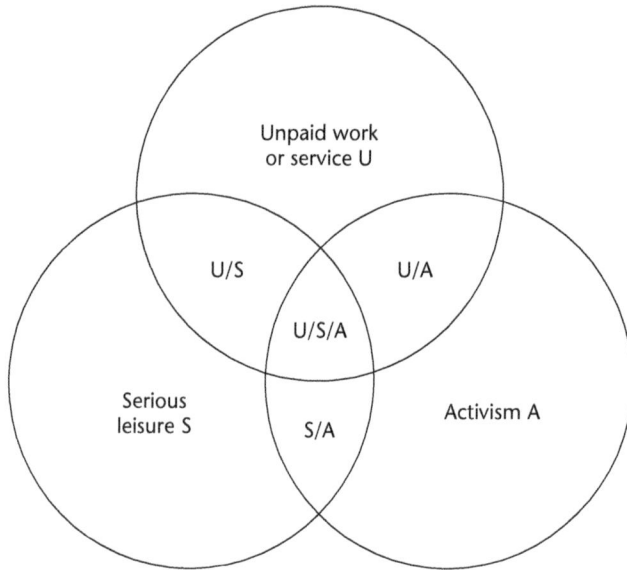

From Rochester (2006); Rochester *et al.*, (2012)

FIGURE 11.1 A three perspective model of volunteering

stand-by job for volunteers – stuffing envelopes – may not appear to be a leisure role. Stebbins uses it to illustrate what casual volunteering might entail, for it hardly fits the criteria for serious leisure. And yet in Edwards' (2007) work on managing leisure-seeking volunteers, this is exactly the role that some volunteers fulfil in the three museums studied. Using the frameworks that Stebbins (2007a) and Rochester (2006) provide, we can begin to ask some questions: is envelope stuffing the only task the volunteer performs? Or maybe it is a small part of the role – so in this case we can concede that there is a larger, primary role that may identify the volunteer as performing a leisure activity? Or maybe it is the organisation – the fact that the role takes place within a museum – that persuades us that this is a leisure role, almost irrespective of the task? But this would suggest that envelope stuffing when a task in a museum is leisure, but not if it is in, say, Greenpeace? Or maybe it is whether the volunteer identifies that they are leisure seeking in their volunteering . This suggests that envelope-stuffing can be a leisure role in a museum and Greenpeace if the volunteer identifies it as such. In fact, Rochester's model allows for this – envelope stuffing in Greenpeace could be a combination of leisure and activism. Perhaps Rochester's work also helps in suggesting that we must learn to live with ambiguity.

Motivations for leisure and volunteering

Setting aside the academic interest in disaggregating this complexity, studying the volunteering/leisure intersection, if it is to have a practical purpose, must have a two-fold purpose. It should help volunteer involving organisations understand why people give their time. And second, it should help enhance the gratification volunteers get from their involvement. In the context of leisure-seeking volunteers the first should lead to the second. It is therefore to motivations and the meanings that leisure-seeking volunteers give to their volunteering that we now turn.

Although academic studies of volunteering and leisure are increasing, many focus, as Lockstone-Binney *et al.* (2010) point out, on tourism, sport and events. Perhaps therefore it is unsurprising that these studies pivot around the link between interest in sport, or museums and volunteering (see for example Burgham and Downward, 2005; Edwards, 2005; Eley, 2003; Green and Jones, 2005; Holmes, 1999; Orr, 2006). This is not to say that the sporting/museum context is the only motivational drive, far from it, as we shall see, many studies draw on a wide motivational literature. Stebbins (2007a) has helped widen this by looking at how volunteering in other fields (the environment, services etc.) also has a leisure component. Rochester's ideas of hybrid forms allow us another relatively simple way to consider a wider range of kinds of volunteering as having a leisure-seeking component – by considering whether the action is a combination of service, or activism. Both help to tease out where leisure lies in an individual's volunteering, and if a key to successfully involving volunteers is to understand their motivation, then the leisure perspective is one that all organisations could benefit from recognising and understanding.

When motivations are considered from a psychological perspective, the context is less important because the motivation is seen to stem from answering a need. Clary, Snyder and Omoto have done some of the best-known work on volunteering from a psychological perspective. A key contribution to the practice of volunteer management is to help address the seemingly endless list of motivations typified by the temptation to believe that there are as many motivations to volunteer as there are volunteers (see Ellis, 2002). Clary and colleagues challenge this by arguing that there are broadly three basic psychological needs: the need to understand the world through acquiring knowledge; the need to act on, and express values and the need to protect the self. Motivation stems from acting to satisfy one (or more) of these needs (see Clary and Snyder, 1991; Clary *et al.* 1992, 1996, 1998; Omoto and Snyder, 1995). In fact, to apply these to volunteering, Clary *et al.* (1996) produced the Volunteer Functions Index (VFI) where they broaden these three needs out into six categories of motivation: Values; Understanding; Career; Social; Protective and Enhancement. Centering motivations on these functions highlights the intrinsic nature of volunteer motivation. Lockstone-Binney *et al.* (2010) showed how Osbourne's (1999) volunteer museums found that intrinsic needs were most important, but when replicated by Edwards (2005), it was found extrinsic motivations were more important. Then in another study of UK museums, intrinsic motivations were important for attracting volunteers, but extrinsic motivations played an equal part when it came to retaining volunteers. Intrinsic motivations also figure in the study by Heo and Lee (2007) where Korean students involved in basketball identified escaping from loneliness, self-image and fun as amongst the reasons they pursued basketball as serous leisure. Although the research used Stebbins' concept, it is unclear whether the students' involvement extended beyond playing – another example of the slipperiness of concepts. Similarly Patterson and Pegg (2009) used a serious leisure perspective to look at the impact of participation on people with intellectual disabilities – some volunteered but not necessarily in the leisure activity they were interviewed about. Fortier *et al.*'s (2007) study of young people in leisure and sports activities in Quebec raised other questions. It is difficult from the study to tell whether the volunteers would qualify as pursuing 'serious leisure'. The sample contained 6 per cent who acted as members of committees, 22 per cent who were responsible for a group or specialised task and 62 per cent who acted in a support capacity – making it tricky to decide which of these could be considered a serious leisure role, which a 'casual' role and which a 'project' role. But also, given that 84 per cent of the sample of volunteers were below 18 years of age, it raises a question about how much experience, knowledge and so forth would we need to see before these volunteers qualify as 'serious'. Nevertheless, the study showed that the motivations were a mix of intrinsic and extrinsic, but with the emphasis on intrinsic. The primary ranked motive was to 'have fun' followed by 'accomplishing something to be proud of', 'serving a cause in which the volunteer believed' and 'enjoying a new experience'. 'Helping out' ranked sixth out of 12 motivations given.

When Gage III and Thapa (2012) studied the motivations and leisure constraints of college students, they found that altruism was important for starting volunteering, but self-interest was more important for continuing. Other studies moved beyond the VFI by including the context; in Bruyere and Rappe's study of organisations involved in the natural environment, 'helping the environment' was the most important find out of 'many motivations'. With expressing values, learning and socialising as 'second order' motivations. Bang *et al.* (2009) in their study of event volunteers identified community involvement and extrinsic rewards as important.

Perhaps we can draw from this that using a distinction between intrinsic and extrinsic motivation is somewhat unhelpful in practice for thinking about managing volunteers. In addition to studies within leisure being inconclusive as to whether volunteers are more likely to exhibit intrinsic or extrinsic motivations (Lockstone-Binney *et al.* 2010), it is not always easy to distinguish between them. Finklestein (2009) tells us that intrinsic motives for volunteering are those satisfied by the activity itself, whereas extrinsic motivations require a separate outcome. Clary and Snyder's VFI seems to split into five intrinsic motivations with just 'career' as extrinsic. But many studies include other elements and it is not clear where something as key as altruism fits. Stebbins (1982, 1998, 2001a) argues that altruism is a key element in recognising career volunteers, while Misener *et al.* (2010, p. 269) point out in their review of literature for their study of older adult volunteers that

'This additional aspect distinguishes volunteers from participants in other forms of serious leisure such as amateurism and hobbyist activities'. While being altruistic may answer a need to 'give', it may also be an extrinsic motivation when organisations use the idea of 'helping out' to attract volunteers. Looking at how volunteers respond to 'the ask' would take us into another theoretical area away from psychological ideas and into sociology. Sociology looks for explanations of the context in which people will respond to 'the ask' and the meaning they attach to volunteering (Musick and Wilson, 2008). A further complication is that, motivations can and do change. In addition to the above examples Eley (2003) in her study of young leaders in sport found that the volunteers were motivated by being involved in sport, over time this remained the key motivation, but the self-awareness of the contribution the young leaders were making in the local community grew considerably over a relatively short time. What might not change however is a volunteer's identity, something alluded to above. We may look to alter typologies, to classify someone as a volunteer or not – but what is important is the identity of the participant as a volunteer, and maybe, as someone identifying a leisure component in their participation.

Rather than trying to distinguish between extrinsic and intrinsic motivations, it may be easier for a volunteer manager to know what rewards people want to accrue from their involvement. Many studies look at this and often benefits and motivations considered together. Lockstone-Binney *et al.* (2010) note that Smith (2002) classifies leisure volunteers by finding that primarily younger volunteers seek experience, while older volunteers seek social opportunities. Social aspects emerge as a key benefit with many studies noting volunteers identifying this. Other benefits include being involved with something that participants are passionate about and interested in and connects with personal values; being able to exercise responsibility; expanding skills and competencies; filling time, learning skills; giving back to the community; feeling better about themselves and enhancing self-image and being recognised for the work they do (for example see Edwards and Graham, 2006; Graham, 2007; Kay *et al.,* 2008; Barnes and Sharpe, 2009; Martinez and McMullin, 2004; Rheberg, 2005).

It is interesting to note that this list corresponds well to volunteering research undertaken outside the serious leisure framework, lending weight to the argument that using Rochester's model of hybridity can help remind us to consider volunteer participation from different perspectives. It is often argued, and seems intuitively right, that knowing the motivations of volunteers will help in the management of volunteers. Given that we have been looking at volunteering slightly differently by drawing on a leisure perspective, what can we now say about management?

Managing volunteers

In her work on museum volunteers, Edwards (2007) draws on Farmer and Fedor's (1999) insight that volunteers place a high value on the work they do and, as a result, look for visible signs that their time is having an impact. This desire appears in a similar form where volunteers base their decision to participate on the efficacy of their volunteer work (Martinez and McMullin, 2004). Edwards develops this to argue that volunteers expect a 'reciprocal' approach: in return for their time, they expect organisations to value their commitment. Edwards found that volunteers were often disappointed appreciation stopped at their 'line manager', and concluded that there is an ethical obligation to address the concerns of volunteers and to manage them appropriately.

The caveat 'appropriately' is important. Edwards (2007, p. 34) for example argues that it requires a '"soft" model of volunteer management based on inclusiveness, commitment, flexibility and relationship building'. And yet, the trend to volunteer management seems to be one of the 'work replacement' model where volunteering is akin to paid work without the pay. Within the workplace model volunteers are an additional resource complementing the role of paid staff. The model is strong in answering some important issues. A 'professional' approach to volunteer management ought to provide the capacity to look at volunteer motivation and put into place policies and structures. In short, it should, as Barnes and Sharpe (2009) note, facilitate an organisation getting 'a job well done by volunteers'. And yet, the thrust of Barnes and Sharpe's paper is addressing a seeming paradox. They examine volunteer involvement in parks and recreation in the context of 'an era of declining volunteerism' (p. 169) noting that human resource practice borrowed from the private sector pervades non-profit organisations. This is leading to isopmorphism of organisations with many displaying formalisation, similar hierarchical structures and the adoption of more sophisticated volunteer screening and application processes. It is a model Rochester et al. (2010) warn against implementing without careful thought. While it may be suitable for some organisations – Holmes (1999) for example argues that the management of volunteers in the heritage sector has become more and more specialised, which may imply more structure and formality – it is not suitable for all. We need again to examine this from a leisure perspective; volunteering in an essentially leisure orientated formal organisation such as a museum might be suitable for more formal volunteer management. But, where volunteering is performed as a leisure activity, then some compromise might be needed. Here we are wrestling with a tension – volunteers may want recognition, but at the same time they will want their leisure motivations fulfilled. Recognition may include items Stebbins suggested make some volunteering 'serious leisure'. But the leisure motivation is also likely to require that volunteering is enjoyable.

The 1997 national survey of volunteering (Davis Smith 1998), reported that 71 per cent of volunteers said that their work could be better organised. This was interpreted as meaning that organising volunteering was in a poor shape. Ten years later the *Helping Out* survey (Low et al., 2007) showed that 31 per cent of regular volunteers felt the same. While it can be argued that this still represents nearly a third of volunteers, the improvement is significant. This improvement came at the same time as (in the UK at least) many programmes to develop volunteer management were implemented (Howlett, 2011). At the same time this improvement in satisfaction of 'organisation' took place, figures for enjoyment remained more stable. In 1997, the number of volunteers reporting that they really enjoyed their volunteering was in the high 80 percentage points, ten years later 96 per cent of volunteers answering the survey said that they enjoyed their volunteering (Low *et al.*, 2007). Can we interpret the high enjoyment satisfaction as having nothing to do with the changing levels of satisfaction with management? It is hard to say without further research – we do not for example know what form this new management has taken. But it does seem that care is needed. Organisations wishing to involve, and keep volunteers, find themselves needing to balance 'management' with keeping volunteering fun. While it should not be assumed that there is a simple correlation between formality and enjoyment, there is research which suggests volunteers do not appreciate overformalisation. Zimmeck (2001) reviewed a host of literature and isolated just two modes of volunteer management – what she calls 'modern' and 'homegrown'. Roughly they accord to formal, bureaucratic organisations and grass-roots organisations. Meijs and Karr (2004), and Meijs and Hoogstad (2001) have a slightly different take. They categorise organisations as essentially service delivery or membership. When it comes to involving volunteers, service delivery organisations define volunteer roles and recruit, membership organisations work from crafting volunteering from the membership.

The point here is *not* that the homegrown model is necessarily better. Indeed research suggests that volunteers *want* management (Gaskin, 2003). But neither do they like the pendulum to swing too far; they are put off by too much management and bureaucracy (Institute for Volunteering Research, 2004). Certainly there seems a favouring for a more organic form of management in some leisure research (Burgham and Downward, 2005; Barnes and Sharpe, 2009). Rochester *et al.* (2012) argue that the available models can be used on a horses for courses approach. Indeed, as Zimmeck (2001) argues, bureaucracy can be a good thing! What seems to be important is combating over formality before it damages the spirit and character of volunteering. The stress must be placed on the idea of 'appropriate' management. It may be that some organisations do need a more formal approach. On the other hand we should remember that in many, many organisations, volunteers are not 'managed' at all. The question here is, should they be? Good practice on involving volunteers effectively suggests that they should be. The key for this chapter is that under whatever circumstances, whether it be a bureaucratic organisation with developed policies and structures, or a 'hobby' club, the imperative to tighten on volunteer management should not be at the expense of the enjoyment of participation. It is very important that organisations look after volunteers, at the same time it is vital that we do not sleepwalk into inappropriate managerialism. Working in the sport and leisure field Nichols (2004) finds that the challenge of managing volunteers is not to adopt business human resource management models too literally. In a study on the pressures on managers in the UK issues of increased professionalisation was identified as a key challenge.

Research using the idea of the psychological contract identified the need for management that allowed volunteers to feel more in control of the relationship between them and their organisation (Nichols and Ojala, 2009).

A survey for the Association of Volunteer Managers in England (AVM, 2007) looked how knowledge is passed between volunteer managers. There is no easy place to acquire knowledge to become a volunteer manager and there is no professional organisation to join. Advice is often passed along through online groups. The survey found that those who said they were in a position to attend events and training and to spend time answering advice online were from larger more structured organisations. The implication is that the knowledge that gets passed on for good practice is that that is best suited to particular structures.

How can we avoid overformalisation and retain the aspect of volunteering that is leisure-like? The role of the volunteer manager is vital, but as mentioned not all organisations have volunteer managers. Not all organisations will want to engage with ideas of management, motivation and levels of formality. Rochester's model of hybridity is useful when we do start to engage with volunteer motivations and want to bring in leisure perspectives. It does seem that there is scope for a greater cross-over between volunteer and leisure research. Much of the literature reviewed in this chapter looks at volunteers in a leisure setting. We can start there and use management models to assess best practice for involvement. But we have also seen that volunteers in other organisational settings characterise their volunteering as leisure, here understanding leisure motivations and rewards will help. Volunteering is a complex mix of motivations and rewards.

Underpinning all this is a notion that volunteers *enjoy* what they do. Aaker *et al.* (2011) find that the relationship between giving time and happiness is undervalued against studies linking money and happiness. The authors find that how someone 'spends' their time can increase happiness and offer five principles of happiness maximisation. They argue that time tends to be more meaning loaded than money and that there is a clear relationship between happiness and the satisfaction a person gets from leisure. They conclude that spending time with the right people and on the right activities is a path to happiness. Those activities need to be 'sticky' – they need to be a 'good investment' and they need to be valued. Not surprisingly, volunteering figures in their work. Maybe it isn't so surprising that Argyle found volunteering such a source of joy. Research findings that show volunteers want management may appear to clash with research that says management puts volunteers off. Except that the tipping point appears to lie in the level and type of management. There is a clear role here for well-informed organisation and management that encourages participation without taking the fun out of everything.

Note

1   Here I am avoiding defining a distinction between voluntary work and volunteering, the way in which Argyle uses it suggests that he is using voluntary work and volunteering synonymously. Notwithstanding, it is necessary to be careful with

terms. Stebbins uses Van Til (1979) to distinguish voluntary action 'uncoerced, and not primarily aimed toward financial gain; it may be individual or group action', and volunteering 'is that form of voluntary action involving helping activities deemed beneficial' (Van Til quoted in Stebbins, 1982, pp. 263–4). Argyle in using voluntary work may be reflecting the fact that he draws on several volunteering surveys and many shy away from using the term volunteering. Voluntary work is often used to avoid an under-counting – respondents understand the idea of unpaid voluntary work more than they do the term 'volunteering' (see Lyons et al., 1998).

12

YOUTH AND LEISURE EXPERIENCES

Youth cultures and social change in Britain since the early twentieth century

Ken Roberts

Introduction

The experience of youth has features that are common across time and place. These arise because youth is always and everywhere a transitional life stage. The life stage may be completed rapidly and its conclusion marked by a formal initiation ceremony, but in present-day modern societies the life stage typically extends over many years, for over two decades in some cases. It involves a series of status transitions: from student to worker, from child to parent, from minor to voter, from having goods and services purchased on one's behalf by an adult to becoming an independent consumer. These changes take place at different ages. Hence the start and end points of the youth life stage are typically fuzzy. Also, to complicate matters further, in complex modern societies the life stage varies by social class, gender and ethnicity among other things.

Leisure plays an important role in young people's lives in all the (modern) societies in which leisure has become a distinct part of life. Leisure is always a site of relative freedom. People can do things purely for the intrinsic satisfaction. This leisure experience is common to all age groups, but there are additional ways in which leisure plays important roles in young people's lives. It is during leisure that young people first make their own decisions such as which music to listen to, which clothes to wear, and where and with whom to spend leisure time. During leisure young people learn to play adult gender and sexual roles. They develop skills and identities which enable them to act responsibly, as they are required to do, when making decisions about their own education and employment careers, and whether and with whom to become a parent. In pre-modern societies, where leisure was not a clearly differentiated part of life, all youth status transitions were normally made under the supervision of families, neighbours, religious communities and work associates. Young people had neither the freedom nor were expected to build their own futures. The experience of leisure is crucial in making this possible.

This chapter examines how the character of the youth life stage has changed continuously throughout the modern era alongside broader economic, political and social changes, including wider changes in the leisure context. Specifically the chapter intervenes in two ongoing debates about changes in the character of youth cultures. The first concerns whether subsequent youth cultures have been more diverse, fragmented, fluid, often hybrid, with greater scope for expressions of individuality, and less squarely based on pre-existing social (class) divisions than the youth subcultures of the 1950s and 1960s (see, for example, Bennett, 1999; Bennett and Kahn-Harris, 2004; Blackman, 2005; Hesmondhalgh, 2005; Miles, 2000; Muggleton, 2000, 2005). This debate has suffered from weak empirical foundations because what are taken as the classic accounts of youth subcultures before the 1970s, produced by sociologists working at or associated with Birmingham University's Centre for Contemporary Cultural Studies (CCCS) (Hall and Jefferson, 1975; Hebdige, 1979; Mungham and Pearson, 1976), were theoretically rich but were based neither on surveys of representative samples of young people nor adequate ethnography. The second debate has arisen as the capitalist market economy has become global alongside the transformation of former communist countries and much of the old third world into emerging market economies. These changes have occurred alongside the advent of digital information and communications technologies (ICT). The over-arching issues have been whether an outcome is a new kind of youth culture, and whether this is a global youth culture (see Lagree, 2002; Nilan and Feixa, 2006).

Both of these alleged changes are set in a longer-term historical context, and Britain is treated as a case study. Britain is in fact the world's most suitable case. It was the world's first modern industrial society. Thus modern youth cultures have a longer history in Britain than in any other country. Britain has also been among the world's principal sources of modern youth movements and cultural products, rivalled in the twentieth century only by the USA. Britain has also been a major contributor throughout the development of the sociology of youth.

Three general conclusions about youth and leisure are developed throughout this chapter. The first is that historical changes usually take many decades to complete, and that youth cultures formed in different eras can co-exist for long periods of time. The second is that new youth cultures are always built on existing foundations. The third conclusion is that changes typically occur unevenly between different social classes. A change in macro-circumstances may affect one class of young people several decades before affecting another class, or only one class may be affected even in the long-term.

Youth cultures in the nineteenth and early twentieth centuries

Middle class youth cultures

Modern youth cultures have never been specifically, and they were not originally, working class creations. Modern childhood and youth were first institutionalised by the English middle classes. This was due to their adoption of the secondary school as the appropriate place to educate middle class children, and as a route into the middle classes for the upwardly mobile. The education had pre-modern origins. The schools' original basic curriculum had been the study of (English) grammar to which the classics (Latin and ancient Greek languages, literature and cultures) were added, then mathematics and other modern subjects as extras or alternatives. During the nineteenth century nearly all these schools became single-sex. A rigorous academic education became essential for middle class boys from the 1850s when the examination system was adopted to regulate admission to the universities, the civil service, the officer ranks in the armed forces and most professions (see Roach, 1971). Schools for middle class girls typically offered a different curriculum, though from the 1850s some exceptional pioneering girls' schools were insisting that girls were as capable as boys of coping with and benefitting from a rigorous academic education (and competitive team sports also). The most prestigious secondary schools were boarding establishments, and in 1871 they formed themselves into a Headmasters Conference and called themselves the public schools (see Garthorne-Hardy, 1979). Until 1902 all secondary education in Britain was private (none was public in the sense of being state provided), and until the 1944 Education Act payment remained the normal way of qualifying for a secondary education. Thus secondary education kept middle class children apart. During the nineteenth century the English upper class (the landed and titled aristocracy) gradually abandoned its former preference for educating its children at home by private tutor in favour of the public schools. Britain's royal family was among the last to abandon the former practice. The current queen and her (now deceased) sister were the last British royals who never went to school.

During the nineteenth century the secondary schools added team sports to the curriculum. Indeed, these schools and the English universities were the sites where many of these sports were invented. Even when the sports were taken-up by the working class, different classes of children, young people and adults continued to play separately. Public schools competed against other public schools, and universities against universities, not against the elementary school, neighbourhood and workplace-based sides composed of working class players. The 'great schism' in rugby football in 1895 (into the union and league codes) was primarily a class split in England (see Dunning and Sheard, 1979).

Jon Savage (2007) claims that 'teenage' first became a public discourse in Europe from the 1870s. His evidence is from diaries: the diaries of middle class teenagers. In 1904 the American psychologist G. Stanley Hall produced the first edition of his famous text on adolescence. This life stage was said to be triggered by the physical changes of puberty, and characterised by inner-strain and turmoil in the course of building an adult identity. Savage admits that teenager was given what became its internationally recognised meaning in the USA in the 1930s, by when completion of high school – normally a public (state) high school – at age 18/19 was becoming normal throughout the country. It was different in England where education became compulsory nationwide only in 1880, up to age 10, subsequently 12/13 and 14 after the 1918 Education Act. Spending the teenage years in education, at its own preferred type of school, continued to set the English middle class apart.

Middle class children and young people were educated and lived separately from the working class (see Davies, 1992). They lived in their own town and city precincts, in houses that were sufficiently large to need servants (though not necessarily servants who lived in). The master-servant relationship was in fact one of the main points of personal contact between the classes at that time. Domestic work was a major source of employment for working class school-leavers. Middle class children and young people grew up in protected environments. Their conduct was policed by their families and schools. Pupils' misbehaviour and student japes were unlikely to receive attention from the police and courts.

The historian David Fowler (2008) claims that youth culture as a public discourse dates from the 1920s when it was first used to describe the efforts of some undergraduates at Cambridge University to revive earlier folk cultures. The flappers, bohemians and other smart young things of the inter-war years were products of England's secondary schools and universities. The middle class lived separately and led other classes in the development of modern youth cultures. Growing up working class was institutionalised differently and much more slowly in industrial England.

Working class youth

At first, lower class rural child-rearing practices continued when families moved into Britain's expanding industrial towns and cities. Children were reared by their families and neighbourhood communities. The employment of young children in mines and factories was common until the 1840s, but by then there were campaigns to exclude children from the moral and physical hazards of adult workplaces. If both mothers and fathers were employed, this meant that young children were left in the care of grandparents, siblings or neighbours, or left to their own devices. During the nineteenth century it became increasingly common for working class children to be sent to an elementary school. Most were run by churches. The basic curriculum was the so-called 3Rs – reading, 'riting, and 'rithmetic – plus hefty doses of religion, all driven home with corporal punishment, as deemed necessary. Provision for all children to attend an elementary school was made only following the 1870 Education Act, and attendance from age 5–10 became compulsory nationwide only in 1880 (see Hunt, 1979; Wardle, 1974). By then, in some places, a mine or factory had been the main employer for 100 years, but by the 1880s efforts were underway to spread 'bourgeois' family practices among the working class (see David, 1980). This meant schooling the working class child, and also paying males a family wage so that women could be full-time wives and mothers. Up to this point the street had been the normal playground for working class children and young people. Male peers formed territory-based gangs, some of which gained national notoriety for their mischief and more serious criminal exploits. Some historians have interpreted such behaviour as a primitive form of class resistance and struggle (see Humphries, 1981), a practice continued up to the present day by some sociologists, and most famously by Paul Willis (1977).

By the end of the nineteenth century the elementary schools had been joined by church Sunday schools, sports clubs and new youth movements – most prominently the Boys Brigade and subsequently the Boy Scouts – as agencies for the socialisation of children and young people. Most sports clubs and other formal youth provisions were for boys. The prevailing view at that time was that the proper place for a girl was in the home, helping her mother (see Evans, 1965). This continued beyond the Second World War: the actors in all the principal working class youth cultures of that period were males. Teenage girls' cultures were then being formed around music records and romance magazines, practising make-up and dance steps in a 'bedroom culture' (see Griffin, 1984). However, following the 1918 Education Act local authorities began to open mixed-sex, 'social' youth clubs. At that time these were regarded as terribly daring and experimental (see Evans, 1965).

The prime targets of the youth organisations were children and juveniles who were deemed to be at risk during their out-of-school hours, and throughout the years between leaving school and becoming settled in marriages and adult jobs. Some working class school-leavers (mainly boys) were apprenticed and trained for skilled employment. Others were hired in juvenile jobs until they became eligible for adult pay and employment at some point between age 18 and 21 (see Bray, 1912; Freeman, 1914; Urwick, 1904). The authorities' main worry throughout these years was that so many young people remained unattached, apparently unclubbable. Their numbers were probably over-estimated. In 1930 the Social Survey of Merseyside found that 38 per cent of boys and 44 per cent of girls aged 11–17 belonged to an organisation affiliated to the Liverpool Junior Organisations Committee (Jones, 1934), but others would have belonged to unaffiliated clubs, sports teams and churches, and we now know from later research that the numbers who have belonged at some time or another have greatly exceeded those who have been members at one specific point in time.

There was little commercial leisure provision suitable and available for working class children and young people in nineteenth and early twentieth century Britain. There were comics, and those who were interested (mainly boys) and who could afford admission could attend spectator sports events. Pubs and music halls were adult places and out-of-bounds for teenagers. Between the world wars a range of new and attractive leisure services became available – light entertainment radio broadcasting, records of popular music and the cinema. However, at that time the wireless and the gramophone were items of lounge furniture, under adult control. The cinema was different, and extremely popular in all age groups, not just among young people. Adults were the majority in cinema audiences, and young people's holidays away from home (if any) were most likely to be either family holidays or organised by churches or adult-led youth groups. The dance palais was different. This was a young people's playground, but those who attended regularly tended to be 20-somethings who could afford the admission and suitable attire. It was then normal for the middle classes to delay marriage until their late 20s. That said, town and city centres became attractive, glamorous, neon-lit places, and young people of all classes could go uptown, downtown or up west (whatever the local expression) if only to hang around the places of entertainment, shops and street stalls.

At the outbreak of the Second World War, two types of working class youth culture had been constructed in Britain. First, there were the cultures of children and teenagers who attended school regularly and 'did well'. They were typically from respectable working class families where the males worked regularly, probably in higher-paid, skilled working class occupations. The children's behaviour was supervised closely by parents who wanted their young people to succeed at school, and afterwards. The young people would typically join sports clubs, attend Sunday school and youth clubs.

The second type of working class youth culture was street-based. These young people were likely to disengage from education at the earliest opportunity. They would progress from school into juvenile jobs, at risk of unemployment, unlikely ever to rise above semi-skilled occupations. These young people were constantly regarded as 'at risk' by the authorities. Despite changes in the contexts, this second type of working class youth culture has survived to the present day, and it is necessary to know the past in order to understand the present, because there is always a youth cultural heritage for upcoming cohorts of young people to work with. 'Rough' working class youth cultures of the streets have often survived since the nineteenth century in the same localities which have continuously been known for their low educational attainments and high crime rates (see MacDonald and Shildrick, 2007 for a twenty-first century example). Some post-1945 youth cultures may have been classless. The pre-1939 boundary between middle and working class cultures has been all but obliterated. However, certain youth cultures have remained emphatically working class. These have always been non-respectable, 'rough' working class youth cultures. A current example is the 'chavs' who, like many of their predecessors, express combinations of difference, pride and defiance with their street demeanour and distinctive attire (see McCulloch et al., 2006; Nayak, 2006).

Youth cultures in the 1950s and 1960s

The circumstances of Britain's young people changed abruptly after 1945. This became a historical landmark and divide in the development of youth cultures. The change was due to the government's adoption of Keynesian economic management which created and maintained a type of full employment which lasted for thirty years (and has not returned since then). There were labour shortages. School-leavers were in demand and their wage levels rose. It became possible for those who entered non-skilled jobs to advance rapidly to full adult earnings, which themselves were rising in real terms year on year. An outcome was to banish the old juvenile jobs into history and the affluent young worker was born. He or she went 'on board' at home on leaving school and retained a historically unparalleled sum for discretionary spending (Abrams, 1959).

Sociology was also reconstituted after the Second World War. A new research-based yet simultaneously theoretically informed sociology began investigating the consequences of the new mass affluence, including the affluence of the young worker, the new teenage consumer. Meanwhile, an older type of social fact gathering/book-keeping social research continued. Its pre-occupation as regards young people, just as before the war, was the numbers who were unattached to any formal youth organisations. These had new commercial competition (see Jephcott, 1954; Reed, 1950; Ward, 1948; Wilkins, 1955). In 1960 a government enquiry deplored the inability of the youth services to compete with smart coffee bars and glitzy dance halls (Albermarle Report, 1960). One response was an expansion of outreach by detached youth workers (Goetschius and Tash, 1967; Lewis *et al.*, 1974; Morse, 1965).

As before the war, the numbers who were unattached, and the extent of any decline in membership, were being exaggerated. At age 16, only 16 per cent of boys and 15 per cent of girls in the 1946 birth cohort had never belonged to a youth club (Douglas, 1968). In the early 1970s Bone (1972) reported that just 26 per cent of 14–20 year olds were currently attending a youth club, but 68 per cent had belonged at some time or another. In 1995 a survey for the Department for Education (1995) found that just 31 per cent of 11–15 year olds were currently participating: this was slightly but not very far beneath the level of participation recorded in in the Social Survey of Merseyside in 1930. A subsequent government survey of 12–19 year olds found that just 20 per cent had attended a youth club or church group in the last six months, but 16 per cent had done some type of voluntary work, 42 per cent had played sport in a club, 35 per cent had taken part in a drama or music group, and 28 per cent had acted in a play or show. The same survey found that 28 per cent had been to a gig or pop concert (Park *et al.*, 2005). The government response was by that time traditional: it declared an urgent need to make it easier for young people to take part in 'positive activities' (Department for Education and Skills, 2005).

A related obsession since the 1960s has been to involve more young people in sport. In 1960 the Wolfenden Report attributed low participation to the limited appeal of Victorian era swimming facilities, water-logged playing fields and waterless changing rooms. Until the 1960s it was rare for girls to play any sport regularly. The only sport played by a substantial number of boys was football, and most dropped out soon after leaving school (Emmett, 1971). However, from the 1960s a new generation of indoor sport and leisure centres was being constructed throughout the country, and participation in sport rose steadily. School children's participation in sport has been monitored regularly since the early 1990s. At that time the vast majority were already playing several hours of sport each week, in and out of school. Every successive enquiry has recorded young people playing even more sport, and on each occasion the response of the sports authorities and government ministers has been to declare that it is still not enough (Sport England, 2003).

Working class youth cultures: the teddy boys and their successors

Ever since the 1950s it has been young people's uses of their new (in the 1950s) affluence that has attracted media attention, and also the attention of sociologists with an interest in youth cultures. The statutory school-leaving age was raised from 14 to 15 in 1947, and until the end of the 1960s 15 was the age when most young people quit full-time education for ever. Those who entered non-skilled jobs could progress quickly to adult earnings. They were the big spenders – the main market for consumer goods and services targeted at young people. Since then young people have become an even larger market for consumer goods and services. Today they are unlikely to hold full-time jobs at age 15 or 16, but they are still spending. The cash is from part-time, then later-on full-time jobs, parents and credit. Also, consumer cultures have been extended downwards into childhood, largely by aggressive consumer advertising, and also upwards due to higher typical ages of first marriages and parenthood. It was different in the 1950s when it was only affluent young workers who could afford regular purchases of fashion clothing, and the outcome at that time was a succession of distinctive styles, all worn by young men. Teddy Boys were followed by the more modern 'Italian' apparel of short-jacketed suits. Affluent teenagers could afford personal transport. The mods and rockers of the early 1960s were distinguished by their dress and also by whether they rode scooters or motor bikes. Skinhead coiffure and 'bovver boots' were associated with hanging out in town centres and on football terraces.

These new types of young people and their preferred music (typically a version of rock 'n roll) attracted intense media scrutiny. Their arrival was associated in media discourse with rising youth crime rates. The recorded crime rate doubled in the 1950s, then doubled again in the 1960s, again in the 1970s, and once more in the 1980s, before stabilising in the 1990s then subsiding. The new youth cultures were also associated (by the media) with rising rates of teenage sexual activity, teen pregnancies and births to unwed mothers. The proportion of births outside wedlock rose to 5 per cent during the 1950s – a very modest figure judged against twenty-first century rates, but alarming in the mid-twentieth century. Teenagers with decently paid jobs could afford to marry if they needed to do so. Typical ages of marriages fell, and a high proportion of teenage brides were already pregnant.

Sociological research showed that the media were correct in associating the new youth cultures with the long-standing 'at risk' group of young people. Being 'on scene' in terms of dress, hairstyle and musical tastes was associated with being anti-school. Teenagers who attended grammar schools, around a quarter of all young people who passed a selection test at age 11 (see below), and those in the examination streams in secondary moderns (the main alternative for those who were not offered places at grammar schools), were usually 'straight' or 'square' (see Sugarman, 1967). It was the same in America at that time (see Coleman, 1961), but the American context was different. By the 1950s over 80 per cent of young Americans were graduating from high school at age 18 or 19. By the end of the 1960s around a half of the age group progressed into college. The young people who failed to graduate high school were drop-outs, and they struggled to establish themselves in employment. Their chronically high rate of unemployment was an ingredient in the 'social dynamite', said to be capable of exploding at any time in America's inner cities (Conant, 1965). In Britain the young people who quit school at age 15 were the majority. It was unnecessary to gain any qualifications to obtain a job in which swift progression to adult earnings was possible. These teenagers could afford to be 'on scene', and could be married and setting up their own households, if they wished to do so, while 'straights' were still in classrooms. Those who were on scene could believe that they were the real winners (as in Willis, 1977).

The initial attempts by UK sociologists to explain the new youth cultures opted for a deviance paradigm (see, for example, Cohen, 1972). This was contested initially by US sociologists who claimed that participation in youth cultures was best understood as a process of continuous socialisation (Elkin and Westley, 1955, 1957; Turner, 1964). This was also the view of the UK's subsequent CCCS sociologists who added that the continuous socialisation was invariably 'classed' (see Cohen, 1976; Willis, 1977).

When the classical accounts of Britain's post-war youth cultures are read today, Teddy Boys and their successors may be mistaken as representing the whole of working class youth of the era. The fact is that most working class young people did not align with any subculture but, if questioned, insisted that they were just 'normal' or 'ordinary' (see Jenkins, 1983; Brown, 1987). One of 'ordinary' young people's big leisure problems throughout the 1950s and 1960s was the sheer boredom of their lives at home and outside (Jephcott, 1954, 1967; Leigh, 1971).

Throughout the 1950s and 1960s the pre-war division between respectable/ straight and rough working class youth cultures remained intact. The spectacular subcultures of that era were reborn versions in a more affluent age of the pre-war street and gang cultures. However, there was a crucial difference. The post-war subcultures were associated with types of music and dress that became instantly recognised throughout the country and beyond. This meant that anyone could become a Ted just by purchasing and wearing the right attire. These types could suddenly appear from 'nowhere' in any small town or village. This was different: it was necessary to have been reared and to live in the territory to belong to a pre-war gang.

Middle class youth cultures

In retrospect we can now see that the 1950s and 1960s were transitional decades. These were the final years in which middle and working class youth cultures remained a world apart. This was because children and young people on working and middle class life trajectories continued to be reared and educated separately. Secondary education was made universal with places available in state schools for everyone following the 1944 Education Act, but around 7 per cent of children (a figure that has remained unchanged to the present day) continued to be educated privately, and pupils in the state education system were divided at age 11 into those allocated to grammar schools while most of the remainder received their secondary education in a new kind of school, the secondary modern. At the grammar schools all pupils were expected to stay until at least age 16 (though it was legally possible to leave at 15 until 1972). Some grammar school pupils stayed on until age 18, gaining the qualifications needed to enter university. They were the sixth formers who became school prefects, role models for younger pupils. Staying on meant deferring gratifications (a much used expression at that time). These teenagers could not match the spending power, and did not have the same status in their families, as 15-year-old leavers from the secondary moderns, especially those who could expect to be earning adult wages by age 18. This kept the middle and working classes apart. There were usually no sporting or cultural contacts between grammar schools and secondary moderns.

Middle class youth grew up separately – physically and socially – but they were exposed to the new working class youth cultures which began to seep into the grammar schools. Parents and teachers might have been opposed and appalled, but it was impossible to prevent pupils styling their hair and wearing their uniforms in ways that expressed defiant cultural affiliations. It was impossible to prevent pupils listening to the latest 'hits' on Radio Luxembourg despite the BBC, the monopoly radio broadcaster within the UK at that time, refusing to dedicate an entire channel to the hit parade until 1967 when Radio 1 was launched. In any case, the expansion in the number of grammar school and university places made it inevitable that many of their pupils and students would be first generation. Allocation to a grammar school and progression to university continued to be class related, but even so the volume of upward mobility through these channels was increasing. The shape of the occupational structure was changing. The proportion of professional and management-grade jobs was increasing at a pace which meant that throughout the second half of the twentieth century the majority of employees in these grades were upwardly mobile (Roberts, 2011a). During this process, from the 1940s onwards, working class pupils and students were importing aspects of their cultures into the grammar schools and universities. Thus began the transformation of the entire middle class from cultural highbrows (or at least not lowbrows) into cultural omnivores (see Bennett *et al.*, 2009; Eijck, 1999; Peterson, 1992).

In the universities the effect was not to turn students into Teddy Boys and rockers. Rather, they adopted their own fashions, usually blue denim, originally a fabric of the labouring classes. An extended historical perspective enables us to see that the student cultures of the 1960s were reworking and updating youth cultures that had existed on university campuses before the Second World War. The beatniks and hippies who suddenly appeared (from nowhere) were reworking student efforts to recover cultures from a pre-materialist age that had been present on campuses at least since the 1920s (Fowler, 2008). The politicos of the 1960s were reworking and updating another long-running strand in student culture. They were successors to students who supported or tried to break the General Strike (which lasted for ten days) that was called by the Trade Union Congress in 1926, those who joined communist and fascist movements in the 1930s, who fought in Spain with the International Brigade, and the members of the Oxford Union (the student debating society) who voted for (in greater numbers than voted against) a proposition in 1933 that they would not fight for king and country. Students in the 1960s took up the political issues of their own day: nuclear disarmament, anti-apartheid, civil rights and opposition to the Vietnam War. University campuses were birth sites of Women's Lib and second-wave feminism. Most students in the 1960s never took part in a sit-in or demonstration (see Blackstone *et al.*, 1970), just as most early school-leavers did not become Teds, skinheads, mods or rockers. That said, it might still be argued that the actors in the spectacular youth cultures were saying significant things about the circumstances, trends and mindsets of the upcoming members of their entire respective classes.

Since the 1970s

Those who claim that there has been a shift from the age of classic youth subcultures (the 1950s and 60s) into a culturally different (hence post-subcultural) age are correct.

- Differences between middle and working class youth cultures have lessened.
- In the process the overwhelming majority of young people have become part of some youth scene.
- Youth cultures have become more diverse, fluid and hybrid. Before the 1970s it was possible to list a limited number of subcultural types. Subsequently youth cultures have become too fluid and too numerous to list and count.
- Since the 1970s most youth cultures have not nested on social class or any other pre-existent social divisions.

However, just as there were continuities between pre-1939 and post-1945 youth cultures, including the middle-working class divide, the above developments that have made post-1960s youth cultures different have been partly outcomes of trends that were underway in the 1950s and 1960s.

Change in education

During the 1960s and 1970s all grammar schools and secondary moderns in Wales and Scotland, and most of those in England, were merged into comprehensive secondary schools. This meant mixing children from all social class origins, and those heading towards all social class destinations. The former division between working and middle class youth cultures could not survive this change. The only class-based youth cultures that have been able to remain intact and clearly apart are those of an upper class, especially those who attend the prestigious fee-paying boarding schools, and at the other extreme a 'rough' lower working class (sometimes since the 1970s described as an underclass or socially excluded) that disengages psychologically from education, often attending school only intermittently during the final years of nominally compulsory education, then faces long-term difficulties in obtaining secure adult employment due to lacking useful qualifications.

Cultural production and distribution

Alongside the mixing of formerly separate social classes of young people in education, there has been a post-1960s expansion and diversification of the production and distribution of cultural products that appeal to young people. In 1973 the BBC lost its radio monopoly. Former 'pirates' who had broadcast 24/7 pop music into Britain from just outside territorial waters were invited onshore and became licensed independent stations using the FM frequencies. Also in the 1970s new technologies were making it possible to produce commercial quality recorded music in 'garage' studios. Audio cassettes could be produced and marketed (often at gigs where the music was played by the artists) by 'independents' (the so-called *indies*). Thus the major record companies forfeited their former market dominance and could remain industry leaders only by absorbing independents and/or signing their artists and diversifying their own catalogues. Hybrid styles and sounds have been created. Thus cultural products have become a resource with which individuals can signal affiliations with wider groups while simultaneously expressing a unique individuality. Rather than groups pre-defined by locality and/or social class acquiring distinctive tastes, the tastes have created their own scenes and crowds composed of young people from diverse backgrounds. These scenes can form and dissolve within a single summer or may last for much longer (see Thornton, 1995; Malbon, 1999). Meanwhile, certain very distinctive youth cultures have endured for decades. These include skinheads, and also the Goths who tend to attract young people on middle class life trajectories (see Hodkinson, 2002, 2011). The ability of some youth fashions to become mainstream, and for young people's music to become family entertainment, enable some youthful tastes and attire to be retained into adulthood which, needless to say, consistently diminishes their attractiveness to new cohorts of young people.

The extension of youth

Coincidentally rather than as cause or effect of the above changes, youth has become a longer life stage. Prolonged education and deferred entry to employment have played minor parts compared with the contraceptive pill. This was first marketed in 1961. Its use then spread gradually, first among married women, and then among young single women from the 1970s onwards. This has enabled marriage and parenthood to be deferred for years, indefinitely if desired, after becoming sexually active. Marriage is now more likely to follow than to precede parenthood, and both are normally preceded by a period of unmarried cohabitation (see Ermisch and Francesconi, 1999).

Housing careers in today's youth life stage typically involve a series of intermediate steps between being a child in one's parents' home and establishing a new child-rearing household. Young people leave their parents' dwellings to live singly or in shared housing (typically rented) prior to becoming sexually cohabiting couples with their own places (see Heath and Kenyon, 2001). Before the 1970s it was not uncommon for young couples to leave their respective parents' homes, marry and begin life in their own marital home, and maybe for both to lose their virginity, all within a single day (Leonard, 1980). These steps have subsequently been stretched over many years.

An effect has been to merge teenage and young singles/couples scenes in a life stage that now extends from teens through the 20s and often into the 30s. Hence the creation of new consumer products such as 18–30 holiday packages. Meanwhile, as indicated above, youth has been starting earlier, largely as a result of 24/7 TV and the new media which market youth fashions and music to the pre-teens. An outcome is that today's youth cultures are multi-graded by age. Mature 16-year-olds will not purchase kids' fashions and music. Those who are 18 plus congregate in adult places from which 16-year-olds are supposed to be excluded. However, every age group supplies role models for younger people, and the extension of the youth life stage has led to the insertion of former adult-only practices into teenage life. This happened initially with alcohol. Youth scenes in the 1950s were alcohol-free. Emerging skiffle groups played in coffee bars. The Liverpool Cavern, where the Beatles played in the early 1960s, was dry. By the 1970s fun pubs were opening, catering for young fun-seekers, and by the early 1970s a half of Britain's 16-year-olds had consumed alcohol during the previous month (Fogelman, 1976).

Continuities

Amid the above changes we must note significant continuities. First, youth is still a transitional life stage. Young people no longer go on scene, find a mate, then depart for ever (Hollands, 1995). Several such relationships are likely to form and dissolve while the actors remain part of young singles/couples scenes. The life stage has been extended, but its characteristic practices are still transitional rites of passage even if they now usually extend over many years although, in principle, they could all be completed within a week (as argued by Northcote, 2006).

The second continuity is the preservation of class relationships and divisions. Particular kinds of music and dress may no longer be associated with the middle and working classes respectively. Today it is only the drop-outs, the NEETs (descendants of the pre-war 'roughs'), who are excluded at one extreme, and at the other the upper class with their hunt balls, regattas and so on. Higher education students and young workers wear similar fashions and both groups go downtown pubbing and clubbing. However, in all cities there are pubs that are used mainly by students (Hollands, 2002), who still have their own student sport facilities, plus religious, political and purely social clubs. Even when they go to the same places, young people on different social class trajectories tend to stick among friends like themselves (MacRae, 2004). If this was not the case it would be impossible to explain the still powerful tendency for social class like to marry like (Blossfeld and Timm, 2003).

We should note that the blurring and blending of middle and working class youth cultures has occurred alongside the formation of an omnivorous middle class in which individuals typically mix lowbrow, middlebrow and highbrow tastes. Meanwhile, the working class remains typically univore (lowbrow and middlebrow) (Bennett et al., 2009). There are still types of (highbrow) cultural consumption, just as there are some (relatively expensive) sports, that keep the middle class separate, while omnivorousness itself acts as a mark of distinction (Erikson, 1996). Meanwhile, middle class youth have become the main producers of all kinds of youth cultural products, and the most active in all kinds of youth scenes (Roberts and Parsell, 1994). The classlessness of present-day youth cultures is of a kind that is compatible with the reproduction over time of class divisions and relationships.

Globalisation and the new media

These interacting developments have affected most aspects of people's lives in every country in the world, but always under specific country and local conditions. In the case of youth cultures, these specifics have been within a broad contrast between the West and the rest.

Globalisation refers to increased flows between countries of goods, services, capital, information and people. Young people are affected by all these flows. Young people from all countries are on the move. In the West they sometimes travel for education, sometimes to work, maybe while backpacking around the world during 'gap years', but most often as tourists. The effect has been to make experience of other countries into normal parts of childhood and youth. Young people move from poorer to richer countries to work for more extended periods, and may settle indefinitely. This has created some new (or even more than in the past) cosmopolitan cities in the West. In 2010 40 per cent of the working age population in London had been born outside the UK (Centre for Economic

Performance, 2010). In other parts of Britain there are hardly any immigrants, but all university students today find themselves part of multi-national, multi-ethnic, multi-faith academic communities. Such environments have become sufficiently common for Ulrich Beck and Elizabeth Beck-Gernsheim (2009) to claim that methodological nationalism in the social sciences is now outdated.

New media owe their new features to their uses of the latest information and communication technologies (ICT). These have accelerated global flows of text, images and sound, and hence cultural products such as music, films and news. This has made cultural production more multi-centric rather than West (or America) centric (Hesmondhalgh, 2007). The new media enable people in all parts of the world to belong to transnational networks based on educational, occupational, political, religious, sporting or any other common interests. Mobile phone take-up by young people soars from zero to near saturation within a few years of the service becoming available in a region. This has happened all over the world. Ownership becomes essential in order to be 'in touch'. Internet take-up is similar. Internet cafes appear on high streets as soon as there is a local service provider, then within a few years the cafes are closing as PC ownership spreads.

Western-type youth cultures have been initially formed in the emerging market economies during the age of globalisation and the latest new media. Youth has thereby become a very different life stage than under communism or when people were relatively isolated in rural villages or shanty towns on the edges of cities. It has been exciting in the emerging market economies to be young amid all these developments; to have been among the first to experience the chance to join transnational online networks and to be able to access the world's top sport, and the latest released films and music. Youth and leisure have been modernised simultaneously.

The recent changes have been experienced differently in the West. In the UK globalisation and the new media have nested on youth cultures with a long history, and their impact has been less dramatic than in new industrial countries and other emerging market economies. The movement of people which has increased the number and size of ethnic minorities in many places has simply added another division and a further source of diversity in cultural production and consumption. The internet has enabled young and older people to add another dimension to their participation in occupational, educational, sporting and other groups. The internet and the mobile phone are additional, and now essential ways of being able to maintain contact with friends. Recorded music can be downloaded using new media, often free of charge, which may have long-term devastating implications for branches of the commercial industry (David, 2010). However, these new features and options have been overshadowed by other developments which have filtered the impact of globalisation and the new media.

Globalisation and the new media are affecting multiple aspects of young people's lives in most countries, but in the UK their impact on young people's leisure is mainly indirect and modest compared with their impact on the economy and labour market. It has become more difficult for young people to obtain jobs. Risks have risen that they will be unable to match the occupational attainments and living standards of their parents (Roberts, 2012). After starting to search for full-time work, young people are at risk of spending years under-employed, and this is now regardless of educational level. The labour market is dividing young people into an upper middle class, mostly higher education graduates who still manage to obtain 'traditional' graduate jobs directly on finishing their studies, a squeezed middle, and a lower class. It was for less than 30 years after 1945 that unqualified early school-leavers could advance quickly to adult earnings, ahead of the rest of their age group, feel that they were winning, and feature as the central actors in their era's youth cultures.

Conclusion

This chapter set out to interrogate claims that there was a major change of character in Britain's youth cultures after the 1950s and 1960s, and that another has been triggered by the joint impact of globalisation and ICT-based new media. The conclusions are that there was indeed a major change after the 1950s and 1960s, but that, unlike in the new industrial countries and other emerging markets, globalisation and the new media have not triggered an equivalent transformation. Also, adopting an extended historical perspective has shown that the post-war youth cultures were not the first, but were built within divisions that had been created in pre-war youth cultures.

Three further conclusions of more general significance follow. The first is that history always matters. Youth cultures are transmitted from cohort to cohort and the impact of any change in circumstances depends on the heritage that is the subject of the impact. Second, the meanings of youth cultural practices are largely products of the contexts. The social class, gender and ethnicity of the actors always impart much of the meaning into their actions. Thus the wider society's reactions to the youth cultures of the 1950s owed much to these being working class youth cultures. Third, youth cultures develop within divisions among young people that are created by the economy-based class structure, the organisation of education, and related family practices. The significance of how young people dress and their favoured melodies and lyrics cannot be found by focusing narrowly upon, then deconstructing these 'texts', or by delving deeply into the minds of the actors. History and context always have over-arching significance.

PART III
Lifelong learning

13

REFLECTIVE LEISURE, FREEDOM AND IDENTITY

Hayden Ramsay

Reflection on the meaning of leisure has taken place over many centuries. The topic of the motivation behind our leisure choices, however, is a matter of fairly recent debate. Leisure studies, psychology and anthropology often focus on the motivational question, which sometimes leaves the question of meaning unaddressed. To debate meaning is to raise philosophical questions. These might include the nature and purpose of leisure, its place within a broadly well-shaped and satisfactory human life, the ethical and social questions to which leisure choices give rise, the opportunity leisure provides for bridging rest and contemplation on the one hand with the benefits of a life of activity on the other, the relation of leisure to work and the ways in which leisure and labour might enable or undermine each other.

The philosophy and (more rarely) theology of leisure is a useful position to explore: grounding questions of meaning philosophically can provide a reasoned basis for addressing and critiquing questions of motivation, access, impact and so on. Beginning with the reflections of Aristotle in ancient Greece through great medieval thinkers such as St Thomas Aquinas up to more contemporary work such as that inspired by the philosopher-commentator Josef Pieper, a small but growing school of thought on the meaning, ethics and spirituality of leisure exists. Key to this approach is the broad thought that leisure is not just about being busily active so as to fill up our time. Rather, leisure is activity that offers tranquillity, revival and recreation, while also developing our tastes and skills for the activities we leisurely perform. This is a thought that will strike some as obvious, but which serves to challenge some contemporary accounts of leisure and leisure practices. The philosophy of leisure implies that people will not realise the full potential of their own leisure, and so of themselves, if they see leisure simply as desire-driven or consumer-driven or mere distraction from labour or the choice simply to increase their personal levels of energy (or of sluggishness). Leisure can serve and accomplish all these goals, but leisure possesses a more profound meaning and structure. How we spend our leisure is therefore a matter of quite serious decision-making and choice.

In this chapter I begin with a classic source – St Thomas Aquinas's *Summa Theologiae* – which I use as an introduction to thinking about boredom and the possibility of meaning in life. I then look at Pieper's account of leisure, in particular leisure's connection with development of a reflective attitude in life. I argue for this view against alternatives. I also look at the role of leisure in enhancing our freedom and helping us express our personal identities in a social world.

One

In his great 'Treatise on Charity' in the *Summa Theologiae* St Thomas Aquinas, sharpest of the philosopher-theologians of the high-medieval period, identifies sloth as an enemy of inner joy. Inner joy according to St Thomas is one of the happy effects of practising true charity: loving God and loving things in the world because of what they reveal about God (Gilby and O'Brien 1964: II–II, 35). Simply put, a sense of charity directs our virtuous acts towards their true end: communion, and ultimately communion with God; and an effect of this communion is spiritual joy. This joy in life and in love can be undermined by various bad acts motivated by human vices – for example, envy which undermines the joy we take in the good of our neighbours, and sloth which undermines the joy we receive from loving God.

This notion of sloth is interesting in coming to think through leisure. Aquinas explains (Gilby and O'Brien 1964, 35, 1) that sloth involves a sense of weariness about daily work, a sluggishness that disinclines us from directed activity and useful employment. This is more than just laziness: sloth is oppressive and sorrowful. Sloth is a serious spiritual and social problem. I suspect that a number of those who pronounce themselves agnostic do so because they find the effort required to think out or pray about ultimate questions debilitating and wearying. We are increasingly slothful about the intellectual life and the value of ideas; hence, the decline in the habits of social philosophising and theologising. What should be joyful and intriguing too often becomes dull and difficult: it's just all too hard, or too boring. Thus with sloth there generally comes agnosticism towards hard beliefs, and not just belief in God.

But sloth is not only a problem about religion. Slothfulness can manifest itself in social life, family life, work life, even leisure – people can and do lead slothful leisure lives. How can this be? One explanation is based on the modern phenomenon of boredom.

We lead our lives in a material universe and learn of it through the senses; yet we are more than mere matter and we are capable of extra-sensory experiences such as reason, love and joy. If we try to live for too long without matter-transcending experiences, we feel boredom and the subsequent need for novelty and stimulation (a cycle which consumerist ideology applauds and consumerist economics serves). Leisure should lead us back to some elements of transcendent experience in life: a sense of who we really are, why we matter and what else truly matters and has worth. Over-zealous attempts to drag leisure back into the realm of mere matter set us up for more boredom.

Commercialisation of leisure often seeks to package unimaginative opportunities for stimulation as if they are great novelties. Of course not all leisure should be high-minded and intellectualist. But where there is repeated denial of transcendence the inner joy in life spoken of by St Thomas will vanish. We are creatures capable of love, of seeing goodness and wonder in the material world around us, and to live without this is great loss.

A materialistic attitude towards leisure sees leisure as just 'spare time' or 'my time' when in fact it is not about time at all but about an attitude of mind that can regard even simple daily activities as of ultimate significance and filled with potential for joy and interest. In certain moods we can listen to a radio programme, make a cup of tea or watch the washing drying in the wind and feel quite 'at one' with everything; not just at peace but with a deep contentment and sense of joy that everything, including ourselves, is presently directed just as it should be. At other times of course the same pattern of daily activities may fill us with a staggering level of boredom.

I want to think a little about the nature of modern boredom and the potential of leisure as a tonic. I will go on to look at the question of personal freedom and identity and the contribution that leisure which is truly a recreation of the person can make towards enhancing our experience of each of these.

Peter Toohey describes common sources of boredom: confinement, monotony, repetition, surfeit, ennui, melancholy, existential doubt (Toohey 2011, Ch. 1). Clearly boredom is one of the human moods: emotional experiences which often have complex causes but usually lack objects (thus whereas an emotion such as jealousy of Fred is *about* the person whose gifts I envy, about Fred, a mood is generally not about anyone or anything in particular). Lars Svendsen notes that boredom 'normally arises when we cannot do what we want to do, or have to do something we do not want to do' (Svendsen 2010, p. 19). This sounds true, but the fact is we are often in these positions *without* being bored: the causality of boredom is complex and need not involve any direct object. Clearly too boredom can be more or less frequent, intense, prolonged and so on; certainly not all boredom amounts to or engenders the intense spiritual sloth Aquinas mentions. Boredom can be brought on by exposing people to confinement, narrow range of choices, diminished opportunities, repeated experiences, frequently disappointed hopes etc. Individuals and whole societies can manufacture these conditions of boredom. Thus part of the paradox of consumerist societies is that while they demonstrate novelty, possibilities, invention, range of choices which are all benefits, they must also create the reverse of these since privation is needed to stimulate continued purchase. These societies then have a natural stake in boredom.

Can we avoid boredom today? Yes, but this requires moral and spiritual effort, particularly in affluent societies. As earth-bound animals living as many of us do in overcrowded cities we are confined; as citizens who choose professions or vocations that then structure all or most of our lives we are exposed to monotony and repetition; with repetition comes surfeit and if we do not effectively fight this, ennui, melancholy and at the last, doubt and despair. Developing a frame of mind so that sometimes at least drinking tea in contentment while watching the washing dry is a joy to us neutralises the threat of boredom that the material condition and need for novelty brings and reminds us that we are wholly physical but not totally physical. We are made for receiving joy through loving people and things because of what they reveal to us about the goodness at the root of everything. We are not made to be bored and slothful. Avoidance of boredom requires great effort in societies that are affluent (and hence interested in the material) yet losing any serious understanding of religion (and hence uninterested in the spiritual).

In ordinary actions – and sometimes in more elevated actions too – we can still find what Svendsen calls the 'personal meaning' which all of us seek in the post-Romantic period (Svendsen 2010, pp. 31–32). The temptation, however, is that to escape the onset of boredom we turn not to what is simpler and more meaningful but to recreational opportunities made available to us by those with a stake in satisfying us quickly so that we soon become bored again and must invest once more in the recreational product. Society tempts us with meaningless activities. The very fact that we are bored means that it appears harder to do what is actually simpler: to alter our frame of mind and start to see daily activities as end-directed and enriching in themselves. It seems more effective to take the manufactured solution which gives a sense of quick fix but which over time is more laborious and less satisfying. It seems likely that the perceived ease and the undoubted success of consumerist responses to boredom is cause not only of spiritual sloth but also of the avalanche in addiction (to real or cyber sex, bad food and harmful drugs), which characterises our world.

So boredom is common because we suffer all the weaknesses of our material nature while due to our matter-transcending minds we cannot be truly satisfied by this but only by insight into the truth of things. A satisfying life then will acknowledge our material limits (life will include confinement and repetition) but will also include times of reflection together with practices of charity, which will hopefully prompt inner experiences of joy, peace and mercy, the benefits St Thomas promised to the actively charitable. Where reflection and charity do develop even confinement and repetition can grow closer to expressing the reflective and charitable life. This is well reflected in the motivation behind certain monastic houses with their voluntary confinement and repeated routines of prayer and work. At their best, these houses achieved just the balance for a satisfactory life: an ideal 'work/life balance' centuries before the concept was framed. Svendsen argues that a collapse in traditional structures of meaning explains the growth of the need for *personal* meaning, and that the impossibility of a fully satisfying personal meaning ushers in the phenomenon of boredom for modernity (Svendsen 2010, pp. 153–154). This seems basically right to me, but where I disagree with Svendsen is in respect of his view of the impossibility of re-introducing traditional structures of meaning. The monasteries are fewer in number but they have not quite gone and opportunities for retreat from the world, albeit temporary, continue to attract even the non-religious. As inspiration for a new attitude towards leisure the monasteries and their secular counterparts are still potent. Augustine and Aquinas in their different ways indicate that full meaning for human persons rests in communion with God; and I think that study of their arguments for this traditional source of meaning suggests a view that is logically compelling and psychologically attractive.

Two

Classic writers see leisure as not only remedy for sloth or boredom but also as opportunity to encounter the divine, grasp spiritual truth and experience personal illumination. In this section I will build on some of the work of Josef Pieper, a mid-twentieth-century philosopher, to indicate the potential leisure contains for a good human life.

For Aristotle, leisure functions not only as personal recovery time but as an actual goal of civil life. Societies and individuals strive and labour and save precisely so as to achieve time for leisure (see discussion in Ramsay 2005 Ch.1). And what is this leisure? At its purest, it is freedom from the mundane and material; and, argues Aristotle, when we are in this condition the natural result for the human person is to contemplate. Freedom from cares, needs and worries means we can let the mind soar (it can of course sink, thus we need to develop some virtues of leisure, a solid set of inner resources, as opposed to developing vices of leisure). Contemplation is for Aristotle the key to the most perfectly happy life and it is also the best consequence of leisure; hence, leisure has a key role in increasing human happiness.

There is surely truth in this view. Much of life directs us towards instrumental activities ('I must do this because if I don't, I won't achieve that …') and social conformity ('I must do this because doing the other would feel embarrassing and look weird …'). From the commuter's morning wait until the quiet end of day TV and the gentle anxiety about how to 'fill' the weekend we sit within a means-end nexus. Self-directed people will park moments or activities aside from this nexus so that they can quietly reflect on their life, their loves, their week, their work, their world and their own place within the world. Unwise people, particularly if post-religious, deny themselves this leisure – often to find the need asserting itself vigorously. No one can escape the need to answer the most basic and 'philosophical' questions for themselves (Who am I? Where did I come from? Is there any truth, or is it all opinion? Is there a purpose to my life? A God? Life after death? Meaning despite suffering …?). And if we are insufficiently self-directed to acknowledge this contemplation in our leisure time, the questions will haunt us and announce themselves dramatically, and often at times of stress or distress when we are least likely to think clearly or give a good answer.

Pieper's conception of leisure involves such periods of calm, time away from urgency, the opportunity to reflect calmly on the world and ourselves (Pieper 1998). For Pieper, the origin of this approach to leisure is Scriptural. In the Bible one day was spent by God quietly reflecting on his great work of creation: He rested. Pieper's suggestion is that we should all take the time after our work to do the same. We should rest and reflect (we should 'study to be quiet', 1 *Thessalonians* 4: 11). Modern people would benefit greatly from a re-emergence of the sense of the sacredness of the Sabbath, a weekly time set aside, ideally for contemplation.

This reflective rest does not mean just doing nothing or navel-gazing. Indeed, reflection often happens most effectively through vigorously performing other activities that we individually find restful: exercise, creating or appreciating imaginative work, study, prayer, the company of loved ones, games and play (Ramsay 2005 pp. 42–49). Of course these activities can also be performed frantically, laboriously or as purely instrumental means to some other ends. But the point is that we *can* jog, dance, sing, cook, read, pray, play purely as activities of contemplation, in a way that frees our minds to reflect restfully and without pain on questions that matter to us, questions of meaning.

Pieper was concerned to explain that true culture and respect for human dignity involve a commitment to spiritually rewarding leisure. His specific targets were totalitarianism and collectivism and his focus was on a renewal of culture after the terrible first half of the twentieth century. His project was to reclaim leisure from the sort of decadent indulgence with which the Marxists regarded it and to critique the view of leisure as vice taken by capitalists (over) fuelled by the work-ethic. Today, we are probably at the other extreme: with Aristotle we see leisure as the rightful goal of our working lives, but unlike Aristotle we now struggle to connect this longed for leisure with any form of contemplative ideal.

The project of taking seriously Pieper's view and the tradition it represents is undermined where contemplation is seen as irrelevant, remote or over-ascetic. This is often the case in post-religious societies, particularly if those societies also possess an anti-intellectual, overtly pragmatic ethos. Hence, it is important to combine Pieper's spiritual and human insight into our transcendent needs with an account of the other, more familiar aspects of leisure – play, fun, rest, recovery, relaxation, recreation. Such a broader account should link up with material routinely explored in psychology, sociology, cultural studies, sports and exercise science and leisure studies. This would undoubtedly make the concept of a more reflective leisure more palatable. But this effort would be useless if it made contemplation attractive only by disguising or falsifying the concept, treating it as a minor element.

To discuss possibilities we can distinguish two distinct and incompatible models of leisure: contemplation through a variety of activities performed in order to let the mind soar; and contemplation as filling one's free time just as one chooses. These are incompatible because the first defines leisure activity by the goal of contemplation and the second strives not to define leisure activity at all.

The justification of the contemplative view of leisure consists in an account of the human person and the human good that includes contemplation as an unavoidable fact of our nature and a necessity for our well-being. As I have argued elsewhere, the theory that best provides this justification is a version of classical natural law theory (Ramsay 2005, Ch. 3). Meanwhile, the justification of the free-time view of leisure consists not only in a philosophical account but also sociological and psychological accounts. The philosophical account consists in one of a cluster of views of the person, human value and society. All views in this cluster have in common the following two features: that the nature of the human good is to be determined by the individual for his or herself, and that that determination is subject to no external limitations except social utility ('harm no others') and social justice ('cause no unjust social burden'). These two features can philosophically justify the view of leisure as free time: work out for yourself how to spend your leisure but ensure it harms no one and creates no unjust social burdens. So justified, this view of leisure has naturally led to a plethora of leisure opportunities judged to be harmless and not unjustly burdensome (debatable though these points may be in connection with specific contemporary leisure activities). And what is wrong with that?

To answer that question we might take one of the very common contemporary leisure activities – shopping, computer games, watching TV, eating out, clubbing … Shopping, for example, is a key leisure activity for many people. It is of high instrumental value (few people can take care of themselves without shopping for some items regularly) but it also provides other forms of value to people: social environment, aesthetic appreciation (design, display colour, music), choice, sense of belonging, information, sense of purpose. What can be wrong with shopping as leisure? The answer is nothing at all as an individual activity – but everything in the world if this is a key activity by which a society aims to create and express its culture and judge itself.

The social environment of shopping is one of strangers: the space is public but commercially operated; design, display, colour and music are actually marketing, directed towards selling as much as possible; choice is free but from a narrow range that market forces have determined as fashionable; the sense of belonging is genuine – at least in shopping malls with their various types of spaces or traditional markets with their conversations – but the community is random, derived from those who happen to gather at any time, and divided into sellers, buyers and those rather charmingly called window-shoppers (or more likely today unemployed people, social misfits, people living on the streets or without homes); information is largely restricted to labels; sense of purpose is the need to possess – which quickly reveals itself as the need to use up so as to be able to replace; it all takes place inside and has no connection to nature, God's 'other revelation' about which human beings are naturally contemplative. Above all is the sense that the proportion of the superficial to the meaningful in leisure shopping is extremely unfavourable. There is little depth of cultural engagement or development of mind, imagination and experience in repeated leisure shopping as mass shopping has developed in the twenty-first century.

But why must our leisure activities be meaningful? They need not always be – but important sources of leisure surely must have the potential for meaning and so for reflection built into them. Key activities that express a culture should be capable of contributing meaning and sense to the lives of those who think and act within that culture. There is no moral difficulty with individual people spending time shopping but there is something profoundly unsatisfactory in a society that encourages shopping as a major leisure activity in the full knowledge that this is nothing to do with bringing people to reflect on their world but everything to do with making money. Something has gone wrong where major leisure activities are intrinsically materialistic. Not every individual leisure activity must be elevated or exalted, but we need a cultural background of thoughtful leisure practices against which more superficial leisure activities occur. Without this what some call the human spirit – the aspect of ourselves made for transcendence and served for centuries by religion and philosophical wisdom – will undoubtedly be repressed and forced to identify as reality what is passing and trivial.

Of course talking about certain activities as superficial or trivial is imprecise, and from the perspective of various personal and political philosophies snobbish, elitist, judgmental, subjective. Yet the fact is that some activities are structured (quite legitimately) to provide instrumental benefit or benefit of fun, rest, relaxation solely, and other activities can do this but also go beyond external goals and surface psychological states and experiences and help us identify questions of depth and issues of complexity and come to an understanding of these. Of course, it could quite legitimately be asked whether shopping and like activities do not supply these opportunities for contemplation as effectively as any other activity. Yet while it is true that we can shop in a daydream thus letting the mind drift, this is a different experience from shopping itself causing the mind to soar. We certainly might notice something while shopping (a beautiful product or lovely display) which causes contemplation; but it is not retail that does this. Rather something else has intervened; we have been taken away briefly from the mission to buy. Whereas a person singing, dancing, praying, making, judging, exercising, reading, writing may by the very rhythm and content of these activities and their lack of extrinsic goals reflect on matters they need or desire to explore.

TV, shopping, computing, clubbing and other massively popular uses of spare time may have certain identifiable features in common that disqualify or undermine their reflective potential. This would no doubt be difficult to justify. But I suspect that two important features of these sorts of activities are passivity and commodification. Naturally, there are senses in which people are always active when doing anything but there is a definite encouragement to passivity or a passive attitude towards life, growth and development which is found in sitting still and watching the narrow (compared to books) range of TV shows or admiring and being tempted by products in shops or playing un-real games on a small screen or experiencing intoxicating atmosphere and substances in clubs and so on. And on commodification, again there is nothing wrong with commodities. We rely on trade and commerce and the utility of manufactured products makes life better for everyone. But simple enjoyment in making things for ourselves and the simple pleasures of time in quiet and natural places is reduced when we live through the heightened, stimulated and simulated, world of TVs, shops, computers, clubs and so on. For that world basically seeks to trade and relies on trade, and as Aristotle taught trade is for the sake of leisure, it is not leisure.

Three

Leisure functions as a potent creative force in the life of human persons, a source of recreation or restoration of our selves. Recreation occurs through using and expressing our freedom, and thereby establishing or confirming our identities. In this section I look briefly at some implications of leisure for freedom and identity.

Freedom is valued by people in different ways and along broadly ideological lines. For convenience, we can divide accounts of freedom into *utility freedom* (freedom is valued because of its role in obtaining some part/s of the human good) and *self-perfecting freedom* (freedom is valued because all or part of the human good consists in the exercise of freedom). On both of these broad accounts an issue of the protection of freedom arises. Whether we value freedom for what it obtains or for what it is, freedom is a significant good and one that must be protected, cultivated and enhanced. The exercise of freedom requires deliberation and choice. These are not inevitable: deliberation takes effort and that is sometimes out of fashion, and choice requires decisiveness, commitment and often courage, and these are not natural but habituated qualities. Part then of protecting freedom is protecting a range of powers and qualities necessary for the exercise of freedom.

But there is an additional aspect of the protection of freedom. Put negatively, this consists in the preservation of areas of life in which we are not readily coerced, not ignorant, not blind, not a victim of others or of fashions, not unfairly or harmfully constrained. Recognising and extending freedom requires preserving as empty certain psychological, social and practical spaces. We need areas for decision-making which have not been filled up with the coercive choices of other individuals or institutions; opportunities for choosing that have not been closed down by violence, threat or intimidation; habits of free choosing that have been built up as personally fulfilling opportunities and not shut down by forces that keep agents ignorant, uneducated or apathetic. Above all perhaps in capitalist-consumerist societies, freedom requires allowing and encouraging people to break with patterns of social conformity and to be different and individual, imaginative and creative.

Individuality and creativity become rarer achievements the more life is commodified or explained and justified in terms of what is for sale. And leisure is as vulnerable as any other dimension of our wellbeing to misdefinition as commodity. This happens primarily when people form the attitude that their leisure-time is a commodity to be 'spent' and that it should not be 'wasted' but spent on activities which are 'worthwhile' as represented by some form of cost. An example of this might be accepting that spending your leisure doing the crossword is less of an investment in your personal recreation than going kayaking or going to the latest movie because crosswords lack dynamic activity, novelty, group involvement, popularity, knowledge and use of equipment or technology, purchase, going outdoors (and instead involve mental repetition and development, solitariness, timeless value, reliance on inner resources, minimum expense, domesticity – itself vital to freedom and identity which develop in the space that privacy affords). Kayaking and movies are good activities of course – and good because they involve other areas of human flourishing as well as leisure (health in the case of the one, aesthetic stimulation or appreciation with the other). Their popularity and image means, however, that in a market economy there is a risk of people being reticent about other options. What has real value is what sells well, what we want to be known for is our support of popular options.

In response to any narrowing of leisure by social forces I suggest that leisure is the area of life in which human persons can be and should be most free, most creative. Most of our lives we exist and function inside networks of obligation. Various forms of necessity constantly constrain us: we are obliged to follow norms of work, social life, family life, expectations of others regarding time, duties, productivity, priorities, convenience. Leisure is precisely the time during which as many forms of necessity as possible are lifted. We cannot be relieved from *all* obligations (moral, legal, religious, natural-physical) but every so often voluntarily assumed or culturally created obligations do 'clear' and in this identified and protected leisure time we are free to do just what we choose to do.

Now part of course of this freedom to choose is freedom to choose commercialised leisure activities. And just because we live in a culture of mass commodification these opportunities will assume disproportionate weight, predominance and influence. Where the range of live and attractive options is limited there can still be free choice in the sense of *choice between alternatives* but what diminishes is *choice of the best option*, what we might call liberty. If the best option does not appear as an alternative or appears only as an unattractive alternative, meaningful freedom to choose that option is reduced or does not exist. Freedom worthy of the name requires a live range of options very different from each other and none of which is made to appear artificially unattractive. And this is precisely what is at risk of being compromised in a consumerist system. There is high risk of reduced options and there is manipulation of the perception of what is attractive.

It is therefore important that as far as possible society and major social institutions continue to present a broad range of leisure options, including those options that are not popular, fashionable, easily made attractive, technologised, for sale and so on. Leisure that allows the mind to soar, that opens up new thoughts about ourselves and our place in the world and new feelings and judgements about that world, should be discussed and explored in schools and colleges. For this leisure is not only directly conducive to wellbeing but is an exercise of freedom that itself encourages greater freedom. It draws our attention to the fact that we are free from what is most popular, really free to be an individual. Leisure can thereby open up opportunities for us to become freer, more aware of the good of freedom and interested in promoting freedom to others.

Identity is another much valued good. Views of the identity of persons divide into those concerned with what we are (a substance? A body? A machine? A soul? A combination?) and how we endure through time (as a physically continuous system? As linked psychological events? As memory? As narrative? As constituted by social recognition?). Across these two categories cuts the broad distinction of persons as matter, persons as spirit or persons as unities of matter and spirit. As with freedom, whichever form of personal identity we tend towards there is a concern to protect and enhance our identities.

If we look at key generic forms of human activity – work, exercise, socialising, study, parenting, art, worship … – a case can be made that the activity in which we are most ourselves is leisure. It is not that these other activities are necessarily alienating. But when we practise them we necessarily encounter contingencies with which we must deal: other people, the limits of our own experience, talents and abilities, the duties that come from morals and manners, our opportunities and so on. In leisure, however, we come closest to being able to act precisely as we choose. With all contingencies that can be removed having been removed from my leisure time, I can be most fully myself and least what I am merely expected to be. My personal identity can be more visible in my leisure life than elsewhere. This is one of the key insights reflected by Pieper's great work. My work and my family life do express my self but they do so in the only ways in which work and family life can express the self: there are limits on what is work and what is family, and I have a role within these institutions which is limited by the institution. With leisure however I stand alone and can choose just as I want to. Therefore, looking at me during genuine leisure ought to be as close to looking at the real me as others can get. This is not to downgrade in the slightest the intimate and personal nature of other activities. People in love can know each other in a unique way – but only in the ways that *lovers* can reveal and understand one another.

This connection between identity and leisure provides another instance of the risk of over-commercialised leisure. Just as lack of options decreases our exercise of freedom, so it decreases the expression of our identities. People do very often choose what is popular, and the reason for the popularity of an activity is its broad appeal, the fact that it is less dependent on one specific type of identity and person but appeals to tastes found across many identities. If this is so, choosing this particular leisure activity does not illustrate anything interesting about me, my specific identity, and does not encourage the development of any specific identity. The activity appeals to 'everyone' and so says nothing much about anyone.

As with freedom, the point is not that there is moral wrongdoing in adopting a highly popular activity but that there may be a loss. People will be less likely to discover unique and personal aspects of themselves. They will be disinclined for idiosyncracy and 'breaking the mould', easily repelled by eccentricity and difference, more judgemental of minority tastes and critical of specialist interests. And in all such attitudes people may be failing to build on something special and worthwhile about themselves, something that would take wits to perceive and courage to express. My personal identity then may become skewed towards my similarity with others, and where this happens it is not that I lose sense of self altogether but that I lose the sense of what is quintessentially me, what makes me different from everyone, interesting to others. Then too my openness to difference in general – either the quixotic differences of unusual characters or the cultural differences of whole classes of strangers – will reduce.

Conclusion

Leisure is unique among the activities that constitute a good human life. It reduces the possibility of boredom: a person who can describe even their aloneness and lack of dramatic activity as being 'at leisure' cannot describe themselves as bored. Because it tackles boredom leisure can act as a preventative for sloth and the sense of oppression it brings. Leisure makes contemplative opportunities and topics available to people who might never contemplate if left to the traditional contemplative activities of prayer and study. And contemplation matters. Serious questions will arise and there is great loss in never learning how to reflect deeply on ourselves, our world and the meaning of our lives – and to do so in ways that are tranquil rather than urgent. Leisure increases the opportunities to practise freedom, calls attention to existential freedom or liberty, and can bring us to reflect on and value freedom more deeply. Leisure allows us to discover important features of our own and others' identities, to work to preserve these and to express identity in choice and action. For these reasons and for others not here discussed, leisure is a matter of moral and spiritual importance in human life and conduct.

14

THE COMPREHENSIVE LEISURE PARTICIPATION FRAMEWORK

Theoretical foundation, cross-cultural variation, and practical implications

Gordon J. Walker

Social scientists often seek to explain and predict human behaviour. Two well-known ways of doing so are Ryan and Deci's (2000) self-determination theory (SDT) and Ajzen's (1991) theory of planned behaviour (TPB). Both SDT and TPB meet commonly espoused criteria for 'good' theory (Popper, 1959, including being parsimonious (e.g., Crawford and Jackson, 2005)). But in striving for parsimony 'theory shyness' may have inadvertently resulted; that is, an over-emphasis on more modest 'midrange' theorizing at the expense of more broad, unitary, or 'grand' theorizing (Kruglanski, 2001). Merton was amongst the first to discuss this trade-off, stating several years ago that:

> I believe – and beliefs are of course notoriously subject to error – that theories of the middle range hold the largest promise, *provided that* the search for them is coupled with a pervasive concern with consolidating special theories into more general sets of concepts and mutually consistent propositions. Even so, we must adopt the provisional outlook of our big brothers and of Tennyson: 'Our little systems have their day; They have their day and cease to be.'
>
> (Merton, 1968, pp. 52–53)

Popper (1959; as cited in Kruglanski, 2001) and Kruglanski (2001) concurred, with both prompting social scientists to have the 'guts' to propose more general theory.

Correspondingly, Crawford and Jackson (2005) held that being 'integrative' was another characteristic of good theory, meaning that midrange theories might 'on some happy future day be assimilated or integrated into "grand" theory' (p. 161). Unfortunately, attempts at such assimilation have been relatively rare; with one of the few exceptions being Hagger, Chatzisarantis, and Harris' (2006) work wherein they combined SDT and TPB. In a more narrow manner, Walker, Courneya, and Deng (2006) identified similarities and differences in some of the variables in TPB and leisure constraints theory (LCT; Crawford *et al.*, 1991); with Kleiber *et al.* (2011) subsequently speculating that LCT itself might be incorporable into Hagger and colleagues' configuration. Just such a likelihood was in fact anticipated by Crawford and Jackson, who stated that they thought it was entirely possible that leisure 'constraints theory itself may some day be completely swallowed up by future theoretical developments, an event that would underscore both the integrative function of theory and the role of theory in science' (p. 161). Based on the above, therefore, the first objective of this chapter is to describe a comprehensive leisure participation framework (CLPF) that incorporates SDT, TPB and LCT.

It is important to remember, however, that in cross-cultural psychology (and, by extension, the cross-cultural psychology of leisure), *universalism* 'adopts the working assumptions that basic psychological processes are likely to be common features of human life everywhere, but that their manifestations are likely to be influenced by culture' (Berry *et al.*, 2002, p. 326). Consequently, in the case of the proposed CLPF, it is expected that some of its components and relationships may also vary across cultures. This expectation, as will be discussed more fully shortly, is based on empirical research that has identified some cross-cultural variation in aspects of SDT (e.g., Iyengar and Lepper, 1999), TPB (e.g., Walker *et al.*, 2006), and LCT (e.g., Walker *et al.*, 2007). Thus, the second objective of this chapter is to describe how the CLPF's components and relationships may potentially be different, but also similar, across cultures.

It must also be kept in mind that, as one of the foundational figures in mainstream social psychology once stated: 'there is nothing so practical as a good theory' (Lewin, 1951, p. 169). The third objective of this chapter, therefore, is to describe how the proposed CLPF could inform leisure education and leisure practice. Because of space limitations, I have chosen to focus on the potential contribution of two specific factors from two different 'origin' theories: psychological needs, from SDT, and constraints and constraint negotiation from LCT.

Self-determination theory

Self-determination theory (SDT; Ryan and Deci, 2000) is one of the principal social psychological models for explaining and predicting behaviour. SDT is composed of various sub-theories, one of which is basic needs theory (BNT). Ryan and Deci (2000) held that there were three needs essential for people's psychological growth and well-being; the: (a) *need for autonomy* (which involves freedom to initiate one's behaviour, typically through personal choice and control); (b) *need for competence* (which involves effective functioning and, in turn, the desire to seek out and conquer ever bigger challenges); and (c) *need for interpersonal relatedness* (which involves people feeling that: (i) they are loved by and connected to others, (ii) those others understand them, and (iii) they are meaningfully involved with the broader social world in which they live). Of these three psychological needs, autonomy is generally considered to be the most important, in part because it and competence are always presumed pertinent whereas relatedness is not (e.g., if you choose to play a computer game by yourself). Unfortunately, to date BNT has largely been overlooked in the leisure studies field. One of the few exceptions is a study (Walker and Wang 2009, cited in Kleiber *et al.*, 2011) that found that when Chinese Canadians were with other people, autonomy, competence and interpersonal relatedness were all satisfied significantly more during leisure than during work.

Another SDT sub-theory – organismic integration theory (OIT) – focuses on behavioural motives rather than psychological needs. Ryan and Deci (2000) held that motivations range from intrinsic to integrated to identified to introjected to external to amotivation; with the first having the greatest degree of perceived 'self-determination' and the last the least. *Intrinsic* motivation involves interest, enjoyment and participation in activities for their own sake (Ryan and Deci, 2000). *Integrated* motivation involves evaluation and assimilation into the self, whereas *identified* motivation involves valuing a goal as being personally important (Ryan and Deci, 2000). In contrast, *introjected* motivations are performed to enhance pride or avoid guilt, whereas *external* motivations are performed to obtain rewards or avoid punishments (Ryan and Deci, 2000). Lastly, *amotivation* entails a person not acting at all, acting but being unaware of why he or she is doing so, or acting but essentially just 'going through the motions' (Ryan and Deci, 2000). OIT has been employed to a greater extent than BNT in our field, and study results have largely been supportive of its ability to explain and predict leisure behaviour. Some of this research will be discussed more fully shortly, but interested readers may also want to peruse, for example, methodological and applied work by Caldwell and associates (e.g., Baldwin and Caldwell, 2003; Caldwell *et al.*, 2010) amongst others.

Theory of planned behaviour

The theory of planned behaviour (TPB; Ajzen, 1991) is another principal social psychological framework for explaining and predicting behaviour. According to TPB (Ajzen, 1991), a person's *behaviour* is largely dependent on his or her *intention* to perform a behaviour which, in turn, is determined by: (a) his or her *attitudes* toward the behaviour, both affective ('Is it enjoyable or unenjoyable?') and instrumental ('Is it wise or unwise?'); (b) the *subjective norms* he or she believes significant others have concerning the behaviour, both injunctive ('Do they approve or disapprove?') and descriptive ('Do they actually do it or not?'); and (c) his or her perception of whether the behaviour can be performed (i.e., *perceived behavioural control*), both in terms of self-efficacy ('Is it easy or difficult?') and *controllability* ('Do I have a little control or a lot?'). On occasion, other variables have been tested in conjunction with attitude, subjective norm and perceived behavioural control; with Ajzen being supportive of such theoretical extension as long these new factors are proven to improve TPB's explanatory ability. TPB, in contrast with the two SDT sub-theories discussed earlier, has been employed to examine a range of leisure activities, including: hunting (Hrubes *et al.*, 2001), playing the lottery (Walker *et al.*, 2006), participating in outdoor recreation (Ajzen and Driver, 1992), and engaging in both physical and sedentary activities (Courneya, 1995, and Rhodes and Dean, 2009, respectively). Overall, study results have been highly supportive of TPB's ability to explain and predict leisure behaviour.

Theoretical integration

Although self-determination theory (Ryan and Deci, 2000) and the theory of planned behaviour (Ajzen, 1991) have been used to explain and predict numerous leisure and non-leisure activities, the relationship between these two theories has been largely unexamined. Recently, however, Hagger *et al.* (2006) proposed that an integrative framework could be created based on Vallerand's (1997) hierarchy, where: (a) TPB is proximally located at the *situational* (or state) level; (b) SDT, in terms of motivations, is located at the *contextual* (or life domain) level; and (c) SDT, in terms of needs, is distally located at the *global* (or personality) level. Hagger *et al.* tested their framework in regard to dieting and exercising and support was found in both instances.

Hagger and associates' (2006) work makes an important contribution to behavioural theorizing. But Kleiber *et al.* (2011) suggested that, by not including leisure constraints theory (LCT) along with SDT and TPB, their framework did not explain or predict human behaviour as well as it could. Leisure constraints are 'factors that are assumed by researchers and/or perceived or experienced by individuals to limit the formation of leisure preferences and/or inhibit or prohibit participation and enjoyment in leisure' (Jackson, 2000, p. 62). LCT (Crawford *et al.*, 1991) proposes that: (a) there are three types of constraints, intrapersonal (e.g., perceived lack of skill), interpersonal (e.g., lack of friends to participate with), and structural (e.g., lack of time or money); and (b) people actively 'negotiate' the constraints they face in order to participate to some degree and/or in some form in their preferred leisure activities (e.g., by budgeting their time so they can engage in an activity).

Anticipation also plays a key role in LCT in that: (a) 'anticipation of one or more insurmountable interpersonal or structural constraints may suppress the desire for participation'; and (b) 'anticipation consists of not simply the anticipation of the presence or intensity of a constraint, but also the anticipation of the ability to negotiate it' (Jackson, 2005, p. 6) The former statement clearly demonstrates that intrapersonal constraint is conceptually distinct from interpersonal and structural constraints (or what is heretofore referred to as 'extrapersonal' constraints). This distinction, in conjunction with Walker and associates' (2007) conjecture that intrapersonal constraints overlap with TPB's attitude, subjective norm, and perceived behavioural control variables, hints that integrating anticipated extrapersonal constraint and anticipated extrapersonal negotiation into Hagger's *et al.* (2006) framework could prove beneficial. Additionally, because 'preference' (as per LCT) and 'intention' (as per TPB) are comparable concepts (Walker *et al.*, 2007), incorporation of the latter component at the most distal part of Vallerand's (1997) situational level seems reasonable (Walker, 2011a). In contrast, actual extrapersonal constraint and actual extrapersonal negotiation would occur after leisure intention but before actual leisure participation (Walker, 2012). Finally, research (Walker, 2012) has found significant relationships exist between anticipated and actual extrapersonal constraints, and anticipated and actual extrapersonal negotiations; a not too surprising finding given humans have the capacity (depending upon on their past experience and assuming they are sufficiently interested) to – to some degree at least – both forecast the future as well plan for its exigencies.

Figure 14.1, adapted from Hagger *et al.* (2006), Kleiber *et al.* (2011), and Walker and Liang (2012), identifies the global (physiological and psychological needs), contextual (i.e., intrinsic motivation, extrinsic motivation and amotivation), and situational (i.e., attitudes, subjective norm, perceived behavioural control, intention, anticipated and actual leisure constraint, anticipated and actual leisure constraint negotiation) components that are presumed to affect actual leisure participation, as well as the presumed relationships among them. It is important

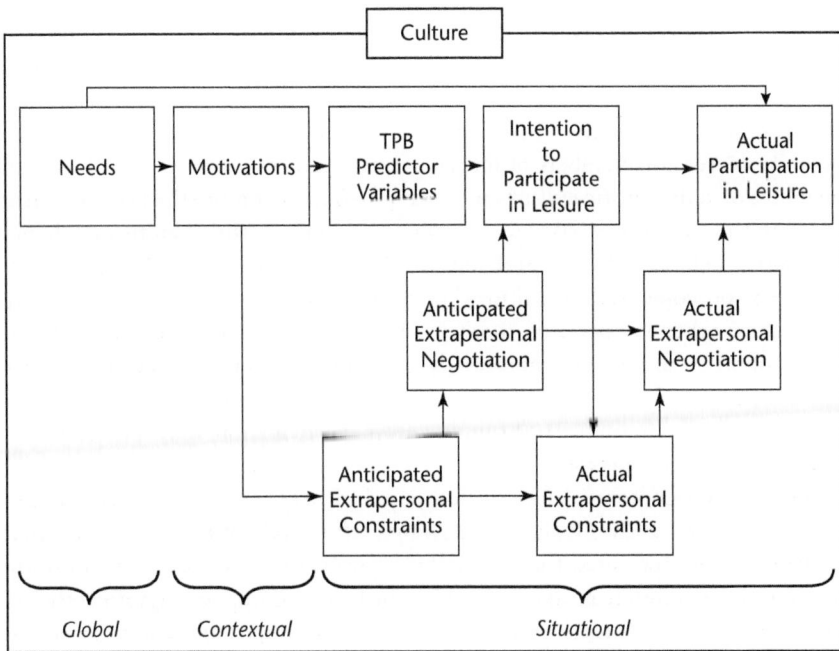

FIGURE 14.1   Comprehensive leisure participation framework

to note here that all three levels are encompassed by culture, which suggests a universalistic approach (Berry *et al.*, 2002) such that these factors and relationships are construed to be largely similar across cultures but that important differences can and do exist. Potential cross-cultural similarities and differences in the comprehensive leisure participation framework are discussed more fully in the next section.

Cross-cultural variation

In this section I: (a) reintroduce the key factors that compose the global, contextual and situational levels of the comprehensive leisure participation framework; (b) discuss how each of these factors has been found to be similar and different across cultural groups; and (c) speculate on what these similarities and differences might mean in regard to leisure participation.

In terms of the CLFP's global level, research suggests that psychological needs vary across cultures and, therefore, so too could leisure participation. For example, Sheldon and colleagues (2001) had American and Korean students rank 10 potential psychological needs. Self-esteem was found to be of primary importance for U.S. students while belonging (i.e., SDT's interpersonal relatedness) was of primary importance for Korean students. This finding is congruent with research (Triandis, 1995) that indicates members of 'collectivistic' cultures (e.g., Chinese, Japanese and Koreans) are generally more focused on the group (and group harmony) whereas members of 'individualistic' cultures (e.g., mainstream Canadians, Americans and Europeans) are more focused on the self. Importantly, this orientation also affects how other key core needs are construed with, for instance, related research suggesting that: (a) members of collectivistic cultures often emphasize self-criticism more than self-esteem, whereas the opposite is true for members of individualistic cultures (Heine *et al.*, 1999); (b) members of collectivistic cultures often emphasize effort more than competence, whereas the opposite is true for members of individualistic cultures (Heine, Kitayama, Lehman, Takata and Ide, as cited in Heine *et al.*, 1999); and (c) members of collectivistic cultures often emphasize group choice (i.e., by significant others, especially those of higher status), whereas members of individualistic cultures are more likely to emphasize personal choice (Iyengar and Lepper, 1999). Interpreted holistically, these results suggest that satisfying the need for belongingness through leisure participation may be especially important for Asian people.

The CLFP's contextual level is composed of SDT's motivations (Ryan and Deci, 2000). A study (Walker and Wang, 2009) of Chinese and Canadian students' leisure indicated that, while both groups were primarily intrinsically motivated (i.e., interesting and enjoyable), the former group was significantly less motivated in terms of identification (i.e., personally important) and introjection (i.e., pride, guilt). These results suggest that leisure's defining attribute, across cultures, is its intrinsic essence (Walker and Wang, 2009). Conversely, leisure's perceived personal value, and its perceived relationship with aspects of the self, likely differs cross-culturally. Based on the above, we would expect to find that: (a) highly intrinsic leisure activities are common around the world, (b) leisure participation overall varies depending upon the importance a culture places upon it; and (c) participation in certain leisure activities varies depending upon whether a culture was more individualistic (and emphasized self-focused emotions such as pride and guilt) or more collectivistic (and did not). There is empirical support for the first (as evidenced by the ubiquity of watching television) and second (as evidenced by various national value surveys; although cohort differences must also be taken into account; see, for example, Sun and Wang, 2010) propositions, whereas empirical testing of the third is currently lacking.

The CLFP's situational level is composed of TPB's (Ajzen, 1991) attitudes, subjective norm, perceived behavioural control, and intention to participate variables; and LCT's (Crawford *et al.*, 1991; Jackson, 2005) anticipated and actual extrapersonal constraint and anticipated and actual extrapersonal constraint negotiation variables. As with SDT, studies that have employed TPB have largely supported its cross-cultural applicability though, at the same time, many have also acknowledged that some of its components are influenced by culture (i.e., universalism; Berry *et al.*, 2002). For example, some researchers (Chan and Lau, 2001; Park and Levine, 1999) have found that attitude was more important for those in individualistic cultures whereas subjective norm was more important for those in collectivistic cultures. This finding, however, may vary depending upon the domain, as Walker's *et al.* (2006) results indicated that attitude was the best predictor of intention to play the lottery for both Chinese Canadians and British Canadians.

As noted earlier, Kleiber *et al.* (2011) proposed that Hagger and associates' (2006) framework would benefit by the incorporation of leisure constraints theory (Crawford *et al.*, 1991). Preliminary research (Walker, 2011a) supports this proposition in terms of predicting intention to casino gamble above and beyond attitude, subjective, norm and perceived behavioural control. Other constraints research supports taking culture into account, with Walker *et al.* (2007) discovering that, when it came to starting a new leisure activity, Chinese students were more intrapersonally and interpersonally, but less structurally, constrained that Canadian students. Chinese students also reported that role fulfillment (i.e., being a good student, friend or son/daughter) was a much more important intrapersonal constraint, which is consistent with Chinese values. Similarly, Liang and Walker (2011) found that face was an intrapersonal constraint to starting a new leisure activity for some Chinese people, particularly those who were less educated.

Additionally, culture could also affect how a person negotiates the factors that constrain his or her leisure. According to Weisz, Rothbaum, and Blackburn (1984) there are two types of control: primary and secondary. Primary control occurs when individuals enhance their rewards by *influencing* existing realities. In contrast, secondary control occurs when individuals enhance their rewards by *accommodating* to existing realities. Cultural differences have been found in regard to control and leisure participation, with American aerobics participants emphasizing primary control and Japanese aerobics participants emphasizing secondary control (Morling, 2000). Thus, non-Westerners may be more apt to use secondary control as a way to deal with their leisure constraints.

Finally, obvious by its absence in the above discussion is the lack of attention paid to the conceptual distinction between anticipated and actual constraints and constraint negotiation. On the one hand, this omission is not surprising given cross-cultural LCT research remains quite rare (Chick and Dong, 2005). On the other hand, a cursory examination of the broader leisure literature suggests that this distinction is seldom (if ever) taken into account in any empirical constraint studies.

Implication for leisure education and practice

Theory integration is important not only for researchers interested in explaining and predicting why people participate in leisure, but also for educators and practitioners who are responsible for encouraging and abetting people to participate in leisure. To briefly illustrate the potential role of the CLPF in this process, I describe how its most distal variable – psychological needs (from SDT) – and its most proximal variable – actual extrapersonal constraints and constraint negotiation (from LCT) – could inform leisure education and practice.

In North America, leisure education has been defined as: 'the process through which individuals acquire the knowledge, skills, and attitudes that motivate and facilitate their leisure functioning' (B. Robertson, 2007, p. 263). Although leisure education occurs across the course of everyone's life, it has traditionally been most closely associated with therapeutic recreation (B. Robertson, 2007). Needs are an acknowledged aspect of both leisure education and therapeutic recreation however, according to Bell (2010): (a) a piecemeal approach has often been taken when using this construct (e.g., by focusing primarily on autonomy); and (b) the effect of need satisfaction on successive factors (e.g., intrinsic motivation) has often been overlooked. After addressing these issues in her own research, Bell concluded that her findings demonstrate 'the danger in choosing one part of a theory to apply as opposed to applying a theory as a whole. It also indicates the value of research in allowing translation of theoretical concepts into practice' (p. 65). I concur with her conclusions, and would hasten to add that because the CLPF includes all three psychological needs; because it identifies how these needs directly impact motives (as well as actual participation); and, most importantly, because it situates these SDT variables within a much larger context (i.e., in relation to TPB and LCT), I also believe that utilization of this framework could greatly improve research on, and the delivery of, leisure education and therapeutic recreation in the future.

Bell (2010) experimentally manipulated autonomy, competence and relatedness in her study; an unusual approach in leisure studies (Kleiber *et al.*,

2011). Unfortunately, equally rare in leisure studies are theory-based discussions of how needs could be fostered in the field as well as actual theory-based empirical studies. An exception to the former can be found in a presentation I made to practitioners attending the 2011 Alberta Recreation and Parks Association Conference (Walker, 2011b). In it I developed 'Eight Simple Need Questions For Front-Line Staff' by adapting items from the SDT General Basic Needs and Basic Needs at Work Scales; and then I recommended front-line staff complete this questionnaire before implementing a new or existing program. Specifically, they should indicate how true they thought each of the following statements would be for their program participants using a seven-point scale (1 = not true at all; 4 = somewhat true; 7 = very true). In terms of *autonomy*: (a) 'They will be able to freely express their ideas and opinions.'; (b) 'Their feelings will be taken into consideration.'; and (c) 'They will pretty much be able to be themselves.' In terms of *relatedness*: (a) 'There will be lots of opportunities for social interaction'; and (b) 'The social environment will be friendly and supportive.' And in terms of *competence*: (a) 'They will feel capable and effective'; (b) 'They will be able to learn interesting new skills'; and (c) 'They will feel a sense of accomplishment from what they do.' Employing this simple measure, I believe, could go a long way toward attracting new participants (assuming they were made aware of how their needs would be satisfied beforehand), and increasing the likelihood that actual participants would continue to engage in the same activity and with the same agency (assuming their needs were indeed satisfied afterwards).

An exception to the latter is an empirical study of adolescent girls attending camp. Gillard, Watts and Witt (2007) outlined a number of practical implications and, albeit camp specific, because of the paucity of recreation research on facilitating need satisfaction, their suggestions are quoted extensively. First, in terms of autonomy:

> Autonomy-supportive interaction styles are characterized by adults being sensitive to young people's needs and providing choices ... Adults can support autonomy by: providing information about options and actions; acknowledging feelings; incorporating student perspectives into activities; providing optimally challenging tasks; providing structure and guidance that demonstrate the reasons for certain behaviors; and minimizing a performance-based climate.

Second, in terms of competence:

> Competence-supporting experiences can lead to self-determined motivation to continue participation ... Contexts that support young people's needs for competence are those that have a high quality of relatedness with adults who appropriately organize activities to maximize skill-building, provide effective positive feedback, and create feelings of self-efficacy.

Third, in terms of interpersonal relatedness:

> While relatedness is a need that can be met within the provision of autonomy and competence, there are some steps that adults can take to meet the needs of young people to feel related and connected to others. For example, Murray (2002) suggests the following for improving relationships: recognize that young people need to feel supported by adults; provide them with opportunities to learn positive relationship skills with adults; learn more about young people's backgrounds, interests, and communities; develop increased awareness of group interactions; and model and expect appropriate behavior. Camp administrators should hire, train, and support staff who are skilled instructors, and who interact with young people in a comfortable, caring, and respectful manner. (p. 157)

Finally, in much the same manner leisure education and practice could benefit from recognizing, and thus facilitating, the CLPF's need component, so too could they benefit from recognizing, but in this instance mitigating, the CLPF's constraint component. Unfortunately, a few years ago Scott (2005, p. 280) lamented that 'there is little indication that practitioners are applying findings from constraints research to improve service delivery' – and I would argue that this lack of application continues today. Perhaps this is because practitioners find the topic too esoteric or uninspiring (Godbey, 1989), or perhaps it is that they simply lack the time to sift through and reflect on the constraints literature. Regardless, for those who do choose to do so an *embarrasse de richesse* awaits. For example, even though practitioners may be aware that time commitments are the most frequently reported constraint, they may not realize that wasting people's time may result in them being shunned by time-conscious constituents (Scott, 2005), to the point of 'committing competitive suicide' (Berry, 1990, p. 31). Additionally, some research (Godbey *et al.*, 1992) indicates that the second most reported barrier to the use of local parks and recreation services is not lack of money but rather lack of information. If correct, the decision to try to help people overcome this constraint would seem commonsensical (even though actually accomplishing the task itself could be quite complicated). Finally, because another study (Hubbard and Mannell, 2001) found that people who are highly motivated to engage in activity are also likely to work hard to negotiate associated constraints, in the same manner discussed earlier in regard to needs, by situating LCT within a much larger context (i.e., in relation to SDT and TPB), I believe utilization of the CLPF could greatly improve research on, and the delivery of, leisure education, programs and services in the future.

Conclusion

The first objective in this chapter was to provide an overview of a comprehensive leisure participation framework based on the work of Hagger *et al.* (2006), Kleiber *et al.* (2011) and Walker and Liang (2012). Over the past decade or so, there have been increasing calls in both social psychology and the social psychology of leisure for less 'theory shyness' (Kruglanski, 2001) and more theoretical integration (Crawford and Jackson, 2005). The latter researchers stated this best when they wrote:

> We may ultimately come to the realization that one of the major issues this line of work faces is not that it has been too brazen, but that it may not have been adventurous enough. Why not be daring and speculate imaginatively now, at this relatively early stage? (p. 165)

The framework outlined herein is both daring and adventurous, and it could make an important contribution to the advancement of leisure studies generally.

The second objective of this chapter was to describe how the CLPF could potentially differ across cultures, while still acknowledging that the factors that affect leisure participation are largely similar cross-culturally. As is evident from what has been written, I am universalistic in perspective (Berry *et al.*, 2002) in that I believe that basic psychological concepts are common to all humans but how they are construed and manifested, and their relative saliency, can be influenced by culture. Moreover, because the comprehensive leisure participation framework (Hagger *et al.*, 2006; Kleiber *et al.*, 2011) described herein reflects this perspective, it is not only daring and adventurous, but it could also make an important contribution to the advancement of cross-cultural leisure studies generally.

The third objective of this chapter was to describe how the proposed CLPF could inform leisure education and practice. Because of space limitations, discussion focused on two components of my framework: psychological needs and constraints and constraint negotiation. But I also hasten to state that there are detriments to practitioners not only taking a piecemeal approach when employing a theory's constructs or its hypothesized relationships (as per Bell, 2010) but also to taking a piecemeal approach by employing a single theory when two or more may provide a more accurate representation of what is really occurring. Also noted in this section was concern that leisure practitioners are still not applying research based on SDT and LCT to the degree that they should, and this bodes even more poorly for an integrated model such as the CLPF. In this case, therefore, it may be that researchers must be daring and adventurous in their attempts to help practitioners negotiate this 'theoretical' constraint, while practitioners must be daring and adventurous in their attempts to incorporate CLPF into practice.

Finally, in the same way TPB grew out of the theory of reasoned action; SDT added relatedness to its initial list of basic needs; and LCT expanded to include not only constraints but the negotiation thereof, it seems inevitable that the CLPF will also continue to evolve. This in fact has already occurred, with my reading of Hagger's *et al.* (2006) 'origin' article first resulting in a cursory description of a basic model (Kleiber *et al.*, 2011), followed shortly thereafter by an expanded discussion of its universalistic aspects (Walker and Liang, 2012). Ultimately, this chapter contributes further to the CLPF's evolution by allowing for continued – and hopefully 'good' – theorizing.

15

LEISURE, IDENTITIES AND PERSONAL GROWTH

Scott A. Cohen

Introduction

Leisure studies have a long history of associating leisure practices and the meanings of leisure with notions of personal growth and self-development. This association is bound up with questions of personal identity and relies on the possibility that we have a stable personal self that we can develop. The prospect of a stable personal self is a distinguishing feature of modernity, and there is now substantial literature from a postmodern perspective suggesting that identities are instead fragmented and transitory. This raises a fundamental tension. If identities are transitory, how can we develop them? And what are the repercussions of this for personal growth through leisure practices? These questions have important implications for the meanings of leisure.

In this chapter I attempt to unpack some of these issues. I begin by discussing personal identities in the context of modernity, drawing out how the challenge of developing a coherent sense of personal identity became a defining feature of the late modern period in the Western world. The discussion leads us to how leisure is implicated in modern developmental approaches to self, particularly through concepts such as 'serious leisure' (Stebbins, 1982) and 'flow experience' (Csikszentmihalyi, 1990). My focus then turns to a divergent postmodern perspective that argues that there is no core self and we instead exist in a world characterized by increasingly fragmented identities. A postmodern perspective argues that the concept of a stable personal identity that we might develop has been a historical social construction. Such a view has little time for notions of personal growth through leisure.

I then turn to how the social sciences have begun to see a middle ground between postmodern 'discourse determinism' (Wearing and Wearing, 2001) on the one hand and an essentialized notion of self on the other. Such a view allows for a re-examination of how we might attempt building a reflective sense of personal identity out of embodied everyday practice. The chapter concludes by reflecting on how positive experiences of leisure, rather than necessarily being viewed as disparate or episodic, may instead constitute a lifestyle in which the accumulation of personally enriching leisure practices engenders perceptions of self-development and growth. It is through this perspective that there may be some reconciliation of modern and postmodern stances on personal identity and scope for assigning value to the importance of subjective lived experience.

Identities in modernity

Self and identity are vast and complicated concepts that are contested within the social sciences. Seigel (2005, p. 3) observes that 'few ideas are both as weighty and slippery as the notion of self', and this is evidenced in that over 30,000 publications on self and identity emerged in social psychology alone (excluding related work in sociology and anthropology) in the 1980s and 1990s (Vaughan and Hogg, 2002). The permeability of self and identity as concepts means they sometimes merge into each other and can be described as co-terminus (Collinson and Hockey, 2007; Seigel, 2005). Although distinctions are at times drawn between collective and personal (self) identity, Breathnach (2006, p. 113) reminds us that identities are 'neither wholly collective nor individual, but are formed in the interaction between the individual and the subject position available to them'. Hence, identities are constructed through difference, in the recognition of what one is not in relation to others (Hall, 1996; Walseth, 2006). Consequently, Hall (1996) defines identities as temporary points of attachment to subject positions constructed through discursive practices. While this definition focuses on how identities are discursively constructed, it is important to remember that our personal identity, or sense of self, while being housed in our physical body and including our emotions, is also an individually experienced reflective construction through which we anchor and position ourselves in the social world. As Gergen (1991, p. x) simply puts it, self refers to 'our ways of understanding who we are and what we are about'.

The challenge of developing a coherent sense of personal identity in the context of an increasing array of life options has been characterized as a defining feature of late modernity in the Western world (Bauman, 2000; Giddens, 1991). Aligning this phenomenon with the Western world gives due recognition to the fact that the Western self is a 'hyperindividualized entity forged under the authoritarian orientation of Judeo-Christian monotheism' (D'Andrea, 2007, p. 112), whereas non-Western understandings of personal identity constructed under different cultural histories have constituted different ways of understanding ourselves in relation to others. Even the word 'self' only first appeared as a noun in the English language at the beginning of the fourteenth century (Danziger, 1997). Burkitt (1991, p. 1) puts it well in stating that the starting point for self as an area of concern in the modern West is the deeply ingrained view of 'human beings as self-contained unitary individuals who carry their uniqueness deep inside themselves, like pearls hidden in their shells' waiting to be found.

The importance attributed to personal identity in the Western world has been the product of this pervasive meta-narrative of 'self' as an inner source that should be cultivated, alongside a loosening of the structures that previously constituted identities (such as social class, religion, gender and 'race') and a consequent accelerating range of options and opportunities for constructing and exploring selves (for some) under conditions of rapid globalization (Gergen, 1991). A consequence of this social opening and pluralization of options has been increasingly transitory and disconnected relationships that may contribute to a fragmented sense of personal identity (ibid.).

Arising out of these conditions, which Bauman (2000) describes as 'liquid modernity', was a growing tendency amongst Western moderns to use personal identity as an 'anchor' or sense-making device (Kuentzel, 2000). Making sense of one's identity thus became understood as a reflexive project of maintaining a coherent narrative or biographical 'story' about the development of one's self (Giddens, 1991). Hence the idea of *self-development*, both reflexively organized and internally referential (ibid.), emerges from the project of the self in late modernity. As McAdams (1997, p. 62) summarizes: '[m]odern men and women routinely adopt a developmental rhetoric in making sense of their own lives'. From this perspective, we can see notions of self-development and personal growth as fundamentally linked to the modern quest for identity. Consequently, humanist ideals in developmental psychology of self-actualization and self-fulfilment (e.g. Maslow, 1971; Rogers, 1969), which suggest that individual (selves) may develop or grow, need to be understood as products of this late modern meta-narrative of identity seeking.

Leisure is centrally implicated in this meta-narrative; Kuentzel (2000) observes that the notion of self-development through the medium of leisure has served as a theoretical starting point in traditional leisure studies. Indeed, mastery, competence and learning through leisure activities have been common themes in leisure research that takes a developmental approach; such research examines the personal benefits that may accrue to individuals through leisure practices, for example through Stebbins' (1982) 'serious leisure' framework and in applications of Csikszentmihalyi's (1990) 'flow theory' (e.g. Priest and Bunting, 1993; Stein *et al.*, 1995). A discourse of self-development is clearly evident in Stebbins' (1982, p. 267) concept of serious leisure: '[i]f leisure is to become, for many, an improvement over work as a way of finding personal fulfilment, identity enhancement, self-expression, and the like, then people must be careful to adopt those forms returning the greatest payoff'. Likewise, Csikszentmihalyi (1990, p. 41) contended that 'following a flow experience, the organization of the self is more complex than it had been before'. Thus he implies that overcoming challenges through the repetition of flow activity results not just in heightened states of being, but a route towards self-fulfilment (ibid.). Such perspectives, in which leisure is imbued with challenge, purpose, goals and growth have been central to conceptions of leisure that position it as much more than just frivolous play or free time.

If we accept, however, that humanist concepts of self-development and personal growth are part and parcel of the meta-narrative of identity seeking in late modernity, then implicitly these concepts are subject to the same critiques levelled by postmodern theory at notions of a unified or core self. It is to this postmodern fragmentation that I now turn.

Postmodern fragmentation of identities

> In the postmodern world there is no individual essence to which one remains true or committed. One's identity is continuously emergent, re-formed, and redirected as one moves through the sea of ever-changing relationships. In the case of 'Who am I?' it is a teeming world of provisional possibilities.
>
> (Gergen, 1991, p. 139)

Gergen's words capture well the possibilities associated with a postmodern perspective. Yet the instability associated with this sea of change, as compared to fixity, also alludes to potential anxieties deriving from our (selves) being set adrift. As aspects of our personal identities become more a matter of choice than social ascription, many individuals are forced to negotiate their sense of self among an increasing range of persons, forms of relationships, options and opportunities that can be transitory, fragmented and unstable (Cote and Levine, 2002; Gergen, 1991; Giddens, 1991). This process is being accelerated with the introduction of technologies that make local face-to-face interactions rarer and contribute further to the fragmentation of social interactions. The result of this pluralization of options and growth in incoherent and disconnected relationships is the supposed fragmentation of our sense of self (Gergen, 1991; Giddens, 1991).

In tension with a modernist view of personal identity as unified and actualizable, these processes of societal change in contrast suggest the emergence of a cacophony of relational selves, as the centre fails to hold and personal identity slides from image to image, being presented on the 'whim of the moment' and eschewing substance (Cote and Levine, 2002). Bauman's (1996, p. 18) words encapsulate well these divergent perspectives between identity in modernity and postmodernity: 'if the modern "problem of identity" was how to construct an identity and keep it solid and stable, the postmodern "problem of identity" is primarily how to avoid fixation and keep options open'. Thus the concept of a core self that 'develops and matures through life's experiences carries little currency in postmodern theory' (Kuentzel, 2000, p. 88). This viewpoint has little time for ideas of self-development and personal growth, including modern associations between development and the meaning of leisure, when that which is to be developed or grown is deemed fractured or unstable to begin with.

The postmodern deconstruction of a core personal identity was taken to its farthest reach by Foucault (1988), who radically argued that the entire notion of a stable reflective self was a historical social construction. Through linguistic practice, or what Foucault (ibid.) referred to as 'technologies of the self', individuals were encouraged to learn socially condoned procedures for systematically reflecting upon their own thoughts, feelings and behaviours (Danziger, 1997). The Catholic practice of confession, keeping a diary and the increase in modern literary productions preoccupied with the idea of an inner core self were given as examples of how these 'technologies of the self' train us to reflect on the 'I' and the 'me' as a unique internal essence (Cohen and Taylor, 1992; Foucault, 1988). Underpinning Foucauldian understandings of reflective identity as linguistically constructed is the observation that technologies of self vary significantly across different cultures where these practices may be instituted and understood in different ways. Thus the modern notion that our core self could be slow and arduously discovered (Cohen and Taylor, 1992) was jettisoned under the pretext that the idea of 'self' is culturally contingent.

Although seeming nihilistic, a postmodern perspective on identity is not intended as a negative outlook. Quite to the contrary, the idea is 'the more selves the merrier' (McAdams, 1997, p. 51). Thus we come back to Gergen's (1991) words on the 'possibilities' opened up by a postmodern perspective, as Seigel (2005, p. 4) attempts to explain the postmodern motivation for deconstructing the idea of a core self: 'they did so on behalf of a vision of transcendent freedom that overwhelms the more modest visions of personal integration and regulated autonomy projected by the ideas and practices they sought to supersede'. Whilst modern and postmodern perspectives on personal identity represent sharply contrasting views, two important questions can and should be asked here: 1) Is there a functional middle ground between these perspectives? and 2) What is the significance of the subjective lived experiences of individuals who use leisure as a field for personal growth? I address these questions in turn in the following sections.

A performative embodied middle ground

Despite a postmodern understanding of personal identities as multiple and fluid, McAdams (1997, p. 47) suggests 'one should not dismiss the possibility that selves nonetheless retain a certain degree of unity and coherence'. Framing the issue in terms of a continuum, Holland (1997) proposes that two poles can be seen in contemporary academic discussions of personal identity, with the range including an extreme 'essentialist' view that fails to take account of the positioning power of discourse (i.e. a modernist perspective) and a completely contrasting ephemeral (i.e. postmodern) position that denies agency. Holland's (ibid.) critique of the latter pole seeks to discredit the Foucauldian (1988) view that language and culture have total power to 'set strict limits to what people are able to think, or deeming consciousness to be so fully constituted by social and cultural relations that mental life becomes a kind of precipitate of collective existence, losing its independence' (Seigel, 2005, p. 21). Levels of autonomy associated with leisure, in relation to the extent that leisure practices are socially constructed (and controlled) by discourse, can also be conceived in these terms.

In contrast to these polarized perspectives, it has been suggested that the difficulty in accurately theorizing the relationship between the individual and the power of discourse has stemmed from self and society having been dichotomized in the literature in the first place (Burkitt, 1991). Butler's (1990) work on the performativity of gender offers a perspective on constructing personal identities that may help to bridge the gap between the determining power of discourse and the agency of embodied selves (Bell, 2008). In applying performativity to identities, Bell (2008, p. 174) explains that 'performativity has come to mean that we perform multiple and shifting identities in history, language, and material embodiments'. Butler (1990, p. 277) observes that the constitution of personal identity is an embodied performance that is processual, wherein individuals are always 'on the stage' and 'within the terms of the performance', however 'just as a script may be enacted in various ways, and just as the play requires both text and interpretation' so can individuals 'expand the cultural field bodily through subversive performances of various kinds' (ibid., p. 282).

Therefore, while all performances of personal identity are citations, or enacted ways of doing, for instance, gender, ethnicity, class, age and abilities, selves are also *performative* in that they are negotiated in and through a process of becoming (Bell, 2008). The theatrical metaphor of 'kinesis', which builds from Goffman's (1959) dramaturgical performance approach to social interaction, offers insight into the performative nature of constituting personal identities as a process of 'breaking and remaking' in which performances not only mirror and sustain normative boundaries but can also subvert and transgress them (Bell, 2008, p. 13). Such notions of performance and performativities are increasingly applied within contemporary leisure theory (e.g., Gilchrist and Ravenscroft, 2013; Waitt and Clifton, 2013), as illustrative of how spaces and discourses are produced, reproduced, resisted and transformed.

A performative perspective denies the existence of a core personal identity, while recognizing that individuals have the power to perform multiple and shifting selves (Bell, 2008). Thus, personal identities are not fixed givens, but are always in process, with individuals having some power in the production and reproduction of their sense of personal identity. Stemming from this perspective, social science research that views personal identities as situational and performed in everyday embodied practice has gained speed.

Allied to this view is the recognition that postmodernity 'is a transitional phenomenon, rather than a novel, well-integrated and permanent cultural system' (Cohen, 1995, p. 24). There is still substantial debate in sociology as to whether Western society can be described by an 'amalgamation' of the characteristics said to form the condition of postmodernity or whether it is still in the throes of late modernity (Sharpley, 2003). Of course, it is more likely that Western society is somewhere between the two, as while aspects of the world might be described as postmodern, it would be inaccurate to assume that all individuals perceive the world through a postmodern lens (Gergen, 1991). Thus, instead of ceasing to believe in one's self as an autonomous agent, wherein one is 'dictated by communal consciousness', many individuals still seek to form 'a patterned collection of social practices that constitute a sense of continuity and stability' (Cote and Levine, 2002, p. 28). It is still common to try to actively construct a coherent sense of personal identity through narratives 'rooted in the human propensity to remember and project' (Seigel, 2005, p. 653), and as such notions of self-development and personal growth do remain highly relevant when examined in the context of subjective lived experience.

Leisure as a field for personal growth

Much of the preceding discussion has focused on personal identity and development more generally, drawing mainly from social psychology and sociology. It is here that I now hone in on the prospects for, and potential benefits from, perceived self-development and personal growth through the vehicle of leisure. I begin with a brief Western historical perspective on the interconnections between leisure and self-development.

Aristotle's classical leisure ideal provided the original theoretical groundwork for leisure studies (Pieper, 1952). With its roots 2,300 years ago in Greek civilization, the classical leisure ideal is a Occidentalocentric or Eurocentric concept that advocates leisure as a way of living which is characterized by a sense of freedom, learning for its own sake and as being undertaken for self-development (de Grazia, 1962). Goodale and Godbey (1988, p. 38) noted these early linkages between leisure, freedom and knowledge: 'importantly, is the link between learning and the leisure ideal held out by the early Greek philosophers ... [k]nowledge has always been related to freedom, and freedom has always been related to leisure'. Despite the classical leisure ideal being overwhelmed by the rise of the Roman Empire and Calvin's Protestant work ethic (and for the sake of this argument ignoring that ancient Greek citizens commonly kept slaves whose work freed up their owners' leisure time), carrying on from ancient Greece into modern leisure discourse were these ideals of freedom, intrinsic motivation, learning and self-development through leisure (Goodale and Godbey, 1988; Neulinger, 1981). Thus, leisure has been associated with a Western meta-narrative of self-development and personal growth for quite some time.

Whilst modern leisure theorists give due recognition to the blurring between intrinsic and extrinsic motivation (Kelly, 1996) and recognize that freedom in leisure is perceived rather than absolute (Neulinger, 1981), the narrative of gaining self-insight and fulfilment through leisure, and particularly through personally challenging and/or 'adventurous' activities, is common in contemporary discourse. Thus, there is a considerable body of literature within leisure and recreation scholarship positing that self-insight or knowledge can be gained through the negotiation of 'risky situations' (e.g., Walle, 1997; Weber, 2001), as individuals may seek subjectively challenging experiences that provide opportunities for perceived learning and self-testing. This has been exhibited in the growth of adventure recreation activities (Ewert and Jamieson, 2003), and although much of the theory concerning motivations for engagement in adventure experiences has focused on the notion of seeking risk (e.g., Ewert, 1989), alternative explanations suggest self-development through subjective challenge is a primary motivation (Walle, 1997; Weber, 2001).

This perspective on adventure recreation brings us back to developmental views on leisure more generally, which at least partially rest on humanist ideals of self-actualization (e.g., Maslow, 1971) that claim we should strive to develop and fulfil our potential. Moments of self-actualization were described by Maslow (ibid., p. 50) as 'peak experiences', paralleling Csikszentmihalyi's (1990) description of flow experiences, characterized as a heightened internal state achieved through challenging situations. These experiences have been represented as experiential states through which individuals may temporarily escape self-consciousness and re-emerge with a 'stronger' sense of self (ibid.). Flow experiences typically accompany activities perceived as intrinsically motivated or freely chosen (Mannell *et al.*, 1988). Ranging from rock climbing to dancing or sculpting, to name but a few leisure examples, Csikszentmihalyi (1990) suggested that nearly any activity that allows for increasing difficulty can lead to flow experiences and a more complex self. In this sense, flow experience has clear synergies with Stebbins' (1982, p. 256) notion of serious leisure, which likewise views perseverance and 'significant personal *effort*' in forms of leisure as potential routes towards enhancing identity and experiencing personal fulfilment.

I will not endeavour to provide here a comprehensive explanation of the reported dimensions of flow experience or the qualities of serious leisure, as my point is not to re-present these concepts in their entirety. Rather I have hoped to demonstrate how flow theory, also called 'optimal experience' (note that optimal denotes 'most favourable'), and the concept of serious leisure have been depicted as vehicles for self-development. Crucially, aspects of personal growth associated with flow experiences through leisure have often taken a back seat to a primary focus on the characteristics of intense individual moments (e.g., Jones *et al.*, 2003), without enough consideration of the implications of the totality of these moments for both an individual's personal identity and sense of overall subjective well-being. Thus, this brings us back to the central tension that has developed in this chapter – in light of postmodern theory that has deconstructed notions of self-development – are subjective experiences of personal growth through leisure practices of enduring significance?

Conclusion

The conditions associated with postmodernity have been accompanied by scepticism towards the meta-narrative of self-development. A postmodern perspective casts doubt on the prospects of taking leisure seriously. However, there are some fundamental gaps in the postmodern deconstruction of a core personal identity that suggest leisure practices can be more than just the enjoyable passage of time: indeed, it can be argued that when the value of leisure is assessed as a product of the mind, perceptions of personal growth and development can accrue as a positive benefit for individuals.

It is helpful here to draw on another one of the qualities that Stebbins (1982) attributed to serious leisure: the tendency for adherents of serious leisure practices to perceive a 'career' in their endeavours. Stebbins (ibid., p. 256) describes these experiences as 'anything but evanescent occurrences devoid of social or psychological continuity'. Thus, at least serious leisure practices, when strongly identified with and carried on over time, may lend an element of continuity to one's personal identity. As social relations in late modernity become increasingly fragmented, leisure experiences may therefore be a route through which individuals seek to structure aspects of their sense of self. Such a perspective inter-relates with the importance of lifestyles under conditions of post-Fordism, in which personal identities become increasingly structured through (leisure) consumption practices (Shields, 1992; Featherstone, 1987). As Giddens (1991, p. 81) went on to suggest: 'lifestyle consumption practices became decisions not only about how to act but who to be'. Hence while 'career' may not be the best analogy for consumption-led leisure lifestyles, Stebbins' (1997, p. 350) later work on the concept of lifestyle is also helpful in suggesting that leisure lifestyles can be comprised of on-going tangible practices, orientations and ways of identifying, constituting 'the basis for a separate, common social identity'.

Turning back to flow experiences, rather than seeing these as disparate and episodic heightened moments, we might instead take the point of view of how the totality of flow experiences accumulated through a particular leisure lifestyle may contribute to a unique sense of personal identity and well-being on the one hand and a distinct and recognizable social identity on the other (Cohen, 2011). My ethnographic research with 'lifestyle travellers' (ibid.) is one example of this, as I found that individuals who backpacked for years on end for the most part experienced this leisure lifestyle as a meaningful source of identity, characterized by high personal investment, challenge and the linking of rewarding episodes into an on-going perception of learning and gaining competencies. Furthermore, Wheaton's (2004) work on lifestyle sports is rife with examples of how re-occurring positive leisure experiences are assembled into a lifestyle, through a particular 'assemblage of goods, clothes, practices, experiences, appearance and bodily dispositions' (Featherstone, 1987, p 59). For our present discussion, the important point to tease out is that the on-going performance of embodied leisure practices not only constitute recognizable leisure lifestyles, but may also be a source of stability and well-being for those taking part.

Through adhering to a particular leisure lifestyle, individuals perform a patterned collection of everyday social practices that may give them a sense of continuity. The accumulation of their on-going subjective lived experience may provide perceptions of personal growth and self-development, possibly through a gestalt effect in which positive perceptions of cumulative experience exceed the sum of its parts. Regardless of postmodern perspectives that may try to objectively devalue these possibilities for development, the perceived psychological benefits of enduring involvement with a meaningful activity may remain intact for individuals. This focus on the psychological benefits of positive experience, taken forward recently in a wider discourse of 'positive psychology' (see Fredrickson, 2001; Seligman and Csikszentmihalyi, 2000), gives renewed emphasis to the subjective experience of positive emotions and how cumulative experience can affect wellbeing and human flourishing. Consequently, just because identity formation and notions of personal growth may be products of the mind, we cannot and should not discard the value of positive leisure experiences as a vehicle towards personal wellbeing.

16

MODELS OF TEACHING IN LEISURE EDUCATION

Sam Elkington and Mike Watkins

Introduction

Leisure and education represent domains of life that have long been identified as significant for human flourishing. This chapter takes as its primary focus the concept of leisure and the challenges associated with educating students in a globalised society. Whilst different learning situations require different curricula, we consider higher education in this chapter where we want to bring about change in learners' understanding of foundation phenomena (e.g., leisure, sport, travel, hospitality, management, and marketing).

This chapter offers a review of several teaching models in leisure education, revealing their approaches and methods. Subsequently, the chapter goes on to consider two additional teaching models as practice based examples of how learners' understandings of leisure can be recognised and embedded in higher education programmes, providing insight into the kinds of learning that might be effective in terms of enhancing their awareness of and sensibility to leisure. This will necessitate a discussion of central challenges at the heart of academic and professional/practitioner debates around the shifting, intermeshing, modalities of higher education and leisure in modern society.

Learning for leisure in higher education

In the context of higher education Leisure Studies has emerged as an increasingly diverse and disjointed collection of programmes, driven by a changing politico-economic landscape and the growing market potential of emergent sub-specialisms such as sport, tourism, hospitality and event management. The declining interest and perceived relevance of the idea of leisure has seen Leisure Studies fade from curricula at many universities. In the UK and Australia, at least part of the decline in such programmes has related to politico-economic initiatives such as the rise of the cultural and creative industries and the decline of public sector leisure provision (Page and Connell, 2010). Henderson (2010) cites issues of disconnect between research and practice as a major reason for the intellectual downturn in leisure-focused degree programmes in the US, caused in large part by a lack of identity that practitioners feel with the field of Leisure Studies. The shifting reality of contemporary leisure practices functions to challenge traditional theory-bound conceptualisations of leisure, with the increasing differentiation of the leisure field leading to growing tension between leisure educators and leisure professionals who no longer share a common vision pertaining to the study and practice of leisure (Hemmingway and Parr, 2000).

The reality with which educators, students and professionals must now contend is one of change and complexity (Barnett, 2004), and for this reason requires continuous evaluation. Available descriptions, especially in a global and pluralist world, multiply and conflict with one another; meaning our hold on the world, and by extension our leisure, is always a fragile one. This form of uncertainty is characteristically internal, primarily to do with how individuals come to understand themselves, with their sense of identity (or lack of it) – with their being in the world (Elkington, 2012). Such uncertainty creates new challenges for a leisure-focused education. Programs must engage with the life-world issues and pedagogical challenges that arise from learning for an uncertain world. The educational task is in principle not epistemological, not one of knowledge or knowing per se, it is not even one of action, or of effective interventions, it is ontological. From an ontological perspective, the task becomes one of emboldening individuals to prosper amid uncertainty in situations in which there are no stable descriptions. Moreover, at a time when leisure research presents a multitude of alternative, contradictory and partial theories, educator-researchers cannot rely on a consistent body of knowledge. The challenge for teachers is now one of being aware of the many alternative and competing theories and practices that can be brought to bear on leisure situations rather than privileging one paradigm of thought or method over another; socio-cultural over psycho-social, liberal arts over vocational, in what becomes an essentially idealised and uni-dimensional view of leisure pedagogy.

Current theorising depicts the reality of modern leisure as abound with subtle complexity. Accounts of modern leisure tend to be rooted in a dominant discourse of individual choice, freedom and self-determination to the extent that it is confined to the immediately engaged situation and to functional and hedonistic needs (Rojek, 2005; 2010). Indeed, it seems much of modern leisure has become conflated with consumption (Rojek, 2006) in the sense that it is marked by individualised consumer patterns with the pursuit of pleasure and happiness much more than work shaping our sense of ourselves. Such processes have been acknowledged as being reflective of the pervasive complexity of people's contemporary life-worlds, and the increasing differentiation and de-differentiation of social life (Bauman, 2000; Blackshaw, 2010). This is a life that is unpatterned rather than patterned, disordered rather than ordered, characterised by the blurring of boundaries that until relatively recently separated self-contained areas of the life-world: work from leisure, leisure from education. It is also a world of multiplying performance indicators and contrasting interpretations, wherein unprecedented advances in digital technologies coupled with the ever-increasing commodification of mainstream leisure participation means people have become drowned in information but starved of knowledge, leading to a deficit of meaning and a condition in which all knowledge is contestable. Modern leisure requires no accompanying self-consciousness; it is performative rather than expressive (Blackshaw, 2010). Similar patterns are beginning to emerge in higher education more broadly which, like leisure, has become another commodity and, in turn, knowledge is no longer determined by its ability to understand, but by its exchange-value (McWilliam, 2005). Mobilised through contemporary discourses of vocationalism, performativity becomes the criterion of the legitimacy of knowledge claims (Barnett, 2004).

Modern leisure has grown to reflect the uncritical, unreflective attitude of daily life. Practice in this sense is concerned with ordinary life as expressed in the routines or taken-for-granted character of daily activities. There is clear need for leisure to be interpreted pragmatically in order to hold any use-value in the world, for this is a world of multiple interpretations and contestable knowledge claims. The challenge for any leisure-focused curriculum in twenty-first-century higher education is one of determining its positioning in relation to learning for the complex and continually changing environment of modern society. But what is it to learn for leisure in such an uncertain world?

Models of teaching in leisure education

In order to address this question it is useful to consider the responses of leisure scholars and the models of teaching they have proposed to deal with such challenges. A review of literature reveals a substantial repertoire of models with most aimed at school and community based programs (cf., Mundy, 1998; Ruskin and Sivan, 1995; Sellick, 2002). Some however, and those we are interested in, are directed toward teaching and learning in higher education. We have chosen to examine four models and for the purposes of this chapter, have labelled these as the Leisure Optimisation Model, Cultural Heritage Model, Humanistic Training Model and Social Justice Model.

As shown in Table 16.1, the conception of a model for teaching in leisure education incorporates two definitional components: an approach to teaching and a method for teaching what is learned. The first component is divided into what we call the pedagogical ideology and deals with the ontological and epistemological world-view that underpins the teaching method as well as the theory of learning that explains how individuals acquire knowledge about leisure and/or related phenomena. The second component considers the relationship between the teacher and student in respect to the role adopted by the teacher in the transfer of knowledge, and the curriculum content or subject matter delivered through learning activities.

TABLE 16.1 A comparative analysis of teaching models in leisure education curricula

Model	Leisure Optimisation Model	Cultural Heritage Model	Humanistic Training Model	Social Justice Model
Exemplar informants	Leitner & Leitner (2004)	Edginton & Chen (2008)	Cohen-Gewerc & Stebbins (2007)	Rojek (2010)
Goal of learning	Increase the quality of well-being	Achieve intellectual & moral experience	Realise human potential	Create a more fair and just society
Pedagogical ideology	Realism & essentialism	Idealism & perennialism	Existentialism & progressivism	Deconstructionism & critical theory
Theory of Learning	Cognitivism	Behaviourism	Individual constructivism	Social constructivism
Role of the teacher	Lecturer & prescriber	Role model & transmitter	Personal guide & cultivator	Advocate & provocateur
Learning activities	Knowledge of leisure concepts, properties, practices & leisure service delivery skills	Cultural literacy in canonical works of social science & leisure literature	Awareness training; knowledge & skills in serious leisure activity	Critical literacy of social leisure issues; skills in social change

In selecting the four models we have chosen titles to distinguish a variety of approaches and methods with the purpose of identifying how they create different learning environments and achieve different outcomes. While depicting important differences, the models should not be read as being mutually exclusive as they can theoretically and practically overlap in their purpose and application. The models can also be considered as components of a broader leisure education programme; in some contexts they provide the basis for teaching one or more courses of study within a programme whilst in other contexts, parts of different models can appear within the one course of study. With these definitions and caveats in mind, the following section expands on the features of models.

The Leisure Optimisation Model represents a synthesis of approaches and methods found in Peterson and Gunn's (1984) *Leisure Ability Model*, the *Time Wise: Learning Lifelong Leisure Skills* curriculum (Caldwell *et al.*, 2004), and Leitner and Leitner's (2012) text on *Leisure Enhancement*. The common feature of these sources is their commitment to using leisure to increase or optimise the quality of individual well-being. In higher education settings, the focus of learning is generally directed toward the vocational outcome of teaching students about the well-being of prospective clients they will engage with in professional practice. In this respect the model conceptualises well-being as a continuum that can be applied to improving deficits in the functioning of individuals with limited well-being; e.g., clients with disabilities or other special needs, to furthering the quality of well-being for normatively functioning individuals.

The ontological component of the model's ideology is consistent with the realist's belief that individuals exist independently of their social worlds. The idea of leisure is therefore objectified as an entity beyond the individual's immediate apprehension. This dualistic perspective is extended to an epistemological stance that favours an essentialist or core body of factual leisure knowledge generated from scientific investigations. The explanation for how individuals acquire knowledge and achieve higher levels of well-being is based on their ability to form a cognitive representation of leisure that is considered normative and deemed worthy of prescription. A normative representation of leisure well-being is characterised by perceptions of freedom, internal locus of control, positive affect and other psychological qualities associated with a leisure state of mind. The teacher in this model adopts the role of lecturer, delivering learning activities that prescribe these qualities to the learner's awareness. In a leisure education curriculum, knowledge about these qualities is generally presented in the form of leisure concepts (history and definitions), social-psychological properties of leisure (motivations, experiences, satisfactions and constraints), leisure activity practices and leisure service delivery skills (recreation leadership, programming and management) that operationalise the possibility for creating and increasing well-being.

Like the previous model, the Cultural Heritage Model aspires to have students learn a core body of knowledge, but one that occurs through transmitting enduring ideas about leisure found in 'great works' of literature. Examples in a leisure education programme might include *The Theory of the Leisure Class, Homo Ludens: A Study of Play Element in Culture, Leisure: The Basis of Culture, Of Time Work and Leisure*, and recent leisure texts such as *The Social Psychology of Leisure and Recreation, All Work and No Play, Leisure Identities and Interactions* and *Decentring Leisure*. This model comes closest to the idea of a classical or liberal arts education, with its goal of developing intellectual and moral excellence.

The Cultural Heritage Model is illustrated in Edginton and Chen's (2008, p. viii–x, 1–16) *Leisure as Transformation*; a text devoted to learning how 'leisure promotes, facilitates, and enables transformation' in the context of living in a 'leisure oriented society'. In establishing the rationale for the text, the authors assert that 'we live in a time when we are subject to great changes on an ongoing and continuous basis' and that 'without question, the world we live in is in a state of constant transformation.' This situation, they suggest, requires a 'universal perspective of transformation' that will enable 'newly engaged leisure service professionals' to proactively address and master change lest they fall victims to its 'ravages' and 'remain unresponsive to the conditions of our time'. Having established the existence and moral significance of a leisure problem, the authors then provide insights from 'great philosophical thinkers of both Eastern and Western cultures', and combine this information with ideas attesting to the power of leisure benefits as a rationale for effecting transformation though leisure.

Reference to the universal existence of ideas and the belief that enduring truth can be found in the wisdom of others' minds locates the ideology of the model within the ontology of idealism and the epistemology of perennialism. Idealism distinguishes between the body and mind with the former offering access to superficial forms of imperfect and transient experience, and the latter to the world of desirable 'perfect and eternal' ideals. The ideal of leisure as an expression of casual mass escapism would thus hold much less value than the nobler Aristotelian ideal of leisure as self improvement, virtue, and civility. Gaining knowledge about leisure – or of 'confoundations' such as how to understand and manage change – is operationalised through transmitting ideas from texts to inspire students to engage their intellects and grapple with phenomena and problems as seen through the eyes of renowned thinkers. When supplemented with introspection, questioning and critical reasoning, the method aims to develop students' understandings and judgements, and thereby bring these capacities more fully into conscious awareness. However this explanation assumes the learner has the necessary pre-understandings or knowledge to engage in such activities – the source of which is debated among idealists. Edginton and Chen (2008) suggest knowledge comes from behavioural modelling via their reference to Oscar Wilde's assertion that 'Most people are other people; (their) thoughts are someone else's opinions, their lives a mimicry, their passions a quotation' (p. x). Thus, like the cognitive explanation in the previous model, the behavioural underpinning in the Cultural Heritage Model contends that learners are relatively passive beings that need to be 'filled-up' or 'conditioned' with the 'right' kind of knowledge in order to 'correctly understand' the world.

The Humanistic Training Model seeks to provide students with the freedom and responsibility for learning through using leisure to cultivate their potential for realising autonomy and authenticity. Two curricula guides informing the model are Cohen-Gewerc and Stebbins's (2007, chapter 3 pp. 33–49) existentially oriented text: *The Pivotal Role of Leisure Education: Finding Fulfilment in this Century* and Priest and Gass's (1997) more pragmatically inclined text: *Effective Leadership in Adventure Programming*. In the former text, the authors discuss the need for a new model of leisure education; highlighting the inadequacies of an 'old era' of education characterised by 'the transmission of knowledge and a detailed repertoire of canonic behaviors', while juxtaposing this modernist tradition to a global society marked by a general increase in free time, growing allure of casual leisure opportunities and the manipulative power of markets. In response Cohen-Gewerc and Stebbins suggest leisure educators 'must conceive of the existential experience that (learners have) in every moment' and to understand learners as 'experimenting with a deep unconscious expectation for something that could inspire them toward achieving a level of consistent meaning in their own existence'. For these authors, the purpose of leisure education is to cater to this expectation and provide students with the skills in 'how to change (and) how to become' in order to avoid the pitfalls of narcissism and 'improve their ... capacity to realise their part in humankind ... and commitment to human solidarity.'

When conceived in these terms, the ideology of the model approximates an existential ontology where the nature of reality and truth are defined by individual choice and standards. In pragmatic applications of the model (e.g., Priest and Gass, 1997) reality is construed as evolving and truth determined by the group in regards to what works best in particular situations. In both cases, working toward a greater good – improvement of the self or society – emphasises a belief in the epistemology of progressivism; the idea that realising one's capacity for becoming a 'whole' and more aware, self realising person represents a desirable and life-long endeavour. This ideology then, marries with an individual constructivist theory of learning that provides the latitude for students to gain knowledge through interpreting social interactions and forming their own personal or self-realised constructions of knowledge. However, achieving self-realisation is recognised in the Cohen-Gewerc and Stebbins perspective as a difficult task and one that requires assistance. By adopting the role of a personal guide the teacher creates opportunities for 'becoming' using activities that challenge and deepen the sense of self through experimentation, risk taking and 'learning by doing'. Serious forms of leisure activity might be particularly useful given they require significant effort and perseverance and produce durable benefits, some of which extend from the individual to social or other directed, domain of life.

The last model to consider adopts an explicitly political orientation in regard to teaching leisure education. The Social Justice Model aims to have students learn how to problematise socially related leisure practices, deconstruct practices in terms of their constituent actors/structures and hierarchies of power relationships, make judgements about the consequences of relationships, and formulate action strategies that produce better (e.g., less problematic, more equitable) relationships. The primary goal of the model is to create a better society by teaching students to acquire a critical consciousness of the complexity and values of social relations framing leisure practice.

The ideology underpinning the Social Justice Model is based on the ontology that reality is socially constructed and imbued with multiple perspectives that require decoding and reading to understand their true meaning. Knowledge of leisure is therefore fashioned out of normative cultural and sub-cultural practices and exists in different forms; from media communicated signs and symbols to embodied forms of personal or group practice that express implicit or explicit meanings of power. Students and other 'actors' appropriate or absorb these meanings as part of their on-going socialisation in the world. While the ideology behind the model is inherently critical in the sense of valuing and contesting meanings, the teacher might adopt the comparatively neutral role of advocating 'consciousness raising' on the grounds it imbues students with a source of power or the more directed role of provocateur who stimulates students to take direct forms of action to resolve social problems. In both cases, learning activities expose students to real world leisure problems, use cross-cultural comparisons of leisure practice to highlight and contrast multiple perspectives, teach students how to critically read meanings of perspectives and consider solutions to problems.

Rojek's (2010) text, *The Labour of Leisure*, illustrates some of the features of the Social Justice Model in addition to indicating the subject content taught in the model. In the first several chapters (1–5), problems relating to the academic study of leisure are outlined and deconstructed. These include the failure of some leisure academics to accept that social divisions position leisure behaviour and therefore invalidate traditional psychological associations between leisure and freedom; the unsustainability of the leisure society thesis as a justification for continuing to support the existence of Leisure Studies programmes; and the inadequacy of an 'old' cultural studies analytic framework that 'essentialised' the role of the State, Corporations, Consumers and Academics (SCCA) in structuring leisure. In pointing to the consequences of these problems, Rojek notes the field's declining relevance for students, leisure organisations and the broader public; the emergence of new specialisations (Sport and Tourism) with the capacity to better influence public debate, and the ensuing need to re-orient the study of leisure. The recommended strategy for resolving these problems is to reconstruct the content of leisure curricula around an expanded number of agents (the State, Corporations, Consumers, Academics, Social Movements and Illegal Leisure); and to 'attune' students of leisure to their multiple, intersecting and shifting influence in positioning leisure.

In summarising the four teaching models we note their collective contribution to teaching students how to engage in leisure in order to improve well-being, how to use leisure as a source for self-realisation and human flourishing, and how to acquire knowledge about the historical ideals and social relations of leisure. These are important and necessary contributions for achieving the goal of educating students *in, for and about* leisure (cf., Henderson, 2007; Kleiber, 2012, Ruskin, 1995). However, we also observe the models give insufficient attention to students' ontological awareness of leisure as a necessary and preliminary object of learning. This claim may seem at odds with the amount of learning activity devoted in the models to providing students with leisure knowledge, skills and attitudes (or values). Nevertheless our claim is based on the tendency of models to assume that exposing students to aspects of leisure as seen from the perspective of the teacher is equivalent to how students will understand leisure. Put another way, the models emphasise didactic instruction in well-being, self-realisation, historical ideals and social relations through the prism of leisure, not the reflexive constitution of leisure as seen through the prism of student awareness. We believe that achieving the latter perspective requires the student's understanding of leisure be made the explicit object of learning. This is an admittedly subtle and contestable distinction, but one that we hope to reinforce through suggesting how leisure educators can complement existing teacher centred teaching models with student centred models of leisure education.

TABLE 16.2 Reflexive teaching models in leisure education curricula

Model	Leisured Pedagogic Model	Learning to Experience Leisure Model
Informants	Elkington (2012)	Watkins (2000)
Goal of learning	Learn how to intuit the essence of leisure as a lived experience	Learn how to discern different essences or ways of experiencing leisure
Pedagogical ideology	Phenomenological & essentialism	Phenomenographic & relationalism
Theory of learning	Experiential learning theory	Variation theory
Role of the teacher	Philosopher & interpreter	Researcher & educator
Learning activity	Descriptive Hermeneutical understanding of the nature and significance of leisure in students' life world experiences	Building a relevance structure & discerning patterns of variation in critical aspects of leisure experiences

The leisured pedagogic orientation (LPO) model

The first model proposed for teaching leisure education, as shown in Table 16.2, aims to teach students how to (re-orient students as to how they) intuit the essence of leisure as a lived experience using their own experiential, practise-based, knowledge as the central pedagogical referent (Elkington, 2012). Ideologically, the LPO model is informed by a phenomenological essentialism – the systematic examination of the types and forms of *lived* experience, and the reduction of their structures to a rich hermeneutic account of their essence – whilst philosophically drawing on Josef Pieper's (1952) reformulation of leisure's educative value and Max Van Manen's (1977; 1990) various work on experience-based writing and narrative phenomenology. For Pieper, the ultimate purpose of a liberal education is the pursuit of leisure, not only critical thinking skills, but to cultivate a contemplative approach to life that transcends the hegemonic ethos of modern living. Freedom through education is not simply the result of critical thinking but also a vigilant receptivity; a stillness from the busy world of work and the restlessness of a discursive mind. To really understand how people experience leisure, an alternative form of human being is required (Pieper, 1952); that is, the subject matter itself must be decentred and an aesthetic approach to viewing leisure taken up. When viewed from this perspective, leisure offers a valuable way of learning, articulating a form of ontological and epistemological guidance that informs a more adequate interpretation of leisure-in-practice. Such an approach sees leisure presented as more than a teaching object (subject-matter to be taught), but as an orientation, bringing with it an implicit social and moral structure comprising beliefs, attitudes, values and dispositions towards leisure. This structure is brought to life by means of an experiential perspective of teaching and learning that is necessarily reflexive and transdisciplinary; moving beyond the false boundaries of sociology, psychology, philosophy and history to free the educated imagination which aims to enhance the whole person rather than merely train the mind. An experiential theory of learning rests on a distinct set of assumptions about the social nature of learning and the role of the teacher – that experiential knowledge already exists in individuals and that learning is best enhanced by the bringing to bear of these personal resources in educationally purposeful and intrinsically meaningful ways. The teacher thus teaches the students as much as they teach the subject matter of leisure.

The concept of orientation can be understood as the existential referent in such phrases as 'having an orientation' in the same sense that a scientist has a particular orientation toward the world. Similarly, teachers and students will inevitably have various orientations (both personal and professional) with respect to certain issues or subject matter of leisure. Thus, the term orientation refers to the specific ways in which an individual looks at the world and to such abilities as receptivity, stillness, thoughtfulness, as well as criticality. Underlying every orientation is a definite ontology, epistemology, axiology; rather, a person's orientation is at once composed of what they believe to be true, to be valuable and to be real (van Manen, 1977). Pedagogically speaking the concept of orientation functions as a device for making visible how the subject matter of leisure constitutes a way of making sense of the world. This means that change with respect to a particular orientation necessitates movement from one orientation to another, usually experienced as a transition between two worlds – a shift from one reality to another (van Manen, 1977). When presented as an orientation, the subsidiary function of leisure is transformed into an interpretative function; learning for leisure becomes a hermeneutic exercise, that of rendering meaning.

Knowledge, from this perspective, is tied to practical educational experiences through a combination of analysis, interpretation and communication. This practical attitude is reflected in work that is focused on interpersonal communication, on group-processes, on practical deliberation, on critical self-reflective analysis of meanings and implications, and is concerned with making visible and understandable (in an existential sense) the leisure experiences, actions and changing perceptions and preoccupations of learners. For this task interpretative devices are needed to tease out the hidden and invariably un-languaged meanings individuals associate with leisure. Interpretative devices include self-reflective analysis of experience, deliberation and rationalisation of choice-making, and qualitative and aesthetic approaches. The attempt here is to guide students to self-reflectively explicate assumptions, preferences and points of view governing their orientation to leisure. Since the LPO model positions the experiential, practice-based, knowledge of students as an alternative starting point for learning, the curriculum cannot be fully formed and set in place in advance of pedagogical activities. Instead the model promotes an open curriculum, wherein the nature and content of learning activities is necessarily shaped by the reflective experiential offerings of students. This is not a total freedom, however, as students are actively involved in collaborative and interactive learning activities facilitated through an integrated network of themed workshops as opposed to a traditional lecture-seminar format.

An effective way of introducing leisure debates to students has been to consider the central problem with the study of leisure: the definition of leisure and its interrelation with other areas of social life, such as work, family, university and personal identity. During these initial stages of the unit students participate in a series of introductory sessions during which they are encouraged to begin thinking, writing and seeking feedback about their leisure through sharing and discussing their experiences in small groups. This initiation of sorts is critical as students will naturally find it challenging to switch between orientations; from the uncritical and unreflective stance of modern leisure to one of critical participation and self-reflection. A focus on lived experience gives students something to contemplate and through contemplation find new things to see. Students are encouraged to think through their experiences using reflective blogs and leisure diaries designed to capture students' experiences and progress for the duration of the programme. These personal reflective accounts function as a formative tool in relation to student learning, shifting emphasis onto student experience of leisure, familiarising students with sharing and discussing their personal experiences, and providing a meaningful understanding of the changing nature of students' orientation toward leisure. Following van Manen (1982) students are encouraged to make use of analogies, metaphors and other literary devices to compose experiential accounts that, when shared, might evoke images and associations that other readers could relate to and reflect upon.

Students' reflective accounts become source material for an overarching leisure narrative task assigned to students in the first week and submitted and graded at the end of the programme. The leisure narrative is intended neither as a position paper, nor as an argument to be defended. Instead it is an extension and reworking of students' reflective accounts wherein it is expected that students demonstrate their ability to respond to suggestions and feedback and critically incorporate and consider the reading and theoretical material in relation to their own learning on the unit. Students describe in what ways they have been changed by the experience, for better or worse, in terms of their 'self' understanding and in relation to their leisure. In this manner, students are expected to incorporate multiple voices in their final leisure narratives: one being first-person, descriptive and particular, the other being third-person and philosophically informed. In this way, the leisure narratives resemble what is termed in social science research as 'narratives of self' (Sparkes, 2002); in the case of the LPO model students articulate their own lived experiences as part of an academic learning journey. What begins for students as a series of descriptive and reflective first-person written accounts of personally significant leisure experiences is progressively developed into a philosophically informed personal narrative of modern leisure.

Utilising such an aesthetic perspective requires for new ideas and information to be met by different means than merely through formal and didactic input. Initial orientation in relation to new topics or material are made through background readings rather than through introductory lectures, with subsequent inclusion of semi-structured interactive sessions then used to discuss and explore initial conceptualisations of the reading. The need to discuss new information is addressed by incorporating group-based work to formulate comments and questions to be raised in further in-class discussion. Presenting material through formal inputs, such as lectures, can be difficult to engage with. Transforming sessions into peer-managed learning activities allows for students to find out what is relevant and helpful to their own learning by collaboratively exploring the reading material. Personally relevant information is then discussed within small groups before being captured in students' reflective leisure diaries. This generates an appreciative approach to addressing relevant aspects of theory for practice, in that rather than the conventional intellectual detachment of the two, leisure theory is utilised as a way of presenting students with a variety of conceptual mirrors and lenses, in and through which they can view themselves (and others) in relation to their leisure practice. While the written text remains important, the open curriculum of the LPO model encourages the use of other 'non-text' media – visuals, animations, sounds – calling them from their currently marginal status in traditionally overwhelmingly text dependent curricula. Seeing in this sense requires students to view leisure in a certain way, this in turn requires that they come prepared with an orientation that allows themselves to become the object of observation and analysis. It is important, therefore, each student develops their own understanding of a topic, building on what they know already, and sometimes requiring the dismantling or re-conceptualisation of existing understandings. In this view, praxis and theory (reflection) are inextricable. The capacity to edit reality – to organise it and re-organise it, to juxtapose through display, to compare to understand differences – is thus valued as a genuine skill to be honed. Making time for structured reflection is central to this process as reflection is the activity which links the personal with the learning, the theory with the practice (van Manen, 1982). Providing regular opportunity to reflect on and make sense of experiences both inwardly and collaboratively with significant others is fundamental to any act of knowing, allowing students to refine self-knowledge through ongoing exploration and articulation of their own leisure practices and meanings. From this perspective, knowing is always an activity and not a thing to be transmitted from tutor to learner, it is always contextually bound and not abstracted, and is representative of an individual's relational-functional stance toward learning that is rarely static and for this reason requires continuous maintenance and evaluation.

The learning to experience leisure (LEL) model

The second model proposed for teaching leisure education aims to teach students how to learn different ways of experiencing leisure (or other phenomena) but to also recognise experiences as a continuum of possible meanings that display increasing levels of developmental complexity in understanding. This goal is achieved by teaching students to: (1) recognise different experiences of leisure and critical aspects or dimensions forming the content of experiences, (2) describe the relational values of dimensions that provide experiences with their qualitative and developmental character, and (3) use the information to develop their capability for expanding their understanding of leisure. Two learning activities for implementing the model are building a *relevance structure* or appreciation of context in students' awareness of leisure, and introducing evidence of *dimensions of variation* into the learning situation to illustrate differences in context. Prior to elaborating these activities, some background information is required to explain the model's approach and method.

The foundations of the LEL model are informed by a research approach called Phenomenography, initially developed by Ference Marton and his colleagues from the University of Goteborg in Sweden in the mid 1970s (Marton and Booth, 1997) and further developed with colleagues at the University of Hong Kong in the early 2000s (Marton and Tsui, 2004). Their collective interests have been directed toward studying the different ways that students experience or make sense of educational phenomena (e.g., the task of interpreting the meaning of a text or learning a new activity skill) and using the knowledge as the foundation for improving student learning outcomes. The rationale for the approach is based on the claim that students' experiences of phenomena are directly related to their capability for understanding the phenomena, and that acquiring more developed or powerful understandings means changing students' awareness of their experiences.

Phenomenographic studies are implemented by collecting written information from students about a phenomenon, and then analysing their responses in terms of *what* the phenomenon means to them and *how* they experience the phenomenon. In respect to exploring understandings of leisure, stimulus questions might ask students to: (1) describe an example of leisure and say what it is about the experience that makes it leisure, (2) identify critical aspects that form the experience, and (3) say how they understand the meaning of aspects. Analysis of responses aims to reveal a limited number of categories of description; e.g., 3–6 qualitatively different experiences, and several critical aspects or dimensions of variation common to experiences. Categories are described using phrases or sentences, capture different essences of experience and map the field of experience for the study group. Dimensions are written as single or several words (e.g., relaxation) and capture one or more relational values in experiences (e.g., physical, mental and emotional relaxation). Interpreting the categories and dimensions according to some justifiable criteria, such the relative inclusiveness of experiences or their conformance to externally recognised standards, enables the categories to be represented as a developmentally related continuum of meanings. The term developmental in this context refers to possibility for some experiences to be partial or less complete understandings compared with other experiences that are relatively more complete or developed. The continuum arrived at from this process provides a heuristic for subsequent pedagogic application.

In addition to being a research approach, phenomenography also incorporates a theoretical framework for defining the nature of an experience and explaining how students learn new experiences (see Watkins, 2000; Watkins and Bond, 2007). An experience of leisure is conceptualised, as an internal relationship formed *between* the student and a situation he or she describes as leisure. The relationship is internal in the sense that it is constituted in awareness as an essence or gestalt and conveys a wholeness of meaning for the student. Meaning is produced from the relational values attached to the dimensions forming the content of the experience. Different experiences and hence meanings therefore reflect different internal relationships comprising different sets of relational values. However, these relations are neither gained from cognitive representations stored in the mind; individual interpretations formed out of inter-personal interactions; nor appropriated from the external world as behavioural habits or socially shared constructions. Rather, the relations reflect the student's experience of being simultaneously in and of the world. In this respect the pedagogical ideology of the model claims a non-dualistic ontology that recognises students' experiences as being both in and of the world. The corresponding epistemological stance favours a relational form of knowing that focuses on context specific or variations in understandings.

Variation Theory is used to explain how students gain a different or new experience of a phenomenon. This theory holds that learning occurs when students demonstrate the capacity to discern and simultaneously hold in their awareness variations in the relational values of an experience that go beyond the relational values they could express at some previous point in time (Marton and Trigwell, 2000). Variation arises from having previously learned to discern the value or meaning of a dimension of experience and then subsequently discerning further differences in meaning of the same dimension. For instance, if students associate leisure with resting the body or physical relaxation, and then experience a different situation in which alleviating intra-personal stress or emotional relaxation becomes important, then they have learned a different way of relating to the dimension of relaxation. Leaning thus becomes a process of progressing from a vague undifferentiated understanding of one or few values to gaining a more differentiated awareness of several values and hence the ability to express different and more inclusive experiences of leisure.

Teachers can use knowledge about different experiences and Variation Theory to increase students' capabilities for acquiring more developed understandings. This occurs through building *relevance structures* and introducing *variations in the relational values* of dimensions. Pang and Marton (2003) use the concept of a Learning Study to operationalise these strategies. A Learning Study requires the teacher to adopt the role of a researcher to first identify different experiences and dimensions of variation in the educational task at hand and second, to adopt the role of an educator by designing theoretically informed learning activities that teach students to recognise and express variations in experience.

An example of a modified learning study to teach students different and more developed understandings of leisure is outlined in the following case study of a first year undergraduate course in leisure theory. The first step required the teacher to establish a relevance structure around students needing to consider the importance of different experiences when designing leisure services. This was achieved by asking students to relate a memorable sporting event and to say what they liked and/or disliked about the event, and how their experience could be improved by event organisers. A survey of sport event satisfaction reporting the reasons and consequence of changing attendance levels was displayed to heighten the topic's importance. The second step asked students to watch a YouTube video of a popular sport event and write a one page synopsis that answered the three stimulus questions described previously. Students were then asked to form groups, read and discuss group members' responses and generate two or more descriptions that categorised different experiences of leisure and their critical dimensions. This step was assisted by adding synopses taken from a broader range of individuals, and which gave the students additional experiences to consider. The third step asked students to order the resulting categories as a developmental continuum of meanings and to justify the positioning of different meanings through explicating their criteria. Immediately prior to implementing this step, the notion of *developmental relativity* in experience was introduced to reinforce the necessary contribution of less developed experiences to the formation of more developed experiences. An additional task required students to identify one meaning that best coincided with the experience of leisure described in their synopsis and to locate the position of the experience on the continuum. Learning activities in subsequent class sessions including studies of textbook concepts of leisure (e.g., time, activity, state of mind and state of being conceptions) and written reviews of contemporary leisure media (e.g., fiction and films) were progressively used and related to the continuum to increase variation in student awareness. As a final step in the process of learning to experience leisure, an end of semester paper asked students to reflect on their learning and answer two questions. The first question asked students to write about a recent experience of leisure, to locate the experience on the continuum of meanings and to say if the experience represented a development in their understanding and if so why. The second question asked students how they would identify and use knowledge about different experiences of leisure (or other phenomena) in future workplace settings to assist in their professional development and service delivery capabilities. Responses to these questions indicated the potential gains in experiencing leisure and in how to learn about leisure for both the student and teacher.

Conclusion

By decentring the concept of leisure as the object of learning in favour of centring the individuals' experiences of leisure as the object of learning, the LPO and LEL teaching models provide an alternative ontological perspective for framing students' explorations of leisure. As described in the explication of the models, this perspective requires students to investigate individuals' orientations toward leisure in the LPO model or individuals' internal relations in the LEL model.

Several advantages are proposed to accompany the application of these models. First, at the commencement of the chapter we identified the challenge of teaching students how to cope with change and uncertainty, particularly as they relate to ideas about leisure in a globalised society. The models respond to this challenge by teaching students a set of skills for acquiring an emerging body of knowledge about how they and other individuals experience leisure and how they might experience leisure differently at some future point in time. This common feature of the models can be contrasted with existing models that primarily teach students a pre-existing body of knowledge about leisure. Learning how to learn about leisure, rather than learning about what leisure is, has the added advantage of incorporating a cross-cultural and therefore global perspective. This is made possible on the grounds that while it is possible to talk about the concept of leisure without referring to its context, it is not conceivable to talk about people's experiences of leisure without talking about the people who are doing the experiencing.

The second advantage is that making students' experiences of leisure the starting point for learning encourages a deeper level of understanding given students are immediately able to relate to what it is they are learning about. Although their initial understandings of leisure might consist of fragments of knowledge gained from self-formed ideas, others' ideas or from a combination of sources, these formative understandings provide the baseline upon which further understandings can develop. To the extent all ways of knowing are partial and therefore incomplete, the inclusion of new knowledge into existing knowledge is likely to reflect deeper qualitative changes in understanding given the aesthetic and relational nature of experience considered in the models.

It logically follows that the type of knowledge produced by the models contributes a third advantage in the form of a first order understanding or 'leisure propaedeutic'. Propaedeutic knowledge explicitly emphasises the 'whatness' of leisure in terms of the phenomenon's *essence* described in the LPO model or *essences* in the LEL model. Such a foundation provides students with the ability to subsequently address second order questions including: *where* is the phenomenon of leisure to be found and where is it not found; *who* owns, influences or controls leisure and who does not; and *why* does leisure occur and why does it not occur or occur in other ways. Whilst we do not necessarily subscribe to a hierarchy in the content of teaching learning activities in leisure education (as implied in the specification of this advantage), the existence of the models suggests answers to second order questions will arise or be better informed from how students understand their own and others' first order experiences of leisure.

A final advantage of the models is they provide teachers with an additional form of knowledge to assess student understanding. Existing models encourage the teacher to measure the magnitude of quantitative change in students' abilities to recall, apply or judge knowledge about leisure provided by the teacher (e.g., in the form of textbook definitions, journal findings, etc). The result is a measure of how much the student has learned about leisure as the phenomenon is *intended* to be seen from the teacher's perspective. Some students will perfectly replicate the teacher's perspective and obtain a perfect grade; others will do so to varying degrees and record varying grades of achievement. In contrast, focusing on students' pre-existing understandings of their experiences of leisure, exposing them to learning activities that seek to vary and broaden their orientations or internal relations, and then measuring gains in their successive understandings, assesses a different kind of knowledge. This knowledge reflects the magnitude of qualitative change in the experience of leisure as it is *lived* or seen from the student's perspective; from the time between when the course of study commenced and when the study formally ended. We propose, therefore, that the distinction between intended knowledge and lived knowledge represents a phenomenally different and important form of knowledge that is accessible to teachers when they adopt the student's perspective as the first order of teaching leisure education. However, it must be added in closing that, in aiming for leisure, we as educators cannot force leisure upon our students, either with the threat of a failing grade or the promise of a reward, neither must we place ourselves between students and the larger world, or between the student and ourselves; we can only invite students by creating spaces for the experience of leisure to be encountered from alterative perspectives.

17

TO BOLDLY GO ...
TALES FROM A LEISURIST

Lesley Lawrence

> He [James Dodson] has accomplished something in Final Rounds that every writer yearns to experience. He has written a story that lives triumphantly on and off the page, one that elevates the craft of writing to mastery. It is not a book about golf. It is a book about where we may be in the best of our moments. And it is unforgettable.
>
> (Kay, cited in Dodson, 1996, back cover)

Preface

A couple of weeks ago I finished re-reading James Dodson's book called '*Final rounds – a father, a son, the golf journey of a lifetime*', a book I'd first come across more than ten years ago; I was hardly able to put it down even the second time round, perhaps a more poignant read this time due to the relatively recent death of my own father. The story had captivated me again just as it had done many years earlier albeit perhaps for different reasons. Such reads are gems that probably don't come along all that often in whatever genre.

If only ... I can't imagine my story of what studying leisure has meant to me in a journey spanning twenty-five years within Higher Education (HE) and the lessons learned en route, having the same unforgettable impact. Yet, hopefully my chapter will arouse some interest and even empower some of you: it's fundamentally about 'boldly going'. You'll spot the linkage with Star Trek as my story unfolds but don't worry, this chapter isn't all about Star Trek! You'll also discover perhaps rather impatiently that it takes a long time for me to actually get to the story itself. Indeed the story shortened the longer I spent developing the chapter, as I discovered what I really wanted to write about, and what importantly, my readers and editors might enjoy and expect respectively. As time elapsed it became less about my story and more about *why* tell the story. I'll eventually get to my abridged, whistle-stop and rather selective self-tour. So bear with me. Perhaps telling the uninterrupted story is for another time.

This chapter *is* about exploration. It's about periodically loosening perceived preordained shackles and exploring who you want to be and what you really want to say, when writing. Select what you want to write about and how you want to write to the extent that it might even take on the characteristics of quality leisure experience: chosen, challenging and usually enjoyable activity (in my mind). It maybe does already? I'll return to 'writing as leisure experience' shortly. Without diminishing the message, why not experiment with your chosen narratives? Maybe try cultivating what some might describe as a playful approach to writing and publishing? Take the odd risk – what's the worst that could happen? It's nothing like the sort of risk some leisure researchers talk of when, through publication, they open their personal worlds or judgements to others (e.g., Johnson, 2009). Ok, your words are in the public domain and can't easily be retractable unlike when having sent an email message, if we get to it in time. I'm definitely a low-risk saver when its money that's at stake, but I do enjoy taking certain perceived risks in other spheres of my life.

Though, maybe we should not talk of risks, but alternatives and opportunity? Within HE for example, I continue to be influenced by a view of quality enhancement that relies on exploring 'alternative approaches to doing things, rather than relying on tried and tested methods' (Brown, 1999, p. 46). One of the co-editors, Sean, and I concluded over ten years ago when researching the student experience that lecturers should be encouraged to *let go of the ledge* and by doing so would find greater reward and satisfaction in teaching (Gammon and Lawrence, 2000). Arguably, doesn't the same apply to our writing? Sword (2012) somewhat dispels the myth of academics not being 'allowed to write outside of strictly prescribed disciplinary formats ... Academic writing is a matter of making appropriate choices, not of following ironclad rules'. I had made that same choice many years previously with my first scary foray into the world of publishing as a PhD student and apprentice leisure researcher that I go on to describe later. I had a conviction that I wanted to do it a particular way and would gain from doing so but hopefully so would the reader. Though, I slightly cringe when I look at it now, for instance, my 'tendency' to overindulge in 'single' quotation 'marks'!

When we write, what legacy do we want to leave? What do we want the reader to get from reading our words? Yes, for sure, for many working in academe today in the UK it's about REFable entries,[1] Kay's use of *unforgettable* about Dodson's book (my starting point above) does raise the question, what draws us, the reader, to read the books that so many academics lovingly craft and/or dispassionately churn out? It's argued that 'we need to understand the full complexity of writing as a situated activity and to recognise its central place in our practices' in universities (Hyland, 2013, p. 69). I don't think it's something we do truly understand or take enough time to unpack. I really liked the double-pronged question posed by Helen Sword: 'Why do so many academics write like jargon-spouting robots rather than human beings with a story to tell?' (Sword,

2012). She prefaces this with a classically different interpretation of the same question to aid her point:

> What theory can be advanced to explicate the propensity of a significant proportion of individuals engaged in the scholarly profession to manufacture writerly texts that exhibit a more substantial resemblance to the technically-replete discursive formations of androidal entities than to the quotidian narrative artefacts of the non-academic populace?

I find what Sword says is so true and resonates with my own experiences. I find many academic books instantly forgettable nor captivating enough to make me read through the night, something I have often done with fiction or autobiographies in my time, books that I'd categorise as leisure time reading or strictly speaking – unobligated time when I should be sleeping. Too often the messages from reading a chapter or book are eclipsed by the often heavy-going, staid, discipline conventions and/or the overly visibly academic format. Apologies to any reader who is a prolific academic writer, no slur is intended and I shall later give examples of academic books or articles that have captivated me. Other than distinguishing books by the colour of their cover, I often distinguish their readability. For instance, when teaching undergraduate leisure studies students I used to say 'it's the yellow book – "Devil Makes Work" – you'll find it an easy read' (Clarke and Critcher, 1985). This was in contrast to other tomes that no doubt had equally significant messages, but in my mind over-jargonised and were difficult reads, especially for students.

I had come across and now regularly use Hunt's imaginatively called 'Travels with a turtle: metaphors and the making of a professional identity' paper (Hunt, 2006) in my teaching on our university's course for new and/or inexperienced lecturers, partly to show the harder scientists on the course that alternatives exist to effectively convey message. Next week I'm giving them a short extract by Alcuin, the Master of the school at York Minster talking about Albert, his predecessor *c.*750 AD containing 'There he moistened thirsty hearts with divers streams of teaching and varied dews of study' (Malcolm and Zukas, 2000, p. 51). I love the idea of moistening thirsty hearts … The authors thought it would help them 'illuminate what has happened to the "communities" of higher education' (p. 52) and I agreed. In my own case, I hope the story behind the telling of my story will provide some illumination, even sharing my self-doubts after accepting the invitation to do so. For example, I don't see myself as a significant figure in the field of leisure studies, my nearest claim to fame being having co-edited Leisure Studies Association (LSA) volumes with Stan Parker, perceived as the most notable founding father of the sociology of leisure in the UK, along with Ken Roberts (Green *et al.*, 1990, p. 11). I don't have particularly weighty propositions or theories to divulge. Nor had I seriously published within the field of Leisure Studies not having RAE/REF expectations in my role, though conversely this does give me a certain degree of freedom to select what I do write about and where. My publications tend to be chapters in either leisure studies or HE teaching and learning books, hopefully not without some value I would hasten to add. When I was struggling somewhat after a first draft, the editors, Sam and Sean, had reassuringly and kindly offered the view that mine was 'a chapter about an academic journey – one we can all learn from'.

Returning to the fold

Being asked to tell my particular story and contribute to the book by the editors, I suspect, was partly sparked off by me having revisited the world of leisure studies and in my mind, returning to the fold where the UK's Leisure Studies Association was concerned after quite a long absence. Studying leisure [and the LSA] has certainly played a hugely significant part in my professional life, but equally I have experienced spells when I have become and felt distanced from its study. I'd started examining the leisure, learning and working worlds of today's academics and particularly for less experienced staff, the management of these, against a backdrop of quality-of-life concerns and calls for more research on work–life balance in academic staff (Kinman and Jones, 2009). I work in a full-time capacity as Head of Academic Professional Development based in the Centre for Learning Excellence (CLE) at the University of Bedfordshire, a university of around 25,000 students and within a short train journey of London. A major purpose of all our roles in the CLE is supporting staff to enhance their teaching practice and in turn, enhance the student learning experience. I lead our Higher Education Academy-accredited certificate route (Postgraduate Certificate in Academic Practice [PgCAP]) for new and inexperienced staff. Similar to Webster-Wright's (2010) health professionals, from ad hoc comments and course feedback I was increasingly sensing that many were 'grappling with how to fit learning into personal and professional lives that were already full' (p. 9). Early findings from piloting a questionnaire confirmed this, and those present in a subsequent conference presentation at the 2012 LSA Conference to test out ideas and concerns, encouraged me to continue. I'm focusing on three of several trends identified by Ken Roberts (2007): long hours culture, work intensification and new technology though ironically the study's on hold at the moment precisely due to these trends, thus, more of an *ongoiiiiinnng* study. Anyway, I felt more comfortable in accepting the invitation to contribute a chapter having had this excursion to a LSA conference. LSA stalwarts and friends I occasionally encountered often asked if I were likely to come to a LSA conference any time soon.

On several counts then, studying leisure and in particular studying the leisure experience has enduring qualities and I've realised you never quite escape from doing so or from the Leisure Studies community, once part of that family. I've always kept leisure in mind throughout my career. Hence why I'm always likely to be interested in the stated aim of this book, namely to 'examine what it means to study leisure and the individual in the context of a potential new era of leisure, seeking to investigate the leisure experience from various theoretical and methodological approaches'. I am a studier of leisure or a *leisurist,* both seriously and dabbling. I first coined the term leisurist in a book chapter where I was commenting on a reduction in face-to-face leisure interaction and a trend towards us being virtual leisurists rather than real ones though I also wondered if it existed as a proper word (Lawrence, 2003). I've concluded that writing this chapter has been a combination of project-based leisure (Stebbins, 2012a), learning and work-related. I'll be sharing some examples of earlier such project-based leisure later, when in story mode. Stebbins defines project-based leisure as: 'short-term, reasonably complicated, one-off or occasional, though infrequent, creative undertaking carried out in free time, or time free of disagreeable obligation' (Stebbins, 2012a, p. 16).

I call writing this chapter work-related rather than work as I might find ways of better supporting those participants on the PgCAP course; yet, I choose not to let it take precedence over more pressing central work priorities. I have written this chapter almost wholly in my leisure-time (weekends), and find myself asking, thus is it leisure? Defining leisure ... shades of my past when I once lovingly wrote a whole chapter of my draft PhD on this perplexing dilemma only for one of my supervisors to tell me I didn't need to include it at all, a real lesson back then to not get too precious about anything you write. 'Activities can be both work and leisure at the same time' (Beatty and Torbert, 2003, p. 248). Stebbins (2006, p. xi) expands believing there:

> can be joy in work just as there is in leisure and that the joy felt is, at bottom, qualitatively the same in both worlds ... this joy is basically a shared sentiment, in that the core activities in work and leisure which are so powerfully attractive – and which foster the joy – are highly similar, and in some instances, literally identical.

Whilst work-related, it is both leisure and learning to me. I quite like the idea of visualising this chapter as developing a potential 'resource for work-related learning' (Isopahkala-Bouret, 2008, p. 387). In a study aiming to determine 'why well-educated professionals invest their leisure time in learning for the purposes of work' (p. 479), Isopahkala-Bouret found that 'a reason to learn at leisure was understood as an intrinsic interest in something' (p. 488). I do not *have* to write this chapter, but I want to learn from doing so, and have selected to do it at the weekend. I have been choosing to do it rather than watch a film or soccer match on the TV or physically go to the cinema or ground, or going and leisurely perusing and spending money in the shops, or going out into the nearby countryside for a long walk. Where I'm concerned, perhaps I am like the teachers described in a study by Delle Fave and Massimini (2003, p. 336) though I'm less sure about artistic hobbies:

> Teachers perceived knowledge acquisition and exchange as part of their life theme, a means for pursuing personal development and growth in

complexity at the psychological level. Apart from teaching, they devoted their attention to books, artistic hobbies, and study.

Not having too consciously thought about this before, I have also increasingly realised as I have written this chapter that the process I undergo – the formulation of the ideas, seeing what others say, and the writing itself is often when I learn best. Yes, I derive some satisfaction from the product, but much more so from the process.

Fortunate that my lifestyle allows me to have choice, I find I am much more selective these days in what I choose to do that I would class as *learning as leisure* or work-related learning. I probably am one of these more elderly workers referred to by Illeris (2011) usually aged between 45 and 65 – I am nicely placed at the midpoint of this period in case you were wondering. He describes us as those who:

> have passed the so-called life turn which is a psychological phenomenon implying a personal perception ... releasing a kind of unconscious recognition that it is no longer worthwhile engaging in everything – one must reserve remaining learning capacity for what really has a personal meaning and value; one has to be selective (p. 151).

It was the pursuit of learning and a new challenge that was also partly responsible for me accepting the invitation to contribute a chapter. I am a fairly inexperienced writer in using what I assumed would be a 'narrative story-form' (akin to Hunt, 2006). Having accepted the invitation, I began to worry about the consequences of venturing into unfamiliar territory and using a largely untried writing style, even after penning a first draft. Was my chapter just going to be a piece of indulgent piecing together of my life to date? Such self-doubt would appear to rather contradict my confident suggestion to the reader at the start that we shouldn't be too opposed to exploring new approaches.

Easing the unease and taking the plunge

To feel a bit more reassured I felt I needed to find out more about the world of telling stories and associated benefits. I'm blaming the time it has taken me to uncover, accumulate and read literature with which I am less familiar for routinely missing the editors' deadlines, ironic given I'm usually quite a punctual person and meet deadlines. Tending to pursue avenues and change tack has detracted from maintaining a clear focus at times, and has not made this an easier writing challenge. I was aware of literature around biography and autobiography in teacher and adult education (e.g., Kridel, 1998; West, 2010), where this sort of enterprise is commonplace. Though it was slightly worrying to read a confession that 'some stories and the lives that inform them intrigue me; others do not' (Bullough, 1998, p. 19). Was it too risky to enter into unknown territory for this sort of higher powered tome? Etherton (2006, p. 85) for example, believes that:

> The academic community has traditionally discouraged the inclusion of our 'selves' in our writing, and academic writers can find this habit hard to break. Writing about ourselves can be experienced as both an opportunity and a risk: the opportunity for personal growth and development, or the risk that accompanies self-disclosure – disclosure of our selves to ourselves and to others.

Having dissected the pioneering work on Leisure Diaries as a PhD student task (Hedges, 1986) and then more recent examples as such methods became more commonplace, I was also aware of criticisms of approaches that rely on retrospective analysis, whether from research respondents or self.

I was not even sure what my intended approach was to be called, and in a sense am still unsure how to accurately depict it. Was it narrative inquiry (e.g., Trahar, 2011); autobiographical narrative or account (e.g., Michelson, 2011); story telling (e.g., Moon, 2010; McDrury and Alterio, 2003); self-study (e.g., Bullough and Pinnegar, 2001)? Or a mixture of these? Or did/does it really matter? Having tried to make sense of the definitional quagmire I was somewhat relieved to find others struggled with the variety of forms of 'writing about self'. Lai (2010) for example, tries to differentiate between the terms narrative and story that are used in academic writing and concludes that it is difficult to define each, as used in qualitative research. In collecting personal narrative from individuals involved in the development of a community garden and 'synthesized the data into a story' (p. 149), Glover (2004) notes the term narrative being used 'ambiguously in the qualitative research literature'. He chose to 'invoke narrative inquiry here, not simply to denote text data, but rather as a descriptor for a particular type of discourse, namely a story' (p. 147). Usefully summing the situation up, Schrader (2004, p. 116) considers: 'The numerous expressions used throughout the literature – autobiography, biography, narrative, life story – embody a common spirit, as they all refer to an account of a person's life', or in my case, a selective account or snapshots of parts of my professional life as represented later in the chapter. I came across the notion of such storytelling acting as learning, and professional development tools (McDrury and Alterio, 2003). They talk of how the emergence of a reflective paradigm in HE over the previous 20 years had 'advanced storytelling's acceptance as a learning tool' (p.8).

This resonated nicely as I'd call myself an avid learner, learning being ever-present in my inter-related worlds of leisure and work. I was pretty sure I would benefit from the process of developing and writing the chapter. It was clearly helping me to make greater sense of my professional decisions and journey, surprisingly unclear to me at times, feeling a bit ad-hoc and lacking connectivity. I found a view that the autobiographical approach 'seems to be ideally suited to revealing experience-based learning and in tracking the development of self as learner' (Usher, 1998: 18). McDrury and Alterio (2003, p. 12) talk of storytelling's 'application to lifelong learning'. I found many examples of personal benefits to the writer e.g., personal and professional transformation (Cortazzi, 1993);

learning about yourself (Shrader, 2004); and, therapeutic and personal development outcomes (Moon, 2010). I was encouraged by Bridges (2006) who likewise had been encouraged by researchers who had been 'discovering and expressing the power of writing for inquiry, creativity, therapy and reflexivity' (p.102). I ran out of time to explore the world of Flow and writing that seems to fit nicely into all of this: in an article on flow writing for example, Gute and Gute (2008) found that 'writing to learn can transform academic anxiety and boredom by facilitating concentration, providing feedback, and enhancing enjoyment' (p.191). For another time. I found I was getting slightly uneasy about balance: *who* do we primarily write for, ourselves and/or our public?

I also revisited the world of leisure studies and found a plea from Snelgrove and Havitx (2010, p. 337): 'An increased focus on alternative theoretical perspectives, methodologies, and methods is needed in leisure studies'. They cite several other researchers in leisure and sport studies who had advocated greater variety and/or were using less widespread methodologies, and present a useful review of the challenges of narrative inquiry, autoethnography and collective memory-work, under the umbrella term of interpretivist research. They refer to the work of Glover (2003, p. 145) for example, who advocates narrative inquiry as offering 'leisure researchers a meaningful way to produce knowledge that deepens and enlarges our understanding of leisure experiences', bemoaning its lack. I found several other examples where the author(s) had referred to their own story and autobiography e.g. an author developing an autobiographic account following the writing of a key concepts textbook in leisure studies (Harris, 2005); authors referring to their intellectual autobiographies when examining their role in researching the leisure lives of South Asian mothers (Watson and Scraton, 2001); and an author exploring triathlon participation in an autoethnographic account (McCarville, 2007). I even found leisure related examples emerging in teacher and adult education. Shannon (2005) for example, considers the value of stories as a learning tool within the adult education literature and how students in a gender and leisure course used 'autobiographical writing as a means of exploring and understanding how gender interacted with their leisure behaviors throughout their lives' (p. 29). In making a case for their greater usage, published autobiographies and the use of the metaphor in sports-related studies were reported as being a 'neglected resource' (Stewart et al., 2011, p. 582). The Leisure Studies Association often gives platforms to emerging and potential leisure scholars and in its newsletter there are often examples e.g. Lawrence's (2013) work-in-progress narrative of fixed gear cycling and online mediatisation. The signs are promising. As an aside, for each edition the newsletter gives voice to two long-standing LSA members and prolific authors: Bob Stebbins with his *Leisure Reflections* and David Crouch with his *And now for a few words from ... David Crouch,* both always informative reads with clear messages. Cut to the chase I hear you murmuring, what about a few words from me and my actual story? I've distilled it into two chunks of experiences: the apprentice leisure researcher and dabbling in project-based leisure.

The apprentice leisure researcher

I fast-forward to when leisure and its meaning and significance became firmly in and on my mind as an apprentice leisure researcher (PhD student) in the broad area of education for leisure in the mid-late 1980s, following five years teaching physical education in schools. Alan Tomlinson considered this orthodox PE background back then as one of the main routes into leisure studies (Andrews, 2006). I was perhaps one of the leisure scholars Sivan (2006, p. 442) describes:

> leisure scholars have examined the relationship between leisure and education over the past few decades, highlighting the theoretical and practice links between the two domains. Leisure has been identified as a significant domain through which education can be best pursued, and education as a lifelong process through which leisure components could be instilled.

I struggled as a relatively inexperienced social scientist and apprentice leisure researcher towards the halfway point in my studentship. There were always more arguments to fuel the debates, more perspectives to be accounted for a more naturally inclined scientist. I was particularly surprised by the number and depth of the interrelated issues and debates to be covered in an investigation of education for leisure. Its definition, justification and implementation all seemed problematic. I started becoming rather critical of the whole notion of education for leisure as a solution to a leisure problem for young people as usually presented, and the view that such leisure had to be acceptable and conform to a stated norm. As I revealed back then:

> At the height of perceived conceptual confusions, writing a cathartic paper entitled 'Education for Leisure: A Confused Issue?', partially succeeded in getting things into perspective. In examining such questions as 'what is the role of leisure in life?' and 'what is leisure?', trying to relate to my own past and present life experiences was also useful. This meant for example, questioning what leisure had meant to me at various key stages, for instance: as school pupil; as student; as PE teacher; and now as research student. Although at the time I was uneasy about utilising one's own life experiences in research work, I felt justified later, in reading how others had utilised life experiences in their work. I was influenced in these early days as an apprentice leisure researcher by the advice aimed at the beginning research student that 'you must learn to use your life experience in your intellectual work: continually to examine and interpret it. In this sense craftsmanship is the centre of yourself and you are personally involved in every intellectual product upon which you may work' (Wright Mills, 1959, p. 196). As an apprentice leisure researcher, I was encouraged by his belief that 'to be able to trust yet to be sceptical of your own experience is one mark of the mature workman' (p. 216). The combination of reflecting on my own life

experiences and the gradual coming to terms with the nature of critical work and the reality of research, must partially explain how quite suddenly, within a short period of time, things seemed to be falling into place.

(Lawrence, 1989, p. 135)[2]

I used the word cathartic back then about my unpublished piece of writing, but it was only when exploring the literature of autobiography and story-telling for the purposes of this chapter that I came across others who describe such activity as cathartic (e.g., Moon, 2010; McDrury and Alterio, 2003). McDrury and Alterio (2003) describe the 'interrelationships between storytelling processes and cathartic/reflective learning outcomes' (p. 16).

Despite some apprehension at the time, I was encouraged by friends to present my perceptions of the research experience at the 1988 LSA annual conference and to then write up a paper for publication in one of the resultant LSA volumes (Lawrence, 1989). I took the plunge and decided to do something that was going to be useful and enjoyable for me, albeit something that I felt was a bit non-conformist. I argued it was what I needed and what I wanted to do, though still felt unease in doing so and going into a public arena. Although I had uncovered some examples of accounts of research experiences (e.g., Bell and Newby, 1984), I had come across the following observation:

> It is rare (if not unknown) for a social scientist to report the truly early stages of a major research project. You will look in vain in professional journals for an account of the dead-ends entered, the fortuitous coincidences discovered or the striking connections made with other problems.
>
> (Wilson, 1979, p. 104)

Howard Newby, in reflecting upon his PhD research, was convinced that many of the problems he encountered were 'familiar to many researchers, yet they are rarely discussed or given the weight they deserve ... consequently the feelings of inadequacy and insecurity often remained entrenched in the mind of the individual research worker' (Newby, 1977, p. 109).

Many years on, there are many more examples to be drawn upon by the novice researcher. I found a much more substantive personal account of a PhD by Nell Bridges (2006), entitled 'Learning and change through a narrative PhD: a personal narrative in progress'. She refers to herself as a novice narrative researcher and reminded me of my own PhD experiences. She talks in a similar way of 'unforeseen trials and tasks' and 'finding my feet' (p. 95). She finishes her chapter telling the story of her lived experience of her narrative PhD with a recommendation: 'This ever-shifting flux of live experiencing and story is at the heart of narrative inquiry, and I thoroughly recommend it' (p. 102). My own much smaller scale writing exercise had several consequences some of which I have already mentioned above. I also found the confidence to switch tack where my PhD was concerned.

I was surprised when I found and revisited the volume more than twenty years later and saw how the editor had kindly described my chapter:

> The last paper in this volume is an autobiographical description of Lawrence's introduction to leisure research. It is an interesting preamble through the process of developing the 'research experience' ... an experiential, educational approach to problem-solving.
>
> (Murphy, 1989, p. 6)

The editor's comments about this being an autobiographical description had not particularly registered at the time or I had forgotten as time elapsed. Yet,

> For many researchers, reflecting on their first major research achievement (perhaps a research Masters or a doctorate), there are powerful autobiographical elements there, and not just those associated with the conventional loneliness of the long-distance researcher ... Talking to researchers about the personal associations and connotations of research, and the things to which they attribute the greatest and most personal sense of meaning, what often emerges are memories, events, trivia, usually highly subjective, more to do with episodic than cognitive memory, part of a kind of autobiographical semantic net based on associations.
>
> (Hannabuss, 2000, p. 105)

It's only now that I realise the true significance of this period on the rest of my professional life. It's where my strong belief in the notion of the importance of the learning process in any research endeavour was formulated. It has underpinned my approach to PhD and undergraduate dissertation supervision, supporting staff in action research projects, and indeed, many facets of my teaching. Whilst the output is important and is probably often perceived as most important, of greater importance to me is the process and learning from the process. When talking to groups of PhD students in introductory teaching and learning workshops, I find myself digressing from the subject of teacher journeys to the subject of the PhD journey and process. I find the similarity striking. As I said over twenty years ago as an apprentice myself:

> the time it takes to appreciate the reality of being a researcher is one of the most important ingredients in the learning process. But the 'coming to terms with reality' could be speeded up and facilitated through, for example, becoming consciously aware of the reality of the research process, through engaging in reflexivity, through utilising personal life experiences and through having access to the written 'research experiences' of other researchers.
>
> (Lawrence, 1989: 138)

Thus for all sorts of reasons my leisure researcher apprenticeship was very much a formative period when my leisure became more than just leisure to be personally experienced 'inconsequentially' (Roberts, 2011b), and became an integral presence in my interrelated worlds of learning and work.

Dabbling in project-based leisure

Following the completion of my PhD and a couple of years working in a leisure research centre at the University of Brighton largely researching leisure preferences and experiences of a range of leisure participants and users, I moved from the south coast when a lecturing opportunity arose at the newly formed University of Luton, just north of London, advertised as suiting somebody inexperienced in lecturing. Research activity and writing took a back seat in the early days of being a leisure studies lecturer as I almost completely focused on teaching, supporting students and course management. I fitted in some doctoral student supervision and external examining, and continued to involve myself in the LSA serving on its executive committee on two separate spells. I only occasionally managed to keep my hand in and do some data collection, writing and publishing within leisure studies, the start of my dabbling period, still continuing today.

Such activity was often triggered when I felt aggrieved or curious about something and found the art of writing not only enabled a sort of cathartic release in certain circumstances but that it allowed me to learn, develop and organise my thinking, and it was fulfilling and enjoyable. I've mentioned earlier, I feel lucky in having choice in what I research and write about, and I do make time for it, within my own (leisure) time. Often it is about my own leisure experiences. Probably the best example came from being a director of studies for a PhD student who was studying football (soccer) fandom. Whilst being a football fan was generally accepted unless you were a hooligan, Star Trek's hardcore audience was portrayed as 'unknowable and irrational' (Tulloch and Jenkins, 1995, p. 3). I was an active fan of each at the time and my interest in collecting some data was triggered by irritation. I had concluded that:

> where Star Trek fans were concerned, their leisure practice is not only marginalised but also trivialised and often ridiculed by 'outsiders' ... Why is it generally accepted to walk around town wearing a football shirt that shows an identification with a favoured football team (or being used simply as a leisure/fashion top) but unacceptable to do so wearing *Star Trek* gear? Moreover, why is going to a football match more acceptable than attending a *Star Trek* convention?
>
> (Lawrence, 2000, pp. 161–2)

The editors (Brackenridge *et al.*, 2000) felt that my 'essay [was] an apposite ending for this volume, in which the reader is invited to reflect on both the just-ness of social inclusion/exclusion in contemporary leisure practices and the significance of leisure in identity formation' (p. ix).

The closure of two science fiction/Star Trek fan clubs, both of which I was a member at the time, also triggered off some related research and I started exploring how the advent of technology impacted upon traditional leisure practice and environments (Lawrence, 2003).

> In February 2001 the British Science Fiction Review ceased publication, citing the immediacy of web-based material as a primary cause ... A similar fate had already befallen a *Star Trek* newsletter, Infinite Diversity in Infinite Combinations (IDIC), which had ceased publication in 1996.
>
> (Lawrence, 2003, p. 303)

I recall fondly one comment: 'I shall sadly miss that bimonthly thud as my fat little envelope hits the doormat! (IDIC newsletter, Edition 47).

I further explored the serious leisure facet of my Star Trek findings a few years later and a scenario of *serious leisure taken too far* or perceived to have been by others; as I coined it 'this serious leisure shadowland' (Lawrence, 2006, p. 78). I found this whole area quite eye-opening as I extended my research into many other fields. The world of collecting unearthed some gems for example, the story of the beer label collector whose obsession led to stealing labels and being sentenced by a judge – the collection numbered 30,000 (Pearce, 1998, p. 162). It was then that I came upon another of my unforgettable books, this time by Richard Askwith (2004), a fell-runner with a personal quest to complete a non-stop circuit of 42 of the Lake District's highest peaks within 24 hours. I was struck by his own questioning of his devotion to a life of fell-running such as 'what madness can have possessed me?' He responds, 'We don't always give ourselves enough credit for doing no harm – and running with like-minded friends in wildernesses that most people consider too bleak and distant to have anything to do with is as harmless a diversion as it's possible to imagine' (p. 321).

It was when I headed up my faculty's Pedagogical Research and Development Unit as part of an Associate Dean (Teaching and Learning) role and was supporting others to engage in research that wasn't just subject/discipline-based that I realised how potent such research could be. I'd found a niche. Wisdom (cited in Cousin, 2009, p. xii) talks of the dual professional in referring to how we study our subject *and* our students. I had begun studying teaching and learning *within* leisure studies a few years earlier, exploring the impact of applying leisure related psychological theory (the concept of Flow) to how a colleague's (Sean) final year 'Leisure in Mind' module was delivered (Gammon and Lawrence, 2000). The teaching strategy Sean had adopted seemed to be making a difference to the student experience and attainment on his module but this perception was unsubstantiated. I was convinced it was down to him purely being an excellent teacher – his student evaluations were outstanding and the best I had seen. But why? The potential reason and benefit of using leisure in learning to re-focus student motivation we had found made us further explore applying Flow, this time to student and lecturer assessment strategies (e.g., Gammon and Lawrence, 2006).

I have since explored the application of Flow in several other settings within HE, for example, personal development planning [PDP] (Lawrence, 2004) and non-specialist teaching (Elkington and Lawrence, 2012). From inconsequential beginnings I would not have predicted this pathway and such unanticipated outcomes when Sean and I wanted to salve our curiosity as to why his student evaluations were so good but needed evidence. It's such meandering that I find enjoyable and fulfilling. I recall Wright Mills' advice to the inexperienced researcher to 'try to be passively receptive to unforeseen and unplanned linkages' (1959, p. 212). I suppose I could never have predicted my career path either.

I moved from faculty to central university posts in student support and teaching quality enhancement, and even more quickly, bypass that period. Emerging from the past few years in my current role in our Centre for Learning Excellence has been an example of project-based leisure that I referred to earlier in the chapter as the *ongoiiiiinnng* study. I have witnessed an increasing number of participants on the PgCAP course that I lead having difficulty finding time to learn whether on the PgCAP or on other courses on which they have embarked, or more informally through workplace learning (Illeris, 2011). This worries me as I do believe in lifelong learning, a strong personal philosophy that transcends both my work and leisure, so the notion that 'learning may stretch out across a lifetime' (Field, 2006, p. 90). Some preliminary findings presented at LSA 2012 were revealing; trying to fit things in was deemed for example, as 'very tricky – lots of leisure/ sleep time sacrifice'. Or, 'Working is priority, PgCAP comes second, and leisure comes last'. Boundaries are blurring. I received some knowing and almost guilty nods and affirmative grunts from some in the audience when talking about 'work creep' (Milliken and Dunn-Jensens, 2004, p. 51). I'd asked did anybody use their mobile devices to be constantly checking emails when on leave? Personally on annual leave, my aim is to switch off as I know I need the recovery time, as some will term, psychological detachment from work during nonwork time (e.g., Park *et al.*, 2011; Sonnentag, 2012).

Outside of such protected space, I think we need to work harder at making and using the space we do create more creatively. I see parallels in what I have been doing in writing this chapter and what Wright-Mills (1959) calls 'loosening your imagination' when talking about rearranging a filing system as part of intellectual craft. Loosening your imagination, Wright-Mills believes:

> occurs by means of your attempt to combine various ideas and notes on different topics. It is a sort of logic of combination, and 'chance' sometimes plays a curiously large part in it. In a relaxed way, you try to engage your intellectual resources, as exemplified in the file, with the new themes. (p. 201)

Why not take time out and in a relaxed way explore and try different or new ventures, even if at times we feel it is a bit indulgent or horrors of horrors we don't have time? Doug Kleiber in 1999 talks of 'the "busy-ness" that is the disease of contemporary life ... we have "hurry sickness", which threatens the health of many who are swept along by the rapids of everyday life' (1999, p. xv). You'll be entertained by a book by the author of *Chaos* (another of my unforgettable books) – James Gleick's *Faster – The Acceleration of Just About Everything*. He asks are we 'just too tired to relax, too tired to have fun' (Gleick, 1999, p. 160)? Bowers (2007, p. 42) believes that:

> there is even less room for a leisurely life, and increasingly our digital lives have locked us into a constant barrage of communications, expectations, multi-tasking and accountability that appears to have traversed all facets of our being, be it at work, in the home or beyond.

Postscript

In the last few years I think I have discovered the ideal sanctuary for writing, a conducive and alternative space cut off from the constant barrage Bowers identifies. Not in the privacy of my house where I sit now at my computer, seeing my neighbours' houses and cars and the occasional person walking past. The scenery is not spectacular unlike where I was in late November – then, the sun was spectacularly setting over a fjord. I was lucky enough to be taking part in an international writing retreat in Iceland, writing as a combination of learning, work and leisure, but with an outcome, a published piece of work. But to me, it works because I am cut off from the world and in a self-imposed email-free zone albeit a chilly experience in this instance. I and a colleague tell the tale of embedding action research into the PgCAP curriculum as a quality enhancement tool (Lawrence and Corkill, 2013). I had convinced myself over the years that I write best when I privately shut myself away, another type of retreat. I now believe that my most productive learning and professional development stems from writing activity, but often when aided through a collaborative and contrasting (from the norm) learning environment. I'd commend writing retreats; they work for me and many others, even in less beautiful locations.

'We live in a speeded up world. But writing has a pace of its own … you need time for the thoughts to emerge'. 'You need to have space for thinking'. These were sentiments I jotted down at a lecture last night at the University of West London by Ron Barnett. It was entitled *'That blinking cursor demands words from me': a wandering scholar reflects on an academic life*. A prolific author on Higher Education, in the marketing blurb for the event Barnett asks the same questions I'd been wondering about:

> Despite its undeniable difficulties and challenges, is writing good for the soul? Just why – in being an academic – might one want to write? How can one embark on such a journey, and in what spirit can one pursue it?

He was sharing his passion, writing. I wasn't sure what to expect but it was illuminating in many ways not least of all when he talked about what had turned him into a writer and the writer he was. In the flyer for the event he reveals 'In a sense, all my academic writing, even though it has been somewhat theoretical and even abstract and philosophical has been *autobiographical*'.

I end by borrowing Usher's (1998, p. x) conclusion to his chapter:

> The past has distended into the present and it is time to bring this narrative to a close. Obviously, a premature closure since much more could be said. Thus this is a text that must necessarily remain unfinished.

I [we] have much more I [we]want to do, more tales to tell and I [we] will somehow find the time.

Acknowledgements

Influential in telling this tale have been many but I'd like to dedicate this chapter to two men who sadly passed away in 2012 – Stan Parker, a stalwart of the LSA, for his humility, strength of conviction and what he taught me, and my father, for just being my dad and always having faith in me.

Notes

1   Research Exercise Framework (REF) is the system for assessing the quality of research in UK HE institutions (see http://www.ref.ac.uk/), previously, the Research Assessment Exercise (RAE).
2   I'm not sure if I'm 'allowed' to do this but I have taken the liberty of removing many single quotation marks given it's my own writing.

BIBLIOGRAPHY

Aaker, L., Rudd, M. and Mogilner, C. (2011) 'If money does not make you happy, consider time', *Journal of Consumer Psychology*, 21(2): 126–130.

Abrams, M. (1959) *The Teenage Consumer*. London: London Press Exchange.

Adams, M., Bell, L. A. and Griffin, P. (eds) (1997) *Teaching for Diversity and Social Justice*. New York: Routledge.

Agyeman, J., Bullard, R. D. and Evans, B. (2002) 'Exploring the nexus: bringing together sustainability, environmental justice and equity', *Space & Polity*, 6: 77–90.

Ahrentzen, S. B. (1992) 'Home as a workplace in the lives of women', in I. Altman and S. Low (eds) *Place Attachment*. London: Plenum Press.

Ajzen, I. (1991) 'The theory of planned behavior', *Organisational Behavior and Human Decision Process*, 50: 179–211.

Ajzen, I. and Driver, B. (1992) 'Application of the theory of planned behavior to leisure choice', *Journal of Leisure Research*, 24: 207–224.

Aitchison, C. C. (2006) 'The critical and the cultural: explaining the divergent paths of leisure studies and tourism studies', *Leisure Studies*, 24: 417–422.

Albermarle Report (1960) *The Youth Service in England and Wales*. London: HMSO.

Algoe, S. and Haidt, J. (2009) 'Witnessing excellence in action: the other-praising emotions of elevation, admiration, and gratitude', *Journal of Positive Psychology*, 4: 105–127.

Allison, M. (2000) 'Leisure, diversity, and social justice', *Journal of Leisure Research*, 32(1): 2–6.

Allison, M. T. and Duncan, M. C. (1987) 'Women, work and leisure: the days of our lives', *Leisure Sciences*, 9: 143–161.

Anderson, J. (1970) *The Ulysses Factor*. London: Hodder & Stoughton.

Andrews, D. (2006) 'Leisure Studies: progress, phases and possibilities – an interview with Alan Tomlinson', *Leisure Studies*, 25: 257–273.

Applebaum, H. A. (1998) *The American Work Ethic and the Changing Work Force: A Historical Perspective*. Westport, CT: Greenwood Press.

Arai, S. and Kivel, B. D. (2009) 'Critical race theory and social justice perspectives on whiteness, difference(s), and (anti)racism: a fourth wave of race research', *Journal of Leisure Research*, 41(4): 459–470.

Argyle, M. (1996) *The Social Psychology of Leisure*. New York: Penguin.

Arnett, J. J. (2004) *Emerging Adulthood: The Winding Road from the Late Teens through the Twenties*. New York: Oxford University Press.

Arnould, E. J. and Price, L. L. (1993) 'River magic: extraordinary experience and the extended service encounter', *Journal of Consumer Research*, 20: 24–45.

Arriaga, P., Esteves, F., Carneiro, P. and Monteiro, M. B. (2008) 'Are the effects of unreal violent video games pronounced when playing with a Virtual Reality System?', *Aggressive Behavior*, 34: 521–538.

Askwith, R. (2004) *Feet in the Clouds – A Tale of Fell-running and Obsession*, London: Aurum Press.

Assmann, J. (2005) *Religion and Cultural Memory*, trans. Rodney Livingston. Stanford, CA: Stanford University Press.

Avis, A. (2007) 'Seek, so you may find', *Turkish Daily News*, November 3, http://www.turkishdailynews.com.tr/article.php?enewsid=87581 (accessed 5 February 2013).

AVM (2007) *Volunteer Manager Survey – Results* http://www.volunteermanagers.org.uk/volunteer-manager-survey-results (accessed 15 August 2012).

Backman, S. and Mannell, R. C. (1986) 'Removing attitudinal barriers to leisure: a field experiment among the institutionalized elderly', *Therapeutic Recreation Journal*, 20: 46–53.

Baldwin, C. and Caldwell, L. (2003) 'Development of the Free Time Motivation Scale for Adolescents', *Journal of Leisure Research*, 35: 129–151.

Bandura, A. (1977) *Social Learning Theory*. New York: Prentice Hall.

Bang, H., Won, D. and Kim, Y. (2009) 'Motivations, commitment, and intentions to continue volunteering for sporting events', *Event Management*, 13(2): 69–81.

Bannert, M. and Arbinger, P. R. (1996) 'Gender-related differences in exposure to and use of computers: results of a survey of secondary school students', *European Journal of Psychology of Education*, 11: 269–282.

Barnes, M. and Sharpe, E. (2009) 'Looking beyond traditional volunteer management: a case study of an alternative approach to volunteer engagement in parks and recreation', *Voluntas*, 20: 169–187.

Barnett, R. (2004) 'Learning for an unknown future', *Higher Education Research and Development*, 23, (3): 247–260.

Bauman, Z. (1996) 'From pilgrim to tourist – or a short history of identity,' in S. Hall and P. du Gay (eds) *Questions of Cultural Identity*. London: Sage.

Bauman, Z. (2000) *Liquid Modernity*. Cambridge: Polity Press.

BBC (1989) *Around the World in 80 Days*, BBC, London, 11/10/89–22/11/89.

BBC (2007) *Long Way Down*, BBC Two, London, 28/10/07–2/12/07.

BBC News (2013) 'Fake girlfriend: I paid for make-believe love on Facebook'. *http://www.bbc.co.uk/news/technology-21446368* (accessed February 2013).

Beatty, J. E. and Torbert, W. R. (2003) 'The false duality of work', *Journal of Management Inquiry*, 12, 3: 239–252.

Beaumont, J. (2011) *Well-being – Discussion Paper on Domains and Measures*. Office for National Statistics Publication.

Beck, U. (2000) *The Brave New World of Work*. Cambridge: Polity.

Beck, U. and Beck-Gernsheim, E. (2002) *Individualization: Individualism and Its Social and Political Consequences*. London: Sage.

Beck, U. and Beck-Gernsheim, E. (2009) 'Global generations and the trap of methodological nationalism for a cosmopolitan turn in the sociology of youth and generation', *European Sociological Review*, 25: 25–36.

Becker, G. (1965) 'A theory of the allocation of time', *Economic Journal* 75: 493–517.

Bednar, R. L., Wells, M. G. and Peterson, S. R. (1989) *Self-esteem: Paradoxes and Innovations in Clinical Theory and Practice*. Washington, DC: American Psychological Association.

Beedie, P. (2010) *Mountain Based Adventure Tourism: Lifestyle Choice and Identity Formation*. Saarbrucken: Lambert Academic Publishing.

Beedie, P. & Hudson, S. (2003) 'The emergence of mountain based adventure tourism', *Annals of Tourism Research*, 30(3): 625–643.

Behnke, K. A. (2012) 'Ladies of Warcraft: changing perceptions of women and technology through productive play', *FDG '12 Proceedings of the International Conference on the Foundations of Digital Games'*, New York: ACM.

Bell, C. and Newby, H. (1984) (eds) *Social Researching – Politics, Problems, Practice*. London: Routledge and Kegan Paul.

Bell, E. (2008) *Theories of Performance*. Los Angeles: Sage.

Bell, G. (2010) 'Self-determination theory and therapeutic recreation: the relevance of autonomy, competence, and relatedness to participant intrinsic motivation' (Doctoral dissertation, Clemson University). Retrieved from http://etd.lib.clemson.edu/documents/1285779192/Bell_clemson_0050D_10720.pdf (accessed 30 July 2012).

Bendle, L. and Patterson, I. (2008) 'Serious leisure, career volunteers and the organisation of arts festivals in a regional Australian city', *International Journal of Event Management Research*, 4(1): 1–10.

Bennett, A. (1999), 'Subcultures or neo-tribes? Rethinking the relationship between youth style and musical taste', *Sociology*, 33: 599–617.

Bennett, A. and Kahn-Harris, K. (2004), 'Introduction', in A. Bennett and K. Kahn-Harris (eds) *After Subculture: Critical Studies in Contemporary Youth Culture*. Basingstoke: Palgrave.

Bennett, T., Savage, M., Silva E., Warde, A., Gayo-Cal, M. and Wright, D. (2009) *Culture, Class, Distinction*. London: Routledge.

Berger, P. (1967) *The Sacred Canopy: Elements of a Sociological Theory of Religion*. New York: Doubleday.

Berleant, A. (2003) 'The aesthetics in place', in S. Menin (ed.) *Constructing Place: Mind and Matter*. London: Routledge.

Berry, J., Poortinga, Y., Segall, M. and Dasen, P. (2002) *Cross-cultural Psychology: Research and Applications* (2nd edn). Cambridge: Cambridge University Press.

Berry, L. L. (1990) 'Market to the perception', *American Demographics*, February.

Bertozzi, E. (2008) '"I am shocked, shocked!": Breaking taboos in digital gameplay', *Loading*, 3.

Billis, D. (1993) *Organising Public and Voluntary Agencies*. London: Routledge.

Billis, D. (2010) 'Towards a theory of welfare hybrids', in D. Billis (ed.) *Hybrid Organizations and the Third Sector. Challenges for Practice, Theory and Policy*. London: Palgrave Macmillan.

Biran, A. and Poria, Y. (2012) 'Reconceptualising dark tourism', in R. Sharpley and P. R. Stone (eds) *Contemporary Tourist Experience: Concepts and Consequences*. Abingdon, Oxon: Routledge.

Biran, A., Poria, Y. and Oren, G. (2011) 'Sought experiences at (dark) heritage sites', *Annals of Tourism Research*, 38(3): 820–841.

Bishop, D. W. and Witt, P. A. (1970) 'Sources of behavioral variance during leisure time', *Journal of Personality and Social Psychology*, 16: 352–360.

Blackman, S. (2005) 'Youth subcultural theory: a critical engagement with the concept, its origins and politics, from the Chicago School to postmodernism', *Journal of Youth Studies*, 8: 1–20.

Blackshaw, T. (2010) *Leisure*. London: Routledge.

Blackstone, T., Gales, K., Hadley, R. and Lewis, W. (1970) *Students in Conflict: LSE in 1967*. London: Weidenfeld and Nicolson.

Bloch, C. (2000) 'Flow: beyond fluidity and rigidity. A phenomenological investigation', *Human Studies*, 23: 43–61.

Blossfeld, H-P. and Timm, A. (eds) (2003) *Who Marries Whom? Educational Systems as Marriage Markets in Modern Societies*. Dordrecht: Kluwer.

Bone, M. (1972) *The Youth Service and Similar Provision for Young People*. London: HMSO.

Borrie, W. T. and Roggenbuck, J. W. (2001) 'The dynamic, emergent, and multi-phasic nature of on-site wilderness experiences', *Journal of Leisure Research*, 33: 202.

Borsay, P. (2006) *A History of Leisure*. New York: Palgrave Macmillan.

Bosserman, P. and Gagan, R. (1972) 'Leisure and voluntary action', in D. H. Smith (ed.) *Voluntary Action Research*. Lexington, MA: D.C. Heath.

Boyd, D. (2007) 'Why youth (heart) social network sites: the role of networked publics in teenage social life', in D. Buckingham (ed.) *MacArthur Foundation Series on Digital Learning – Youth, Identity, and Digital Media*. Cambridge, MA: MIT Press.

Bowen, D. and Clarke, J. (2009) *Contemporary Tourist Behaviour: Yourself and Others and Tourists*. Oxford: CBI International.

Bowers, T. (2007) 'Cultivating a leisurely life in a culture of crowded time: rethinking the work/leisure dichotomy', *World Leisure Journal*, 49, 1: 30–43.

Brackenridge, C., Howe, D. and Jordan, F. (2000) 'Editors' introduction' in C. Brackenridge, D. Howe, and F. Jordan (eds) *JUST Leisure: Equity, Social Exclusion and Identity*, LSA Publication, No. 72.

Bradley, W. and Mannell, R. C. (1984) 'Sensitivity of intrinsic motivation to reward procedure instructions', *Personality and Social Psychology Bulletin*, 10: 426–431.

Braun-Courville, D. K. and Rojas, M. (2009) 'Exposure to sexually explicit web sites and adolescent sexual attitudes and behaviours', *Journal of Adolescent Health*, 45: 156–162.

Bray, R. A. (1912) *Boy Labour and Apprenticeship*. London: Constable.

Breathnach, T. (2006) 'Looking for the real me: locating the self in heritage tourism', *Journal of Heritage Tourism*, 1(2): 100–120.

Bricker, K. and Kerstetter, D. (2000) 'Level of specialisation and place attachment: an exploratory study of white-water recreationists', *Leisure Sciences*, 22: 233–257.

Bridges, N. (2006) 'Learning and change through a narrative PhD: a personal narrative in progress', in S. Trahar (ed.) *Narrative Research on Learning: Comparative and International Perspectives*. Oxford: Symposium Books.

Brooks, J. J., Wallace, G. N. and Williams, D. R. (2006) 'Place as relationship partner: an alternative metaphor for understanding the quality of visitor experience in a backcountry setting', *Leisure Sciences*, 28, 331–349.

Brown, J. D. (2000) 'Adolescents' sexual media diets', *Journal of Adolescent Health*, 27: 35–40.

Brown, J. D. (2006) 'Emerging adults in a media-saturated world', in J. J. Arnett and J. L. Tanner (eds) *Emerging Adults in America: Coming of Age in the 21st Century*. Washington, DC: American Psychological Association.

Brown, J. D. and L'Engle, K. L. (2009) 'X-Rated: sexual attitudes and behaviors associated with U.S. early adolescents' exposure to sexually explicit media', *Communication Research*, 36: 129–151.

Brown, K. W. and Ryan, R. M. (2003) 'The benefits of being present: mindfulness and its role in psychological well-being', *Journal of Personality and Social Psychology*, 84: 822–848.

Brown, P. (1987) *Schooling Ordinary Kids*. London: Tavistock.

Brown, S. (1999) 'How can threshold standards assure and enhance quality', in H. Smith, M. Armstrong, and S. Brown (eds) *Benchmarking and Threshold Standards in Higher Education*. London: Kogan Page.

Bruyere, B. L. and Rappe, S. (2007) 'The motivations of outdoor volunteers', *Journal of Environmental Planning and Management*, 50, (4): 503–516.

Bryant, C. D. (ed.) (2011) *The Routledge Handbook of Deviant Behaviour*. London: Routledge.

Bryant, F. and Veroff, J. (2007) *Savoring: A New Model of Positive Experience*. Mahwah, NJ: Erlbaum.

Bryce, J. (2001) 'The technological transformation of leisure', *Social Science Computer Review*, 19: 7–16.

Bryce, J. (2010) 'Online sexual exploitation of children and young people', in Y. Jewkes and M. Yar (eds) *Handbook of Internet Crime*. London: Willan.

Bryce, J. and Haworth, J. T. (2002) 'Well-being and flow in a sample of male and female office workers', *Leisure Studies*, 21 249–263.

Bryce, J. and Kaye, L. K. (2011) 'Computer and videogames', in G. Brewer (ed.) *Media Psychology*, London: Palgrave Macmillan.

Bryce, J. and Klang, M. (2009) 'Young people, disclosure of personal information and online privacy: control, choice and consequences', *Information Security Technical Report*: 14: 160–166.

Bryce, J. and Rutter, J. (2003) 'The gendering of computer gaming: experience and space', in S. Fleming and I. Jones (eds) *Leisure Cultures: Investigations in Sport, Media and Technology*. Eastbourne: Leisure Studies Association.

Bryce, J. and Rutter, J. (2006) 'Digital games and the violence debate', in J. Bryce and J. Rutter (eds) *Understanding Digital Games*. London: Sage.

Bullough, R. V. (1998) 'Musings on life writing: biography and case studies in teacher education', in C. Kridel (ed.) *Writing Educational Biography – Explorations in Qualitative Research*. New York and London: Garland Publishing, pp. 19–32.

Bullough, R. V. and Pinnegar, S. (2001) 'Guidelines for quality in autobiographical forms of self-study research', *Educational Researcher*, 30, 3: 13–21.

Burgham, M. and Downward, P. (2005) 'Why volunteer, time to volunteer? A case study from swimming', *Managing Leisure*, 10(2): 79–93.

Burkhalter, B. (1999) 'Reading race online: discovering racial identity in Usenet groups', in M. A. Smith and P. Kollock (eds) *Communities in Cyberspace*. London: Routledge.

Burkitt, I. (1991) *Social Selves: Theories of the Social Formation of Personality*. London: Sage.

Burns, T. (1992) *Erving Goffman*, London: Routledge.

Buss, A. H. and Briggs, S. (1984) 'Drama and the self in social interaction', *Journal of Personality and Social Psychology*, 47: 1310–1324.

Butler, J. (1990) 'Performative acts and gender constitution: an essay in phenomenology and feminist theory', in S. Case (ed.) *Performing Feminisms: Feminist Critical Theory and Theatre*. Baltimore, MD: Johns Hopkins University Press.

Byrd, R. (1938) *Alone*. New York: G.P. Putnam's Sons.

Caldwell, L. and Witt, P. (2011) 'Leisure, recreation, and play from a developmental context', *New Directions for Youth Development*, 130: 13–27.

Caldwell, L., Baldwin, C., Walls, T. and Smith, E. (2004) 'Preliminary effects of a leisure education program to promote healthy use of free time among middle school adolescents', *Journal of Leisure Research*, 36, (3): 310–335.

Caldwell, L. L., Patrick, M. E., Smith, E. A., Palen, L. A. and Wegner, L. (2010) 'Influencing adolescent leisure motivation: intervention effects of *HealthWise* South Africa', *Journal of Leisure Research*, 42: 203–220.

Caltabiano, M. (1995) 'Main and stress-moderating health benefits of leisure', *Society and Leisure*, 18: 33–52.

Campbell, A. (1980) *The Sense of Well-Being in America*. New York: McGraw-Hill.

Carroll, J. S., Padilla-Walker, L. M., Nelson, L. J., Olson, C. D., McNamara, B. C. and Madsen, S. D. (2008) 'Generation XXX: pornography acceptance and use among emerging adults', *Journal of Adolescent Research*, 23: 6–30.

Cassell, J. and Jenkins, H. (1998) *From Barbie to Mortal Kombat: Gender and Computer Games*. Cambridge, MA: The MIT Press.

Cassidy, W., Jackson, M. and Brown, K. (2009) 'Sticks and stones can break my bones, but how can pixels hurt me? Students' experiences with cyber-bullying', *School Psychology International*, 30: 383–402.

Centre for Economic Performance (2010) *Immigration and the UK Labour Market: The Evidence from Economic Research*. London: Centre for Economic Performance, London School of Economics.

Ceron, J. and Dubois, G. (2007) 'Limits to tourism? A backcasting scenario for sustainable tourism mobility in 2050', *Tourism and Hospitality Planning and Development*, 4(3): 189–208.

Chan, R. and Lau, L. (2001) 'Explaining green purchase behavior: a cross-cultural study on American and Chinese consumers', *Journal of International Consumer Marketing*, 14: 9–40.

Chick, G. and Dong, E. (2005) 'Cultural constraints on leisure', in E. L. Jackson (ed.) *Constraints to Leisure*. State College, PA: Venture.

Cialdini, R. B., Borden, R. J., Thorne, A., Walker, M. R., Freeman, S. and Cloan, L. R. (1976) 'Basking in reflected glory: three (football) field studies', *Journal of Personality and Social Psychology*, 34: 366–375.

Clapham, D., Buckley, K., Mackie, P., Orford, S. and Stafford I. (2010) *Young People and Housing in 2020: Identifying Key Drivers for Change*. York: Joseph Rowntree Foundation.

Clarke, J. and Critcher, C. (1985) *The Devil Makes Work – Leisure in Capitalist Britain.* Basingstoke: MacMillan Press.

Clarke, S. G. and Haworth, J. T. (1994) 'Flow experience in the daily lives of sixth form students', *British Journal of Psychology*, 85: 511–523.

Clary, E. G. and Snyder, M. (1991) 'A functional analysis of altruism and prosocial behaviour: the case of volunteerism', in M. Clark (ed.) *Review of Personality and Social Psychology.* Newbury Park, CA: Sage.

Clary, E. G., Snyder, M. and Ridge, R. (1992) 'Volunteers' motivations: a functional strategy for the recruitment, placement and retention of volunteers', *Nonprofit Management and Leadership*, 2: 333–350.

Clary, E. G., Snyder. M. and Stukas, A. (1996) 'Volunteers' motivations: findings from a national survey', *Nonprofit and Voluntary Sector Quarterly*, 25: 485–505.

Clary, E. G., Snyder, M., Ridge, R., Copeland, J., Stukas. A., Haugen, J. and Miene, P. (1998) 'Understanding and assessing the motivation of volunteers: a functionalist approach', *Journal of Personality and Social Psychology*, 74: 1516–1530.

Clawson, M. and Knetsch, J. L. (1966). *Economics of Outdoor Recreation.* Baltimore, MD: John Hopkins Press.

Coatsworth, D., Sharp, E., Palen, L., Darling, N., Cumsille, P. Marta, E. (2005) 'Exploring adolescent self-defining leisure activities and identity experiences across three countries', *International Journal of Behavioral Development*, 29, (5): 361–370.

Cockburn, C. (1986) 'The material of male power', in *Feminist Review* (ed.) *Waged Work: A Reader.* London: Virago.

Cohen, E. (1992) 'Pilgrimage centers: concentric and excentric', *Annals of Tourism Research*, 19, (1): 33–50.

Cohen, E. (1995) 'Contemporary tourism – trends and challenges: sustainable authenticity or contrived post-modernity?' in R. Butler and D. Pearce (eds) *Change in Tourism: People, Places, Processes.* London: Routledge.

Cohen, P. (1976) 'Sub-cultural conflict and working class community', in A. Hammersley and P. Woods (eds) *The Process of Schooling.* London: Routledge.

Cohen, S. (1972) *Folk Devils and Moral Panics.* London: MacGibbon and Kee.

Cohen, S. and Taylor, L. (1992) *Escape Attempts: The Theory and Practice of Resistance to Everyday Life.* London: Routledge.

Cohen, S. A. (2011) 'Lifestyle travellers: backpacking as a way of life', *Annals of Tourism Research*, 38(4): 1535–1555.

Cole, H. and Griffiths, M. D. (2007) 'Social interactions in Massively Multiplayer Online Role-playing Games', *CyberPsychology and Behavior*, 10: 575–583.

Coleman, J. S. (1961) *The Adolescent Society: The Social Life of the Teenager and Its Impact on Education.* New York: Free Press.

Collinson, J. A. and Hockey, J. (2007) '"Working out" identity: distance runners and the management of disrupted identity', *Leisure Studies*, 26(4): 381–398.

Colwell, J. (2007) 'Needs met through computer game play among adolescents', *Personality and Individual Differences*, 43: 2072–2082.

Colwell, J. and Kato, M. (2003) 'Investigation of the relationship between social isolation, self-esteem, aggression and computer game play in Japanese adolescents', *Asian Journal of Social Psychology*, 6: 149–158.

Colwell, J. and Payne, J. (2000) 'Negative correlates of computer game play in adolescents', *British Journal of Psychology*, 91: 295–310.

Conant, J. B. (1965) 'Social dynamite in our large cities: unemployed out-of-school youth', in A. Kerber and B. Bommarito (eds) *Schools and the Urban Crisis.* New York: Holt, Rinehart and Winston.

Conrad, P. and Schneider, J. (1992) *Deviance and Medicalization: From Badness to Sickness.* Philadelphia: Temple University Press.

Cortazzi, M. (1993) *Narrative Analysis*, Social Research and Educational Studies Series: 12. London: The Falmer Press.

Cote, J. E. and Levine, C. G. (2002) *Identity Formation, Agency, and Culture: A Social Psychological Synthesis.* Mahwah: Lawrence Erlbaum Associates.

Courneya, K. (1995) 'Understanding readiness for regular physical activity in older individuals: an application of the theory of planned behavior', *Health Psychology,* 14: 80–87.

Cousin, G. (2009) *Researching Learning in Higher Education – An Introduction to Contemporary Methods and Approaches.* London: Routledge.

Crawford, D. and Jackson, E. (2005) 'Leisure constraints theory: dimensions, directions, and dilemmas', in E. Jackson (ed.) *Constraints to Leisure.* State College, PA: Venture Publishing.

Crawford, D., Jackson, E. and Godbey, G. (1991) 'A hierarchical model of leisure constraints', *Leisure Sciences,* 13: 309–320.

Cross, E. J., Richardson, B., Douglas, T. and von Kaenel-Flatt, J. (2009) *Virtual Violence: Protecting Children from Cyberbullying.* London: Beatbullying.

Cross, G. (1993) *Time and Money.* London: Routledge.

Crouch, D. (2000) 'Places around us: embodied lay geographies in leisure and tourism', *Leisure Studies,* 19: 63–76.

Csikszentmihalyi, M. (1975) *Beyond Boredom and Anxiety.* San Francisco: Jossey-Bass.

Csikszentmihalyi, M. (1990) *Flow: The Psychology of Optimal Experience.* New York, NY: Harper & Row.

Csikszentmihalyi, M. (1992) *Flow: The Psychology of Happiness.* London: Rider.

Csikszentmihalyi, M. (1997) *Finding Flow: The Psychology of Engagement with Everyday Life.* New York: Basic Books.

Csikszentmihalyi, M. (2002) *Flow.* London: Random House.

Csikszentmihalyi, M. (2003) *Good Business: Leadership, Flow and the Making of Meaning.* London: Hodder & Stoughton.

Csikszentmihalyi, M. and Csikszentmihalyi, I. S. (eds) (1988) *Optimal Experience: Psychological Studies of Flow in Consciousness.* New York: Cambridge University Press.

Csikszentmihalyi, M. and Csikszentmihalyi, I. S. (eds) (2006) *A Life Worth Living: Contributions to Positive Psychology.* Oxford: OUP.

Csikszentmihalyi, M. and LeFevre, J. (1989) 'Optimal experience in work and leisure', *Journal of Personality and Social Psychology,* 56: 815–822.

Currie, D. H., Kelly, D. M. and Pomerantz, S. (2006) '"The Geeks shall inherit the earth": girls' agency, subjectivity and empowerment', *Journal of Youth Studies,* 9: 419–436.

D'Andrea, A. (2007) 'Osho international meditation resort (Pune, 2000s): an anthropological analysis of Sannyasin therapies and the Rajneesh legacy', *Journal of Humanistic Psychology,* 47(1): 91–116.

Daley, A. J. (2009) 'Can Exergaming contribute to improved physical activity levels and health outcomes in children?' *Paediatrics,* 124: 763–771.

Danziger, K. (1997) 'The historical formation of selves', in R. D. Ashmore and L. Jussim (eds) *Self and Identity: Fundamental Issues.* New York: Oxford University.

Datablog (2010) www.guardian.co.uk, 14 November, retrieved 14 June 2011.

David, M. (2010) *Peer to Peer and the Music Industry: The Criminalisation of Sharing.* London: Sage.

David, M. E. (1980) *The State, the Family and Education.* London: Routledge.

Davies, A. (1992) *Leisure, Gender and Poverty.* Buckingham: Open University Press.

Davis Smith, J. (1998) *The 1997 National Survey of Volunteering.* London: National Centre for Volunteering.

DeBotton, A. (2002) *The Art of Travel.* London: Penguin.

de Grazia, S. (1962) *Of Time, Work and Leisure.* New York: The Twentieth Century Fund.

Delle Fave, A. and Massimini, F. (2003) 'Optimal experience in work and leisure among teachers and physicians: individual and bio-cultural implications', *Leisure Studies,* 22: 323–342.

Department for Education (1995) *Young People's Participation in the Youth Service,* Statistical Bulletin 1/95, London: Department for Education.

Department for Education and Skills (2005) *Youth Matters*. London: Department for Education and Skills.

Dewey, J. (1916) *Democracy and Education*. New York: Macmillan.

Dickinson, J. and Lumsdon, L. (2010) *Slow Travel and Tourism*. London: Earthscan.

Dickinson, J., Lumsdon, L. and Robbins, D. (2011) 'Slow travel: issues for tourism and climate change', *Journal of Sustainable Tourism*, 19, (3): 281–300.

Diener, E. (2000) 'Subjective well-being: the science of happiness and a proposal for a national index', *American Psychologist*, 55: 34–43.

Dietz, T. L. (1998) 'An examination of violence and gender role portrayals in video games: implications for gender socialization and aggressive behavior', *Sex Roles*, 38: 425–442.

Dodson, J. (1996) *Final Rounds – A Father, a Son, the Golf Journey of a Lifetime*. London: Arrow.

Donath, J. (1998) 'Identity and deception in the virtual community', in M. Smith and P. Kollack (eds) *Communities in Cyberspace*. London: Routledge.

Donnelly, P. (2004) 'Playing with gravity: mountains and mountaineering', in P. Vertinsky and J. Bale (eds) *Sites of Sport: Space, Place and Experience*. London: Routledge.

Donovan, N., Halpern, D. and Sargeant, R. (2002) *Life Satisfaction: The State of Knowledge and Implications for Government*, Strategy Unit. London: Cabinet Office.

Dorling, D. (2010) *Injustice: Why Social Inequality Persists*. Cambridge: Polity Press.

Dossey, L. (1982) *Space, Time & Medicine*. Boston, MA: Shambhala Publications.

Douglas, J. W. B. (1968) *All Our Future*. London: P. Davies.

Drasdo, H. (1978) 'Margins of safety', in K. Wilson (ed.) *The Games Climbers Play*. London: Diadem.

Driver, B. L. and Brown, P. J. (1984) 'Contributions of behavioral scientists to recreation resource management', in I. Altman and J. F. Wohlwill (eds) *Behavior and the National Environment*. New York: Plenum Press.

Driver, B. L. and Tocher, S. R. (1970) 'Toward a behavioral interpretation of recreational engagements, with implications for planning', in B. L. Driver (ed.) *Elements of Outdoor Recreation Planning*. Ann Arbor: University of Michigan Press.

Driver, B. L., Tinsley, H. E. A. and Manfredo, M. J. (1991) 'The paragraphs about leisure and recreation experience preference scales: results from two inventories designed to assess the breadth of the perceived psychological benefits of leisure', in B. L. Driver, P. J. Brown and G. L. Peterson (eds) *Benefits of Leisure*. State College, PA: Venture Publishing.

Dubrovsky, V. J., Kiesler, S. and Sethna, B. N. (1991) 'The equalization phenomenon: status effects in computer-mediated and face-to-face decision-making groups', *Human Computer Interaction*, 6: 119–146.

Dunning, E. and Sheard, K. (1979) *Barbarians, Gentlemen and Players*. London: Martin Robertson.

Durkheim, E. (2001 [1912]) *The Elementary Forms of Religious Life* (translated by C. Cosman). Oxford: Oxford University Press.

Earth Charter Commission (1992) *The Earth Charter*. http://www.earthcharterinaction.org/content/pages/Read-the-Charter.html (accessed December 1, 2012).

Easterbrook, G. (2003) *The Progress Paradox: How Life Gets Better While People Feel Worse*. New York: Random House.

Edginton, C. E. and Chen, P (2008) *Leisure as Transformation*. Champaign, IL: Sagamore Publishing.

Edwards, D. (2005) 'It's mostly about me: reasons why volunteers contribute their time to museums and art museums', *Tourism Review International*, 9: 21–31.

Edwards, D. (2007) 'Leisure-seeking volunteers: ethical implications', *Voluntary Action*, 8, (3): 19–39.

Edwards, D. and Graham, M. (2006) 'Museum volunteers. A discussion of challenges facing managers in the cultural and heritage sector', *Australian Journal of Volunteering*, 11(1): 19–27.

Eijck, K. van (1999) 'Socialisation, education and lifestyle: how social mobility increases the cultural heterogeneity of status groups', *Poetics*, 26: 309–328.

Eley, D. (2003) 'Perceptions and reflections on volunteering: the impact of community service on citizenship in students', *Voluntary Action*, 5(3): 27–45.

Elgin, D. (1981) *Voluntary Simplicity: Toward a Way of Life that is Outwardly Simple, Inwardly Rich*. New York: William Morrow and Company, Inc.

Elgin, D. (2010) *Voluntary Simplicity: Toward a Way of Life that is Outwardly Simple, Inwardly Rich, (2nd edn)*. New York: Harper Collins.

Elkin, F. and Westley, W. A. (1955) 'The myth of the adolescent culture', *American Sociological Review*, 20: 680–684.

Elkin, F. and Westley W. A. (1957) 'Protective environment and adolescent socialization', *Social Forces*, 35: 243–249.

Elkington, S. (2010) 'Articulating a systematic phenomenology of flow: an experience-process perspective', *Leisure/Loisir*, 34: 327–360.

Elkington, S. (2011) 'What it is to take the flow of leisure seriously', *Leisure/Loisir*, 35: 253–282.

Elkington, S. (2012) 'Ways of seeing degrees of leisure: from practice to pedagogy', *Leisure Studies*, 31: 1–15.

Elkington, S. and Lawrence, L. (2012) 'Non-specialism and shifting academic identities: a sign of the times?,' *Innovations in Education and Teaching International*, 49, 1: 51–61.

Ellis, S. (2002) *The Volunteer Recruitment Book*, 3rd edn. Philadelphia: EnergizeInc.

Emmett, I. (1971) *Youth and Leisure in an Urban Sprawl*. Manchester: Manchester University Press.

Erikson, B. H. (1996) 'Culture, class and connections', *American Journal of Sociology*, 102: 217–251.

Erikson, E. H. (1968) *Identity: Youth and Crisis*. New York: Norton.

Ermisch, J. and Francesconi, M. (1999) *Cohabitation in Britain: Not for Long but Here to Stay*, Working Paper, Institute for Social and Economic Research. Colchester: University of Essex.

Etherton, K. (2006) 'Reflexivity: using our "selves" in narrative research', in S. Trahar (ed.) *Narrative Research on Learning: Comparative and International Perspectives*. Oxford: Symposium Books.

Evans, D. (2012) *Risk Intelligence: How to Live With Uncertainty*. London: Atlantic Books.

Evans, W. M. (1965) *Young People in Society*. Oxford: Blackwell.

Ewert, A. (1989) *Outdoor Adventure Pursuits: Foundations, Models, and Theories*. Columbus: Publishing Horizons.

Ewert. A. and Jamieson, L. (2003) 'Current status and future directions in the adventure tourism industry', in J. Wilks and S. J. Page (eds) *Managing Tourist Health and Safety in the New Millennium*. Amsterdam: Pergamon.

Fain, G. S. (1991) 'Moral leisure', in G. S. Fain (ed.) *Leisure and Ethics: Reflections on the Philosophy of Leisure*. Reston, VA: American Association for Leisure and Recreation.

Farmer, S. and Fedor, D. (1999) 'Volunteer participation and withdrawal: a psychological contract perspective on the role of satisfaction, expectations, and organization support', *Nonprofit Management and Leadership*, 9: 349–367.

Featherstone, M. (1987) 'Lifestyle and consumer culture', *Theory, Culture and Society*, 4(1): 55–70.

Ferguson, C. J. (2010) 'Blazing angels or resident evil? Can violent videogames be a force for good?', *Review of General Psychology*, 14: 68–81.

Ferguson, C. J. and Kilburn, J. (2010) 'Much ado about nothing: the misestimation and overinterpretation of violent video game effects in Eastern and Western nations: comment on Anderson *et al.*, (2010)', *Psychological Bulletin*, 136: 174–178.

Ferguson, C. J. and Rueda, S. M. (2010) 'The Hitman study: violent video game exposure effects on aggressive behaviour, hostile feelings and depression', *European Psychologist*, 15: 99–108.

Ferguson, C. J., Rueda, S. M., Cruz, A. M., Ferguson, D. E., Fritz, S. and Smith, S. M. (2008) 'Violent video games and aggression: causal relationships or by-product of family violence and intrinsic violence motivation?', *Criminal Justice and Behavior*, 35: 311–332.

Ferguson, K. (2012) *Bradt Travel Guide, Slow Cornwall & the Isles of Scilly*. Guilford, CT: Globe Pequot Press Inc.

Field, J. (2006) *Lifelong Learning and the New Educational Order* (2nd edn). Stoke on Trent: Trentham Books.

Filiciak, M. (2003) 'Hyperidentities: postmodern identity patterns in massively multiplayer online role-playing games', in M. J. P. Wolf and B. Perron (eds) *Video Game Theory Reader*. New York: Routledge.

Finklestein, M. (2009) 'Intrinsic vs. extrinsic motivational orientations and the volunteer process', *Personality and Individual Differences*, 46: 653–658.

Fletcher, R. (2008) 'Living on the edge: the appeal of risk sports for the professional middle class', *Sociology of Sport Journal*, 25: 310–330.

Fletcher, R. (2010) 'The emperor's new adventure: public secrecy and the paradox of adventure tourism', *Journal of Contemporary Ethnography*, 39, (1): 6–33.

Fogelman, K. (1976) *Britain's Sixteen Year Olds*. London: National Children's Bureau.

Fortier, J., Auger, D. and Froment-Prévesto, C. (2007) 'The motivations and satisfactions of youth volunteers in leisure and sport activities in Quebec: the perspective of the volunteer and the organisation', *Voluntary Action*, 8, (3): 79–97.

Foucault, M. (1988) 'Technologies of the self', in L. Martin, H. Gutman and P. Hutton (eds) *Technologies of the Self: A Seminar with Michel Foucault*. London: Tavistock.

Fowler, D. (2008) *Youth Culture in Modern Britain, c1920–c1970*. Basingstoke: Palgrave Macmillan.

Franklin, S. S. (2010) *The Psychology of Happiness: A Good Human Life*. Cambridge, MA: Cambridge University Press.

Fredrickson, B. L. (2001) 'The role of positive emotions in positive psychology: the broaden-and-build theory of positive emotions', *American Psychologist*, 56, (3): 218–226.

Fredrickson, B. L. (2006) 'The Broaden-and-Build theory of positive emotions', in Y. Harahousou, 'Leisure and aging', in C. Rojek, S. M. Shaw and A. J. Veal (eds) *A Handbook of Leisure Studies*. Basingstoke and New York: Palgrave Macmillan.

Freeman, A. (1914) *Boy Life and Labour*. London: King.

Freire, P. (1971) *Pedagogy of the Oppressed*. New York: Bloomsbury Publishing.

Frey, B. S. (2008) *Happiness: A Revolution in Economics*. Cambridge, MA: MIT Press.

Furedi, F. (2007) 'The only thing we have to fear is the culture of fear itself', Spiked On-Line Essay www.spiked-online.com/index.php?/site/article/3053 (accessed December 2012).

Gage III, R. and Thapa, B. (2012) 'Volunteer motivations and constraints among college students: analysis of the volunteer function inventory and leisure constraints models', *Nonprofit and Voluntary Sector Quarterly*, 41: 405–430.

Gailey, C. W. (1993) 'Mediated messages – gender, class, and cosmos in home video games', *Journal of Popular Culture*, 27: 81–97.

Gammon, S. (2012) 'Sports events: typologies, people and place', in S. Page and J. Connell (eds) *The Routledge Handbook of Events*, London: Routledge, pp 101–119.

Gammon, S. and Lawrence, L. (2000) 'Using leisure in learning to re-focus student motivation: "letting go of the ledge"', in *Teaching and Learning Conference Proceedings*, University of Luton.

Gammon, S. and Lawrence, L. (2006) 'Improving student experience through making assessments "flow"', in C. Bryan and K. Clegg (eds) *Innovative Assessment in Higher Education*. London: Routledge.

Gardner, N. (2009) 'A manifesto for slow travel', *Hidden Europe Magazine, 25:* 10–14.

Garthorne-Hardy, J. (1979) *The Public School Phenomenon*. Harmondsworth: Penguin.

Gaskin, K. (2003) *A Choice Blend: What Volunteers Want from Organisation and Management*. London: Institute for Volunteering Research.

Gentile, D. (2009) 'Pathological video-game use among youth ages 8 to 18: a national study', *Psychological Science*, 20: 594–602.

Gentile, D. A. and Anderson, C. A. (2003) 'Violent video games: the newest media violence hazard', in D. A. Gentile (ed.) *Media Violence and Children: A Complete Guide for Parents and Professionals*. Westport, CT: Praeger Publishing.

Gentile, D. A., Lynch, P. J., Linder, J. R. and Walsh, D. A. (2004) 'The effects of violent video game habits on adolescent aggressive attitudes and behaviors', *Journal of Adolescence*, 27: 5–22.

Gergen, K. J. (1991) *The Saturated Self: Dilemmas of Identity in Contemporary Life*. USA: Basic Books.

Gewerc-Cohen, E. and Stebbins, R. (2007) *The Pivotal Role of Leisure Education: Finding Personal Fulfilment in This Century*, State College, PA: Venture Publishing.

Ghazi, P. and Jones, J. (1997) *Getting a Life: The Downshifters' Guide to Happier, Simpler Living*. London: Hodder and Stoughton.

Giddens, A. (1991) *Modernity and Self-identity: Self and Society in the Late Modern Age*. Cambridge: Polity Press.

Gilby, T. and O'Brien, T. C. (1964) *St. Thomas Aquinas Summa Theologiae*. London: Blackfriars translation. Oxford: McGraw Hill.

Gilchrist, P. and Ravenscroft, N. (2013) 'Space hijacking and the anarcho-politics of leisure', *Leisure Studies*, DOI: 10.1080/02614367.2012.680069.

Gillard, A., Watts, C. and Witt, P. (2007) 'The effect of perceptions of support for autonomy, relatedness, and competence on interest in camp for adolescent girls', in C. LeBlanc and C. Vogt (compilers) *Proceedings of the 2007 Northeastern Recreation Research Symposium*. Newton Square, PA: USDA Forest Service.

Gilpin, W. (2005) *Observations of the River Wye*. London: Pallas Athene Arts.

Gim, J. (2009) 'Toward a quality leisure experience: the practice of mindfulness', *World Leisure Journal*, 51: 105–109.

Gleick, J. (1999) *Faster – The Acceleration of Just About Everything*. London: Little, Brown and Company.

Glover, T. D. (2003) 'Taking the narrative turn: the value of stories in leisure research', *Society and Leisure*, 26, 1: 145–167.

Glover, T. D. (2004) 'Social capital in the lived experiences of community gardeners', *Leisure Sciences*, 26, 2: 143–162.

Godbey, G. (1989) 'Implications of recreation and leisure research for professionals', in E. Jackson and T. Burton (eds) *Understanding Leisure and Recreation: Mapping the Past, Charting the Future*. State College, PA: Venture Publishing.

Godbey, G., Graefe, A. and James, S. (1992) *The Benefits of Local Recreation and Park Services: A Nationwide Study of the Perceptions of the American Public*. Washington, DC: National Recreation and Park Association.

Goetschius, G. W. and Tash, M. J. (1967) *Working with Unattached Youth*. London: Routledge.

Goffman, E. (1956) 'Embarassment and social interaction', *The American Journal of Sociology*, 62, (3): 264–271.

Goffman, E. (1959) *The Presentation of Self in Everyday Life*. New York: Doubleday.

Goffman, E. (1963) *Behaviour in Public Places*. London: Collier-Macmillan Limited.

Goffman, E. (1983) 'The interaction order', *American Sociological Review*, 48: 1–17.

Goodale, T. L. and Godbey, G. C. (1988) *The Evolution of Leisure: Historical and Philosophical Perspectives*. State College, PA: Venture Publishing.

Gottlieb, A. (1982) 'Americans' vacations', *Annals of Tourism Research*, 9(2): 165–187.

Graef, R., Csikszentmihalyi, M. and Gianinno, S. M. (1983) 'Measuring intrinsic motivation in everyday life', *Leisure Studies*, 2: 155–168.

Graf, D. L., Pratt, L. V., Hester, C. N. and Short, K. R. (2009) 'Playing active video games increases energy expenditure in children', *Pediatrics*, 124: 534–540.

Graham, M. (2007) 'Volunteering for tourism: discordance and commonality within a serious leisure context', *Voluntary Action*, 8, (3): 3–18.

Graves, L., Stratton, G., Ridgers, N. D. and Cable, N. T. (2007) 'Energy expenditure in adolescents playing new generation computer games', *British Medical Journal*, 335: 1282–1284.

Green, B. C. and Jones. I. (2005) 'Serious leisure, social identity and sport tourism', *Sport and Society*, 8(2): 164–181.

Green, E., Hebron, S. and Woodward, D. (1990) *Women's Leisure, What Leisure?* Basingstoke: MacMillan.

Greenwood, D. N. and Long, C. R. (2009) 'Mood specific media use and emotion regulation: patterns and individual differences', *Personality and Individual Differences*, 46: 616–621.

Griffin, C. (1984) *Typical Girls?* London: Routledge.

Gunn, L. and Caissie, L. T. (2002) *Deviant Leisure and Serial Murder: Exploring the Unknown*. Tenth Canadian Congress on Leisure Research, University of Alberta, Edmonton, Alberta.

Gunter, B. G. (1987) 'The leisure experience: selected properties', *Journal of Leisure Research*, 19: 115–130.

Gunter, B. and Furnham, A. (1998) *Children as Consumers: A Psychological Analysis of the Young People's Market*. London: Routledge.

Gute, D. and Gute, G. (2008). 'Flow writing in the liberal arts core and across the disciplines: a vehicle for confronting and transforming academic disengagement', *Journal of General Education*, 57: 191–222.

Haggard, L. M. and Williams, D. R. (1992) 'Identity affirmation through leisure activities: leisure symbols of the self', *Journal of Leisure Research*, 24, (1): 1–18.

Hagger, M., Chatzisarantis, N. and Harris, J. (2006) 'From psychological need satisfaction to intentional behavior: testing a motivational sequence in two behavioral contexts', *Personality and Social Psychology Bulletin*, 32: 131–148.

Hald, G. M. and Malamuth, N. M. (2008) 'Self-perceived effects of pornography consumption', *Archives of Sexual Behavior*, 37: 614–625.

Hall, G. S. (1904) *Adolescence*. New York: Appleton.

Hall, S. (1996) 'Introduction: who needs "identity"?', in S. Hall and P. du Gay (eds) *Questions of Cultural Identity*. London: Sage Publications.

Hall, S. and Jefferson, T. (eds) (1975) *Resistance Through Rituals*. London: Hutchinson.

Halley, G. (2004) 'Grief tourists lap up other people's pain', *The Sunday Independent* (Ireland), March 14.

Halman, L. (1996) 'Individualism in individualized society? Results from the European Values Surveys', *International Journal of Comparative Sociology*, 37, (3–4): 195–214.

Halpin, B. and Tak Wing Chan (2003) 'Educational homogamy in Ireland and Britain', *British Journal of Sociology*, 54: 473– 495.

Hamilton, C. and Mail, E. (2003) *Downshifting in Australia: A Sea Change in the Pursuit of Happiness*. Discussion Paper Number 50, The Australia Institute.

Hamilton-Smith, E. (1991). *The Construction of Leisure. Benefits of Leisure*. State College, PA: Venture Publishing.

Hammitt, W. E. (1980) 'Outdoor recreation: is it a multi-phase experience?', *Journal of Leisure Research*, 12: 107–115.

Hammit, W. E., Backlund, E. A. and Bixler, R. D. (2004) 'Experience use history, place bonding and resource substitution among trout anglers during recreation engagements', *Journal of Leisure Research*, 36: 356–278.

Handy, F, Brodeur, N. and Cnaan, R. (2006) 'Summer on the island: episodic volunteering', *Voluntary Action*, 7(3): 31–46.

Hannabuss, S. (2000) 'Being there: ethnographic research and autobiography', *Library Management*, 21(2): 99 – 107.

Harahousou, Y. (2006) 'Leisure and aging', in C. Rojek, S. M. Shaw and A. J. Veal (eds) *A Handbook of Leisure Studies*. Basingstoke and New York: Palgrave Macmillan

Harman, G. (1975) 'Moral relativism defended', *The Philosophical Review*, 84(1): 3–22.

Harris, D. (2005) 'Leisure studies as a teaching object', *Journal of Hospitality, Leisure, Sport and Tourism Education*, 4, (1): 30–41.

Hartmann, T. and Klimmt, C. (2006) 'Gender and computer games: exploring females' dislikes', *Journal of Computer-Mediated Communication*, 11: 910–931.

Havitz, M. and Mannell, R. C. (2005) 'Enduring involvement, situational involvement, and flow in leisure and non-leisure activities', *Journal of Leisure Research*, 37: 152–177.

Haworth, J. T. (1997) *Work, Leisure and Well-being*. London: Routledge.

Haworth, J. T. (2004) 'Work, leisure and well-being', in J. T. Haworth and A. J. Veal (eds) *Work and Leisure*. London: Routledge.

Haworth, J. T. (2011) 'Life, work, leisure, and enjoyment: the role of social institutions', *Leisure Studies Association Newsletter*, 88 (March): 72–80.

Haworth, J. T. and Evans, S. (1995) 'Challenge, skill and positive subjective states in the daily life of YTS students', *Journal of Occupational and Organisational Psychology*, 68: 109–121.

Haworth, J. T. and Hart, G. (eds) (2007/2011) *Well-Being: Individual, Community and Social Perspectives*. Basingstoke: Palgrave Macmillan.

Haworth, J. T. and Hill, S. (1992) 'Work, leisure and psychological well-being in a sample of young adults', *Journal of Community and Applied Psychology*, 2, (2): 147–160.

Haworth, J. T. and Lewis, S. (2005) 'Work, leisure and wellbeing', *British Journal of Guidance and Counselling*, 33(1): 67–79.

Haworth, J. T. and Roberts, K. (2007) 'Leisure: the next 25 years', *Science Review for the DTI Foresight Project on Mental Capital and Mental Wellbeing*, July.

Haworth, J. T., Jarman, M. and Lee, S. (1997) 'Positive psychological states in the daily life of a sample of working women', *Journal of Applied Social Psychology*, 27: 345–370.

Heath, S. and Kenyon, L. (2001), 'Single young professionals and shared household living', *Journal of Youth Studies*, 4, 83–100.

Hebdige, D. (1979) *Sub-culture: The Meaning of Style*. London: Methuen.

Hedges, B. (1986) *Personal Leisure Histories*. London: ESRC/Sports Council.

Heidegger, M. (1962) *Being and Time*. New York: Harper and Row.

Heine, S., Lehman, D., Markus, H. and Kitayama, S. (1999) 'Is there a universal need for positive self-regard?', *Psychological Review, 106*: 766–794.

Hemmingway, J. L. and Parr, M. G. (2000) 'Leisure research and leisure practice: three perspectives on constructing the research–practice relation', *Leisure Sciences, 22*: 139–162.

Henderson, K. A. (1997) 'Just recreation: ethics, gender, and equity', *Journal of Park and Recreation Administration,* 15(2): 16–31.

Henderson, K. A. (1998) 'Researching diverse populations', *Journal of Leisure Research,* 30(1): 157–170.

Henderson, K. A. (2000) 'Just leisure, ethical fitness, and ecophilosophical issues', in M. McNamee, C. Jennings and M. Reeves (eds) *Just Leisure: Policy, Ethics, and Professionalism (No. 17)*. Eastbourne: Leisure Studies Association Publication.

Henderson, K. A. (2007) 'Quality of life and leisure education: implications for tourism economies', *World Leisure Journal*, 49(2): 89–93.

Henderson, K. A. (2009) 'Just research and physical activity: diversity is more than an independent variable (research reflection)', *Leisure Sciences*, 31: 100–105.

Henderson, K. A. (2010) 'Leisure studies in the 21st century: the sky is falling?' *Leisure Sciences*, 32: 391–400.

Henderson, K. A. (2012) *Justice in Leisure Research: Have the Easy Questions been Answered?'* Keynote presentation to Leisure Studies Association Conference in Edinburgh, Scotland.

Henderson, K. A. and Ainsworth, B. E. (2003) 'A synthesis of perceptions about physical activity among older African American and American Indian women', *American Journal of Public Health,* 93(2): 313–317.

Henderson, K. A. and Hickerson, B. D. (2007) 'Women and leisure: premises and performances uncovered in an integrated review', *Journal of Leisure Research*, 39: 591–610.

Henderson, K. A., Bialeschki, M. D., Hemingway, J., Hodges, J. S., Kivel, B. and Sessoms, H. D. (2001) *Introduction to Recreation and Leisure Services*, 8th edn. State College, PA: Venture Publishing.

Henderson, K. A., Bialeschki, M. D., Shaw, S. M. and Freysinger, V. J. (1996) *Both Gains and Gaps: Feminist Perspectives on Women's Leisure*. State College, PA: Venture Publishing.

Heo, J. and Lee, Y. (2007) '"I don't want to feel like a stranger": Korean students who play basketball seriously', *Leisure/Loisir*, 31(1): 133–154.

Herring, S. C. (1993) 'Gender and democracy in computer-mediated communication', *Electronic Journal of Communication/Revue Electronique de Communication*, 3: 1–29.

Hesmondhalgh, D. (2005) 'Subcultures, scenes or tribes? None of the above', *Journal of Youth Studies*, 8: 21–40.

Hesmondhalgh, D. (2007) *The Cultural Industries*. London: Sage.

Hey, V. (1984) *Pubs and Patriarchy*. London: Tavistock.

Hodgkin, R. (1978) 'Skills and safety', in K. Wilson (ed.) *The Games Climbers Play*. London: Diadem.

Hodkinson, P. (2002) *Goth: Identity, Style and Subculture*. Oxford: Berg.

Hodkinson, P. (2011) 'Ageing in a spectacular "youth culture": continuity, change and community amongst older goths', *British Journal of Sociology*, 62: 262–282.

Hogan, B. (2010) 'The presentation of self in the age of social media: distinguishing performances and exhibitions online', *Bulletin of Science Technology and Society*, 30(6): 377–386.

Hollands, R. (1995) *Friday Night, Saturday Night*. Newcastle-upon Tyne: University of Newcastle, Department of Social Policy.

Hollands, R. (2002) 'Divisions in the dark: youth cultures, transitions and segmented consumption spaces in the night-time economy', *Journal of Youth Studies*, 5: 153–171.

Holmes, K. (1999) 'Changing times: volunteering in the heritage sector 1984–1998', *Voluntary Action*, 1(2): 21–35.

Honoré, C. (2004) *In Praise of Slowness: How a Worldwide Movement is Challenging the Cult of Speed*. San Franscisco: Harper.

Hooks, B. (1994) *Teaching to Transgress: Education as the Practice of Freedom*. New York: Routledge.

Hope, A. (2007) 'Risk taking, boundary performance and intentional school internet "misuse"', *Discourse*, 28: 87–99.

Horna, J. (1994) *The Study of Leisure: An Introduction*. Toronto: Oxford University Press.

Horney, K. (1950) *Neurosis and Human Growth: The Struggle toward Self-realization*. New York: Norton.

Howlett, S. (2010) 'Developing volunteer management as a profession', *Voluntary Sector Review*, 1(3): 355–61.

Hrubes, D., Ajzen, I. and Daigle, J. (2001) 'Predicting hunting intentions and behavior: an application of the theory of planned behavior', *Leisure Sciences*, 23: 165–178.

Hubbard, J. and Mannell, R. (2001) 'Testing competing models of the leisure constraint negotiation process in a corporate employee recreation setting', *Leisure Sciences*, 23: 145–163.

Hull, R. B., Michael, S. E., Walker, G. J. and Roggenbuck, J. W. (1996) 'Ebb and flow of brief leisure experiences', *Leisure Sciences*, 18: 299–314.

Hull, R. B., Stewart, W. P. and Yi, Y. K. (1992) 'Experience patterns, explaining the dynamic nature of a recreation experience', *Journal of Leisure Research*, 2: 240–252.

Humphries, S. (1981) *Hooligans or Rebels? An Oral History of Working Class Childhood and Youth, 1889–1939*. Oxford: Blackwell.

Hunt, C. (2006) 'Travels with a turtle: metaphors and the making of a professional identity', *Reflective Practice*, 7 (3): 315–332.

Hunt, J. S. (1979) *Elementary Schooling and the Working Classes*. London: Routledge.

Hutton, W. and Schneider, P. (2009) 'The failure of market failure: towards a 21st century Keynesianism', *NESTA: National Endowment for Science, Technology and the Arts* www.nesta.org.uk/the-failure-o-market-failure/ (accessed 11 April 2012).

Hyland, K. (2013) 'Writing in the university: education, knowledge and reputation', *Language Teaching*. Cambridge: Cambridge University Press 2011, 1: 53–70. (doi:10.1017/S0261444811000036 first published online 2 March 2011) (accessed online 2013 edition 5 March 2013).

Hyun-Sook, K. (2006) 'Educating in a post-conventional society', *Religious Education*, Fall http://findarticles.com/p/articles/mi_qa3783/is_200610/ai_n17194917?tag=art Body;col1 (accessed 15 January 2013).

Illeris, K. (2011) *The Fundamentals of Workplace Learning – Understanding How People Learn in Working Life*. London: Routledge.

Ingham, R. (1986) 'Psychological contributions to the study of leisure – part one', *Leisure Studies*, 5: 255–279.

Ingham, R. (1987) 'Psychological contributions to the study of leisure – part two', *Leisure Studies*, 6: 1–14.

Institute for Volunteering Research (2004) *Volunteering for All? Exploring the Link between Volunteering and Social Exclusion*. London: Institute for Volunteering Research.

Iso-Ahola, S. E. (1979) 'Some social psychological determinants of perceptions of leisure: preliminary evidence', *Leisure Sciences*, 2: 305–314.

Iso-Ahola, S. E. (1997) 'A psychological analysis of leisure and health', in J. T. Haworth (ed.) *Work, Leisure and Well-Being*. London: Routledge.

Iso-Ahola, S. E. and Mannell, R. C. (2004) 'Leisure and health', in J. T. Haworth and A. J. Veal (eds) *Work and Leisure*. London: Routledge.

Isopahkala-Bouret, U. (2008) 'Developmental leisure: why work-related learning takes place outside of working hours', *Human Resource Developmental International*, 11(5): 479–491.

Iwasaki, Y. and Mannell, R. C. (1999) 'Situational and personality influences on intrinsically motivated leisure behavior: interaction effects and cognitive processes', *Leisure Sciences*, 21: 287–306.

Iyengar, S. and Lepper, M. (1999) 'Rethinking the value of choice: a cultural perspective on intrinsic motivation', *Journal of Personality and Social Psychology*, 76: 349–366.

Jackson, E. L. (2000) 'Will research on leisure constraints still be relevant in the twenty-first century?', *Journal of Leisure Research*, 32: 62–68.

Jackson, E. L. (2005) 'Leisure constraint research: overview of a developing theme in leisure Studies', in E. Jackson (ed.), *Constraints to Leisure*. State College, PA: Venture Publishing.

Jackson, E. L. and Henderson, K. (1995) 'Gender-based analysis of leisure constraints', *Leisure Sciences*, 17: 31–54.

Jackson, E. L., Crawford, D. and Godbey, G. (1993) 'Negotiation of leisure constraints', *Leisure Sciences*, 15: 1–11.

Jackson, S. A. (1992) 'Athletes in flow: a qualitative investigation of flow states in elite figure skaters', *Journal of Applied Sport Psychology*, 4: 161–180.

Jackson, S. A. and Eklund, R. C. (2002) 'Assessing flow in physical activity: the Flow State Scale-2 and the Dispositional Flow Scale-2', *Journal of Sport and Exercise Psychology*, 24: 133–150.

Jacob, J., Jovic, E. and Brinkerhoff, M. B. (2009) 'Personal and planetary well-being: mindfulness meditation, pro-environmental behaviour, and personal quality of life in a survey from the social justice and ecological sustainability movement', *Social Indicators Research*, 93: 275–294.

Jahoda, M. (1982) *Employment and Unemployment: A Social Psychological Analysis*. Cambridge: Cambridge University Press.

Jahoda, M. (1984) 'Social institutions and human needs: a comment on Fryer and Payne', *Leisure Studies* 3: 297–99.

Jahoda, M. (1986) 'In defence of a non-reductionist social psychology', *Social Behaviour*, 1: 25–9.

James, W. (1890) *The Principles of Psychology*. New York: Henry Holt.

Jansz, J. and Tanis, M. (2007) 'The appeal of playing online first person shooter games', *Cyberpsychology & Behavior*, 10: 133–136.

Jephcott, P. (1954) *Some Young People*. London: Allen and Unwin.

Jephcott, P. (1967) *Time of One's Own*. London: Oliver and Boyd.

Jenkins, J. (1996) *Social Identity*. London: Routledge.

Jenkins, R. (1983) *Lads, Citizens and Ordinary Kids*. London: Routledge.

Johnson, C. W. (2009) 'Writing ourselves at risk: using self-narrative in working for social justice', *Leisure Sciences*, 31: 483–489.

Jones, C. D. (2008) 'Examining interactions between adventure seeking and states of the four channel flow model', *Leisure/Loisir*, 32: 139–162.

Jones, C. D., Hollenhorst, S. J. and Perna, F. (2003) 'An empirical comparison of the four channel flow model and adventure experience paradigm', *Leisure Sciences*, 25: 17–31.

Jones, D. C. (1934) *The Social Survey of Merseyside*. Liverpool: Liverpool University Press.

Jones, G. (1995) *Leaving Home*. Buckingham: Open University Press.

Kafai, Y. B. (1996) 'Electronic play worlds: gender differences in children's construction of video games', in Y. B. Kafai and M. Resnick (eds) *Constructionism in Practice: Designing, Thinking, and Learning in a Digital World*. Mahwah, NJ: Ablex.

Kafai, Y. B., Heeter, C., Denner, J. and Sun, J. Y. (2008) *Beyond Barbie and Mortal Kombat: New Perspectives on Gender and Gaming*. Cambridge, MA: MIT Press.

Kapidzic, S. and Herring, S. C. (2011) 'Gender, communication, and self-presentation in teen chatrooms revisited: have patterns changed?', *Journal of Computer-Mediated Communication*, 17: 39–59.

Katz, J. (1988) *Seductions of Crime*. New York: Basic Books.

Kay, P., Hede, A., Inglis, J. and Polonky, M. (2008) *Applicability of Leisure Theory to Managerial Views on Volunteerism in a Volunteer Managed Non-Profit Organisation: Some Preliminary Findings*. ANZMAC Marketing: Shifting the Focus from Mainstream to Offbeat. Promaco Conventions P/L, Western Sydney.

Kay, T. (2001) *Leisure, Gender and Family: Challenges for Work-life Integration*. ESRC seminar series 'Wellbeing: situational and individual determinants' (2001–2002) www.wellbeing-esrc.com (accessed 11 July 2012).

Kaye, L. K. (2011) *Motivations, Experiences and Outcomes of Playing Videogames*. Unpublished doctoral thesis, Preston: University of Central Lancashire.

Kaye, L. K. and Bryce, J. (2012) 'Putting the fun factor into gaming', *International Journal of Internet Science*, 7: 23–37.

Kelly, J. (1983) *Leisure Identities and Interactions*. London: George Allen & Unwin.

Kelly, J. (1996) *Leisure*. Boston: Allyn and Bacon.

Kerr, A. (2003) 'Women just want to have fun: a study of adult female gamers', in M. Copier and J. Raessens (eds) *Level Up: Digital Games Research Conference*. Utrecht: University of Utrecht.

Keyes, C. L. M. (1998) 'Social well-being', *Social Psychology Quarterly*, 61: 121–40.

Kim, J. L. and Ward, L. M. (2004) 'Pleasure reading: associations between young women's sexual attitudes and their reading of contemporary women's magazines', *Psychology of Women Quarterly*, 28: 48–58.

Kim, Y. and Ross, S. D. (2006) 'An exploration of motives in sport video gaming', *International Journal of Sports Marketing and Sponsorship*, 8: 34–46.

Kinman, G. and Jones, F. (2009) 'A life beyond work? Job demands, work-life balance, and wellbeing in UK academics' in D. R. Buckholdt and G. E. Miller (eds) *Faculty Stress*. London: Routledge.

Kirkwood, T. (2001) *The End of Age. Reith Lectures*. London: BBC.

Kivel, B. D. and Kleiber, D. A. (2000) 'Leisure in the identity formation of lesbian/gay youth: personal, but not social', *Leisure Sciences*, 22: 215–232.

Kleiber, D. A. (1999) *Leisure Experience and Human Development*. New York: Basic Books.

Kleiber, D. A. (2000) 'The neglect of relaxation', *Journal of Leisure Research*, 32: 82–86.

Kleiber, D. A. (2012) 'Taking leisure seriously: new and older considerations about leisure education', *World Leisure, 54*, (1): 5–15.

Kleiber, D. A., Larson, R. W. and Csikszentmihalyi, M. (1986) 'The experience of leisure in adolescence', *Journal of Leisure Research*, 18: 169–176.

Kleiber, D. A., Walker, G. J. and Mannell, R. C. (2011) *A Social Psychology of Leisure*. State College, PA: Venture Publishing.

Klimmt, C., Hartmann, T. and Frey, A. (2007) 'Effectance and control as determinants of video game enjoyment', *CyberPsychology and Behavior*, 10: 845–848.

Kofoed, J. and Ringrose, J. (2012) 'Travelling and sticky affects: exploring the meanings of sexualized cyberbullying among UK and Danish teens', *Discourse*, 33: 5–20.

Kohn, M. and Schooler, M. (1983) *Work and Personality: An Enquiry into the Impact of Social Stratification*. Norwood, NJ: Ablex.

Kridel, C. (1998) (ed.) *Writing Educational Biography – Explorations in Qualitative Research*. New York and London: Garland Publishing.

Krippendorf, J. (1984) *The Holiday Makers*. London: Heinemann.

Kroger, J. (1989) *Identity in Adolescence: The Balance between Self and Other*. London: Routledge.

Kruglanski, A. (2001) 'That "vision thing": the state of theory in social and personality psychology at the edge of the new millennium', *Journal of Personality and Social Psychology*, 80: 871–875.

Krugman, P. (2012) *End This Depression Now*. London: WW. Norton & Co.

Kubey, R. and Czikszentmihalyi, M. (1990) *Television and the Quality of Life: How Viewing Shapes Everyday Experience*. Hillsdale, NJ: Erlbaum.

Kuentzel, W. F. (2000) 'Self-identity, modernity, and the rational actor in leisure research', *Journal of Leisure Research*, 32(1): 87–92.

Kyle, G. T. and Chick, G. (2002) 'The social construction of place', *Leisure Sciences*, 29: 209–25.

Kyle, G. T., Absher, J. D. and Graefe, A. R. (2003) 'The moderating roles of place attachment on the relationship between attitudes toward fees and spending preferences', *Leisure Sciences*, 25: 1–18.

Lagree, J-C. (ed.) (2002) *Rolling Youth, Rocking Society: Youth Take Part in the Post-Modern debate on Globalization*. Paris: UNESCO.

Lai, C. K. Y. (2010) 'Narrative and narrative enquiry in health and social sciences', *Nurse Researcher*, 17(3): 72–84.

Langer, E. J. (1989) *Mindfulness*, Reading, MA: Addison Wesley.

Larsen, J. (2001) 'Tourism mobilities and the travel glance: experiences of being on the move', *Scandinavian Journal of Hospitality and Tourism*, 1: 80–98.

Larson, R. W. (2000) 'Toward a psychology of positive youth development', *American Psychologist*, 55(1): 170–183.

Larson, R. W. and Csikszentmihalyi, M. (1983) 'The experience sampling method', in H. T. Reis (ed.) *Naturalistic Approaches to Studying Social Interaction*. San Fransisco, CA: Jossey-Bass.

Larson, R. W., Mannell, R. C. and Zuzanek, J. (1986) 'The daily experience of older adults with friends versus family and its relation to global well-being', *Journal of Psychology and Aging*, 1: 117–126.

Laurencic, J. (2013) 'From the keyboard to the road: a narrative of fixed gear cycling and online mediatisation in Leeds, UK' (LSA Leisure Research Showcase No.3 – Research in progress). *Leisure Studies Associaton Newsletter*, 94: 12–13.

Lawrence, L. (1989) 'Investigating leisure aims in the teaching of physical education: perceptions of the research experience', in W. Murphy (ed.) *Children, Schooling and Education for Leisure*. Eastbourne: Leisure Studies Association Publications, 36.

Lawrence, L. (2000) 'Who are these people? And what on earth are they doing?', in C. Brackenridge, D. Howe and F. Jordan (eds) *Just Leisure: Equity, Identity and Social Inclusion*. Eastbourne: Leisure Studies Association Publications, 72.

Lawrence, L. (2003) '"These are the voyages …": interaction in real and virtual space environments in leisure', *Leisure Studies*, 22: 301–315.

Lawrence, L. (2004) 'Enhancing PDP by adopting flow', *On reflection*, Issue 8 [Online]. http://www.recordingachievement.org (assessed 01 June 2012).

Lawrence, L. (2006) 'To obsessively go … exploring serious leisure and the "other" side of leisure in cult fandom', in S. Elkington, I. Jones and L. Lawrence (eds)

Serious and Casual Leisure: Extensions and Applications. Eastbourne Leisure Studies Publications, 95.

Lawrence, L. and Corkill, H. (2013 forthcoming) 'Enhancing the enhancers: action research as a quality enhancement tool', in C. Nygaard., N. Courtney and P. Bartholomew (eds) *Quality Enhancement in University Teaching and Learning: Theories and Cases.* LIHE, Libra Publishing.

Layard, R. (2003) *Happiness: Has Social Science a Clue?* A series of three lectures which can be accessed at the website www.cep.lse.ac.uk (accessed 05 May 2012).

Layard, R. (2005) *Happiness: Lessons from a New Science.* New York: Penguin.

Leary, M. R. (1995) *Self-Presentation: Impression Management and Interpersonal Behaviour.* Iowa: Brown and Benchmark Publishers.

Leary, M. R. and Kowalski, R. M. (1990) 'Impression management: a literature review and two-factor model', *Psychological Bulletin*, 107: 34–47.

Lee, B. B. and Shafer, C. S. (2002) 'The dynamic nature of leisure experience: an application of affect control theory', *Journal of Leisure Research*, 34: 290–310.

Lee, Y., Dattilo, J. and Howard, D. (1994) 'The complex and dynamic nature of leisure experience', *Journal of Leisure Research,* 26: 195–211.

Lefkowitz, E. S. and Gillen, M. M. (2006) '"Sex is just a normal part of life": sexuality in emerging adulthood', in J. J. Arnett and J. L. Tanner (eds) *Emerging Adults in America: Coming of Age in the 21st Century.* Washington, DC: American Psychological Association.

Leigh, J. (1971) *Young People and Leisure.* London: Routledge.

Leitner, J. and Leitner, S. (2012) *Leisure Enhancement.* Urbana, IL: Sagamore.

Leitner, M. J. and Leitner, S. F. (2004) 'Personal leisure philosophy', in M. J. Leitner (ed.) *Leisure Enhancement* (3rd edn). Binghamton, NY: Haworth Press.

Lennon, J. and Foley, R. (2000) *Dark Tourism: The Attraction of Death and Disaster.* London: Continuum.

Leonard, D. (1980) *Sex and Generation.* London: Tavistock.

Lewin, K. (1951) *Field Theory in Social Science: Selected Theoretical Papers by Kurt Lewin.* London: Tavistock.

Lewis, B., Chisnall, A. and Hall, A. (1974) *Unattached Youth.* London: Blond and Briggs.

Lewis, K., Kaufman, J. and Christakis, N. (2008) 'The taste for privacy: an analysis of college student privacy settings in an online social network', *Journal of Computer-Mediated Communication*, 14: 79–100.

Lewis, S. and Purcel, C. (2007) 'Well-being, paid work and personal life', in J. Haworth and G. Hart (eds) *Well-being: Individual, Community, and Social Perspectives.* Basingstoke: Palgrave Macmillan.

Liang, H. and Walker, G. J. (2011) 'Does "face" constrain Mainland Chinese people from starting new leisure activities?' *Leisure/Loisir*, 35: 211–225.

Liau, A. K., Khoo, A. and Ang, P. H. (2005) 'Factors influencing adolescents engagement in risky internet behavior', *CyberPsychology and Behavior*, 8: 513–520.

Livingstone, S. (2008) 'Taking risky opportunities in the creation of youthful content creation: teenagers' use of social networking sites for intimacy, privacy and self-expression', *New Media and Society*, 10: 393–411.

Livingstone, S. and Haddon, L. (2008) 'Risky experiences for European children online: charting research strengths and research gaps', *Children and Society*, 22: 314–23.

Livingstone, S., Haddon, L., Görzig, A. and Olafsson, K. (2011) *Risks and Safety on the Internet: The UK Report, LSE.* London: EU Kids Online.

Lockstone-Binney, L., Holmes, K., Smith, K. M. and Baum, T. G. (2010) 'Volunteers and volunteering in leisure: social science perspectives', *Leisure Studies*, 29, (4): 435–455.

Lounsbury, K., Mitchell, K. J. and Finkelhor, D. (2011) *The True Prevalence of 'Sexting',* Crimes Against Children Research Centre, University of New Hampshire. https://www.unh.edu/ccrc/pdf/Sexting%20Fact%20Sheet%204_29_11.pdf (accessed 6 July 2012).

Low, N., Butt, S., Ellis Paine, A. and Davis Smith, J. (2007) *Helping Out: A National Survey of Volunteering and Charitable Giving*. London: Cabinet Office.

Low, S. M. and Altman, I. (1992) 'Place attachment: a conceptual inquiry', in I. Altman and S. M. Low (eds) *Place Attachment*. New York: Plenum Press.

Luder, M. T., Pittet, I., Berchtold, A., Akré, C., Michaud, P. A. and Suris, J. C. (2011) 'Associations between online pornography and sexual behavior among adolescents: myth or reality?', *Archives of Sexual Behavior*, 40: 1027–1035.

Lumsdon, L. and McGrath, P. (2011) 'Developing a conceptual framework for slow travel: a grounded theory approach', *Journal of Sustainable Tourism*, 19, (3): 265–279.

Lyng, S. (1990) 'Edgework: a social-psychological analysis of voluntary risk taking', *American Journal of Sociology*, 95: 851–86.

Lyons, M., Wijkstrom, P. and Clary, G. (1998) 'Comparative studies of volunteering: what is being studied?', *Voluntary Action*, 1(1): 45–54.

MacDonald, R. and Shildrick, T. (2007) 'Street corner society: leisure careers, youth (sub)culture and social exclusion', *Leisure Studies*, 26: 339–355.

Macduff, N. (2005) 'Societal changes and the rise of the episodic volunteer', in J. Brudney (ed.) *Emerging Areas of Volunteering*. Indianapolis: Association for Research on Nonprofit Organizations and Voluntary Associations.

Mackenzie, S. H., Hodge, K. and Boyes, M. (2011) 'Expanding the flow model in adventure activities: a reversal theory perspective', *Journal of Leisure Research*, 43: 519–544.

MacRae, R. (2004) 'Notions of "us" and "them": markers of stratification in clubbing lifestyles', *Journal of Youth Studies*, 7: 55–71.

Maffesoli, M. (1996) *The Time of the Tribes: The Decline of Individualism in Mass Society*. London: Sage.

Malamuth, N. M. and Impett, E. A. (2001) 'Research on sex and media: What do we know on the effects on children and adolescents?', in D. G. Singer and J. L. Singer (eds) *Handbook of Children and Media*. Thousand Oaks, CA: Sage.

Malamuth, N. M., Addison, T. and Koss, M. (2000) 'Pornography and sexual aggression: are there reliable effects and can we understand them?', *Annual Review of Sex Research*, 11: 26–91.

Malbon, B. (1999) *Clubbing, Dancing, Ecstasy and Vitality*. London: Routledge.

Malcolm, J. and Zukas, M. (2000) 'Becoming an educator: communities of practice in Higher Education', in I. McNay (ed.) *Higher Education and its Communities*. Buckingham: SRHE/OU Press.

Malpas, J. E. (2001) 'Comparing tolographies: across paths/around places: a reply to Casey', *Philosophy and Geography*, 4(2): 231–238.

Manago, A., Graham, M., Greenfield, P. and Salimkhan, G. (2008) 'Self-presentation and gender on MySpace', *Journal of Applied Developmental Psychology*, 29: 446–458.

Manfredo, M. J. (1992) *Influencing human behavior*. Champaign, IL: Sagamore.

Manfredo, M. J., Driver, B. L. and Brown, P. J. (1983) 'A test of concepts inherent in experience based setting management for outdoor recreation areas', *Journal of Leisure Research*, 15: 263–283.

Mannell, R. C. (1979) 'A conceptual and experimental basis for research in the psychology of leisure', *Society and Leisure*, 2: 179–194.

Mannell, R. C. (1980) 'Social psychological techniques and strategies in studying leisure experiences', in S. Iso-Ahola (ed.) *Social Psychological Perspectives of Leisure and Recreation*. Springfield, IL: Charles C. Thomas.

Mannell, R. C. (1993) 'High investment activity and life satisfaction among older adults: committed, serious leisure and flow activities', in J. R. Kelly (ed.) *Activity and Aging*. Newbury Park, CA: Sage.

Mannell, R. C. (1999) 'Leisure experience and satisfaction', in E. L. Jackson and T. L. Burton (eds) *Leisure Studies: Prospects for the Twenty-first Century*. State College, PA: Venture.

Mannell, R. C. and Bradley, W. (1986) 'Does greater freedom always lead to greater leisure? Testing a person X environment model of freedom and leisure', *Journal of Leisure Research,* 18: 215–230.

Mannell, R. C. and Iso-Ahola, S. E. (1987) 'Psychological nature of leisure and tourism experience', *Annals of Tourism Research,* 14: 314–331.

Mannell, R. C. and Kleiber, D. A. (1997) *A Social Psychology of Leisure.* State College, PA: Venture Publishing Inc.

Mannell, R. C. and Kleiber, D. A. (2013) 'Psychology of leisure', in T. Blackshaw (ed.) *The Routledge International Handbook of Leisure Studies.* London: Taylor and Francis.

Mannell, R. C., Kaczynski, A. T. and Aronson, R. M. (2005) 'Adolescent participation and flow experience in physically active leisure and electronic media activities: testing the displacement hypothesis', *Society and Leisure,* 28: 653–675.

Mannell, R. C., Kleiber, D. A. and Staempfli, M. (2006) 'Psychology and social psychology and the study of leisure', in C. Rojek, S. M. Shaw, and A. J. Veal (eds) *A handbook of leisure studies,* New York: Palgrave Macmillan.

Mannell, R. C., Zuzanek, J. and Larson, R. (1988) 'Leisure states and "flow" experiences: testing freedom and intrinsic motivation hypotheses', *Journal of Leisure Research,* 20: 289–304.

Manning, R. (1986) *Studies in Outdoor Recreation: A Review and Synthesis of the Social Science Literature in Outdoor Recreation.* Corvallis, OR: Oregon State University Press.

Marcel, J. (2004) 'Death makes a holiday', *The American Reporter,* 21 January, 10: 2273.

Marcia, J. E. (1966) 'Development and validation of ego identity status', *Journal of Personality and Social Psychology,* 3, 551–558.

Markey, P. M. and Scherer, K. (2009) 'An examination of psychoticism and motion capture as moderators of the effects of violent video games', *Computers in Human Behavior,* 25: 407–411.

Markwell, K., Fullagar, S. and Wilson, E. (2012) 'Reflecting upon slow travel and tourism experiences', in S. Fullagar, K. Markwell, and E. Wilson (eds) *Slow Tourism: Experiences and Mobilities.* Bristol: Channel View Publications.

Marshall, W. L. and Fernandez, Y. M. (2000) 'Phallometric testing with sexual offenders: limits to its validity', *Clinical Psychology Review,* 20: 807–822.

Martinez. T. A. and McMullin, S. L. (2004) 'Factors affecting decisions to volunteer in nongovernmental organizations', *Environment and Behavior,* 36(1): 112–126.

Marton, F. and Booth, S. (1997) *Learning and Awareness.* Mahwah, NJ: Lawrence Erlbaum.

Marton, F. and Trigwell, K. (2000) 'Variatio est mater studorium', *Higher Education Research & Development,* 19: 381–395.

Marton, F. and Tsui, A. B. M. (2004) *Classroom Discourse and the Space of Learning.* Mahwah, NJ: Lawrence Erlbaum.

Maslow, A. H. (1968) *Toward a Psychology of Being.* Toronto: Van Nos Reinhold.

Maslow, A. H. (1971) *The Farther Reaches of Human Nature.* Middlesex: Penguin Books.

Matos, R. (2004) 'can slow tourism bring new life to Alpine regions?' in K. Weiermair and C. Mathies (eds) *The Tourism and Leisure Industry: Shaping the Future.* New York: Haworth Press.

Matthew, D. (2010) *Peer to Peer and the Music Industry: The Criminalisation of Sharing.* London: Sage.

McAdams, D. P. (1997) 'The case for unity in the (post)modern self: a modest proposal', in R. D. Ashmore and L. Jussim (eds) *Self and Identity: Fundamental Issues.* New York: Oxford University Press.

McCarville, R. (2007) 'From a fall in the mall to a run in the sun: one journey to Ironman triathlon', *Leisure Sciences,* 29, (2): 159–173.

McCulloch, K., Stewart, A. and Lovegreen, N. (2006) '"We just hang out together": youth cultures and social class', *Journal of Youth Studies,* 9: 539–556.

McDrury, J. and Alterio, M. (2003) *Learning Through Storytelling in Higher Education – Using Reflection and Experience to Improve Learning.* London: Kogan Page.

McGillivray, D. and Frew, M. (2007) 'Capturing adventure: trading experiences in the symbolic economy', *Annals of Leisure Research*, 10(3): 54–78.

McIntyre, N. (1998) 'Person and environment transaction during brief wilderness trips: an exploration', in A. E. Watson, G. H. Aplet and J. C. Hendee (comps) *Personal, Societal, and Ecological Values of Wilderness: Sixth World Wilderness Congress Proceedings on Research, Management, and Allocation*, Volume 1. USDA Forest Service Proceedings RMRS-P-4. Ogden, UT: Rocky Mountain Research Station, pp. 79–84.

McNamee, M. (2000) 'Just leisure? The ethics of recognition', *Leisure Studies*, 19: 125–126.

McRobbie, A. (1991, 2000) *Feminism and Youth Culture*. London: Routledge.

McWilliam, E. L. (2005) 'Unlearning pedagogy', *Journal of Learning Design*, 1(1): 1–11.

Meijs, L. P. C. M and Hoogstad, E. (2001) 'New ways of managing volunteers: combining membership management and programme management', *Voluntary Action*, 3(3): 41–61.

Meijs, L. C. P. M. and Karr, L. B. (2004) 'Managing volunteers in different settings: membership and programmes management', in R. A. Stebbins and M. Graham (eds) *Volunteering as Leisure, Leisure as Volunteering. An International Assessment*. Wallingford: CABI Publishing.

Meiser, T. (2011) 'Much pain, little gain? Paradigm-specific models and methods in experimental psychology', *Perspectives on Psychological Science*, 6: 183–191.

Melucci, A. (1996) *The Playing Self: Person and Meaning in the Planetary Society*. Cambridge: Cambridge University Press.

Meredith, B. and Storm, E. (2011) *Slow Living*. http://www.create-the-good-life.com/slow_living.html (accessed 17 January 2013).

Merton, R. (1968) *Social Theory and Structure* (rev. edn). Glencoe, IL: Free Press.

Michelson, E. (2011) 'Autobiography and selfhood in the practice of adult learning', *Adult Education Quarterly*, 61, (1): 3–21.

Miles, S. (2000) *Youth Lifestyles in a Changing World*. Buckingham: Open University Press.

Milliken, F. J. and Dunn-Jensen, L. M. (2005) 'The changing time demands of managerial and professional work: implications for managing the work-life boundary', in E. E. Kossek and S. J. Lambert (eds) *Work and Life Integration – Organizational, Cultural, and Individual Perspectives*. Mahwah, NJ: Lawrence Erlbaum Associates.

Miriam, D. (1980) *The State, the Family and Education*. London: Routledge.

Misener, K., Doherty, A. and Hamm-Kerwin, S. (2010) 'Learning from the experience of older adult volunteers in sport: a serious leisure perspective', *Journal of Leisure Research*, 42(2): 267–289.

Mitas, O., Yarnal, C., Adams, R. and Ram, N. (2012) 'Taking a "peak" at leisure travelers' positive emotions', *Leisure Sciences*, 34: 115–135.

Mitchell, K. J., Finkelhor, D. and Wolak, J. (2007) 'Online requests for sexual pictures from youth: Risk factors and incident characteristics', *Journal of Adolescent Health*, 41: 196–203.

Mitchell K. J., Finkelhor, D., Jones, L. M. and Wolak J. (2012) 'Prevalence and characteristics of youth sexting: a national study', *Pediatrics*, 129, 13–20.

Mitchell, K. J., Ybarra, M. and Finkelhor, D. (2007) 'The relative importance of online victimization in understanding depression, delinquency and substance use', *Child Maltreatment*, 12: 314–324.

Moon, J. (2010) *Using Story in Higher Education and Professional Development*. London: Routledge.

Moorehead, B. (1995) *Words Aptly Spoken*. Redmond, WA: Overlake Christian Bookstore.

More, T. A. and Payne, B. R. (1978) 'Affective responses to natural areas near cities', *Journal of Leisure Research*, 10: 7–12.

Morling, B. (2000) '"Taking" an aerobics class in the U.S. and "entering" an aerobics class in Japan: primary and secondary control in a fitness context', *Asian Journal of Social Psychology*, 3: 73–85.

Morris, S. (1998) 'Gender and online gaming' http://www.gamegirlz.com/articles/quakewomen.shtml (accessed 3 March 2012).

Morse, M. (1965) *The Unattached.* Harmondsworth: Penguin.

Mortlock, C. (1984) *The Adventure Alternative.* Milnthorpe: Cicerone Press.

Muggleton, D. (2000) *Inside Subculture: The Postmodern Meaning of Style.* Oxford: Berg.

Muggleton, D. (2005) 'From classlessness to clubculture: a genealogy of post-war British youth cultural analysis', *Young,* 13: 205–219.

Mundy, J. (1998) *Leisure Education: Theory and Practice.* Champaign, IL: Sagamore.

Mungham, G. and Pearson, G. (eds) (1976) *Working Class Youth Culture.* London: Routledge.

Murphy, W. (1989) 'Editor's introduction', in W. Murphy (ed.) *Children, Schooling and Education for Leisure.* Eastbourne: Leisure Studies Association Publications, 36.

Murray, C. (2002) 'Supportive teacher-student relationships: promoting the social and emotional health of early adolescents with high incidence disabilities', *Childhood Education,* 78: 285–291.

Musick, M. and Wilson, J. (2008) *Volunteers: A Social Profile.* Bloomington: Indiana University Press.

Nabi, R. L., Stitt, C. R., Halford, J. and Finnerty, K. L. (2006) 'Emotional and cognitive predictors of the enjoyment of reality-based and fictional programming: an elaboration of the uses and gratifications perspective', *Media Psychology,* 8: 421–447.

Nakamura, J. and Csikszentmihalyi, M. (2001) 'The concept of flow', in C. R. Snyder and S. J. Lopez (eds) *Handbook of Positive Psychology.* Oxford: Oxford University Press.

Nardi, B. A. (2008) 'Mixed realities: Information spaces then and now', *Information Research,* 13. http://informationr.net/ir/13–4/paper354.html (accessed 23 November 2011).

Nayak, A. (2006) 'Displaced masculinities: chavs, youth and class in the postmodern city', *Sociology,* 40: 813–831.

Neulinger, J. (1974) *The Psychology of Leisure.* Springfield, IL: Charles C. Thomas.

Neulinger, J. (1981) *The Psychology of Leisure,* (2nd edn). Springfield, IL: Charles C. Thomas.

New Economics Foundation (2013) *New Macroeconomic Strategy* www.neweconomics.org (accessed 11 May 2012).

Newby, H. (1977) 'In the farm: reflections on the study of Suffolk farm workers', in C. Bell and H. Newby (eds) *Doing Sociological Research.* London: Allen and Unwin.

Ng, B. D. and Wiemer-Hastings, P. (2005) 'Addiction to the internet and online gaming', *CyberPsychology and Behavior,* 8: 110–113.

Nichols, G. (2004) 'Pressures on volunteers in the UK', in R. A. Stebbins and M. Graham, (eds) *Volunteering as Leisure, Leisure as Volunteering. An International Assessment.* Wallingford: CABI Publishing.

Nichols, G. and Ojala, E. (2009) 'Understanding the management of sports events volunteers through psychological contract theory', *Voluntas,* 20: 369–387.

Nijkamp, P. and Baaijens, S. (1999) 'Time pioneers and travel behavior: an investigation into the viability of "slow motion"', *Growth and Change,* 30, (2): 237–263.

Nilan, P. and Feixa, L. (eds) (2006) *Global Youth? Hybrid Identities, Plural Worlds.* London: Routledge.

Northcote, J. (2006) 'Nightclubbing and the search for identity: making the transition from childhood to adulthood in an urban milieu', *Journal of Youth Studies,* 9: 1–16.

Norton, D. L. (1976) *Personal Destinies.* Princeton, NJ: Princeton University Press.

Novak, T. P., Hoffman, D. L. and Duhachek, A. (2003) 'The influence of goal-directed and experiential activities on online flow experiences', *Journal of Consumer Psychology,* 13: 3–16.

Ofcom (2011) *Children and Parents: Media Use and Attitudes Report.* London: Ofcom.

Ogletree, S. M. and Drake, R. (2007) 'College students' video game participation and perceptions: gender differences and implications', *Sex Roles: A Journal of Research,* 56: 537–542.

Olson, C. K. (2010) 'Children's motivations for video game play in the context of normal development', *Review of General Psychology*, 14: 180–187.

Omoto, A. M. and Snyder, M. (1995) 'Sustained helping without obligation. Motivation, longevity of service and perceived attitude change among AIDS volunteers', *Journal of Personality and Social Psychology*, 68: 671–686.

Ornstein, R. (1969). *On the Experience of Time.* Middlesex: Penguin Books.

Orr, N. (2006) 'Museum volunteering: heritage as "serious leisure"', *International Journal of Heritage Studies*, 12(2): 194–210.

Osborne, K. (1999) '"When they are good they are very, very good, but ..." The challenges of motivating retried volunteers in small museums', in K. Moore (ed.) *Management in Museums.* London: Athlone Press.

Oviedo, L. (2005) 'Whom to blame for the charge of secularization?', *Zygon*, 40(2): 351–361.

Page, S. J. and Connell, J. (2010) *Leisure: An Introduction.* London: Prentice-Hall.

Pang, M. F. and Marton, F. (2003) 'Beyond lesson study: comparing two ways of facilitating the grasp of economic concepts', *Instructional Science*, 31: 175–194.

Park, A., Phillips, M. and Johnson, M. (2005) *Young People in Britain: The Attitudes and Experiences of 12–19 Year Olds*, Research Report RR564. Nottingham: Department for Education and Skills.

Park, H. and Levine, T. (1999) 'The theory of reasoned action and self-construal: evidence from three cultures', *Communication Monographs*, 66: 199–216.

Park, Y., Fritz, C. and Jex, S. M. (2011) 'Relationship between work-home segmentation and psychological detachment from work: the role of communication technology use at home', *Journal of Occupational Health Psychology*, 16(4): 457–467.

Parkins, W. (2004) 'At home in Tuscany: slow living and the cosmopolitan subject', *Home Cultures*, 1(3): 257–74.

Parr, M. G. (2009) 'Repositioning the position: revisiting Pieper's argument for a leisure ethic', *Leisure*, 33: 79–94.

Patterson, I. and Pegg, S. (2009) 'Serious leisure and people with intellectual disabilities: benefits and opportunities', *Leisure Studies*, 28: 387–402.

Pearce, C. (2006) *Playing Ethnography: A Study of Emergent Behaviour in Online Games.* London: Central Saint Martin's College of Art and Design.

Pearce, S. M. (1998) *Collecting in Contemporary Practice.* London: Sage.

Peeters, P., Gossling, S. and Becken, S. (2006) 'Innovation towards tourism sustainability: climate change and aviation', *International Journal of Innovation and Sustainable Development*, 1, 3: 184–200.

Pempek, T., Yermolayeva, Y. and Calvert, S. (2009) 'College students' social networking experiences on Facebook', *Journal of Applied Developmental Psychology*, 30: 227–238.

Peter, J. and Valkenburg, P. M. (2006) '"Adolescents" exposure to sexually explicit online material and recreational attitudes toward sex', *Journal of Communication*, 56: 639–660.

Peter, J. and Valkenburg, P. M. (2007) '"Adolescents" exposure to a sexualized media environment and their notions of women as sex objects', *Sex Roles*, 56: 381–395.

Peter, J. and Valkenburg, P. M. (2009) '"Adolescents" exposure to sexually explicit Internet material and sexual satisfaction: a longitudinal study', *Human Communication Research*, 35: 171–194.

Peterson, C. and Gunn, S. (1984) *Therapeutic Recreation Program Design: Principles and Practices.* Englewood Cliffs, NJ: Prentice Hall.

Peterson, R. A. (1992) 'Understanding audience segmentation: from elite and mass to omnivore and univore', *Poetics*, 21: 243–282.

Petrini, C. (2001) *Slow Food: The Case for Taste.* New York: Columbia University Press.

Pieper, J. (1952) *Leisure: The Basis of Culture.* New York: Pantheon Books.

Pieper, J. (1998) *Leisure, the Basis of Culture,* trans. Gerald Malsbary. South Bend IN: St Augustine's Press.

Ponton, L. E. and Judice, S. (2004) 'Typical adolescent sexual development', *Child Adolesc Psychiatric Clin N Am*, 13, 497–511.

Poon, A. (1994) 'The "new tourism" revolution', *Tourism Management*, 15(2): 91–92.

Pope, K. S. and Singer, J. L. (1978) *The Stream of Consciousness: Scientific Investigations into the Flow of Human Experience*. New York: Plenum.

Popper, K. (1959) *The Logic of Scientific Discovery*. New York: Harper. (Original work published as *Logik der Forschung*, 1935).

Postmes, T. and Spears, R. (2002) 'Behavior online: does anonymous computer communication reduce gender inequality?', *Personality and Social Psychology Bulletin*, 28: 1073.

Pressman, S. D., Matthews, K. A., Cohen, S., Martire, L. M., Scheier, M., Baum, A. and Schulz, R. (2009) 'Association of enjoyable leisure activities with psychological and physical well-being', *Psychosomatic Medicine*, 71: 725–732.

Priest, S. and Bunting, C. (1993) 'Changes in perceived risk and competence during whitewater canoeing', *Journal of Applied Recreation Research*, 18(4): 265–280.

Priest, S. and Gass, M. (1997) *Effective leadership in Adventure Programming*. Champaign, IL: Human Kinetics.

Prilleltensky, I. and Prilleltensky, O. (2007) 'Webs of well-being: the interdependence of personal, relational, organizational and communal well-being', in J. T. Haworth and G. Hart (eds) *Well-Being: Individual, Community and Social Perspectives*. Basingstoke: Palgrave Macmillan.

Ramsay, H. (2005) *Reclaiming Leisure*. London: Macmillan.

Reed, B. H. (1950) *Eighty Thousand Adolescents*. London: Allen and Unwin.

Reible, H. L. (2005) 'Deviant leisure: uncovering the "goods" in transgressive behaviour', *Eleventh Canadian Congress on Leisure Research*, Malaspina University-College, Nanaimo, B.C., 17–20 May.

Reisch, L. A. (2001) 'Time and wealth: the role of time and temporalities for sustainable patterns of consumption', *Time & Society*, 10: 367–85.

Relph, E. (1976) *Place and Placelessness*. London: Pion.

Rheberg, W. (2005) 'Altruistic individualists: motivations for international volunteering among young adults in Switzerland', *Voluntas*, 16(2): 109–122.

Rhodes, R. and Dean, R. (2009) 'Understanding physical inactivity: prediction of four sedentary leisure behaviors', *Leisure Sciences*, 31: 124–135.

Rickly-Boyd, J. (2012) 'Lifestyle climbing: toward existential authenticity', *Journal of Sport & Tourism*, 17, (2): 85–104.

Ringrose, J., Gill, R., Livingstone, S. and Harvey, L. (2012) *A Qualitative Study of Children, Young People and 'Sexting'*. London: NSPCC.

Roach, J. (1971) *Public Examinations in England*. London: Cambridge University Press.

Robbins Report (1963) *Higher Education*, Committee on Higher Education. London: HMSO.

Roberts, D. F., Foehr, U. G. and Rideout, V. (2005) *Generation M: Media in the Lives of 8–18 Year-Olds*, Kaiser Family Foundation Study. http://www.kff.org/entmedia/upload/generation-m-media-in-the-lives-of-8-18-year-olds-report.pdf (accessed 12 December 2012).

Roberts, E. (1996) 'Place and spirit in public land management', in B. Driver, D. Dustin, T. Baltic, G. Elsner and G. Peterson (eds) *Nature and the Human Spirit: Toward an Expanded Land Management Ethic*. State College, PA: Venture Publishing.

Roberts, K. (2007) 'Work-life balance – the sources of the contemporary problem and the probably outcomes: a review and interpretation of the evidence', *Employee Relations* 29(4): 334–351.

Roberts, K. (2011a) *Class in Contemporary Britain*. Basingstoke: Palgrave Macmillan.

Roberts, K. (2011b) 'Leisure: the importance of being inconsequential', *Leisure Studies*, 30: 5–20.

Roberts, K. (2012) 'The end of the long baby boomer generation', *Journal of Youth Studies*, 15: 479–497.

Roberts, K. and Parsell, G. (1994) 'Youth cultures in Britain: the middle class take-over', *Leisure Studies,* 13: 33–48.

Robertson, B. (2007) 'Leisure education', in R. McCarville and K. MacKay (eds) *Leisure for Canadians.* State College, PA: Venture Publishing.

Robinson, L. (2007) 'The cyberself: the self-ing project goes online, symbolic interaction in the digital age', *New Media and Society,* 9: 93–110.

Rochester, C. (2006) *Making Sense of Volunteering: A Literature Review.* London: The Commission on the Future of Volunteering.

Rochester, C., Ellis Paine, A. and Howlett, S. (2012) *Volunteering and Society in the 21st Century.* London: Palgrave Macmillan.

Rogers, C. R. (1969) *Freedom to learn.* Columbus: Charles E. Merrill.

Rojek, C. (1997) 'Leisure theory: retrospect and prospect,' *Society and Leisure,* 20: 383–400.

Rojek, C. (1999a) *Leisure and Culture.* New York: St. Martin's Press.

Rojek, C. (1999b) 'Deviant leisure: the dark side of free-time activity', in E. L. Jackson and T. L. Burton (eds) *Leisure Studies: Prospects for the XXI Century.* State College, PA: Venture Publishing.

Rojek, C. (1999c) 'Abnormal leisure: invasive, mephitic, and wild forms', *Society and Leisure,* 22, (1): 21–37.

Rojek, C. (2000) *Leisure and Culture.* London: Macmillan.

Rojek, C. (2004) 'Postmodern work and leisure', in J. T. Haworth and A. J. Veal (eds) *Work and Leisure.* London: Routledge.

Rojek, C. (2005) *Leisure Theory: Principles and Practice.* New York: Palgrave-Macmillan.

Rojek, C. (2006) 'Leisure and consumption', *Leisure/Loisir,* 30,(1): 475–486.

Rojek, C. (2010) *The Labour of Leisure: The Culture of Free Time.* London: Sage.

Rojek, C., Shaw, S. M. and Veal, A. J. (eds) (2006) *A Handbook of Leisure Studies.* Basingstoke and New York: Palgrave Macmillan.

Rotter, J. B. (1966) 'Generalised expectancies for internal versus external control of reinforcement', *Psychological Monographs,* 80: 609.

Ruskin, H. (1995) 'Conceptual approaches in policy development in leisure education', in H. Ruskin and A. Sivan (eds) *Leisure Education towards the 21st Century.* Provo, UT: Department of Recreation Management and Youth Leadership, Brigham Young University.

Ruskin, H. and Sivan, A. (1995) *Leisure Education towards the 21st Century.* Provo, UT: Department of Recreation Management and Youth Leadership, Brigham Young University.

Russoniello, C., O'Brien, K. and Parks, J. (2009) 'The effectiveness of casual video games in improving mood and decreasing stress', *Journal of CyberTherapy and Rehabilitation,* 2: 53–66.

Ryan, R. M. and Deci, E. (2000) 'Self-determination theory and the facilitation of intrinsic motivation, social development, and well-being', *American Psychologist,* 55: 68–78.

Ryan, R. M., Rigby, C. S. and Przybylski, A. (2006) 'The motivational pull of video games: a self determination theory approach', *Motivation and Emotion,* 30: 347–363.

Sabina, C., Wolak, J. and Finkelhor, D. (2008) 'The nature and dynamics of internet pornography exposure for youth', *Cyberpsychology and Behavior,* 11: 691–693.

Samdahl, D. (1988) 'A symbolic interactionist model of leisure: theory and empirical support', *Leisure Sciences,* 10: 27–39.

Sato, I. (1988) 'Bosozoku: flow in Japanese motorcycle gangs', in M. Csikszentmihalyi and I. Csikszentmihalyi (eds) *Optimal Experience: Psychological Studies of Flow in Consciousness.* Cambridge: Cambridge University Press.

Savage, J. (2007) *Teenage: The Creation of Youth Culture.* London: Chatto and Windus.

Sawday, A. (2010) *Go Slow France.* Bristol: Sawday's.

Schachter, S. and Singer, J. (1962) 'Cognitive, social, and physiological determinants of emotional state', *Psychological Review,* 69: 379–399.

Schatzki, T. R. (2002) *The Site of the Social: A Philosophical Account of the Constitution of Social Life and Change*. Pennsylvania: Pennsylvania State University Press.

Schatzki, T. R. (2006) 'Peripheral vision: on organisations as they happen', *Organisation Studies*, 27: 1863–1873.

Schau, H. J. and Gilly, M. C. (2003) 'We are what we post? Self-presentation in personal web space', *Journal of Consumer Research*, 30: 385–404.

Scherl, L. M. (1988) 'Constructions of a wilderness experience: using the repertory grid technique in the natural setting', *Australian Psychologist*, 23: 225–242.

Schlenker, B. R. (1980) *Impression Management: The Self-Concept, Social Identity, and Interpersonal Relations*. Monterey, CA: Brooks/Cole.

Schlenker, B. R. (1984) 'Identities, identification, and relationships', in V. Derlaga (ed.) *Communication, Intimacy and Close Relationships*. New York: Academic Press.

Schlenker, B. R. and Weigold, M. F. (1992) 'Interpersonal processes involving impression management', *Annual Review of Psychology*, 43: 133–168.

Schneider, B., Ainbinder, A. M. and Csikszentmihalyi, M. (2004) 'Stress and working parents', in J. T. Haworth and A. J. Veal (eds) *Work and Leisure*. London: Routledge.

Schofield, M. (1965) *The Sexual Behaviour of Young People*. London: Longman.

Schofield, M. (1973) *The Sexual Behaviour of Young Adults*. London: Allen Lane.

Schor, J. (1992) *The Over-Worked American*. New York: Basic Books.

Schor, J. (1998) 'Beyond work and spend: time, leisure and consumption', in S. Scraton (ed.) *Leisure, Time and Space: Meanings and Values in People's Lives*. Eastbourne: Leisure Studies Association.

Schor, J. (2006) 'Overturning the modernist predictions: recent trends in work and leisure in the OECD', in C. Rojek, S. M. Shaw and A. J. Veal (eds) *A Handbook of Leisure Studies*. Basingstoke and New York: Palgrave MacMillan.

Schott, G. R. and Horrell, K. R. (2000) 'Girl gamers and their relationship with the gaming culture', *Convergence*, 6: 36–53.

Schrader, C. (2004) 'The power of autobiography', *Changing English*, 11(1): 115–124.

Schumacher, P. and Morahan-Martin, J. (2001) 'Gender, internet and computer attitudes and experiences', *Computers in Human Behavior*, 17: 95–110.

Scott, D. (2005) 'The relevance of constraints research to leisure service delivery', in E. Jackson (ed.) *Constraints to Leisure*. State College, PA: Venture Publishing.

Seaton, A. and Lennon, J. (2004) 'Moral panics, ulterior motives and alterior desires: thanatourism in the early 21st century', in T. Singh (ed.) *New Horizons in Tourism: Strange Experiences and Stranger Practices*. Wallingford: CABI Publishing.

Seigel, J. (2005) *The Idea of the Self: Thought and Experience in Western Europe since the Seventeenth Century*. Cambridge: Cambridge University.

Seligman, M. E. P. (2002) *Authentic Happiness: Using the New Positive Psychology to Realize Your Potential for Lasting Fulfillment*. New York: Free Press.

Seligman, M. E. P. (2011) *Flourish: A Visionary New Understanding of Happiness and Wellbeing*. London: Free Press.

Seligman, M. E. P. and Csikszentmihalyi, M. (2000) 'Positive psychology: an introduction', *American Psychologist*, 55, (1): 5–14.

Sellick, J. (2002) *Leisure Education: Models and Curriculum Development* http://www.cprs.org/membersonly/LeisureEducation_Models.doc (accessed 2 July 2012).

Seto, M. C., Marıç, A. and Darbaree, H. E. (2001) 'The role of pornography in the aetiology of sexual aggression', *Aggression and Violent Behaviour*, 6: 35–53.

Shamir, B. (1992) 'Some correlates of leisure identity salience: three exploratory studies', *Journal of Leisure Research*, 24: 301–23.

Shannon, C. S. (2005) '"Oh, I get it now!" – autobiographical writing as fostering understanding of gender and leisure interactions', *Schole: Journal of Leisure Studies and Recreation Education*, 20: 29–42.

Sharpley, R. (2003) *Tourism, Tourists and Society*. Huntingdon: Elm Publications.

Sharpley, R. and Stone, P. R. (eds) (2009) *The Darker Side of Travel: The Theory and Practice of Dark Tourism*. Aspects of Tourism Series. Bristol: Channel View Publications.

Shaw, S. M. (1984) 'The measurement of leisure: a quality of life issue', *Society and Leisure*, 7: 91–107.

Shaw, S. M. (1994) 'Gender, leisure and constraint: towards a framework for the analysis of women's leisure', *Journal of Leisure Research*, 26: 8–22.

Shaw, S. M. (1999) 'Men's leisure and women's lives: the impact of pornography on women', *Leisure Studies*, 18: 197–212.

Shaw, S. M. (2001) 'Conceptualising resistance: women's leisure as political practice', *Journal of Leisure Research*, 33: 186–201.

Sheldon, K., Elliot, A., Kim, Y. and Kasser, T. (2001) 'What is satisfying abut satisfying events? Testing 10 candidate psychological needs', *Journal of Personality and Social Psychology*, 80: 325–339.

Shen, X. and Yarnal, C. (2010) 'Blowing open the serious leisure-casual leisure dichotomy: what's in there?' *Leisure Sciences*, 32: 162–179.

Shields, R. (1992) 'Spaces for the subject of consumption', in R. Shields (ed.) *Lifestyle Shopping: The Subject of Consumption*. London: Routledge.

Shildrick, T. and MacDonald, R. (2006) 'In defence of subculture: young people's leisure and social divisions', *Journal of Youth Studies*, 9: 125–140.

Shilling, C. (2005) 'Embodiment, emotions and the foundations of social order: Durkheim's enduring contribution', in J. Alexander and P. Smith (eds) *The Cambridge Companion to Durkheim*. Cambridge: Cambridge University Press.

Shilling, C. and Mellor, P. (1998) 'Durkheim, morality and modernity: collective effervescence, Homo Duplex and the sources of moral action', *The British Journal of Sociology*, 49(2): 193–209.

Shipton, E. (1944) *Upon That Mountain*. London: Hodder & Stoughton.

Shrader, C. (2004) 'The power of autobiography', *Changing English*, 11(1): 115–124.

Siddiquee, A., Sixsmith, J., Lawthom, R. and Haworth, J. T. (forthcoming) 'Paid work, life work and leisure', *Leisure Studies*.

Siekpe, J. S. (2005) 'An examination of the multidimensionality of flow construct in a computer-mediated environment', *Journal of Electronic Commerce Research*, 6: 31–43.

Sivan, A. (2006) 'Leisure and education', in C. Rojek, S. M. Shaw, and A. J. Veal (eds) *A Handbook of Leisure Studies*. Basingstoke: Palgrave Macmillan.

Sixsmith, J. and Boneham, M. (2002) 'Exploring social capital in narrative accounts of life transitions', *Auto/Biography*, 10(1–2): 123–30.

Sixsmith, J. and Boneham, M (2007) 'Health, well-being and social capital', in J. T. Haworth and G. Hart (eds) *Well-Being: Individual, Community and Social Perspectives*. Basingstoke and New York: Palgrave Macmillan.

Skolnick, J. and Gordon, P. (2005) 'Editor's introduction: secularization and disenchantment', *New German Critique*, 94: 3–17.

Sky One (2004) *Long Way Round*, Sky One, London, 18/10/04–1/02/05.

Slow Food (1989) The Slow Food Manifesto http://www.slowfood.com/about_us/eng/manifesto.lasso (accessed 8 January 2013).

Smith, D. H. (1975) 'Voluntary action and voluntary groups', *Annual Review of Sociology*, 1: 247–270.

Smith, K. A. (2002) 'Modelling the volunteer experience: findings from the heritage sector', *Voluntary Action*, 4(2): 9–30.

Smith, M. A. and Kollock, P. (1999) *Communities in Cyberspace*. London: Routledge.

Snape, R. and Pussard, H. (2011) 'Theorisations of leisure in inter-war Britain', paper presented at *Leisure Studies Association Conference*, Southampton Solent University.

Snelgrove, R. and Havitx, M. E. (2010) 'Looking back in time: the pitfalls and potential of retrospective methods in leisure studies', *Leisure Sciences*, 32: 337–351.

Snyder, C. R. and Lopez, J. (2007) *Positive Psychology: The Scientific and Practical Explorations of Human Strengths*. Thousand Oaks, CA: Sage.

Soloman, I. (2006) *Karen Horney and Character Disorder for the Modern Practitioner*. New York: Springer Publishing Company.

Solomon, S., Qin, D., Manning, M., Chen, Z., Marquis, M., Averyt, K. B., Tignor, M. and Miller, H. L. (eds) (2007) *Contribution of Working Group I to the Fourth Assessment Report of the Intergovernmental Panel on Climate Change.* Cambridge: Cambridge University Press.

Sonnentag, S. (2012) 'Psychological detachment from work during leisure time: the benefits of mentally disengaging from work', *Current Directions in Psychological Science,* 21, (2): 114–118.

Sparkes, A. (2002) *Telling Tales in Sport and Physical Activity: A Qualitative Journey.* Champaign, IL: Human Kinetics Press.

Sport England (2003) *Young People and Sport in England: Trends in Participation 1994–2002.* London: Sport England.

Sproull, L. and Kiesler, S. (1991) *Connections: New Ways of Working in the Networked Organization.* Cambridge, MA: MIT Press.

Stavrou, N. A., Jackson, S. A., Zervas, Y. and Karteroliotis, K. (2007) 'Flow experience and athletes' performance with reference to the orthogonal model of flow', *The Sport Psychologist,* 21: 438–457.

Stebbins, R. A. (1982) 'Serious leisure: a conceptual statement', *The Pacific Sociological Review,* 25(2): 251–272.

Stebbins, R. A. (1992a) *Amateurs, Professionals, and Serious Leisure.* Montreal and Kingston: McGill-Queen's University Press.

Stebbins, R. A. (1992b) 'Costs and rewards in barbershop singing', *Leisure Studies,* 11: 123–133.

Stebbins, R. A. (1996a) *Tolerable Differences: Living with Deviance* (2nd edn). Toronto: McGraw-Hill Ryerson Limited.

Stebbins, R. A. (1996b) 'Volunteering: a serious leisure perspective', *Nonprofit and Voluntary Sector Quarterly,* 25(2): 211–224.

Stebbins, R. A. (1997) 'Casual leisure: a conceptual statement', *Leisure Studies,* 16: 17–25.

Stebbins, R. A. (1998) *After Work: The Search for an Optimal Leisure Lifestyle.* Calgary: Detselig.

Stebbins, R. A. (2001a) 'Volunteering – mainstream and marginal: preserving the leisure experience', in M. Graham and M. Foley (eds) *Volunteering in Leisure: Marginal or Inclusive?* (LSA Publication No. 75). Eastbourne: Leisure Studies Association.

Stebbins, R. A. (2001b) 'Serious leisure', *Society,* 38, (4): 53–57.

Stebbins, R. A. (2003) 'Boredom in free time', *Leisure Studies Association Newsletter,* 64, (March): 29–31 (also available at www.seriousleisure.net – Digital Library, 'Leisure Reflections No. 2').

Stebbins, R. A. (2004a) *Between Work and Leisure: The Common Ground of Two Separate Worlds.* New Brunswick, NJ: Transaction.

Stebbins, R. A. (2004b) 'Introduction', in R. A. Stebbins and M. Graham (eds) *Volunteering as Leisure, Leisure as Volunteering. An International Assessment.* Wallingford: CABI Publishing.

Stebbins, R. A. (2004c) 'Serious leisure, volunteerism and quality of life', in J. T. Haworth and A. J. Veal (eds) *Work and Leisure.* London: Routledge.

Stebbins, R. A. (2005a) *Challenging Mountain Nature: Risk, Motive and Lifestyle in Three Hobbyist Sports.* Calgary: Detselig Enterprises.

Stebbins, R. A. (2005b) 'Project-based leisure: theoretical neglect of a common use of free time', *Leisure Studies* 24: 1–11.

Stebbins, R. A. (2006) *Between Work and Leisure – The Common Ground of Two Separate Worlds.* New Brunswick, NJ/London: Transaction Publishers.

Stebbins, R. A. (2007a) 'A leisure-based, theoretical typology of volunteer and volunteering', *Leisure Reflections...No.16 LSA Newsletter No. 78 – November 2007* available at http://www.seriousleisure.net/uploads/8/3/3/8/8338986/reflections16. pdf (accessed 23 April 2012).

Stebbins, R. A. (2007b) *Serious Leisure: A Perspective For Our Time.* Brunswick, NJ: Transaction.

Stebbins, R. A. (2008) 'Leisure abandonment: quitting free time activity that we love', *Leisure Studies Association Newsletter* 81 (November): 14–19 (also available at www.seriousleisure.net – Digital Library, 'Leisure Reflections No. 19').

Stebbins, R. A. (2009a) *Leisure and Consumption: Common Ground, Separate Worlds.* Basingstoke: Palgrave Macmillan.

Stebbins, R. A. (2009b) *Personal Decisions in the Public Square: Beyond Problem Solving into a Positive Sociology.* New Brunswick, NJ: Transaction.

Stebbins, R. A. (2009c) 'Would you volunteer?', *Social Science and Public Policy*, 46: 155–159.

Stebbins, R. A. (2010) 'Flow in serious leisure: nature and prevalence', *Leisure Studies Association Newsletter* 87, (November): 21–3 (also available at www.seriousleisure.net – Digital Library, 'Leisure Reflections No. 25').

Stebbins, R. A. (2012a) 'Leisure Reflections No. 29 – Self-directed learning as a foundation for complex leisure', *Leisure Studies Association Newsletter*, 91: 15–17.

Stebbins, R. A. (2012b). *The Idea of Leisure.* Brunswick, NJ: Transation Publications.

Stebbins, R. A. (2013). 'Leisure Reflections No. 33 – The spaces of the serious pursuits: a typology', *Leisure Studies Association Newsletter*, 95.

Stebbins, R. A. and Graham, M. (eds) (2004) *Volunteering as Leisure, Leisure as Volunteering. An International Assessment.* Wallingford: CABI Publishing.

Stebbins, R. A., Rojek, C. and Sullivan, A. M. (eds) (2006) *Leisure/Loisir*, 30: 3–231.

Stedman, R. (2003) 'Is it really social construction?: the contribution of the physical environment to sense of place', *Society and Natural Resources*, 16: 671–685.

Stein, G. L., Kimiecik, J. C, Daniels, J. and Jackson, S. A. (1995) 'Psychological antecedents of flow in recreational sport', *Personality and Social Psychology Bulletin*, 21(2): 125–135.

Stenseng, F., Rise, J. and Kraft, P. (2011) 'The dark side of leisure: obsessive passion and its covariates and outcomes', *Leisure Studies*, 30, (1): 49–62.

Stewart, C., Smith, B. and Sparkes, A. C. (2011) 'Sporting autobiographies of illness and the role of metaphor', *Sport in Society: Cultures, Commerce, Media, Politics*, 14(5): 581–597.

Stewart, W. P. (1998) 'Leisure as multiphase experiences: challenging traditions', *Journal of Leisure Research*, 30: 391–400.

Stewart, W. P. and Hull, R. B. (1992) 'Satisfaction of what? Post hoc versus real-time construct validity', *Leisure Sciences*, 14: 195–209.

Stokols, D. (1992) 'Establishing and maintaining healthy environments', *American Psychologist*, 47, (6): 6–22.

Stone, P. R. (2009) 'Dark tourism: morality and new moral spaces', in R. Sharpley and P. R. Stone (eds) *The Darker Side of Travel: The Theory and Practice of Dark Tourism*, Aspect of Tourism Series. Bristol: Channel View Publications.

Stone, P. R. (2011) 'Dark tourism: towards a new post-disciplinary research agenda', *International Journal of Tourism Anthropology*, 1(3/4): 318–332.

Stone, P. R. (2012) 'Dark tourism and significant other death: towards a model of mortality mediation', *Annals of Tourism Research*, 39(3): 1565–1587.

Stone, P. R. and Sharpley, R. (2008) 'Consuming dark tourism: a thanatological perspective', *Annals of Tourism Research*, 35(2): 574–595.

Storry, T. (2003) 'Ours to reason why', *Journal of Adventure Education and Outdoor Learning*, 3(2): 133–143.

Stulhofer, A., Busko, V. and Landripet, I. (2010) 'Pornography, sexual socialization, and satisfaction among young men', *Archives of Sexual Behavior*, 39: 168–178.

Subrahmanyam, K., Garcia, E. C. M., Harsono, L. S., Li, J. S. and Lipana, L. (2010) 'In their words: connecting on-line weblogs to developmental processes', *British Journal of Developmental Psychology*, 27: 219–245.

Sugarman, B. (1967) 'Involvement in youth culture, academic achievement and conformity in school', *British Journal of Sociology*, 18: 151–164.

Sun, J. and Wang, X. (2010) 'Value differences between generations in China: a study of Shanghai', *Journal of Youth Studies*, 13: 65–81.

Svendsen, L. (2010) *A Philosophy of Boredom*. London: Reaktion.

Sword, H. (2012) 'Narrative trust', *Times Higher Education* http://www.timeshighereducation. co.uk/features/narrative-trust/421045.article (accessed 5 November 2012).

Tarrant, M., North, A. C., Endridge, M., Kirk, L. E., Smith, E. A. and Turner, R. E. (2001) 'Social identity in adolescence', *Journal of Adolescence*, 24(5): 597–609.

Taylor, R. (2002) 'Britain's world of work-myths and realities', *ESRC Future of Work Programme Seminar Series*. Economic and Social Research Council, Polaris House, Swindon.

Taylor, W. C., Floyd, M. F., Whitt-Glover, M. C. and Brooks, J. (2007) 'Environmental justice: a framework for collaboration between the public health and parks and recreation fields to study disparities in physical activity', *Journal of Physical Activity and Health*, 4 (Suppl 1): S50–S63.

Tejada-Flores, L. (1978) 'Games climbers play', in K. Wilson (ed.) *The Games Climbers Play*. London: Diadem.

Thatcher, A., Wretschko, G. and Fridjhon, P. (2008) 'Online flow experiences, problematic Internet use and Internet procrastination', *Computers in Human Behavior*, 24: 2236–2254.

Thompson, J. (2007) *Massacre at Virginia Tech: Interview with MSNBC* http://www.msnbc. msn.com/id/18220228/ (accessed 10 September 2010).

Thornton, S. (1995) *Club Cultures: Music, Media and Subcultural Capital*. Cambridge: Polity Press.

Tinsley, H. E. A. and Tinsley, D. J. (1986) 'A theory of the attributes, benefits, and causes of leisure experience', *Leisure Sciences*, 8: 1–45.

Toohey, P. (2011) *Boredom: A Lively History*. New Haven, CT: Yale University Press.

Towner, J. (2002) 'Literature, tourism and the grand tour', in M. Robinson and H.-L. Andersen (eds), *Literature and Tourism Essays in the Reading and Writing of Tourism* London: Thomson, pp. 226–238.

Træen, B., Sørheim-Nilsen, T. and Stigum, H. (2006) 'Use of pornography in traditional media and on the Internet in Norway', *Journal of Sex Research*, 43: 245–254.

Trahar, S. (ed.) (2011) *Learning and Teaching Narrative Inquiry: Travelling in the Borderlands*. Amsterdam: John Benjamins Publishing.

Triandis, H. (1995) *Individualism & Collectivism*. Boulder, CO: Westview Press.

Trainor, S., Delfabbro, P. Anderson, S. and Winefield, A. (2010) 'Leisure activities and adolescent psychological well-being', *Journal of Adolescence*, 33: 173–186.

Tuan, Y. F. (1975) 'Place: an experiential perspective', *The Geographical Review*, 65(2): 151.

Tuan, Y. F. (1977) *Space and Place*. Minneapolis: University of Minneapolis Press.

Tuan, Y. F. (1980) 'Rootedness versus sense of place', *Landscapes*, 25: 3–8.

Tulloch, J. and Jenkins, H. (1995) *Science Fiction Audiences*. London: Routledge.

Turner, R. H. (1964) *The Social Context of Ambition: A Study of High School Teenagers in Los Angeles*. San Francisco, NC: Chandler.

Turner, V. (1992) *Blazing the Trail*. Tucson, AZ: University of Arizona Press.

Urban Dictionary (2013) http://www.urbandictionary.com/define.php?term=fakenger (accessed November 2012).

Urwick, E. J. (ed.) (1904) *Studies of Boy Life in our Cities*. London: Dent.

Usher, R. (1998) 'The story of the self: education, experience and autobiography', in M. Erben (ed.) *Biography and Education: A Reader*. London: Falmer Press.

Valadez, J. J. and Ferguson, C. J. (2012) 'Just a game after all: violent video game exposure and time spent playing effects on hostile feelings, depression and visuospatial cognition', *Computers and Human Behavior*, 28: 608–616.

Vallerand, R. (1997) 'Towards a hierarchical model of intrinsic and extrinsic motivation', in M. Zanna (ed.), *Advances in Experimental Psychology*. New York: Academic Press.

Van Manen, M. (1977) 'Linking ways of knowing with ways of being practical', *Curriculum Inquiry*, 6(3): 205–228

Van Manen, M. (1982) 'Phenomenological pedagogy', *Curriculum Inquiry*, 12(3): 293–299

Van Manen, M. (1990) *Researching Lived Experience: Human Science for an Action Sensitive Pedagogy* (2nd edn). Ontario: Althouse Press.

Van Til, J. (1979) 'In search of volunt–ism', *Volunteer Administration*, 12: 8–20.

Varley, P. (2006) 'Confecting adventure and playing with meaning: the adventure commodification continuum', *Journal of Sport & Tourism*, 11(2): 173–194.

Vaughan, G. M. and Hogg, M. A. (2002) *Introduction to Social Psychology* (3rd edn). Frenches Forest: Pearson Education.

Veenhoven, R. (2009) 'Enjoyment of life lengthens life. Findings and consequences', in T. Freire (ed.) *Understanding Positive Life: Research and Practice on Positive Psychology.* Lisboa: Escolar Editora.

Vega, V. and Malamuth, N. M. (2007) 'Predicting sexual aggression: the role of pornography in the context of general and specific risk factors', *Aggressive Behaviour*, 33: 104–107.

Virilio, P. (1991) *La Vitesse*. Paris, Flammarion.

Vorhaus, M. (2008) 'Internet and TV lead list of ways men pass the time', *Advertising Age*, 79: 17.

Waitt, G. and Clifton, D. (2013) '"Stand out, not up": bodyboarders, gendered hierarchies and negotiating the dynamics of pride/shame', *Leisure Studies*, DOI: 10.1080/02614367.2012.684397.

Walle, A. H. (1997) 'Pursuing risk or insight: marketing adventures', *Annals of Tourism Research*, 24(2): 265–282.

Walker, C. J. (2010) 'Experiencing flow: is doing it together better than doing it alone?', *The Journal of Positive Psychology*, 5: 3–11.

Walker, G. J. (2011a) 'Incorporating leisure constraints theory into Hagger's *et al.* (2006) multi-theory framework: the roles of anticipated constraint and anticipated constraint negotiation', *Proceedings from the First International Conference on Emerging Research Paradigms in Business and Social Sciences.* [CD]. Dubai, UAE: Middlesex University Dubai.

Walker, G. J. (2011b) *Are We Really Satisfying People's Needs?* Lake Louise, AB: Alberta Recreation and Parks Association Conference. Presentation available from the author.

Walker, G. J. (2012) 'Effects of willingness, constraints, and constraint negotiation on casino gambling', in M. Stodolska and J. Bocarro (comps) *2012 Leisure Research Symposium Book of Abstracts*. National Recreation and Park Association Congress and Exhibition, Anaheim, CA, pp. 72a–72d.

Walker, G. J. and Deng, J. (2003) 'Comparing leisure as a subjective experience with the Chinese experience of rùmí', *Leisure/Loisir*, 28, 245–276.

Walker, G. J. and Liang, H. (2012) 'An overview of a comprehensive leisure participation framework and its application for cross-cultural leisure research. (Published in Chinese as 概述: 综合休闲参与理论框架及其对跨文化休闲研究的影响). *Journal of Zhejiang University (Humanities and Social Sciences)*, 42, 22–30.

Walker, G. J. and Wang, X. (2009) 'The meaning of leisure for Chinese/Canadians', *Leisure Sciences*, 31: 1–18.

Walker, G. J., Courneya, K. S. and Deng, J. (2006) 'Ethnicity, gender, and the theory of planned behavior: the case of playing the lottery', *Journal of Leisure Research*, 38: 224–248.

Walker, G. J., Jackson, E. L. and Deng, J. (2007) 'Culture and leisure constraints: a comparison of Canadian and Mainland Chinese university students', *Journal of Leisure Research*, 39: 567–590.

Walker, G. J., Halpenny, E., Spiers, S. and Deng, J. (2011) 'A prospective panel study of Chinese-Canadian immigrants' leisure participation and leisure satisfaction', *Leisure Sciences*, 33: 349–365.

Walseth, K. (2006) 'Young Muslim women and sport: the impact of identity work', *Leisure Studies*, 25(1): 75–94.

Walter, J. (1984) 'Death as recreation: armchair mountaineering', *Leisure Studies*, 3(1): 67–76.

Wan, C. and Chiou, W. (2006) 'Psychological motives and online games addiction: a test of flow theory and humanistic needs. Theory for Taiwanese adolescents', *CyberPsychology and Behavior*, 9: 317–324.

Ward, J. (1948) *Children Out of School*. London: Central Advisory Council for Education.

Ward, L. (2003) 'Understanding the role of entertainment media in the sexual socialization of American youth: a review of empirical research', *Developmental Review*, 23: 347–388.

Wardle, D. (1974) *The Rise of the Schooled Society*. London: Routledge.

Warr, P. (1987) *Work, Unemployment and Mental Health*. Oxford: Clarendon Press.

Warr, P. (1999) 'Well-being and the workplace', in D. Kahneman, E. Diener and N. Schwarz (eds) *Well-Being: The Foundations of Hedonic Psychology*. New York: Russell Sage Foundation.

Warr, P. (2007) *Work, Happiness, and Unhappiness*. London: Routledge.

Warren, K. (1996) 'Educating for environmental justice', *Journal of Experiential Education*, 19(3): 135–140.

Waterman, A. S. (1990) 'Personal expressiveness: philosophical and psychological foundations', *Journal of Mind and Behavior*, 11: 47–74

Waterman. A. S. (1993) 'Finding Something to do or someone to be: a Eudaimonist perspective on identity formation', in J. Kroger (ed.) *Discussions on Ego Identity*, London: Lawrence Erlbaum Associates.

Waterman, A. S., Schwartz, S. J. and Conti, R. (2006) 'The implications of two conceptions of happiness (hedonic enjoyment and eudaimonia) for the understanding of intrinsic motivation', *Journal of Happiness Studies*, 9: 41–79.

Watkins, M. (2000) 'Ways of learning about leisure meanings', *Leisure Sciences, 22*: 93–107.

Watkins, M. (2008) 'A follow-up study into different ways of experiencing leisure', *Annals of Leisure Research*, 11: 205–224.

Watkins, M. and Bond, C. (2007) 'Ways of experiencing leisure', *Leisure Sciences, 29*: 287–307.

Watson, B. and Scraton, S. (2001) 'Confronting Whiteness: researching the leisure lives of South Asian mothers', *Journal of Gender Studies*, 10(3): 265–277.

Wearing, B. (1998) *Leisure and Feminist Theory*. London: Sage Publications.

Wearing, S. and Wearing B. (2001) 'Conceptualizing the selves of tourism', *Leisure Studies*, 20(2): 143–159.

Weber, K. (2001) 'Outdoor adventure tourism: a review of research approaches', *Annals of Tourism Research*, 28(2): 360–377.

Webster-Wright, A. (2010) *Authentic Professional Learning – Making a Difference through Learning at Work*. Dordrecht: Springer.

Weibel, D., Wissmath, B., Habeggar, S., Steiner, Y. and Groner, R. (2008) 'Playing online games against computer-versus-human-controlled opponents: effects on presence, flow and enjoyment', *Computers in Human Behavior*, 24: 2274–2291.

Weisz, J., Rothbaum, F. and Blackburn, T. (1984) 'Standing out and standing in: the psychology of control in America and Japan', *American Psychologist*, 39: 955–969.

West, L. (2010) 'Challenging boundaries: an auto/biographical imagination and the subject of learning', *International Journal of Continuing Education and Lifelong Learning*, 2(2): 74–87.

West, P. (2004) *Conspicuous Compassion: When Sometimes It Really Is Cruel to Be Kind*. London: CIVITAS.

West, P., Sweeting, H., Young, R. and Robins, M. (2006) 'A material paradox: socioeconomic status, young people's disposable income and consumer culture', *Journal of Youth Studies*, 9: 437–462.

Wheaton, B. (2004) *Understanding Lifestyle Sports: Consumption, Identity and Difference*. London: Routledge.

Whitty, M. T. (2008) 'Liberating or debilitating? An examination of romantic relationships, sexual relationships and friendships on the Net', *Computers in Human Behavior*, 24: 1837–1850.

Whitty, M. T., Young, G. and Goodings, L. (2011) 'What I won't do in pixels: examining the limits of taboo violation in MMORPGs', *Computers in Human Behavior*, 27: 268–275.

Wilkins, L. T. (1955) *The Adolescent in Britain*. London: Central Office of Information.

Wilkinson, R. and Pickett, K. (2009) *The Spirit Level: Why More Equal Societies Always Do Better*. London: Allen Lane.

Williams, D. J. (2009) 'Deviant leisure: rethinking "the good, the bad, and ugly"', *Leisure Sciences*, 31: 207–213.

Williams, D. R. and Roggenbuck, J. W. (1989) 'Measuring place attachment: some preliminary results', in L. H. McAvoy and D. Howard (eds) *Abstracts: 1989 Leisure Research Symposium*. Arlington, VA: National Recreation and Park Association.

Williams, D. R., Patterson, M. E., Roggenbuck, J. W. and Watson, A. (1992) 'Beyond the commodity metaphor: examining emotional and symbolic attachment to place', *Leisure Sciences*, 14: 29–46.

Willis, P. (1977) *Learning to Labour*. Farnborough: Saxon House.

Wilson, M. J. (1979) 'Introduction to Reading 6', in M. J. Wilson (ed.) *Social and Educational Research in Action: A Book of Readings*. London: Longman/Open University Press.

Wingood, G. M., Di Clemente, R. J., Harrington, K., Davies, S., Hook, E. W. and Oh, M. K. (2001) 'Exposure to X-rated movies and adolescents' sexual and contraceptive-related attitudes and behaviors', *Paediatrics*, 107: 116–119.

Winn, J. and Heeter, C. (2009) 'Gaming, gender, and time: who makes time to play?', *Sex Roles*, 61: 1–13.

Wolak, J., Mitchell, K. and Finkelhor, D. (2007) 'Unwanted and wanted exposure to online pornography in a national sample of youth Internet users', *Pediatrics*, 119: 247–257.

Wolfenden Report (1960) *Sport and the Community*. London: HMSO.

Womack, S. (2012) 'Chore wars', *Society Now* Swindon: ESRC 12: 10–11.

Wood, R. T. (2003) 'The straightedge youth sub-culture: observations on the complexity of sub-cultural identity', *Journal of Youth Studies*, 6: 33–52.

Woodward, K. (2002) *Understanding Identity*. London: Arnold.

World Leisure (2005) *Charter for Leisure* http://www.worldleisure.org (accessed 1 December 2012).

World Wildlife Federation (2012) *Living Planet Report 2012* http://awsassets.panda.org/downloads/lpr_2012_summary_booklet_final.pdf (accessed 1 December 2012).

Wright Mills, C. (1959) *The Sociological Imagination*. Oxford: Oxford University Press.

Yates S. J. and Littleton, K. (1999) 'Understanding computer game cultures: a situated approach', *Information, Communication and Society*, 2: 566–583.

Ybarra, M. L. and Mitchell, K. J. (2005) 'Exposure to Internet pornography among children and adolescents: a national survey', *Cyber Psychology and Behavior*, 8: 473–486.

Ybarra, M. L., Mitchell, K., Finkelhor, D. and Wolak, J. (2007) 'Internet prevention messages: are we targeting the right online behaviors?', *Archives of Pediatric and Adolescent Medicine*, 161: 138–145.

Ybarra, M. L., Mitchell, K. J., Hamburger, M., Diener-West, M. and Leaf, P. J. (2011) 'X-rated material and perpetration of sexually aggressive behavior among children and adolescents: is there a link?', *Aggressive Behaviour*, 37: 1–18.

Yee, N. (2006) 'The demographics, motivations and derived experiences of users of massively-multiuser online graphical environments', *Presence: Teleoperators and Virtual Environments*, 15: 309–329.

Yee, N. (2007) 'Motivations of play in online games', *CyberPsychology and Behavior*, 9: 772–775.

Young, M. D. and Schuller, T. (1988) 'Introduction: towards chronosociology', in M. Young and T. Schuller (ed.) *The Rhythms of Society*. London: Routledge.

Yuan, M. S. and McEwen, D. (1989) 'Test for campers' experience preference differences among three ROS setting classes', *Leisure Sciences*, 11: 177–185.

Zhao, S. (2005) 'The digital self: through the looking glass of telecopresent others', *Symbolic Interaction*, 28(3): 387–405.

Zhao, S., Grasmuck, S. and Martin, J. (2008) 'Identity construction on Facebook: digital empowerment in anchored relationships', *Computers in Human Behavior*, 24: 1816–1836.

Zillmann, D. (1988a) 'Mood management: using entertainment to full advantage', in L. Donohew, H. E. Sypher and E. T. Higgins (ed.) *Communication, Social Cognition and Affect*. Hillsdale, NJ: Lawrence Erlbaum Associates.

Zillmann, D. (1988b) 'Mood management through communication choices', *American Behavioral Scientist*, 31: 327–340.

Zimmeck, M. (2001) *The Right Stuff: New Ways of Thinking about Managing Volunteers*. London: Institute for Volunteering Research.

Zuzanek, J. (2004) 'Work, leisure, time pressure and stress', in J. T. Haworth and A. J. Veal (eds) *Work and Leisure*. London: Routledge.

Zuzanek, J. and Mannell, R. C. (1993) 'Leisure behavior and experiences as part of everyday life: the weekly rhythm', *Society and Leisure*, 16: 31–57.

INDEX

References in **bold** indicate tables and in *italic* indicate figures.